The Politics of Contemporary Spain

The Politics of Contemporary Spain charts the trajectory of Spanish politics from the transition to democracy through to the present day, including the aftermath of the Madrid bombings of March 2004 and the elections that followed three days later. It offers new insights into the main political parties and the political system, into the monarchy, corruption, terrorism, regional and conservative nationalism and into Spain's policies in the Mediterranean and the European Union. It challenges many existing assumptions about politics in Spain, reaching beyond systems and practices to look at identities and political cultures. It brings to bear on the analysis the latest empirical data and theoretical perspectives.

Providing a detailed political analysis in an historical context, this book is of vital importance to students and researchers of Spanish studies and politics. It is also essential reading for all those interested in contemporary Spain.

Sebastian Balfour is Professor of Contemporary Spanish Studies at the London School of Economics and Political Science. His research interests cover the history and politics of twentieth-century Spain. Recent publications include: *The End of the Spanish Empire 1898–1923* and *Deadly Embrace: Morocco and the road to the Spanish Civil War*.

The Politics of Contemporary Spain

Edited by Sebastian Balfour

LONDON AND NEW YORK

First published 2005
by Routledge
2 Park Square, Milton Park, Abingdon, Oxon OX14 4RN

Simultaneously published in the USA and Canada
by Routledge
270 Madison Ave, New York, NY 10016

Routledge is an imprint of the Taylor & Francis Group

Typeset in Times by
Book Now Ltd
Printed and bound in Great Britain by
Cromwell Press, Trowbridge, Wiltshire

British Library Cataloguing in Publication Data
A catalogue record for this book is available from the British Library

Library of Congress Cataloging in Publication Data
The politics of contemporary Spain/edited by Sebastian Balfour.
 p. c.m.
 Includes bibliographical references and index.
 1. Spain–Politics and government–1975– I. Balfour, Sebastian.
 DP272.P653 2005
 320.946′09′0511–dc22   2004014085

ISBN 0–415–35677–6 (hbk)
ISBN 0–415–35678–4 (pbk)

Contents

List of illustrations   vii
List of contributors   ix
Acknowledgements   xi

Introduction: Spain since the transition to democracy: an overview   1
SEBASTIAN BALFOUR

1 **From consensus to competition: the changing nature of
   democracy in the Spanish transition**   6
   JONATHAN HOPKIN

2 **The monarchy of Juan Carlos: from dictator's dreams to
   democratic realities**   27
   PAUL PRESTON

3 **Corruption, democracy and governance in contemporary Spain**   39
   PAUL M. HEYWOOD

4 **Using terror against terrorists: the Spanish experience**   61
   PADDY WOODWORTH

5 **Terrorism and nationalist conflict: the weakness of democracy
   in the Basque Country**   81
   JOSÉ MANUEL MATA

6 **Convergència i Unió, Catalonia and the new Catalanism**   106
   ANDREW DOWLING

7 **From National-Catholic nostalgia to constitutional patriotism:
   conservative Spanish nationalism since the early 1990s**   121
   XOSÉ-MANOEL NÚÑEZ SEIXAS

8 **The reinvention of Spanish conservatism: the Popular Party since 1989**   146
SEBASTIAN BALFOUR

9 **The Socialist Party in government and in opposition**   169
MÓNICA MÉNDEZ-LAGO

10 **Between ambition and insecurity: Spanish politics and the Mediterranean**   198
RICHARD GILLESPIE

11 **Spain in the new European Union: in search of a new role and identity**   215
MARY FARRELL

Index   235

Illustrations

Tables

1.1 The Spanish party system – some base indicators (1977–2000)   11
1.2 Shares of votes and seats in Spanish parliamentary elections,
      1977–2000   13
3.1 The 2003 Corruption Perceptions Index (Western Europe)   40
5.1 Basque satisfaction with the Statute of Autonomy   85
5.2 Preferences regarding the state framework in the Basque
      Autonomous Community   85
5.3 Basque national identity   93
5.4 Basque nationalist identification   95
5.5 Fear of active participation in politics   96
5.6 Feeling free to talk about politics   96
5.7 Evolution of attitudes towards ETA   101
9.1 Total number of candidatures and percentage out of the total
      number of municipalities   172
9.2 Federal Executive Committee (FEC)   182
9.3 Degree of renewal (Federal Executive Committee, FEC)   182

Figures

1.1 Percentage of overall vote, and percentage of vote for statewide
      parties, won by the two largest parties in Spain, 1977–2000   11
1.2 Percentage of overall vote won by non-statewide parties, in
      Spain, 1977–2000   12
3.1 CPI rankings of Spain, 1980–2003   41
3.2 Self-sustaining relationships between social capital and
      governance   50
5.1 Putative structure of the Basque National Liberation
      Movement (BNLM)'s basic network 2004: activities and
      organisations   98
9.1 Yearly growth in members of PSOE and in local branches   180
9.2 Number of members of PSOE (male and female), 1977–96   181
9.3 Evolution of public opinion regarding the performance of the
      PP in government and the role of the PSOE in opposition   191

Contributors

Sebastian Balfour is Professor of Contemporary Spanish Studies and Deputy Director of the Cañada Blanch Centre for Contemporary Spanish Studies at the London School of Economics and Political Science. His recent publications include *The End of the Spanish Empire 1898–1923* (OUP, 1997) and *Deadly Embrace: Morocco and the Road to the Spanish Civil War* (OUP, 2002)

Andrew Dowling is lecturer in Hispanic Studies at the University of Cardiff and co-author of the book *The Catalans*, to be published at the end of 2004 as part of a series on European peoples.

Mary Farrell is Senior Researcher in Comparative Regional Integration Studies at the United Nations University. She worked for eight years in the University of North London, School of Area and Language Studies. Recent publications include *Spain in the EU. The Road to Economic Convergence* (Palgrave, 2001), and M. Farrell, A. Verdun and Erik Jones, eds, *Political Economy and the Study of European Integration* (Routledge, 2003)

Richard Gillespie is Professor of Politics at the University of Liverpool, Director (and founder) of the Europe in the World Centre and has been editor of the journal *Mediterranean Politics* since 1996. He recently published *Spain and the Mediterranean: Developing a European Policy towards the South* (Macmillan, 2000) and co-edited *Spain: The European and International Challenges* (Cass, 2001).

Paul M. Heywood is Dean of the Graduate School and Sir Francis Hill Professor of European Politics at the University of Nottingham. His publications include *The Government and Politics of Spain* (Macmillan, 1995) and *Spain and European Union* (with Carlos Closa) (Palgrave, 2004).

Jonathan Hopkin is lecturer in the Department of Government at the London School of Economics and Political Science. He is the author of *Party Formation and Democratic Transition in Spain* (Macmillan, 1999), and has published a variety of articles on comparative European politics in journals such as *Party Politics*, *West European Politics*, the *European Journal of Political Research*, the *Review of International Political Economy* and *European Urban and Regional Studies*.

José Manuel Mata is Professor and Dean of the Faculty of Social and Communication Sciences, University of the Basque Country, and author of *El nacionalismo vasco radical* (UPV, 1993) and *Las elecciones municipales y forales en el País Vasco: fracaso táctico del nacionalismo vasco en la escala local* (CIS, 2004).

Mónica Méndez-Lago has been Profesor Titular in Politics at the University of Murcia since 1999. Her Ph.D. thesis analysed the organisational strategy of the Spanish Socialist Workers' Party between 1975 and 1996 and she is author of *La estrategia organizativa del Partido Socialista Obrero Español, 1975–1996* (CIS, 2000) among other publications.

Xosé-Manoel Núñez Seixas is Profesor Titular in Modern History at the University of Santiago de Compostela. His recent books include *Entre Ginebra y Berlín. La cuestión de las minorías nacionales y la política internacional en Europa, 1914–1939* (Akal, 2001) and *O inmigrante imaxinario* (University of Santiago, 2002).

Paul Preston is Príncipe de Asturias Professor of Contemporary Spanish History and Director of the Cañada Blanch Centre for Contemporary Spanish Studies at the London School of Economics and Political Science. His numerous publications include *Franco: A Biography* (HarperCollins, 1993) and *Juan Carlos: A People's King* (HarperCollins, 2004).

Paddy Woodworth has written extensively for the *Irish Times,* where he was a staff journalist from 1988 to 2002. He has worked for numerous other publications, as well as in radio and television. His first full-length book, *Dirty War, Clean Hands* (Cork University Press, 2001 and Yale University Press, 2003), is a study of the consequences, for contemporary Spanish democracy, of the use of state terrorist methods to combat the terrorism of the Basque separatist group ETA. In 2003 he was the William B. Quarton Fellow on the International Writing Program at the University of Iowa.

Acknowledgements

The original idea of publishing this collection of essays, mostly based on seminar papers, came from Professor Paul Preston, Director of the Cañada Blanch Centre of Contemporary Spanish Studies at the London School of Economics and Political Science. I am grateful also to Joe Whiting, from the beginning and for several years the editor at Routledge responsible for the joint Routledge/Cañada Blanch Centre series of publications on contemporary Spain, for recommending the publication of this book to his successor, Terry Clague, and to Craig Fowlie and Heidi Bagtazo, the editorial team at Routledge in charge of politics and international studies. I would also like to thank Grace McInnes for her assistance in preparing the manuscript for publication. At the Cañada Blanch Centre, I am grateful to its administrator, Gerry Blaney, for his highly efficient help in the numerous peripheral tasks associated with this book.

Of all those who helped to put this book together, I am particularly grateful to the authors, many of whom were happy to revise their chapters at short notice in the light of unfolding events in Spain.

Introduction

Spain since the transition to democracy: an overview

Sebastian Balfour

The bomb outrage in Madrid on 11 March 2004 caused the world's media to focus their lenses briefly on Spain. What they witnessed was a society with a continued power to mobilise. This mobilisation took new forms. Text messaging and mobile phone calls brought people out into the streets and squares of the cities in solidarity and protest, and helped to rally voters for the election. Far from being intimidated by the terrorists, Spanish voters turned out in unprecedented numbers a few days later on 14 March to make their electoral choices (some 2.5 million more people voted than in the 2000 elections, a rise in voter turnout of 8.5 per cent). Against most predictions, the Socialists won a majority of votes and formed a new government to replace that of the Popular Party, which had been in power since 1996. The startling alternation of government represented a sea-change in political culture because the political system had become increasingly polarised. Twenty-seven years earlier, the transition to democracy, on the contrary, had been characterised by a high level of consensus.

One of the aims of this book is to explain why. *The Politics of Contemporary Spain* charts the trajectory of Spanish politics since the transition to the present day, looking inwards as well as outwards. It does so by focusing in depth on a number of key political processes, policies and parties. It thus goes beyond the textbook summaries about Spanish politics that are beginning to appear in response to a growing international interest in Spain. The authors, largely historians and political scientists from Spain and the UK, are either well-known experts in specific fields of contemporary Spain or young academics with fresh perspectives, many of whom first presented some of their ideas in a seminar series with the same title as this book organised by the Cañada Blanch Centre for Contemporary Spanish Studies at the London School of Economics and Political Science.

In his chapter on the politics of the transition and consolidation, for example, Jonathan Hopkin argues against the widely held view that Spain provides a model for a well-oiled evolution from consensus to majoritarian democracy. On the contrary, he claims that the emergence of a competitive, rather than collusive, party system was the result to a great extent of contingency, and that Spain was fortunate that the hasty abandonment of consensual decision-making in 1980–1 did not fatally destabilise the delicate transition process. Paul Preston traces the reasons why Juan Carlos became a popular monarch in a society with weak monarchical roots. In the course of the dictator's final years, motivated by a healthy instinct for self-preservation, Juan Carlos dramatically redefined his role. Throughout the process, there was an element of cynicism and calculation and a considerable contribution from a number of shrewd political advisers. Through his intervention against the attempted coup of 1981, the king cleared the monarchy of the stigma of Francoism and earned the right to be head of state. But Preston argues that his legitimacy is a very personal one and not necessarily a guarantee of the legitimacy of the crown. For his part, Paul Heywood examines political corruption in Spain and argues that traditional analytical approaches emphasising structural factors and the influence of social capital are insufficient as explanations. Instead, he emphasises the importance of incentives and opportunity structures associated with the changing nature of governance in Spain since democracy. The apparent fluctuations in the level of corruption are due more to oversaturation in the media and 'cycles of contestation' than any real diminution of corrupt practices.

The three following chapters about regional nationalism and the state also challenge existing analyses about Spanish politics. In the first, the Irish writer and journalist Paddy Woodworth looks back on the war against terrorism which Spain has been fighting for many years, examining in particular the state's use of dirty war tactics against ETA in the 1980s and the consequences for Spanish democracy since then. He argues that this dirty war undermined the democratic struggle against political violence but that this lesson seems to have been assimilated by policy-makers and counter-terrorist strategists alike. The relative success of the Spanish media and judiciary in exposing it was a remarkably mature achievement for Spain's young democracy. In a sombre analysis, José Manuel Mata examines the present-day situation in the Basque Country in which nationalist terrorism and persecution continue with the support of important sections of the Basque population, whose political culture, he maintains, is anti-democratic. Ethno-political discrimination against non-nationalist Basques, who number half the population, is rooted in a retrograde and essentialist nationalism that has succeeded in destroying the consensus vital to the functioning of democracy. Andrew Dowling, on the other hand, looks at the relatively successful trajectory of political Catalanism from the end of Francoism to the left-wing rainbow coalition that won the regional elections of 2003. He focuses in particular on the party that dominated Catalan politics in all that period, Convergència i Unió (CiU), as a result of a series of conjunctural factors, from strategic errors on the part of Spanish and Catalan social democracy to the role of Catalan communism in the shaping of the democratic environment in Catalonia. The CiU, he argues, transformed the terrain of politics in Catalonia to such an extent that the new government led by the Socialists has adopted Catalanisation as its flagship policy.

Xosé-Manoel Núñez and I both bring new perspectives to bear on the phenomenon of rehabilitated conservatism in contemporary Spain. Nuñez gives an overview of the new 'patriotic' discourse of Spanish conservative intellectuals and policy-makers linked to the Popular Party since the early 1990s, particularly during its two terms of office between 1996 and 2004. He argues that the renovation of this discourse is more apparent than real and that it still suffers from legitimacy deficits, above all in its failure to condemn the Francoist regime. This makes a common understanding with the left difficult in matters such as national symbols, liturgy and particularly the defence of Spain's territorial unity against peripheral nationalisms. Indeed, the absence of politics of memory plays a very important role in Spain's present-day public opinion. I examine the reinvention of Spanish conservatism since the transition to democracy, arguing that the Popular Party is not old wine in a new bottle but has undergone considerable renewal in its engagement with democratic politics. Nevertheless, authoritarian and right-wing mentalities persist in the party, matched by an incomplete assimilation of parliamentary democracy, as exemplified in the decision to join the Iraq war coalition. In the post-Aznar regime, the party, with a new unelected leader, found itself unexpectedly in opposition and isolated in a parliament celebrating the post-electoral honeymoon of its rival, the Socialist Party.

Mónica Méndez-Lago demonstrates that the effect of governmental power on the Socialist Party when it won the elections of 1982 was extreme because it had little time to develop its organisation before assuming office. Although attaining power was a catalyst for membership growth, it also hindered the internal dynamism of party organisation and shaped its growth in a way that had diminishing returns over time. Reliance on the resources made available by government constrained the party's organisational capacity to react to new environments, particularly once it lost most of those resources. Its unexpected victory in the 2004 general elections opened up a new phase both in Spanish politics and in the development of the party.

The last two chapters look at Spain's external relations. Richard Gillespie examines the growing importance to Spain of the Mediterranean, particularly in terms of national security concerns relating to immigration, the challenge posed by Islamist movements in North Africa, and Moroccan claims to Spanish territorial possessions. He identifies the main trends in Spanish Mediterranean policy since the death of Franco, looking at both domestic and exogenous factors such as the collapse of the Middle East peace process, 9/11, the war on Iraq, the bomb outrage in Madrid and the electoral victory of the Socialists. Mary Farrell argues that while Spain has benefited hugely from the European Union both economically and politically since its accession in 1986, Spain's alignment in the war in Iraq under the Aznar government, EU enlargement and internal regional tensions have threatened internal unity and external consensus. With the new Socialist-led government in office comes a return to the philosophy that shaped the national policy of their predecessors who took the country into the European Community; that it is through constructing and consolidating Europe's role in the world that member states, and Spain in particular, can define the national interest.

To go back to the opening words of this introduction, the elections of 14 March 2004 were a sign of the strength of the democratic process in Spain today; and it is a measure of the success of the transition to and consolidation of democracy over three decades. The unsung heroes of the transition were those who organised mass protests against the Dictatorship of Franco, many of whom suffered torture and imprisonment. They helped to create the conditions in which authoritarian rule became untenable and democracy virtually irrepressible. The political system that emerged was the result of tough and protracted bargaining between political elites of the centre and the left and those on the right willing to accept democracy. The dynamics of this pacted transaction have been the subject of intense investigation. But it is usually forgotten in the abundant literature that elite accommodation was conditioned by mass pro-democracy mobilisations in the streets and squares of urban Spain.

Another aspect of the transition that is often ignored is that Spaniards embraced democracy so easily not because of the skills of the negotiators but because they had already embraced the civic values that underpin democratic organisation and this, in turn, was partly the result of the accelerated modernisation of the 1950s and 1960s and Spain's economic assimilation into Europe. That does not mean that civil society emerged ready made. Indeed the relative weakness of civil networks and the lack of pluralist traditions and associational activity in Spain remained for some time, and still remains to some extent, one of the deficits of Spanish political life.

The democratic transaction that ensued was impelled by pragmatism and rational choice and based on a calculation of the balance of power between right and left and changing electoral opportunities. With the reluctant compliance of its politicians, the Dictatorship of Franco was eased out of existence rather than overthrown, as the left had hoped. A price was exacted by the right for the new democracy, part of which was a tacit agreement that reconciliation in the present did not have to entail reconciliation with the past. Franco's torturers were quietly pensioned off and the injustices of the past remained shrouded in silence. The revival of civil society is exemplified by the recent efforts of the nationwide popular organisation, the Association for the Recuperation of Historical Memory, to uncover the mass graves of those murdered by the rebels in 1936 and to bury the victims. Acknowledging the crimes of the recent past can only strengthen democracy.

The Constitution was itself a model of consensual politics but where agreement could not be reached crucial issues were left ambiguous, to be resolved when democracy was fully consolidated. At least in one area, the price of ambiguity is still being paid today. The thorny question of the real nature of the semi-federal model adopted during the transition after much compromise has not been resolved and may turn out to be a major headache for the government of the Socialist PSOE. In principle, the Constitution envisages the eventual integration of all Spain's regions, both the historic and the semi-invented, into a symmetrical, quasi-federal system. But the Catalan government seeks to maintain the existing asymmetry by deepening the process of devolution to its region, while the Basque government seeks to go beyond the Constitution to establish a new relationship of de facto independence from Spain. In the absence of any compensatory measures, the renegotiation of their statutes of autonomy agreed by the Socialist government (which falls short of Basque nationalist demands) entails not just the widening of the differential between the regions but also the risk of a substantial deficit in the financial system of the state of the autonomies as a whole.

Yet the Socialist government has demonstrated its willingness to address many of the issues left unresolved since the transitional pact, some of which require constitutional reform, such as the need to transform the Senate into a genuine chamber of regional representation. It would be rash to suggest that the transition to and consolidation of democracy may finally be completed soon (when it won power in 1996 the Popular Party government unwisely proclaimed the beginning of the second transition), but for all the continued belligerence of the PP and the residue of presidentialism in the Socialist government, the signs are positive for democracy in that a new spirit of dialogue permeates political life in Spain.

1 From consensus to competition

The changing nature of democracy in the Spanish transition

Jonathan Hopkin[1]

Introduction

The Spanish transition to democracy attracted a wave of scholarly interest in the late 1970s and early 1980s, and few aspects of the process remain unstudied. The juridical mechanisms and political negotiations underpinning the reform,[2] the emergence of parties and electoral politics,[3] the role of the military,[4] and the attempts to address territorial tensions[5] all received extensive attention. Subsequent work focused on the concept of consolidation, with threats to democratic stability itself constituting the main concern.[6]

Now that the dust has settled and no one doubts the sustainability of Spanish democracy, it seems appropriate to look into what kind of democracy has emerged in Spain, and why. Despite the predominant role played by negotiation and consensus in the process of regime change, by the early 1980s the new political system had developed the key characteristics of a majoritarian democracy.[7] In other words, although cooperation and negotiation between political forces was necessary to establish democracy in Spain, cooperation gave way to free, and sometimes intense, competition for power once democracy was perceived as consolidated. Rather than the coalitional form of government characteristic of countries such as Italy, Belgium or the Netherlands, Spain has been governed by single-party administrations, alternating between left and right: a qualified version of the 'Westminster model'.

This shift from 'consensus' to 'majoritarian' democracy makes the Spanish case central to recent debates on building and consolidating new democratic regimes. The literature on democratization posits an intractable dilemma between democracy as cooperation and democracy as competition. On the one hand, scholars have argued that ideological polarization threatens democratic consolidation, and that institutions should therefore be designed in such a way as to avoid political competition becoming too conflictual.[8] Juan Linz, for example, has argued powerfully that presidential democracies tend to polarize political positions, putting democracy at risk.[9]

On similar lines, much of the literature on transitions has emphasized the importance of elite pacts and consensus in building support for new democratic regimes.[10] On the other hand, an alternative view emphasizes the dangers for democracy if political competition is restricted or suppressed. For example, Hagopian took issue with the 'elite settlement' route to democracy as adopted in Brazil, arguing that it entrenched non-democratic practices and protected the positions of privileged groups, undermining the quality of the emerging democracy.[11]

The debate therefore seems to draw two conflicting conclusions: democratization is most likely to succeed if political competition is constrained, but the quality of the resulting democracy will suffer if collusion between political elites becomes institutionalized.[12] The process of democratization in Spain, however, has benefited from the 'best of both worlds'. The Spanish 'model' of pacted transition has been lavishly praised for its success in overcoming what most observers believe was a significant potential for political conflict at the end of the Franco era. Yet this consensual transition to democracy quickly gave way to a competitive battle for power between government and opposition, averting the ills of collusive democracy that have afflicted Italy, for example.

This chapter is concerned with how the contest between competing types of democracy was resolved in post-Franco Spain. It shows how, as the transition period drew to a close, Spain underwent a shift from a 'consensual' mode of democratic government to a more competitive or 'majoritarian' kind of democracy, to use Arend Lijphart's terminology. It explores the reasons for this shift, emphasizing the importance of contingent strategic choices made by political and social elites, and concludes by assessing the implications of the Spanish case for theories of democratization.

The rise and fall of consensus in the Spanish transition

Lijphart's definition of consensus and majoritarian democracy is based on two dimensions: the *executive-parties* dimension, which looks at the nature of party competition and government formation, and the *federal-unitary* dimension, which focuses on the territorial structure of the state and the type of constitution. Lijphart found that democracies tended to cluster into two types: consensus democracies, characterized by multi-party systems, balanced executive-legislative relations, and decentralized constitutional structures, and majoritarian democracies, in which a smaller number of parties compete for control over a relatively strong executive in a basically centralized, unitary state.[13]

In the Spanish case, there has been movement on both the executive-parties dimension and the federal-unitary dimension in the quarter of a century of democratic government. There is little dispute that Spain has become a more 'federal' state since the transition to democracy, as the 1978 constitution provided for the transfer of significant powers from the centre to the autonomous regions.[14] On this dimension Spain is closer to the consensual end of the scale. However on the executive-parties dimension Spain has moved in the opposite direction, to such an extent that it appears closer to the majoritarian than to the consensus model, with a pattern of 'government and opposition', in which two large parties alternate in power. This shift has taken place without constitutional changes, and under the same electoral system (a form of proportional representation with a majoritarian bias which penalizes small parties with dispersed support).[15] This can be seen in three areas: the composition of government, the pattern of executive-legislative relations, and the party system.

From government by consensus to single-party rule

Clearly Spain's transition was not the work of a broad multi-party coalition. On Franco's death in November 1975, a single-party authoritarian state was in place, and none of its institutions were composed of freely elected representatives – indeed, political parties were at that time illegal. The transition was initiated and implemented by a government nominated by the dictator's successor King Juan Carlos in July 1976. But in spite of its undemocratic origins, the government of Adolfo Suárez in fact consulted widely with all the relevant political forces. Suárez had secret talks with opposition leaders, including the leader of the banned Communist Party (PCE), Carrillo, to convince them that he intended to establish full democracy in Spain. At the same time, he convinced the components of the Dictatorship that his plans would respect the constitutional order and maintain political stability. A Law for Political Reform was passed, within the Francoist constitutional framework, which envisaged free elections with an electoral law designed in consultation with both regime conservatives and opposition leaders. Such was the degree of consultation on the reform that the text was described as 'cross-eyed' (*estrábico*), since it appeared simultaneously to satisfy incompatible demands: full democracy for the opposition and constitutional continuity for regime conservatives.[16]

This consensual theme continued after the first democratic elections. Adolfo Suárez's hastily organized party, the Union of Democratic Centre (UCD), won the elections, allowing him to remain in power to direct the remainder of the transition. Although the UCD governments of 1977–82 were not formally coalitions, they fell into the 'consensus' category in a number of ways. The party itself was heterogeneous, originating as a coalition and following a broadly factional dynamic in the distribution of power both in the party and in the government.[17] Moreover, especially in the 1977–9 period, a number of prestigious independents served in the UCD governments, undermining its 'partisan' quality. The high levels of cabinet instability – five mid-legislature reshuffles in as many years – and extensive policy disagreements reflect a lack of party discipline inside the government.

Moreover, as minority administrations, the UCD governments were obliged to build coalitions in order to pass legislation. In the 1977–9 period, supermajorities integrating virtually all the parliamentary groups were commonplace (this has been described as a 'consociational model of transition').[18] Despite the sometimes fractious nature of interparty relations in the 1979–82 parliament, analyses of legislative votes reveal a persistently high level of interparty collaboration in parliamentary votes.[19] This was partly a response to the need to update Spanish legislation in a variety of areas, but partly a consequence of the UCD's vocation as a centrist party seeking to govern 'for all Spaniards'.

The PSOE governments from 1982 to 1993 were, in contrast, almost exclusively partisan, highly cohesive and supported by solid single-party majorities which allowed them to push through very partisan legislative programmes. Although, like any party, the PSOE had its own internal factional dynamics, there was no detectable pattern of proportional allocation of portfolios to structured party factions. Although a degree of interparty cooperation on some legislation persisted, governments in this period followed a party programme and rarely bothered to seek support from other parliamentary groups.[20] Between 1993 and 2000, first the PSOE and then the PP fell short of parliamentary majorities, and were forced into pacts with 'peripheral nationalists' to maintain their minority administrations, although the executive remained strongly partisan in both cases. In the 2000–4 parliament the PP enjoyed an overall majority, and the pattern of single-party majority government returned.

Executive-legislative relations: the weakening of parliament

The constitutional framework governing executive-legislative relations in post-Franco Spain has facilitated executive dominance over parliament, both under the Francoist Fundamental Laws, but also under the democratic 1978 constitution.[21] However, there has been considerable variation in the balance of power under the democratic institutional framework: the executive-legislative relationship was relatively balanced between 1977 and 1982, whilst the executive has clearly dominated since 1982 (again with a parenthesis in 1993–2000).[22]

The 1977–9 parliament was in effect a constituent assembly, and Suárez used his party's plurality status to negotiate consensual solutions to divisive constitutional issues, rather than imposing a partisan text. The pattern of executive-legislative relations was therefore rather balanced, although Suárez used his dominant position within the UCD to deny his own parliamentary group any real influence over government policy. The most critical negotiations over contentious constitutional issues took place outside parliament, and the UCD parliamentarians with formal responsibility for the constituent process were marginalized.[23] Paradoxically, however, Suárez's neglect of his own parliamentary supporters served the purpose of integrating the parliamentary opposition more fully into the process of drafting the constitution. Suárez's objective was to pass a constitution with the overwhelming support of the parliament. As a result, the other parliamentary groups had an effective power of veto over some government proposals.[24]

After 1979, the deterioration of Suárez's leadership position strengthened parliament. The end of the constituent process made it more difficult to build supermajorities, and the UCD's minority status left it vulnerable to parliamentary defeats. Growing divisions within the party undermined the discipline of the UCD parliamentary group. Consensus was maintained for the passing of Autonomy Statutes for the pressing cases of the Basque Country and Catalonia, but broke down for some of the remaining regions. The UCD minority government began to suffer regular parliamentary defeats, and attempts to find consensual solutions for divisive questions such as education, workers' rights and family law failed, although there was a brief revival of consensus after the 1981 coup attempt. In short, between 1979 and 1982 the executive was in no position to impose policy on parliament. The difficult investiture votes of March 1979 and February 1981 and the censure motion of May 1980 testify to this executive weakness and the resurgence of the legislature.

After 1982 the González governments had cohesive parliamentary majorities which obviated the need for consensus or consultation with the ideologically antagonistic opposition, AP (Alianza Popular).[25] Executive dominance permitted a series of highly partisan and potentially divisive measures (the legalization of abortion, educational reforms favouring the state sector, significant increases in taxation) to be implemented with little parliamentary difficulty. González's position as Prime Minister remained secure even after major political setbacks, such as his change of heart over NATO, soaring unemployment and a successful general strike. Only with the loss of its majority in 1993 was the González government's authority curtailed. In 2000–4, the Aznar government had a solid majority, and parliament reverted to a subordinate role. A quantitative study of the proportion of legislation originating from the executive rather than parliament during these different periods, reported by Lynn Maurer,[26] confirms this picture.

The emergence of an 'adulterated' two-party system

Spain has had a multi-party system throughout the post-Franco period. However the nature of that system has changed over time, with significant shifts occurring both in 1982 and in 1993. Measures such as the number of effective parliamentary parties and the number of issue dimensions fail to capture the extent of this shift (Table 1.1). So what has happened to the Spanish party system to make it more majoritarian?

The best way to illustrate the shift is to look at the proportion of the vote won by the two largest parties in the system (Figure 1.1). In the first two democratic elections (1977 and 1979), the two biggest parties, the PSOE and

Table 1.1 The Spanish party system – some basic indicators (1977–2000)

Election	Number of parties (Congress)	Effective number of parties (Electoral)	Effective number of parties (Congress)
1977	11	4.16	2.85
1979	14	4.16	2.77
1982	10	3.33	2.32
1986	12	3.57	2.63
1989	13	4.16	2.77
1993	11	3.53	2.70
1996	11	3.28	2.72
2000	12	3.12	2.48
Average	11.8	3.66	2.66

Sources: José Ramón Montero, 'Stabilizing the Democratic Order: Electoral Behaviour in Spain', in Paul Heywood (ed.), *Politics and Policy in Democratic Spain: No Longer Different?* (London: Frank Cass, 1999), pp. 53–79; José Ramón Montero and Juan Linz, 'The Party Systems of Spain: Old Cleavages and New Challenges', in Lauri Karvonen and Stein Kuhnle (eds), *Party Systems and Voter Alignments Revisited* (London: Routledge, 2001), pp. 150–96.

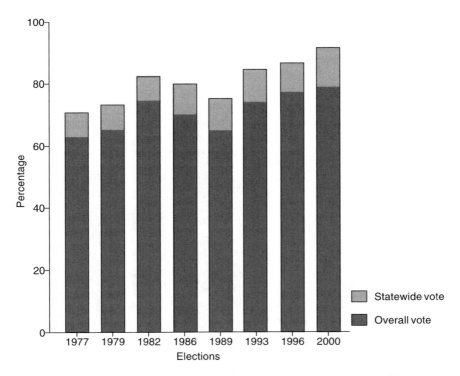

Figure 1.1 Percentage of overall vote, and percentage of vote for statewide parties, won by the two largest parties in Spain, 1977–2000.

the UCD, together won just short of two-thirds of the total votes. In 1982, the proportion of the vote won by the two largest parties (this time the PSOE and the AP) leapt to 74.5 per cent. Although this number dropped back a little during the rest of the 1980s, it rose again through the 1990s, reaching a new peak of 78.6 per cent in the 2000 elections. There is therefore a clear tendency towards a bipolar system, in which the two most powerful parties win over three-quarters of the total vote – a situation roughly equivalent to that of the United Kingdom.

This tendency is in part disguised by the persistently large number of parties winning parliamentary representation in Spain (Table 1.1). Party system fragmentation has been maintained at high levels by the strong performance of non-statewide parties, whose vote share has grown steadily from around 10 per cent in the first democratic elections to just under 15 per cent in 2000. In short, the Spanish party system has displayed two contra-dictory trends: an increasing concentration of the vote around the two large statewide parties, and a growth (and increasing dispersion) of the vote for non-statewide parties.

The changes in the distribution of votes amongst statewide parties, which win around 90 per cent of the parliamentary seats, have fundamentally altered the dynamic of the party system (see the changing vote shares in Table 1.2). The pre-1982 party system could be classified as moderate

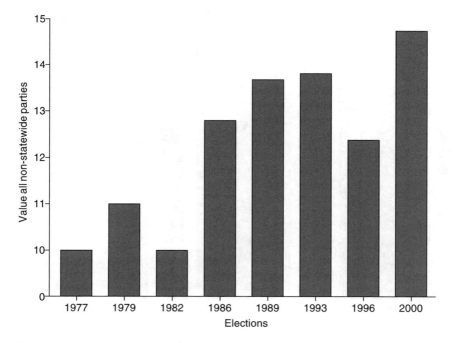

Figure 1.2 Percentage of overall vote won by non-statewide parties, in Spain, 1977–2000.

Table 1.2 Shares of votes and seats in Spanish parliamentary elections, 1977–2000

	1977		1979		1982		1986		1989		1993		1996		2000	
	%V	%S	%V	%S	%V	%S	%V	%S	%V	%S	%V	%S	%V	%S	%V	%S
PSOE	29.3	33.7	30.4	34.6	48.1	57.7	44.1	52.6	39.6	50.0	38.8	45.4	37.5	40.3	34.1	35.7
AP/PP	8.2	4.6	6.1	2.9	26.4	30.6	26.0	30.0	25.8	30.6	34.7	40.3	38.9	44.6	44.5	52.3
UCD	34.4	47.4	34.8	48.0	6.8	3.1	–	–	–	–	–	–	–	–	–	–
CDS	–	–	–	–	2.9	0.6	9.2	5.4	7.9	4.0	1.8	0.0	–	–	–	–
PCE/IU	9.3	5.4	10.8	6.6	4.0	1.1	4.6	1.7	9.1	4.9	9.6	5.1	10.6	6.0	5.5	2.3
Other SW	8.8	1.8	6.9	0.3	1.8	0	3.4	0	4.0	0	1.4	0	0.6	0	1.3	0
CiU	2.8	3.1	2.7	2.3	3.7	3.4	5.0	5.1	5.0	5.1	4.9	4.9	4.6	4.6	4.2	4.3
EAJ–PNV	1.6	2.3	1.7	2.0	1.9	2.3	1.5	1.7	1.2	1.4	1.2	1.4	1.3	1.4	1.5	2.0
Other NSW	5.6	1.8	6.6	3.3	4.4	1.2	6.2	3.4	7.4	4.0	7.6	2.9	6.5	3.1	8.9	3.4
Total	100	100	100	100	100	100	100	100	100	100	100	100	100	100	100	100

Source: Spanish Ministry of Interior, elaboration Ingrid van Biezen and Jonathan Hopkin.

Notes
%V = share of votes cast.
%S = share of seats in Congress of Deputies.
Other SW = other statewide parties.
Other NSW = other non-statewide parties.

pluralism, with two large centre-oriented parties both potentially capable of governing (the UCD and the PSOE) flanked by two smaller less moderate parties (the AP and the PCE), neither of which were genuine anti-system parties. The presence of four relevant statewide parties imposed a coalitional logic on party interactions.

After 1982, this balance was overturned as the PSOE obtained a comfortable and sustainable single-party governing majority. The UCD's disappearance allowed the Socialists to monopolize the pivotal centre space in the party system, whilst the PCE's decline minimized the threats to its left wing. In short, the system shifted from a balanced and fluid moderate pluralism with a coalitional dynamic to a dominant party system with higher levels of polarization and interparty antagonism. But as the Socialist vote entered into decline, a further shift in 1993 brought greater balance to the system. The disappearance of the centrist CDS mostly benefited the PP, which emerged as a potential governing party to rival the PSOE. In 1996 it overtook the PSOE, and in 2000 won an overall majority. The recent 2004 election resulted in a further alternation.

The Spanish party system has therefore developed into what could be described as an 'adulterated' two-party system. Despite quite a high number of parties represented in parliament, the party system essentially revolves around a bipolar competition between two large statewide parties. The strong presence of non-statewide parties, and the nature of the electoral system, place obstacles in the way of the winning party achieving an overall majority. However, the post-1982 pattern of alternating single-party majority or minority administrations places Spain closer to the majoritarian than to the consensual end of the scale.

From consensus to majoritarian democracy: a natural move?

It could be argued that these changes are unremarkable. Parties will obviously form coalitions and alliances if they fail to achieve parliamentary majorities to govern alone; if electoral rules are held constant, 'consensus' and 'majoritarian' democracy may just be neat ways of describing the outcomes of general elections. Moreover, consensus democracy in Spain coincided with the transition to democracy – what could be more natural than a move to 'real' party competition once this delicate phase was over?

However, the outcomes of general elections are dependent as well as independent variables, and movements between 'consensual' and 'majoritarian' behaviour on the part of party elites determine party system characteristics as well as being determined by them.[27] In fact, there is compelling evidence that 'majoritarianism' in the Spanish case in fact resulted from conscious choices on the part of some political and social elites, despite a number of factors favourable to a 'consensus' type of democracy (in particular, the persistence of important divisions in Spanish society). These choices are all the more puzzling in view of the lack of enthusiasm for majoritarian democracy amongst the most prominent political leaders involved in the transition process.

The main supporters of majoritarianism were the conservative reformers led by Manuel Fraga who admired the British path to democracy through gradual reform, and hoped to establish the two-party Westminster model in Spain.[28] This group was sufficiently influential within the Francoist institutions to introduce a majoritarian bias into the new electoral system, although its influence waned after the AP's poor electoral showing in 1977–9.

The remaining political forces backed an electoral system based on the principle of proportional representation. Reformist Prime Minister Suárez saw a proportional electoral system as a precondition of his reform strategy based around consensus, and generally favoured a more consensual style of democracy based on continuous negotiation as an antidote to the disastrous consequences of a confrontational style of politics in the 1930s.[29] Key UCD factions supported this line.[30]

The forces of opposition to the Franco regime rejected negotiations with the Dictatorship, insisting instead on the immediate formation of a provisional government. However, they strongly supported the maximum degree of proportionality in the electoral system.[31] The Communist PCE was unlikely to enjoy the kind of broad social support necessary for it to benefit from a majoritarian system, and until the first elections the Socialists could not be sure of benefiting either, since they faced strong competition from both the Communists and other Socialist parties (such as the PSP) for their political space. Non-statewide parties also favoured proportional representation, since single-party government would marginalize them in the national parliament. In sum, all the major political forces in the 1977 elections favoured proportional representation, with the sole exception of AP. The emergence of majoritarian democracy is therefore best understood in terms of the changing strategic environment facing the various political forces.

Why transition through consensus?: the constituent period

The electoral law negotiated between these forces was itself a product of consensus, as Suárez's stated aim was a law 'acceptable to all'.[32] In the first democratic elections in 1977 this law produced the ideal parliament for a consensual transition, with a plurality, but not a majority, of seats going to the UCD, a party committed to a negotiated constitution. The UCD's plurality in the chamber allowed it to dominate legislative activity, whilst its inability to govern on its own obliged it to seek agreements with other forces, allowing Suárez to resist pressures from the conservative sector of the UCD to limit political change. The Socialists' domination of the left political space meant that any measure the UCD agreed with them would have an unassailable majority. More radical forces, such as the AP and the PCE, had limited parliamentary clout. The parliamentary arithmetic turned out to be ideal for a consensual constituent process directed by the two largest parties.

Consensus was further assisted by the positions adopted by parties which could potentially destabilize the process, such as the PCE. Despite the strong Communist presence in the trade union movement, the party's 9 per cent vote share in 1977 undermined any ambition to condition Suárez's transition project,[33] and its position in the party system left it few options. It was isolated on the left, and had historically poor relations with the PSOE, which had little interest in forming a broad left front.[34] González's view as early as June 1976 was that 'any bilateral alliance which could provoke reactions against us and undermine the process of stability we are aiming for would be an error'.[35] Only a broad-based 'national government' (*gobierno de concertación*) could provide the PCE with any real influence. The Communists' willingness to participate in consensus is therefore easily explained in terms of its strategic position.

The Socialists' position was far more complex, and led to regular changes in strategy throughout the 1976–82 period. Strategy was driven by the aspiration to form an electoral majority, an aspiration made possible by the promising 1977 results and encouraged by the overwhelming influence in the PSOE of the German Social Democrats, who opposed alliances with forces such as the Communist Party.[36] The Socialists faced conflicting incentives. On the one hand, the PSOE had a clear interest in participating in the elaboration of the new constitution, in order to shape the future institutions and impress its electorate. At the same time, collaboration with the UCD would undermine the Socialists' profile as the alternative governing party, and would favour their opponents in the subsequent elections.

Ultimately, however, the Socialists had to be incorporated if the constitution was to achieve broad parliamentary backing, and the Socialists themselves were not prepared to jeopardize the transition by blocking the constituent process. The UCD's ability to form majority coalitions with both the PCE and the AP constituted a useful threat to push the Socialists into compromise positions. When the draft constitution began its passage through the parliamentary commission, the UCD negotiated the first 25 articles with the AP, forming a conservative majority. The PSOE protested furiously, and the rest of the constitutional text was drawn up through joint negotiations between the two major parties.[37] Once the uncomfortable issue of the monarchy had been overcome, the Socialists participated in the constitutional consensus – with occasional slamming of doors to emphasize their distinctiveness from the governing party[38] – and profited from a substantial input into the constitutional text. The UCD, for its part, benefited from having piloted a successful constituent process in which practically all-party agreement had been reached. Among the most significant parties, only the Basque Nationalists (PNV) and part of the AP failed to ratify the text. Cross-party agreement was also reached on a package of measures to address the economic crisis (the Moncloa Pacts, September 1977). However, this consensual relationship was, as we see below, fundamentally unstable.

Interparty competition and the decline of the centre

The new constitution came into force in December 1978, and elections were called for March 1979, producing largely similar results to 1977. But despite the essential continuity of the party system format, consensus quickly began to falter. This change of climate can be explained in terms of the changing opportunity structure.

Perhaps the most important change in the strategic scenario was the apparent resolution of the constitutional question. The success of the referendum on the new constitution (only in the Basque Country did a majority fail to support it) and the agreement of Statutes of Autonomy for the Basque Country and Catalonia in the summer of 1979, gave the impression that the transition was over. One UCD politician recalled: 'it was generally a feeling in public opinion, exaggerated by the media, that consensus politics were for the constituent period, and that after that, parties should take up their real positions'.[39] The fear of civil war in Spain, based on the traumatic memory of the 1936–9 conflict,[40] was sufficiently real for the key political elites to compromise on contentious issues rather than risk confrontation during the transition period. With the success of the constituent process in 1977–8, and the failure of Francoist hardliners to destabilize the democratization process, this fear began to fade, providing an incentive for parties such as the Socialists to abandon restraint and adopt opportunistic electoral strategies.

The UCD, despite reaffirming its position as the largest party in the 1979 elections, suddenly found itself in a vulnerable position. Suárez aimed to continue governing as a minority administration after March 1979, seeking consensus on broad constitutional issues and ad hoc alliances on other matters. The strategy was reflected in the UCD's failure to publish any partisan programme of government, and in its post-election commitment to 'carry out a moderate set of policies, in a spirit of service to the whole Spanish people, accepting all the responsibilities deriving from its popular mandate and in full respect of the other political forces'.[41] This strategy ran into trouble as early as the investiture vote, when Suárez struggled to find the eight votes necessary to achieve majority backing. The AP offered its parliamentary support, but on the understanding that Suárez 'abandoned the ambiguities of his previous government and the concessions to the left', adding that 'it is our intention to clear the path so that Adolfo Suárez can adopt a proper right-wing programme, without concessions'.[42] At the same time, the PSOE began to adopt a tougher line towards the UCD, representing it as a party of the classic conservative right,[43] and announcing the end of consensus, which 'would remain in the archives of history'.[44] In the end Suárez was forced to hammer out a deal with regionalist parties.

The shift in strategic incentives fatally undermined Suárez's consensus strategy. On the part of the Socialists, the rationale for adopting an aggressive strategy of opposition was clear enough: they had confirmed their position as the hegemonic party of the left in the 1979 poll, but had made little progress towards replacing the UCD as the governing party. The kind of electoral growth the PSOE needed in order to win elections could only come from the right, and taking votes from the UCD would also weaken the only other potential party of government. A prerequisite for this strategy was a shift towards the ideological centre, achieved by the abandonment of Marxism in an Extraordinary Congress in September 1979,[45] and contacts with the Spanish 'power elites' (the big banks, the church and sectors of the military) and Washington to establish the PSOE's credentials as a 'responsible' party of government.[46] The party could then set about attacking the UCD government for its failure to respond to the pressing economic and public order problems facing Spain in 1979–80. Consensus had threatened the PSOE's identity as an alternative party of government,[47] so the Socialists became selectively unavailable for agreements with the UCD. An example of this was the UCD's attempt to contain the process of political decentralization by imposing a restrictive Statute of Autonomy on the regions of Galicia and Andalusia. The Socialist leadership reneged on an agreement over Galicia, and then ran a demagogical campaign for increased autonomy in Andalusia, sensing an opportunity for electoral growth in Spain's most populous region.[48]

Rather more complex changes were also taking place on the right of the political spectrum. The UCD contained a conservative sector of mainly Christian Democrats and Liberals who had had little option but to join Suárez in 1977, but were far less enthusiastic about consensus with the parties of the left; as one party leader recalled in an interview, 'consensus was very strongly attacked; it provoked a great deal of tension within the party'.[49] During the constituent period, these groups were too weak to challenge Suárez, as the Liberal faction leader admitted in 1978:

> Adolfo Suárez is at the moment the only man inside the UCD who possesses sufficient political capital to exercise the functions of president of the party and of the government . . . I think that we should support him, since he continues to represent the safest option for the consolidation of democracy.[50]

By 1979 this support was running out, and other options became open to UCD conservatives.

The changing mood amongst Spanish business elites was fundamental in this respect. One UCD leader neatly explained the shifting position of conservative interests in Spain in the course of the transition period:

> The Spanish right was, in 1974–75, terrified at what might happen after Franco's death; the feeling of a 'leap in the dark' was widespread. When Suárez offered them a possibility of change without trauma, they went along with that. But when they found that instead of a right-wing policy he was adopting policies which only partly satisfied that electorate, then these circles went out for revenge. It's obvious! If only we could have gone all out instead of making concessions. So then there is a movement to support Fraga, thinking that instead of giving up '30 per cent' they could have got away with just giving up 'five per cent', so to speak.[51]

This contrasted sharply with the UCD leadership's strategy of negotiating broad cross-party agreements on contentious issues such as the decentralization process, family law, labour law and education. One UCD leader defended this strategy in the following terms: 'party interests could not be allowed to prevail. The interest of the state had to prevail and that interest was to consolidate a system of freedoms in which all Spaniards would have a comfortable and secure place'; 'there are a series of laws which have to be passed in consensus between the major political forces, because they are permanent laws . . . Without that consensus there is no way of creating an integrated society.'[52]

UCD conservatives tried to push for an end to Suárez's strategy of consensus, and on a number of occasions used their parliamentary leverage to push for more partisan policies.[53] Their position within the UCD did not permit them to take over the party leadership, so instead they sought to push Suárez into a parliamentary deal with Fraga's AP, a strategy known as the 'natural majority' (*mayoría natural*) and strongly supported by business interests (the big banks and the employers' federation CEOE). Suárez resisted such a deal, which would have undermined his consensus strategy and his electoral appeal to centrist voters. At this point the strategies of the conservative right and the PSOE coincided, as one UCD leader explained:

> On the one hand AP is aware that unless UCD becomes weaker it cannot gain support... On the other the Socialist Party understands that anything that weakens UCD and helps it gain a moderate image will bring electoral advantage, so there is a kind of tacit understanding between AP and the PSOE to weaken UCD and encourage internal divisions in UCD.[54]

This collusion found its clearest expression in a parliamentary censure motion tabled by the Socialists in May 1980. Ostensibly this formed part of the Socialist strategy of distancing itself from consensus and presenting itself as an alternative governing party, capitalizing on Suárez's increasing weakness. In practice it developed into a curious pincer movement involving both the PSOE and the AP. On the one hand, the Socialist Guerra denounced Suárez as a throwback to Francoism, incapable of governing democratically; on the other, Fraga denounced Suárez for being too weak and failing to impose public order.[55] At the same time, the two parties complimented each other, with González suggesting that 'with that brain big enough to fit the state inside, if Mr Fraga was on the left, this country would have a great leader of the left',[56] and Fraga offering his counterpart similar praise. The two parties shared a common interest: by undermining the UCD, they could push interparty relations towards a competitive majoritarian dynamic which would improve the position of both.

The 1982 elections and the triumph of majoritarianism

The final push towards majoritarianism required the UCD to become a more clearly conservative party tied to Alianza Popular, and to abandon its strategy of consensus with an increasingly aggressive Socialist Party. Suárez's opposition to majoritarianism and his close control over the party machinery were a formidable obstacle to this. Moreover, the coup attempt of February 1981 temporarily restored consensus as the Socialists and conservatives took fright and called off their assault on the government. Agreement was reached to slow down the decentralization process, and unions and employers reached a deal on wages and working conditions. The perceived negative consequences of mutual intransigence in the aftermath of military intervention were responsible for this, but fear of a further coup quickly subsided and consensus collapsed again in the summer of 1981.

The bipolar majoritarian competition between socialism and conservativism in the 1982 elections became possible as a result of the UCD's implosion. The causes of this implosion were in large part internal,[57] but a decisive contribution was made by both the PSOE and the conservative interests backing Fraga. Both stood to gain from the UCD's collapse: around a fifth of the UCD's 1979 electorate voted Socialist in 1982, and around half voted for the AP.[58] The Socialists' contribution was to entice prominent figures in the UCD's Social Democrat faction to cross the floor with offers of ministries in a future PSOE government, whilst the AP, with the encouragement of the CEOE, offered conservative sectors of the UCD prime places on its electoral lists if they defected. The business elite, which had bankrolled the UCD from the beginning, had long criticized the Suárez governments' economic policies, but in the tense transition period felt that the UCD represented the safest bet for political stability. Their perception of strategic opportunities had shifted by 1981, according to one UCD minister:

> Between 1981 and 1982 an important sector of Spanish public life, and particularly in financial circles, organized a manoeuvre which would involve splitting UCD and electing Manuel Fraga as the leader of the new formation . . . Reagan and Thatcher's election victories had a big impact in this; they made the CEOE believe that given the world climate it was possible for a clearly right-wing party to win here.[59]

A senior UCD figure recognized that the Socialists' increasingly centrist strategy made a high-risk strategy more attractive to conservative circles: 'the PSOE now has a much more moderate image, and for this reason conservative sectors feel they don't have to accept the UCD's reformist position just for fear of a Socialist victory'.[60] Business interests were also much better organized than at the beginning of the transition: by 1981 the CEOE represented 80 per cent of private sector employment in Spain.[61] The CEOE threw its weight behind the AP in regional elections in Galicia and Andalusia, and the AP managed to overtake the UCD's vote share in both these regional elections. Business circles also bankrolled the 'critical' movement within the UCD, which attempted to push the UCD into the 'natural majority' alliance with the AP.[62]

Once it became clear that they would not be able to take control of the UCD (at the party congress in early 1981) and convert it into a more right-wing party, these conservative Liberals and Christian Democrats set out to weaken the UCD as a prelude to crossing over to the AP. One minister recalls that:

> After the Palma congress the critics had given up on UCD, and they were already making different plans. There was a decision to change UCD, a view that UCD's purpose had been fulfilled, that the idea of a broad-based party was no longer viable and that there needed to be a much more precise definition of the political space, and that that definition could be achieved through AP.[63]

The same minister also explained how this would be done: 'there were meetings, hosted by the CEOE, in which they more or less reached the conclusion that since it was not possible to reform and change UCD, it was necessary to do everything possible to destroy it'.[64] The CEOE's president Ferrer Salat made thinly veiled threats in public, stating that 'if [the UCD's] leaders do not manage to move beyond the illogical conception of the centre as a mixture of disparate ideologies . . . we foresee an inevitable election defeat in the next elections'.[65] This prophecy was fulfilled in 1982, with the help of significant defections from the UCD to Coalición Popular, the electoral alliance constituted by Fraga's AP. The Christian Democrat group formed a separate party, the PDP, in order to make the shift. According to one AP provincial leader interviewed by Richard Gunther, 'the PDP was an operation designed to destroy the UCD'.[66]

The business circles which backed the Suárez reform operation had grown tired of a formula in which they bankrolled a centre-right party which then governed through consensus with the left. They preferred to push for the UCD to be replaced by a more conservative party, thus reconstituting party competition into a left–right battle in which they were confident their money and social influence would prevail. The AP and the tiny conservative factions marginalized within the UCD were only too happy to join this operation. The Socialists realized that a clearly right-wing party would be a much less dangerous competitor than the UCD, given the broadly centre-left orientation of the Spanish electorate,[67] and welcomed these developments. One UCD leader complained bitterly that the PSOE and the AP combined to deny the small UCD parliamentary group access to its state funding after the 1982 elections: 'The Socialist Party did nothing to help us out, to stop UCD disappearing as a political force. Why? . . . Because the PSOE is happier with Fraga in opposition than with UCD.'[68]

Another UCD leader with particular responsibility for financial affairs told the author that 'important figures in the banking sector told me that if you dissolve, then there will be no problem, there won't be anyone to pay us, and that will be that. But if you intend to carry on, we are going to call in your debts – which were 5,000 million pesetas'.[69] The 1982 elections were not simply an alternation in government between political parties, or even a case of a particularly heavy electoral defeat by an unpopular governing party (although the UCD did have plenty of responsibility for its own decline). It was also the outcome of a deliberate and sustained campaign by two political parties and influential business interests to realign the Spanish party system on a bipolar basis, in which 'the best of the left could compete with the best of the centre'.[70] The UCD was duly dissolved in early 1983, and Spain had, at the statewide level at least, taken a decisive step towards a majoritarian pattern of party competition.

Conclusions

This account of the shift from consensus to majoritarian democracy in post-Franco Spain rests largely on political forces' perceptions of their strategic opportunities, and the ways in which these strategic opportunities changed over the transition period, within a more or less constant institutional framework. The thrust of my argument is that the Socialists' unexpected electoral success and the Communists' corresponding failure provided a rationale for the PSOE to switch to a majoritarian strategy, abandoning consensus politics and collaborating with conservative forces in undermining the UCD, the party around which consensus politics had been based. The conservative AP's preference for majoritarian democracy remained constant throughout the period; what changed were the resources available to them, and in particular the changing position of Spanish business elites. The electoral stagnation of communism, and the aimless leadership of the UCD after 1978, provided the Socialists and the AP with the opportunity to reshape the party system in terms of their own electoral interests.

What does this tell us about how majoritarian and consensus democracy come about? First of all, consensus democracy was difficult to sustain in Spain because of the way in which a fairly disproportional electoral system interacted with the electoral choices made by Spanish voters. The concentration of electoral support around the two most centre-oriented statewide parties, the UCD and the PSOE, gave the party system a centripetal dynamic, as both parties had to adopt centrist strategies in order to increase their parliamentary representation. Had the Communists become the largest party on the left, there would have been strong incentives for the UCD and the PSOE to coalesce in a centre-oriented governing majority, as in the Italian case after 1962. Instead, in the party system that emerged in 1977 the Socialists had an incentive to adopt an aggressive strategy of opposition to the UCD in order to win power.

Second, the incentives produced by the party system did not, in the Spanish case, lead directly to a predictable outcome. The Socialist leadership refrained from adopting a competitive strategy during the early stages of the transition, cooperating with the UCD government in maintaining the consensual pattern of decision-making Suárez had initiated in 1976. Fears about military intervention and a reversal of the democratization process contributed to this decision. But a decline in the fear of civil confrontation after 1979 led political actors to perceive intransigent positions as less dangerous than they had been in the initial phase of the transition. The attempted coup of 1981 suggests that this was a dangerous miscalculation, and that continued cooperation may well have been a more appropriate strategy. The strategic shift of 1979–80 ultimately paid off for the Socialist leadership, but only after they spent several hours at gunpoint on 23 February 1981. This shows that the ways in which institutional engineering feeds through into political outcomes are conditioned by moments of fine political judgment, impossible for constitution-writers to foresee.

It is therefore difficult to argue that Spain constitutes a model for a well-timed move from consensus to competition. The fortunate outcome was serendipity – many of the decisions were taken in terms of partisan interest, and the balance of forces, plus the broad support of the population and a bit of luck, secured democracy. The constitutional framework cannot alone explain this shift, since it could comfortably accommodate both types of democracy. In sum, the consolidation of a particular type of democracy in Spain was indeterminate, subject to a substantial degree of contingency.

This case study bears out some of Lijphart's own comparative conclusions. First, 'the institutions of consensus democracy on the executive-parties dimension do not depend as directly on constitutional provisions as the divided-power institutions'.[71] The emergence of an 'adulterated two-party system' in Spain depended as much on the contingent choices of party leaders and voters as on the choice of electoral system. Second, Lijphart concluded that 'both institutional and cultural traditions may present strong resistance to consensus democracy', and that 'consensus democracy may not be able to take root and thrive unless it is supported by a consensual political culture'.[72] Statements cited in this chapter suggest that, for some key political actors, democracy was largely conceptualized in terms of the features of majoritarian party politics: government and opposition, highly competitive electoral contests, and clear, cohesive governing majorities. In particular, Spanish business elites were quick to reject consensus as a mode of economic decision-making, and complained bitterly that UCD ministers were following policies dictated by the Socialist opposition.

Consensus democracy may indeed require a consensual political culture, and a consensual political culture requires social as well as political actors to be willing to engage in negotiation and compromise. Spain is perhaps fortunate that the more intransigent sectors of its political and social elite held off their fire until the most dangerous phases of the transition had passed.

Notes

1 The author would like to thank Peter Mair for helpful comments on an earlier version of this chapter, Richard Gunther for allowing me to cite from elite interviews he carried out during the Spanish transition, and Ingrid van Biezen for some help with electoral data. The usual disclaimer applies.
2 Richard Gunther, 'Spain: The Very Model of a Modern Elite Settlement', in Richard Gunther and John Higley (eds), *Elites and Democratic Consolidation in Latin America and Southern Europe* (Cambridge: Cambridge University Press, 1992), pp. 38–80.
3 Richard Gunther, Giacomo Sani and Goldie Shabad, *Spain After Franco. The Making of a Competitive Party System* (Berkeley: University of California Press, 1986); Juan Linz and José Ramón Montero (eds), *Crisis y cambio: Electores y partidos en la España de los años 80* (Madrid: Centro de Estudios Constitucionales, 1986).
4 Paul Preston, *The Triumph of Democracy in Spain* (London: Methuen, 1986); Felipe Agüero, *Soldiers, Civilians, and Democracy: Post-Franco Spain in Comparative Perspective* (Baltimore: Johns Hopkins University Press, 1995).
5 See, for example, Jordi Solé Tura, *Nacionalidades y nacionalismos en España* (Madrid: Alianza Editorial, 1985).

6 Leonardo Morlino, 'Political Parties and Democratic Consolidation in Southern Europe', in Richard Gunther, Nikiforos Diamandouros and Hans-Juergen Puhle (eds), *The Politics of Democratic Consolidation. Southern Europe in Comparative Perspective* (Baltimore: Johns Hopkins University Press, 1995), pp. 315–88; and Leonardo Morlino, *Democracy Between Consolidation and Crisis. Parties, Groups and Citizens in Southern Europe* (Oxford: Oxford University Press, 1998); see also Paul Heywood, 'The Emergence of New Party Systems and Transitions to Democracy: Spain in Comparative Perspective', in Geoffrey Pridham and Paul Lewis (eds), *Stabilizing Fragile Democracies. Comparing New Party Systems in Southern and Eastern Europe* (London: Routledge, 1996), pp. 145–66.

7 To use the terminology of Lijphart; see Arend Lijphart, *Democracies. Patterns of Majoritarian and Consensus Government in Twenty-One Countries* (New Haven: Yale University Press, 1984); Arend Lijphart, *Patterns of Democracy. Government Forms and Performance in Thirty-Six Countries* (New Haven: Yale University Press, 1999). See also Jordi Capo Giol, Ramón Cotarelo, Diego López Garrido and Joan Subirats, 'By Consociationalism to a Majoritarian Parliamentary System: The Rise and Decline of the Spanish Cortes', in Ulrike Liebert and Maurizio Cotta (eds), *Parliament and Democratic Consolidation in Southern Europe: Greece, Italy, Portugal, Spain and Turkey* (London: Pinter, 1990), pp. 92–111.

8 Giovanni Sartori, *Parties and Party Systems* (Cambridge: Cambridge University Press), 1976; and *Comparative Constitutional Engineering* (London: Macmillan, 1994). See also J. Samuel Valenzuela, 'Democratic Consolidation in Post-Transitional Settings: Notion, Process, and Facilitating Conditions', in Scott Mainwaring, Guillermo O'Donnell and J. Samuel Valenzuela (eds), *Issues in Democratic Consolidation: The New South American Democracies in Comparative Perspective* (Notre Dame, IN: University of Notre Dame Press, 1992), pp. 57–104.

9 Juan Linz, 'Transitions to Democracy', *The Washington Quarterly* 13 (1990), pp. 143–64; 'The Perils of Presidentialism', *Journal of Democracy* 1 (1990), pp. 51–9; and 'Presidential or Parliamentary Democracy: Does it Make a Difference?', in Juan Linz and J. Samuel Valenzuela (eds), *The Failure of Presidential Democracy* (Baltimore: Johns Hopkins University Press, 1994), pp. 3–87.

10 Giuseppe Di Palma, *To Craft Democracies* (Berkeley: University of California Press, 1990); Terry Lynn Karl and Philippe Schmitter, 'Modes of Transition in Southern and Eastern Europe, Southern and Central America', *International Social Science Journal* 43 (1991), pp. 269–84; Michael Burton, Richard Gunther and John Higley, 'Introduction: Elite Transformations and Democratic Regimes', in Gunther and Higley (eds), *Elites and Democratic Consolidation*, pp. 1–37.

11 Frances Hagopian, 'Democracy by Undemocratic Means? Elites, Political Pacts, and Regime Transition in Brazil', *Comparative Political Studies* 23 (1990), pp. 147–70; Frances Hagopian, *Traditional Politics and Regime Change in Brazil* (Cambridge: Cambridge University Press, 1996). See also Terry Lynn Karl, 'Petroleum and Political Pacts', *Latin American Research Review* 22 (1987), pp. 63–94.

12 Bonnie Field, 'Frozen Democracy? Pacting and the Consolidation of Democracy: The Spanish and Argentine Democracies in Comparative Perspective'. Paper presented to the 2000 Meeting of the Latin American Studies Association, Miami, 16–18 March 2000.

13 Lijphart, *Patterns of Democracy*, chapter 1.

14 Luis Moreno, *The Federalization of Spain* (London: Frank Cass, 2001); Eliseo Aja, *El estado autonómico* (Madrid: Alianza Editorial, 1999).

15 Gunther *et al.*, *Spain After Franco*, pp. 43–53; José Ramón Montero, 'Stabilizing the Democratic Order: Electoral Behaviour in Spain', in Paul Heywood (ed.),

Politics and Policy in Democratic Spain: No Longer Different? (London: Frank Cass, 1999), pp. 53–79; Jonathan Hopkin, 'Spain: Proportional Representation with Majoritarian Outcomes', in Michael Gallagher and Paul Mitchell (eds), *The Politics of Electoral Systems* (Oxford: Oxford University Press, forthcoming).

16 Pablo Lucas Verdú, *La octava ley fundamental* (Madrid: Tecnos, 1976).

17 Carlos Huneeus, *La Unión de Centro Democrático y la transición a la democracia en España* (Madrid: Centro de Investigaciones Sociológicas, 1985); Jonathan Hopkin, *Party Formation and Democratic Transition in Spain* (Basingstoke: Macmillan, 1999).

18 Huneeus, *La Unión de Centro Democrático.*

19 Lynn Maurer, 'Parliamentary Influence in a New Democracy: The Spanish Congress', *Journal of Legislative Studies* 5/2 (1999), pp. 24–45; Field, 'Frozen Democracy?'

20 Field, 'Frozen Democracy', also Maurer, 'Parliamentary Influence'.

21 Paul Heywood, *The Government and Politics of Spain* (Basingstoke: Macmillan, 1995); Paul Heywood, 'Power Diffusion or Concentration? In Search of the Spanish Policy Process', in Heywood, *Politics and Policy in Democratic Spain*, pp. 103–23.

22 See also Ingrid van Biezen and Jonathan Hopkin, 'The Presidentialization of Spanish Democracy: Sources of Prime Ministerial Power in Post-Franco Spain', in Thomas Poguntke and Paul Webb (eds), *The Presidentialization of Politics in Democratic Societies?* (Oxford: Oxford University Press, forthcoming).

23 Emilio Attard, *La Constitución por dentro* (Barcelona: Argos Vergara, 1983); Miguel Herrero de Miñón, *Memorias de estío* (Madrid: Temas de Hoy, 1993); Hopkin, *Party Formation and Democratic Transition*, chapter 3.

24 Hopkin, *Party Formation and Democratic Transition*, chapter 3.

25 Gianfranco Pasquino, 'Executive-Legislative Relations', in Gunther, Diamandouros and Puhle, *The Politics of Democratic Consolidation*, pp. 261–83.

26 Maurer, 'Parliamentary Influence in a New Democracy'.

27 See Sartori, *Parties and Party Systems.*

28 For example, Manuel Fraga, *El gabinete inglés* (Salamanca: University of Salamanca, 1954) and *Cánovas, Maeztu y otros discursos de la segunda Restauración* (Madrid: Sala Editorial, 1976).

29 See Adolfo Suárez, *Un nuevo horizonte para España. Discursos del Presidente del Gobierno 1976–78* (Madrid: Colección Informe, 1978); Josep Meliá, *Así cayó Adolfo Suárez* (Barcelona: Planeta, 1981).

30 See, for example, Tácito, *Tácito* (Madrid: Ibérico Europeo Ediciones, 1975).

31 Jordi Capo Giol, 'To Reform the Electoral System in Spain?', in Serge Noiret (ed.), *Political Strategies and Electoral Reforms: Origins of Voting Systems in Europe in the 19th and 20th Centuries* (Baden-Baden: Nomos Verlagsgesellschaft, 1990), pp. 403–22, at p. 408.

32 Gunther *et al.*, *Spain After Franco*, p. 45.

33 Nancy Bermeo, 'Myths of Moderation: Confrontation and Conflict in Democratic Transitions', in Lisa Anderson (ed.), *Transitions to Democracy* (New York: Columbia University Press, 1999), pp. 120–37, at p. 136.

34 Richard Gillespie, *The Spanish Socialist Party. A History of Factionalism* (Oxford: Clarendon, 1989).

35 Santos Juliá, *Los socialistas en la política española, 1879–1982* (Madrid: Taurus, 1997), p. 452.

36 Ibid., p. 472.

37 Bonifacio de la Cuadra and Soledad Gallego-Díaz, *Del consenso al desencanto* (Madrid: Saltés, 1981), p. 44.

38 Juliá, *Los socialistas en la política española*, pp. 486–504.

39 Richard Gunther interview, 1981 (Juan March Institute, Madrid).

40 Paloma Aguilar, 'The Memory of the Civil War in the Transition to Democracy: The Peculiarity of the Basque Case', in Heywood, *Politics and Policy in Democratic Spain*, pp. 5–25.
41 'UCD favorecerá la modificación del reglamento del Congreso', *El País*, 4 March 1979, p. 12.
42 'Coalición Democrática apoyará a UCD sin exigir contrapartidas', *El País*, 8 March 1979, p. 13.
43 See, for instance, the article by Socialist Luis Solana, 'Ya no hay centro', *El País*, 18 March 1979, p. 14.
44 Juliá, *Los socialistas en la política española*, p. 520.
45 Gillespie, *The Spanish Socialist Party*, pp. 337–56; Santos Juliá, 'The Ideological Conversion of the Leaders of the PSOE, 1976–79', in Frances Lannon and Paul Preston (eds), *Elites and Power in Twentieth Century Spain: Essays in Honour of Sir Raymond Carr* (Oxford: Clarendon, 1990), pp. 269–85.
46 Juliá, *Los socialistas en la política española*, p. 523.
47 Jordi Giol Capo, 'Estrategias para un sistema de partidos', *Revista de Estudios Políticos* 23 (1981), pp. 153–67, at p. 158.
48 Hopkin, *Party Formation and Democratic Transition*, chapter 4.
49 Richard Gunther interview, 1983 (Juan March Institute, Madrid).
50 Joaquín Garrigues Walker, *Un año antes, un año después* (Madrid: Unión Editorial, 1978), pp. 126–8.
51 Richard Gunther interview, 1983 (Juan March Institute, Madrid).
52 Ibid.
53 For example, on the position of religious schools and on divorce; see Hopkin, *Party Formation and Democratic Transition*, chapter 5.
54 Richard Gunther interview, 1983 (Juan March Institute, Madrid).
55 See *Diario de Sesiones del Congreso de los Diputados*, 91–5, 20–30 May 1980, pp. 5949–6294.
56 Ibid., 94, 29 May 1980, pp. 6170–1.
57 Hopkin, *Party Formation and Democratic Transition*.
58 Giacomo Sani, 'Los desplazamientos del electorado: anatomía del cambio', in Linz and Montero (eds), *Crisis y cambio*, pp. 1–26, at p. 13.
59 Interview by the author, 1993. See also Meliá, *Así cayó Adolfo Suárez*.
60 Luis Gámir, 'La tentación conservadora/2', *El País*, 12 September 1981, p. 14.
61 Robert Martínez and Rafael Pardo Avellanada, 'El asociacionismo empresarial español en la transición', *Papeles de Economía Española* 22 (1985), pp. 84–115, at p. 84.
62 Herrero de Miñón, *Memorias de estío*, p. 228.
63 Interview by the author, 1992.
64 Ibid.
65 CEOE, *Discurso del Presidente a la Asamblea Electoral, 9 setiembre 1981* (Madrid: CEOE, 1981), p. 21. This was not simply a piece of advice – shortly afterwards the CEOE withdrew campaign funding from the UCD.
66 Cited in Richard Gunther, 'Electoral Laws, Party Systems, and Elites: The Case of Spain', *American Political Science Review* 83 (1989), pp. 835–58, at p. 851.
67 José María Maravall, *The Transition to Democracy in Spain* (London: Croom Helm, 1982), chapter 2.
68 Richard Gunther interview, 1983 (Juan March Institute, Madrid).
69 Interview by the author, 1992.
70 Oscar Alzaga, 'Reflexiones sobre una crisis política grave', *Revista de Derecho Político* 10 (1981), pp. 133–44.
71 Lijphart, *Patterns of Democracy*, p. 303.
72 Ibid., pp. 305–6.

2   The monarchy of Juan Carlos

From dictator's dreams to democratic realities

Paul Preston

King Juan Carlos has been described by a recent biographer as a 'self-made monarch'. Had such a phrase been used to describe any of his predecessors over the last two centuries, it would have provoked reactions along the lines of 'yet another example of shoddy Spanish workmanship'. The claim is justified in that Juan Carlos played a crucial part during the relatively pacific transition to democracy between 1975 and 1977, in his subsequent role as head of the armed forces in restraining *golpismo*, and finally, and most courageously, intervening on the night of 23 February 1981 to stifle the attempted coup.

It would, however, be wrong to give the impression that Juan Carlos was the prince born to bring Spain back to democracy and a democratic monarchy back to Spain. Numerous interviewers of the king and some scholars have interpreted the entire transition process as a consequence of the clairvoyance of the king and his advisers. The very presence of Juan Carlos on the throne was the culmination of a process whereby Franco set out to construct a 'Francoist' monarchy to ensure the continuation of his regime after his death. That role was willingly accepted by Juan Carlos, although, in the course of the dictator's final years, motivated by a healthy instinct for self-preservation, he dramatically redefined his role. Throughout the process there was an element of cynicism and calculation and a considerable contribution from a number of shrewd political advisers. That does not mean that the transition to democracy in Spain was made possible by political engineering carried out by a group of experts in the employ of a far-sighted king. This is not the place to explain the process in detail, but suffice it to say that there would have been no transition had it not been for the profound social changes of the preceding 20 years. The mass pressure of workers, students, women's groups and the traditional anti-Francoist opposition obliged the king's advisers to see that real concessions would have to be made if the monarchy were to survive more than a few months after the death of the dictator. However, that in turn, does not mean that the role of democratic protagonism played by the king did not signify 'earning' not the restoration of the monarchy – that was Franco's work – but the right to remain on merit as head of state.

In order to understand what was involved in Juan Carlos's redefinition of his role it is necessary to focus on General Franco's contribution to the process of bringing back the monarchy to Spain. Franco's attitude towards the Borbón family was a complex mixture of slavish adulation underlain with an intensely critical perception of its historical failures. He had been born in the naval port of El Ferrol which felt with particular bitterness the loss of the remnants of empire in 1898. In 1941, believing himself to be on the verge of creating a new empire, he declared: 'when we began our life . . . we saw our childhood dominated by the contemptible incompetence of those men who abandoned half of the fatherland's territory to foreigners'.[1] Although he had accepted very considerable preferment from King Alfonso XIII, he did nothing to defend him in April 1931 when the Second Republic was established. Deeply tainted by his acquiescence in the establishment of the military dictatorship of General Miguel Primo de Rivera, Alfonso had been unable to survive its failure. Lacking the will – or brutality – to hold onto his throne by violence, he had withdrawn from Spain – not abdicated – in the hope that his followers would be able to destroy the Republic and call him back. Throughout the Spanish Civil War, the conviction grew in Franco that he was doing what Alfonso XIII had been incapable of doing: definitely eradicating the poisons of liberalism, democracy, freemasonry, socialism, communism and anarchism from Spain. Nevertheless, his damning view of Alfonso was never voiced publicly. Most army officers believed that they were fighting in order to restore the monarchy. Franco always gave the impression that he shared that ambition although he was to devote massive effort to ensuring that the monarchy would not return until 36 years after the end of the war. Even then, there would be no restoration of the monarchy that came to an end in April 1931, but rather, to use Francoist terms, the installation of a new institution.

On 15 August 1936, Franco had announced in Seville the adoption of the red and yellow monarchist flag as the banner of the Nationalists. This gesture was one factor which clinched the support of key monarchist generals for Franco to become commander-in-chief of the Nationalist forces and then, on 1 October 1936, head of state of Nationalist Spain. On 7 December 1936, the then heir to the throne, Alfonso XIII's third son, Don Juan, wrote to Franco to express his desire to fight for the military rebels by joining the crew of a Nationalist warship. As son of the English queen of Spain, Victoria Eugenia, and having served in the Royal Navy, Don Juan was irremediably tainted with all the 'isms' that he wanted to eradicate from Spain. More immediately, Franco sensed the danger to himself in having the heir to the throne as a potential focus for monarchist agitation and he responded with consummate cunning:

It would have given me great pleasure to accede to your request . . . However, the need to keep you safe would not permit you to live as a simple officer . . . the place which you occupy in the dynastic order and the obligations which arise from that impose upon us all, and demand of you, the sacrifice of desires which are as patriotic as they are noble and deeply felt, in the interests of the Patria.

He told the monarchist daily, *ABC* of Seville:

> My responsibilities are great and among them is the duty not to put his life in danger, since one day it may be precious to us . . . If one day a King returns to rule over the State, he will have to come as a peace-maker and should not be found among the victors.

The cynicism of such sentiments could be appreciated only after nearly four decades had elapsed during which Franco had dedicated his efforts to institutionalizing the division of Spain into victors and vanquished and omitting to restore the monarchy.[2]

Had they been a little more suspicious, Spanish monarchists might have been alarmed to note that the newly installed head of state began to comport himself as if he were the king rather than simply the praetorian guard responsible for bringing back the monarchy. With the support of the Catholic Church which had blessed the Nationalist war effort as a religious crusade, Franco began to project himself as the defender of Spain and the defender of the universal faith, both roles normally associated with the great kings of the past. Religious ritual was used to legitimize his power as it had those of the medieval king. The liturgy and iconography of his regime presented him as a holy crusader, he had a personal chaplain and he usurped the royal prerogative of entering and leaving churches under a canopy. The confidence in himself and his office generated by such ceremonial was revealed in a letter to Alfonso XIII who had written to him expressing concern about the low priority being given to the restoration of the monarchy. Franco's reply, on 4 December 1937, was harsh and dismissive: insinuating that the problems which caused the Civil War were of the king's own making and outlining both his own achievements and the tasks remaining to be carried out after the war. He made it clear that Alfonso XIII could expect to play no part in that future: 'the new Spain which we are forging has so little in common with the liberal and constitutional Spain over which you ruled that your training and old-fashioned political practices necessarily provoke the anxieties and resentments of Spaniards'.

At the end of the Civil War, Franco failed to send Alfonso XIII a telegram announcing the capture of Madrid which the king took as an unequivocal sign that he had no intention of restoring the monarchy. Rather, in all kinds of ways, Franco revealed his own monarchical pretensions, insisting on the right to name bishops, on the royal march being played every time his wife arrived at any official ceremony, and planning, until dissuaded by his brother-in-law, to establish his residence in the massive Palacio Real in Madrid. The *Ley de la Jefatura del Estado* on 8 August 1939 gave him legislative power to make laws and decrees without consulting the cabinet. It gave him 'the supreme power to issue laws of a general nature', and to issue specific decrees and laws without discussing them first with the cabinet 'when reasons of urgency so advise'. According to the exegetes of his controlled press, the 'supreme chief' was simply assuming the powers necessary to allow him to fulfil his historic destiny of national reconstruction. It was power of a kind previously enjoyed only by the kings of medieval Spain.[3]

During the Second World War, external dangers and an internal power struggle between Falangists and monarchists gave Franco ample excuse not to pursue the subject of the restoration of the monarchy. In fact, Alfonso XIII had finally abdicated on 15 January 1941 and died six weeks late on 28 February. The Caudillo gave little thought to the heir to the throne until the fall of Mussolini on 25 July 1943. Seizing this opportunity, Don Juan sent Franco a telegram recommending the restoration of the monarchy as the only way in which he might avoid the fate of the Duce. It was the beginning of a long duel between the two. Mortified, but storing his resentment for a better moment, Franco replied with an appeal to Don Juan's patriotism, begging him not to make any public statement which might weaken the regime.[4] At the end of 1943, the Dictatorship's intelligence service intercepted a letter from Don Juan to one of his followers calling upon them to break publicly with the regime. The Caudillo wrote to him again in terms which made it brutally clear that he considered his own right to rule Spain as infinitely superior to that of Juan III: 'Among the rights that underlie sovereign authority are the rights of occupation and conquest, not to mention that which is engendered by saving an entire society.'

Despite his virtually limitless confidence in his own superiority over the House of Borbón, and his belief in the legitimacy of his power by dint of the right of conquest, he felt seriously threatened by Don Juan's so-called Manifesto of Lausanne. With the defeat of the Axis imminent, this document, broadcast by the BBC on 19 March 1945, was a denunciation of the fascist origins and the totalitarian nature of the regime. It called upon Franco to withdraw and make way for a moderate, democratic, constitutional monarchy. It infuriated Franco and set in stone his prior determination that Don Juan would never be king of Spain. He was, as usual, publicly prudent although he privately told the monarchist General Alfredo Kindelán: 'as long as I live, I will never be a queen mother.'[5] He called a meeting of his military high command on the next day and dismissed suggestions that he stand down with a boast that the Western powers, eaten up with jealousy of his success, would soon imitate his regime.[6] However, in response to the hostility of the democratic powers and to the monarchist ambitions of his own generals, he began to take practical steps to give substance to his claims to be the best hope for the monarchy.

At a cabinet meeting held in early April, he talked of adopting 'a monarchical form of government'. A 'Council of the Kingdom' would be set up to establish the eventual succession. It was an idea whose daring was matched only by its duplicity. Franco would continue as head of state and, whoever the eventual monarchist successor might be, the candidate would not take the crown until Franco either died or abandoned power. Speaking on 1 May 1945 to his future Minister of Foreign Affairs (from 18 July 1945), the influential Catholic and monarchist, Alberto Martín Artajo, Franco outlined this plan for surviving the fall of the Axis. He would produce a law which turned Spain into a kingdom, but that would not necessarily mean bringing back the Bourbons. When Martín Artajo referred to Don Juan as the king and suggested that the proposed law should be discussed with him, Franco replied 'Don Juan is a pretender. It is up to me to decide.' In brutal language, he expressed his contempt for the track record of the decadent constitutional monarchy which had ended with Alfonso XIII by reference to the notorious immorality of the latter's grandmother, the nineteenth-century Queen Isabel II. It will be recalled that Isabel was noted for the eclectic nature of her sexual predilections which ranged broadly across the social spectrum and throughout the animal kingdom. There are those who believe that she was the inspiration behind Tom Lehrer's much-quoted remark about the literal meaning of the phrase 'animal husbandry'. Franco said 'The last man to sleep with Doña Isabel cannot be the father of the king and what comes out of the belly of the Queen must be examined to see if it is fit.' Clearly, Franco did not regard Don Juan de Borbón as fit to be king – 'he has neither will nor character'. A monarchical restoration would take place, declared Franco, only when he, the Caudillo, decided and the pretender had sworn an oath to uphold the fundamental laws of the regime.[7]

In an attempt to neutralize Don Juan, Franco had been suggesting that he take up residence in Spain. However, the heir to the throne was determined not to return until Franco left and, at the beginning of February 1946, he took up residence in the fashionable Portuguese resort of Estoril near Lisbon. His arrival in the Iberian peninsula set off a wave of monarchist enthusiasm which was expressed in various ways. Most worryingly from Franco's point of view was a collective letter of greeting signed by 458 of the most important figures of the Spanish establishment, including 20 ex-ministers, the presidents of the country's five biggest banks, many aristo-crats and prominent university professors. It expressed their wish to see the restoration of the monarchy, 'incarnated by Your Majesty'.[8] Published on 13 January 1946, it infuriated Franco. He reacted violently, telling a cabinet meeting on 15 February, 'This is a declaration of war, they must be crushed like worms.' His first reaction was say that he would put all the signatories in prison without trial. Advised by ministers of the potentially damaging international repercussions of such a move, he then went through the list of signatories, writing next to their names different ways of punishing them, by withdrawing passports, tax inspections or dismissal from their posts. In the case of General Kindelán, Franco had him exiled to the Canary Islands.[9] He instructed elements of the Falangist *Sindicato Español Universitario* to disrupt the classes of the professors who had signed the document and sent a note to Don Juan in which he announced that relations between them were broken.[10]

He drew the conclusion from the incident, and the broad range of support manifested for Don Juan from Carlists on the extreme right to Socialists on the left, that he must accelerate his plans to 'monarchize' his regime. This took the form of the 'Law of Succession' on 31 March 1947. The first article declared that 'Spain, as a political unit, is a Catholic, social and representative state which, in keeping with her tradition, declares herself constituted as a kingdom'. The second article declared that 'the Head of State is the Caudillo of Spain and of the Crusade, Generalísimo of the Armed Forces, Don Francisco Franco Bahamonde'. The declaration that Franco would govern until prevented by death or incapacity, the Caudillo's right to name his own royal successor, the lack of any indication that the royal family had any rights of dynastic succession, the statement that the future king must uphold the fundamental laws of the regime and could be removed if he departed from them – all this showed that nothing but the label had changed. However, when the Korean War broke out three years later, that repackaging was virtually all that would be needed to put an end to international ostracism and open the way to incorporation into the Western community.

The Law of Succession received considerable popular backing in the referendum of 6 July 1947. Nevertheless, Franco was sufficiently concerned by the threat to his position constituted by Don Juan that he went to great lengths to organize a meeting with him on his yacht, *Azor*, on 25 August 1948. He quickly dashed any hopes that Don Juan might have still entertained of ascending the throne by telling him that he had excellent health and expected to rule Spain for at least another 20 years. His excuse for not restoring the monarchy was a concern that Don Juan would not have the firmness of command (*mando*) necessary. In contrast to what he imagined would be Don Juan's practice, he declared 'I do not permit my ministers to answer me back. I give them orders and they obey.' Franco's real purpose in arranging the meeting finally became apparent when he showed immense interest in the pretender's ten-year-old son Juan Carlos completing his education in Spain. Juan Carlos in Spain would be a hostage to justify Franco's indefinite assumption of the role of regent and an instrument to control the political direction of any future monarchical restoration. Franco spoke with a mixture of cunning and prejudice of the dangers run by princes under foreign influence (*príncipes extranjerizados*). Although no agreement had been reached on the subject, Franco leaked the news that the young prince was to be educated in Spain. Fearful of the consequences for a future restoration, Don Juan was forced to agree, knowing full well that any announcement that Juan Carlos was going to live under Franco's tutelage would be used by the regime to imply that he had abdicated. The ten-year-old prince arrived in Spain on 9 November 1948 to a barrage of regime publicity which gave the impression that the monarchy was in every way subordinate to the wishes of the dictator.[11]

The contempt with which he was treated by Franco inclined Don Juan to flex his muscles one last time. Juan Carlos had finished the secondary education imparted by his private tutors and, on 16 July 1954, Don Juan sent a *note verbale* to the Caudillo to say that it was time for his son to begin his university education at Louvain. Franco had his own plans for Juan Carlos to enter the military academy at Zaragoza for a period, followed by time at the naval and air academies, the social science and engineering faculties of Madrid University and then some practice in the art of government 'at the side of the Caudillo'. His reply to Don Juan coldly stated that those who hoped to govern Spain should be educated in Spain. The contemptuous implication was that Don Juan did not figure in his plans for any future monarchical restoration. Franco's letter also threatened that if Don Juan did not accept the programme for Juan Carlos, he would be 'closing the natural and viable road that could be offered for the installation of the monarchy in our *Patria*'.[12]

Nevertheless, innumerable outbursts of monarchist fervour inclined Franco to meet Don Juan again in December 1954. As with the *Azor* meeting in 1948, he simply wanted to convey to royalists inside Spain an illusion of his own good faith as a monarchist, but behind closed doors Franco left no room for doubt that he would hand over only on his death or total incapacity and then only to a king who was committed to the unconditional maintenance of the Dictatorship. Not to accept that his son Juan Carlos should be educated entirely within the values of Franco's system would be taken as a renunciation of the throne.[13]

In his end-of-year message on 31 December 1954, Franco, using the 'royal we' declared that, 'if . . . we took from our traditions the form of a kingdom, which gave unity and authority to our Golden Age, this does not mean under any circumstances the resuscitation of the vices and defects which in the last centuries ruined it'. In Francoist code, this meant that there would be no restoration of the Bourbon dynasty.[14] To Falangist concerns that he might be considering an early transition to the monarchy, Franco responded with a widely reproduced interview which dispelled hopes of his early departure. 'Although my magistracy is for life', he declared pompously, 'it is to be hoped that there are many years before me, and the immediate interest of the issue is diluted in time.' The message was that any future monarchy would be a Falangist one devoid of the constitutional weaknesses of that which fell in 1931.[15]

It seemed in the mid-1950s as if, having rejected the possibility of a transition to Don Juan, Franco planned to withdraw into hard-line Falangism. It took the joint efforts of two of his servants to get the monarchy back on the agenda for a post-Francoist Spain. His *éminence grise* and cabinet secretary, Admiral Carrero Blanco, together with the Opus Dei technocrat Laureano López Rodó, pushed the idea of an authoritarian monarchy which would guarantee the continuity of Francoism. The first draft of their constitutional scheme for the post-Franco succession was given to Franco by Carrero Blanco on 7 March 1959, together with a sycophantic note urging the completion of the 'constitutional process':

> If the king were to inherit the powers which Your Excellency has, we would find it alarming since he will change everything. We must ratify the life-time character of the magistracy of Your Excellency who is Caudillo which is greater than king because you are founding a monarchy.[16]

So hostile was Franco to the idea of bringing nearer his own departure from the political scene that he did nothing with the draft for nearly eight years.

Franco finally permitted the law drafted so long ago be presented to the Cortes in November 1966 as the *Ley Orgánica del Estado* which created the mechanisms for the future without specifically naming a candidate. As beneficiary, the Caudillo's immediate entourage favoured the more reliably Falangist *príncipe azul*, Alfonso de Borbón Dampierre (who was the fiancé of Franco's granddaughter María del Carmen, whom he was to marry on 18 March 1972). The job of implementing the law in favour of Juan Carlos fell to Admiral Carrero Blanco, whom, on 21 September 1967, Franco named vice-president of the government.[17] For his part, to ensure that he would be the favoured candidate on 8 January 1969, in an interview with the official news agency EFE, Juan Carlos declared his unreserved commitment to the Francoist principle of monarchical installation rather than restoration. López Rodó said to Franco: 'The Prince has burned his boats. Now all that is lacking is Your Excellency's decision.'

When he took the decision in July 1969, Franco wrote to Don Juan asking for his formal acceptance of his son's designation as 'the coronation of the political process of the regime'. Don Juan declined with dignity, pointing out that the monarch should be king of all Spaniards, above groups and parties, based on popular support and committed to individual and collective liberties. He thereby condemned implicitly his son's monarchy as irrevocably linked to the dictatorship. [18] Bestowing upon Juan Carlos of the title of *Príncipe de España*, and not *Príncipe de Asturias*, the traditional title of the heir to the throne, was Franco's device to severe both the continuity and the legitimacy of the Borbón line. The new monarchy would be his and his alone. In the Cortes, on 22 July 1969, the prince swore fidelity to the principles of the *Movimiento*.[19]

In the summer of 1973 Franco handed over the powers of head of the government to Admiral Carrero Blanco, whose job was to be the political bodyguard of the prince. There has been considerable recent debate over the commitment of Carrero to ushering in a constitutional monarchy under Juan Carlos.[20] However, the tone of his political thought can be derived from his statement that 'to attempt to liberalize Spain would be like offering a reformed alcoholic a drink'.[21] It did not matter, since Carrero Blanco was assassinated on 20 December 1973. It was hardly surprising that, in the two years preceding Franco's death on 20 November 1975, the brutal incompetence which poisoned relations with the Basques, the clergy and the workers caused growing disquiet among supporters of Juan Carlos, who began to fear that his future was being irrevocably compromised. During that period, Juan Carlos twice became provisional head of state. In July 1974, he assumed the position for barely six weeks. On 20 October 1975, Article 11 of the Ley Orgánica was reactivated. The first experience was sufficiently distressing for him to endeavour to insist on it not being provisional this time. It was rumoured that when he asked Franco if this time it would be for good, the dictator was alleged to have replied, 'Well, it can be until you die but then I will resume my rule.' In fact he was too ill to reply one way or the other.

Success for the monarchy could be measured only in terms of permanence, and that required freeing it of its Francoist stigma. The ultra-rightist Blas Piñar expressed the dilemma facing the new king when he declared: 'This is no monarchical restoration, but the installation of a new Francoist monarchy which has no other thought behind it than the Nationalist victory in the Civil War.'[22] It is hardly surprising that the clandestine opposition press greeted Juan Carlos's coronation with headlines like '¡No a un Rey impuesto!' and '¡No a un Rey franquista!'[23] Considerable popular goodwill greeted the beginnings of Juan Carlos's reign, but the bunker remained powerful, entrenched in the Army, the police and the Civil Guard. Throughout the next few years, Juan Carlos would make careful use of his position as commander-in-chief of the armed forces. Three weeks before Franco died, he had flown his own aircraft to El Aaiún in Spanish Sahara under threat from Morocco and visited the garrison there, which provoked considerable praise and enthusiasm among the officer corps.[24] The problem was illustrated starkly on 22 November when Juan Carlos addressed the Francoist Cortes. His mildly progressive speech, which ostentatiously omitted references to 18 July 1936, was received coldly by the *procuradores*, who then gave an ecstatic ovation to Franco's daughter.

The survival of the monarchy, let alone the bloodless resolution of the crisis in which Spain found itself at the death of Franco, depended on the skill of Juan Carlos, of the ministers that he chose and, lest it be forgotten, of the leaders of the opposition. Juan Carlos knew that important sectors of Spanish capitalism were anxious to ditch the political mechanisms of Francoism. Through his wife, he was equally conscious of the consequences of the Greek royal family's costly errors. The views of his father were also influential. By opting boldly for progress, he would be assured of mass support for the monarchy. If his long-term survival depended on him responding to the overwhelming popular urge for democracy, Franco had rigged the constitutional cards to prevent him doing so.

The regime's institutions, the Consejo del Reino, the Consejo Nacional del Movimiento and the Cortes were in the hands of hard-line Francoists and behind them stood the Army and the Civil Guard. Aware of the strength, determination and ill-will of the bunker in the early days of his reign, Juan Carlos opted for caution and severely disappointed those who had placed their hopes in him by asking Franco's last prime minister, Carlos Arias Navarro, to stay on. He would have preferred to appoint his one-time tutor, the expert in Francoist constitutional law, Torcuato Fernández Miranda. The Talleyrand-like Fernández Miranda was hardly a liberal but his expertise would make him the brains behind the reform project. Fernandez Miranda and the king agreed that he would be more use as president of the Cortes (which would have to ratify any reform scheme) and of the Consejo del Reino (which chose prime ministers), from which positions he could facilitate a 'legal' reform.[25] His first crucial move was to use his position to persuade Arias Navarro to include the young Adolfo Suárez in his cabinet as Minister-Secretary of the Movimiento. When Juan Carlos finally felt strong enough to replace Arias in the summer of 1976, Torcuato also used his power within the Consejo del Reino to ensure that Suárez was in the *terna* from which the candidates were to be picked.[26] Thereafter, with Fernández Miranda as a shrewd script-writer, Suárez fronted the complex operation whereby the Francoist establishment effectively dismantled itself.

During the transition, the king kept a relatively low profile and accepted that if the reform programme planned by Torcuato Fernández Miranda and Suárez were to be successful, it would leave the monarchy effectively powerless. The particular contribution of Juan Carlos lay first of all in persuading relatively heavy-weight figures to join Suárez's first cabinet,[27] in riding out the storm of opprobrium provoked by his nomination of a Falangist and, above all, in the skill with which he neutralized the high command of the army. Throughout the entire transition process, he travelled indefatigably throughout Spain, which did much to generate support for the reform.

He made a very considerable effort to make contact with members of the opposition and, when he did so, treated them with great affability. On their first meeting in 1976, Juan Carlos said to Miquel Roca i Junyent, 'Tu y yo, por edad, no somos monárquicos.' In a similar vein, during the period in 1978 when the new democratic Constitution was being elaborated by a parliamentary commission or Ponencia of which Roca was a member, there was a reception for Giscard d'Estaing who was visiting Madrid. At one point, Juan Carlos sidled over to Miquel Roca and whispered 'Parece más rey que yo, ¿verdad?'[28] Indeed, while it might be said that the transition was about the interaction of broad social forces and was merely articulated through the political roles of the negotiators from each side, Juan Carlos's role was one of persuading the opposition that he could eventually play a role in democratization while still maintaining the support of Francoists by dint of continuing to respect the Leyes Fundamentales on which, for the moment, his 'legitimacy' rested. Through his intermediaries, he was able to give Socialists and Communists the hint that he might be able to take the risk of breaking with the Francoist institutions.

However, it was precisely this process which caused the greatest problem. The legalization of the Communist Party on 9 April 1977 triggered the military's belief that its job was not so much to defend Spain from external enemies but to safeguard Franco's Civil War victory. From 1977 until 1982, barely a month went by in which Juan Carlos did not have to impose all of his authority as commander-in-chief of the armed forces on senior officers who were outraged at Suárez's government promoting liberal officers out of turn. The situation was perilous because of the relentless provocation of ETA murders of officers. The response of the ultras within the army was *golpismo*. Juan Carlos received senior officers at the Zarzuela and visited garrisons to take the message that the only acceptable response was unity and discipline. The crisis intensified and in late 1980 the plot which culminated in the Tejerazo of 23 February 1981 was hatched. The ex-secretary general of the royal household, General Alfonso Armada, persuaded other generals, most notably the captain-general of Valencia, the ultra Jaime Milans del Bosch, that he had royal approval for a military coup. On 29 January 1981, with his own party, Unión de Centro Democrático crumbling, Adolfo Suárez resigned as prime minister. This left the king as the most visible guarantor of democracy, but a series of meetings with Armada enabled the latter to give the impression of royal collusion in what was being plotted. On 23 February 1981, Lieutenant-Colonel Antonio Tejero seized the entire Spanish political elite as they attended the Cortes ceremony of the investiture of a new cabinet under Leopoldo Calvo Sotelo, and Milans del Bosch ordered tanks into the streets of Valencia. Alone with his immediate staff, the king courageously took charge of the operation to dismantle the coup. In the course of a tense night, he made it quite clear to the military that he would be upholding the Constitution, appearing on television and personally informing Milans 'No *golpe de estado* of any kind can shelter behind the person of the king. It is against the king.' He effectively told Milans that he would have to kill him in order to succeed: 'I swear to you that I will neither abdicate nor leave Spain.' Thereafter, he was insistent that, while the culprits should be brought to justice, there should be no generalized grudge against the military. He had cleared the monarchy of the stigma of Francoism and earned the right to be head of state. Thereafter, it could be said that Spain had become a Juancarlista country. Whether it has become monarchist remains to be seen.

Notes

1 *La Vanguardia Española*, 18 July 1941.
2 *ABC* (Seville), 18 July 1937.
3 *Boletín Oficial del Estado*, 9 August; *Arriba*, 9 August; *Ya*, 9 August 1939.
4 Laureano López Rodó, *La larga marcha hacia la monarquía* (Barcelona: Noguer, 1977), pp. 515–19; José María Gil Robles, *La monarquía por la que yo luché: páginas de un diario 1941–1954* (Madrid, 1976), p. 55.
5 Manuel Vázquez Montalbán, *Los demonios familiares de Franco* (Barcelona: Dopesa, 1978), p. 105.

6 Bowker, the British chargé d'affaires, to Eden, the British Foreign Minister, 27 March 1945, PRO FO371/49587, Z4137/233/41.

7 Javier Tusell, *Franco y los católicos: la política interior española entre 1945 y 1957* (Madrid: Alianza Editorial, 1984), pp. 56–9.

8 Luis Suárez Fernández, *Francisco Franco y su tiempo*, vol. IV (Madrid: Fundación Nacional Francisco Franco, 1984), pp. 53, 62–3. López Rodó, *La larga marcha*, p. 62; Javier Tusell, *La oposición democrática al franquismo 1939–1962* (Barcelona: Planeta, 1977), pp. 114–16.

9 Alfredo Kindelán Duany, *La verdad de mis relaciones con Franco* (Barcelona: Planeta, 1981), pp. 128–30, 254; Tusell, *Franco y los católicos*, pp. 150–1.

10 Javier Tusell, *La oposición democrática al franquismo*, pp. 114–16; Gil Robles, *La monarquía*, pp. 163, 168–9.

11 Tusell, *La oposición democrática*, pp. 197–202; Suárez Fernández, *Franco*, vol. IV, pp. 249–51.

12 Diary entries for 13 May, 21, 22 June, 25 July, 7 September 1954; Don Juan to Franco, 16 July, Franco to Don Juan 17, 20 July 1954, in Gil Robles, *La monarquía*, pp. 327–8, 411–18; López Rodó, *La larga marcha*, pp. 115–17, 554–5.

13 Mallet, the British ambassador, to Eden, 11 January 1955, FO371/117914, RS1942/4; Pedro Sáinz Rodríguez, *Un reinado en la sombra* (Barcelona: Planeta, 1981), pp. 222–35; Jean Créac'h, *Le coeur et l'épée* (Paris: Plon, 1958), pp. 341–5.

14 Francisco Franco, *Discursos y mensajes del Jefe del Estado 1951–1954* (Madrid: Publicaciones Españolas, 1955), pp. 551–3.

15 *Arriba*, 23, 27 January 1955; *ABC*, 1 March 1955.

16 Suárez Fernández, *Franco*, vol. VI, p. 96.

17 Ricardo de la Cierva, *Historia del franquismo: il aislamiento, transformación, agonía (1945–1975)* (Barcelona: Planeta, 1978), pp. 250–1; Manuel Fraga Iribarne, *Memoria breve de una vida pública* (Barcelona: Planeta, 1980), p. 194; López Rodó, *La larga marcha*, pp. 263–5; Laureano López Rodó, *Memorias: años decisivos* (Barcelona: Plaza y Janés, 1991), p. 207.

18 López Rodó, *Memorias*, pp. 456–66.

19 Joaquín Bardavío, *Los silencios del Rey* (Madrid: Strips Editores, 1979), pp. 49–50.

20 Javier Tusell, *Carrero. La eminencia gris del régimen de Franco* (Madrid: Ediciones Temas de Hoy, 1993).

21 Writing as Ginés de Buitrago, *ABC*, 2 April 1970.

22 *Cambio 16*, no. 206, 17 November 1975.

23 *Mundo Obrero*, no. 38, 25 November 1975; *Servir al Pueblo* (Movimiento Comunista Español), no. 45, November 1975. See also *Frente Libertario*, no. 57, December 1975 and *Correo del Pueblo* (Partido de Trabajo de España), nos 21 and 22, 18 November, 6 December 1975.

24 Alfonso Armada, *Al servicio de la Corona* (Barcelona: Planeta, 1983), pp. 190–2.

25 Joaquín Bardavío, *El dilema: un pequeño caudillo o un gran rey* (Madrid: Strips Editores, 1978), pp. 20–4, 42–6; Gregorio Moran, *Adolfo Suárez: historia de una ambición* (Barcelona: Planeta, 1979), p. 16.

26 *El País*, 2, 4 July 1976; Alfonso Osorio, *Trayectoria política de un ministro de la corona* (Barcelona: Planeta, 1980), pp. 126–9; Morán, *Suárez*, pp. 55–61; Bardavío, *El dilema*, pp. 150–5; Antonio Izquierdo, *Yo, testigo de cargo* (Barcelona: Planeta, 1981), p. 41.

27 Osorio, *Trayectoria*, pp. 130–4.

28 Author's interview with Miquel Roca, London, 23 March 1995.

3 Corruption, democracy and governance in contemporary Spain

Paul M. Heywood

There is no doubt that Spain's post-Franco transition from dictatorship to democracy represents a remarkable political achievement. Indeed, the Spanish transition has often been invoked as a 'model' for achieving the successful reconciliation of opposing forces and demands: not only were competing visions of the country's future accommodated within a flexible constitutional settlement, but there was also a widespread consensus over the need to draw a line under the past and avoid apportioning blame and responsibility. However, whilst Spain's transition has been almost universally hailed as a triumph, there is less consensus over the quality of the democracy which resulted. In technical terms, contemporary Spain is unquestionably a fully fledged democratic member of the European and international communities, meeting such generally accepted indicators as open and widespread participation in the political system and its decision-making processes, defence of civil liberties and human rights, relative freedom of information, and the rule of law. At the very least, Spain stands comparison in these areas with its European neighbours.

Yet, none the less, concerns continue to be expressed about various aspects of how democracy functions in Spain. Questions have been raised over the supposed poor development of civil society, the 'hijacking' of decision-making by a reduced elite, the marginalisation of trade unions, the continued tension between the centre and the regions, and the low standard of corporate governance.[1] Of particular note, however, have been the accusations of corruption levelled at governments – especially during the final years of the Socialist (PSOE) administrations of Felipe González (1982–96). Although there were fewer high-profile corruption scandals following the accession to power in 1996 of José María Aznar's right-wing Popular Party (PP), the Gescartera investment company and the BBVA Bank cases which emerged respectively in 2001 and 2002 ensured that the issue of corruption has remained high on the agenda of critics of Spain's democratic functioning. Indeed, Spain tends to be bracketed with its neighbours 'below the olive line' as being 'more corrupt' than northern European countries (see Table 3.1).

Table 3.1 The 2003 Corruption Perceptions Index (Western Europe)

Overall country rank	Country	2003CPI score	Surveys used	Standard deviation	High–low range
3	Denmark	9.5	9	0.4	8.8–9.9
6	Sweden	9.3	11	0.2	8.8–9.6
7	Netherlands	8.9	9	0.3	8.5–9.3
8	Norway	8.8	8	0.5	8.0–9.3
8	Switzerland	8.8	9	0.8	6.9–9.4
11	Luxembourg	8.7	6	0.4	8.0–9.2
11	United Kingdom	8.7	13	0.5	7.8–9.2
14	Austria	8.0	9	0.7	7.3–9.3
16	Germany	7.7	11	1.2	4.9–9.2
17	Belgium	7.6	9	0.9	6.6–9.2
18	Ireland	7.5	9	0.7	6.5–8.8
23	Spain	6.9	11	0.8	5.2–7.8
23	France	6.9	12	1.1	4.8–9.0
25	Portugal	6.6	9	1.2	4.9–8.1
35	Italy	5.3	11	1.1	3.3–7.3
50	Greece	4.3	9	0.8	3.7–5.6

That corruption should be a particular concern is understandable, given the clear and growing evidence that it not only undermines economic efficiency and good governance, but can also lead to public disillusionment with the very process of democracy.[2] Transparency International's Corruption Perception Index (CPI), published annually since 1995, is probably the most widely used benchmark to measure corruption. CPI rankings of corruption in Spain since 1980 show a clear perception that the problem worsened markedly under the Socialist administrations of the mid-1990s, when there was a host of high-profile scandals involving senior government figures (see Figure 3.1). This is certainly consistent with the view expressed in September 2001 by Vicente Martínez Pujalte, PP spokesman on the economy: 'There are two facts that are radically different. Under the Socialist government, corruption was possible. Under the Popular Party government, corruption is not possible.'[3] Can we therefore simply conclude that corruption in contemporary Spain has been a problem primarily linked to and caused by the Socialist Party in power, and that following the March 2004 general elections we should expect to see another upsurge in corruption scandals? Or can we learn more from other explanatory approaches? The thrust of much recent research into the variables which best explain a country's corruption propensity points to more structural and long-term factors. Amongst the clearest – or at least most statistically robust – findings are that corruption tends to be correlated with Catholicism, a civil law legal tradition, low levels of economic development, federal rather than unitary state structures, limited exposure to or experience of democracy, and economic protectionism. Such factors not only suggest that levels of

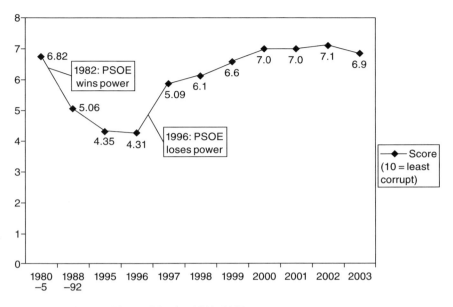

Figure 3.1 CPI rankings of Spain, 1980–2003.

corruption should be fairly consistent in any given country, or else change only gradually, but also that we might well *expect* Spain to have a problem with corruption. An alternative approach, which has received considerable recent attention, stresses the role of social capital in protecting against corruption: is Spain characterised by a clientelistic tradition which has hindered the development of those crucial networks of civic engagement which promote trust and norms of reciprocity?

This chapter argues that all these approaches to analysing political corruption have serious drawbacks when applied to Spain, and fail to provide a convincing account of either the reasons for, or the nature of, its development. The argument is developed in four sections. The first discusses the use of perceptions indices to measure corruption and some of the key explanatory variables which have been derived from them. In the second section, structural factors, as well as the influence of social capital in explaining corruption, are explored and also found to be wanting. The third section argues that we need to deploy more nuanced definitions of the concept of corruption, and the reasons for its emergence. Particular emphasis is placed on the importance of incentives and opportunity structures, associated with the changing nature of governance in Spain since the return of democracy. The final section discusses the mobilisation of scandal, and argues that 'cycles of contestation' may help to explain the apparent fluctuations in the level of corruption in contemporary Spain.

Perceptions of corruption in Spain

As shown in Table 3.1, Spain was ranked twelfth out of sixteen established European democracies, and twenty-third overall, in the 2003 Transparency International Corruption Perception Index. The 2003 ranking reflects the steady improvement in perceptions of corruption in Spain since the index was first published in its present form in 1995, with its CPI score rising from a poor 4.35 to a more positive 7.1 (in 2002) over the period in question. Prior to then, however, in the composite indices for 1980–5 and for 1988–92 respectively, Spain's score fell from 6.82 and 5.06, suggesting a clear downward trend which paralleled the Socialist Party's accession to office in 1982 (see Figure 3.1). Spain's position amongst the sixteen countries listed in Table 3.1 remained more or less constant, rising from thirteenth in 1995 to twelfth in 2003. The global ranking also improved marginally, although these last figures must be treated with considerable caution as the number of countries covered in each index has not been constant. Overall, then, it appears that perceptions of corruption in Spain have reduced in recent years, bringing the country more into line with (though still somewhat distant from) most of its European counterparts: only Italy and Greece have consistently received lower scores, joined more recently by Portugal and France.

Such findings may seem at first sight to be unsurprising, given the corruption scandals which dogged Spanish politics from the early 1990s. Accusations of corrupt or underhand practices by the PSOE government had simmered in a rather inchoate fashion since 1982, but the catalyst for an upsurge in media interest in the issue was the emergence of the so-called 'Juan Guerra case' at the start of 1990, when it was alleged that the then deputy prime minister's brother had used official PSOE premises in Seville for private business purposes. Alfonso Guerra was eventually forced to resign in January 1991, his departure signalling the start of a full-scale assault on the probity of the PSOE government – but it was only after the 'Mani Pulite' investigations and the emergence of the Tangentopoli scandals in Italy during 1992 that political corruption became the dominant focus of attention in Spain, as journalists sought out evidence of parallel news-grabbing (and copy-selling) scandals. The PSOE government became a particular target of the newspaper, *El Mundo*, launched in 1989 by Pedro J. Ramírez. Appointed editor of *Diario16* in 1980 at the age of twenty-eight, Ramírez's previous newspaper had started to investigate the PSOE government's links to the GAL (anti-terrorist liberation groups), which fought a dirty war against ETA separatists between 1983 and 1987 and which would become the source of a major scandal during the 1990s. He was fired from the editorship at the start of 1989, and remained convinced that his dismissal had been engineered by the government.

Whilst Ramírez and *El Mundo* were key players in the revelation of scandals, the PSOE government seemed almost to harbour a perverse wish to offer all possible assistance. An array of major corruption stories rocked the Socialists in early 1994, the low point of what was beginning to look like a never-ending saga of scandal and sleaze.[4] Most spectacular was the fall from grace of two high-profile PSOE appointees: Mariano Rubio, the former governor of the Bank of Spain, who was accused of tax fraud and insider dealing, and Luis Roldán, first civilian head of the Civil Guard, who was arrested for bribery and misappropriation of funds. To compound matters, Roldán managed to escape from custody in farcical circumstances, before being re-arrested in Laos. The Rubio and Roldán cases led directly to the political downfall of Carlos Solchaga, minister of the economy and a key player in the González administration, José Luis Corcuera, former minister of justice, and Antonio Asunción, minister of the interior. A further scandal led to the resignation of Vicente Alberón, minister of agriculture, who was implicated in a financial scam set up by Rubio's financial adviser, Manuel de la Concha.

The 1994 scandals were just the latest in a growing list of improprieties by figures associated with the PSOE. For instance, in 1991 investigations began into a party funding racket in which it emerged that elected Socialist representatives ran a group of front companies (called Filesa, Malesa and Time Export) that paid bills for the PSOE with money obtained by charging sympathetic companies and banks for fictitious consultancy work. The following year it was reported that the national railway, Renfe, had been involved in land speculation, leading to the resignation of the health minister and former Renfe president, Julián García Valverde. Further questions were raised over the award of contracts relating to the high-speed rail link between Madrid and Seville, as well as the Expo92 site and other infrastructure projects in Andalusia. A senior PSOE figure, Aida Alvarez, was prosecuted for collecting bribes in connection with the award of public sector contracts to foreign firms such as Volkswagen and Siemens. In 1993, the director-general of the state's official journal of record, the *BOE*, resigned after it was revealed that she had siphoned off funds by massively overcharging for the purchase of paper.

Most damaging of all, though, was the scandal surrounding the use of Ministry of Interior secret funds to set up the GAL, which re-emerged as an issue during 1994 and came to dominate the final two years of the PSOE administration. Ultimately, the GAL case led in 1998 to the imprisonment of the former minister of the interior, José Barrionuevo, and former director of state security, Rafael Vera, for illegal detention and misappropriation of state funds.[5] Probably more than any other issue, the GAL scandal served to undermine the credibility and reputation of the Socialist government and contributed directly to the PSOE's defeat in the 1996 general election. Ironically, the key figure in re-opening investigations into the GAL affair in 1994 was the investigating magistrate, Baltasar Garzón, who had been included in second place behind Felipe González as an independent candidate on the PSOE's electoral list for Madrid in the 1993 general elections. Seen at the time as a cunning move to co-opt the highly popular judge (dubbed 'Super Garzón' in the press) and demonstrate the government's commitment to combat corruption, the move backfired badly. Garzón resigned in May 1994, accusing the government of lacking sincerity, and immediately became one of the major thorns in the PSOE's flesh, alongside Pedro J. Ramírez.

In the context of such a catalogue of corruption-related scandals, it therefore seems only logical to expect the Transparency International index to reflect a change in perceptions during the mid-1990s. But the compilers of the CPI have explicitly adopted a methodology designed to avoid such short-term variations: it 'combines assessments from the previous three years to reduce abrupt variations in scoring. Such changes might be due to high-level political scandals that affect perceptions, but do not reflect actual changing levels of corruption.'[6] But what exactly does the CPI show? Is it an accurate reflection of levels of corruption? There are several reasons why the index should be treated with caution. First, it should be stressed that the index measures *perceptions*, not actual instances, of corruption.[7] One key issue for any such index is exactly whose perceptions are counted and measured. The CPI is a composite index, drawing on various different sampling frames, data sources and methodologies to provide what it considers is a statistically robust overall result. For the 2003 index, for instance, seventeen data sources were used, provided by the World Economic Forum, the World Bank's World Business Environment Survey, the Institute of Management Development (Lausanne), Pricewaterhouse-Coopers, the Political and Economic Risk Consultancy (Hong Kong), Information International, World Markets Research Centre, Columbia University, 'a multilateral development bank', the Economist Intelligence Unit and Freedom House. The range of sources looks impressively wide, but the CPI appendix on sources reveals that the respondents comprised 'expatriate business executives', 'top and middle company management', 'senior managers', 'chief finance officers', 'expert expatriate staff', and 'senior business leaders'.[8] In other words, the index almost certainly privileges the views of western business leaders, and we might therefore expect there to be a north–south, as well as east–west, division in the rankings.

Whilst the CPI cautions that comparisons with figures in previous years can be misleading, because the sources and methodology change from year to year, it is striking that, in practice, most countries have very consistent scores. As Manion has pointed out:

> The scores span more than two decades, from 1980 through 2001. If … we collapse the index to form three categories defined by thirds of the ten-point scale, few scores change enough to cross categories: more than 90 per cent of the 54 countries for which scores are available for the entire period have basically consistent high, low, or intermediate scores.[9]

Spain is one of the 10 per cent and does cross categories (twice): from low (just) in the 1980–5 period, to intermediate between 1988 and 1998, to low again since 1999. How can we explain this? Given the nature of the surveys and the respondents, it seems highly plausible (though it cannot be proved) that perceptions of corruption were indeed influenced by the kinds of headlines being produced in Spain: indeed, it is hard to imagine how it could be otherwise. Thus it is possible – even likely in the case of Spain – that the CPI can operate more as a measure of headline-grabbing scandals than of actual cases of corruption.[10] Not all corruption results in scandals, of course, and not all scandals are to do with corruption. Thus the fact that there was undoubtedly a marked rise in the number of reported scandals in Spain under the Socialist administrations of 1982–96 does not in itself prove that there was actually more corruption during that period (which is not to deny that there may well have been).

Linked to the issue of whose perceptions matter is the question of what survey respondents actually understand by 'corruption'. Like the elephant which is difficult to describe, but recognised when seen, so corruption is often understood in an intuitive sense but remains difficult to define precisely. Transparency International operates with a straightforward definition: 'the misuse of public power for private benefit'.[11] But perceptions of 'misuse' (and 'benefit') may vary: what is acceptable to one person may be anathema to another. In practice, the focus of most of the surveys used in the CPI is on bribes and unofficial payments connected with licences, permits and contracts, and the extent to which these operate as constraints on the business environment.[12] Such a focus may well capture a very important aspect of corruption, but may also completely miss other dimensions of what is actually a highly complex phenomenon. It will be argued below that we need a more precise understanding of what we mean by corruption, but the point to note here is that only some (and probably not the most shocking) of the scandals which emerged during the PSOE period in office fit the framework of side-payments and bribery for contracts and so forth. The GAL scandal, for instance, certainly appears to have involved a misuse of power, but not for 'private' or financial benefit. As will be seen, a key issue in various scandals involving not just the PSOE was the attempt to generate income for political parties rather than for individuals.[13] It remains a question for empirical research whether the business environment in Spain has actually changed for the better since the mid-1990s in terms of any need to pay bribes or make irregular extra payments when dealing with public officials – and, if it has, how can this be explained?

A final concern about interpretations of the CPI relates to the interval scales used: although the methodology used to standardise the data sources before arriving at a mean value is clearly explained,[14] what cannot be controlled is what the estimations of respondents mean in the original surveys. We have no way of knowing whether respondents have similar conceptions of what any particular point on a scale means in terms of how much corruption they perceive to be taking place: what may be a poor score for one person could be a perfectly acceptable one for another. The questions used in surveys often invite relatively imprecise judgements, such as 'How do you rate corruption in terms of its quality or contribution to the overall living/working environment?' (Political and Economic Risk Consultancy) or 'Assess whether bribing and corruption prevail or do not prevail in the public sphere' (Institute for Management Development). We might therefore expect CPI rankings to be quite impressionistic, but they are presented with what appears to be a high degree of precision, supported by seemingly sophisticated quantitative analytic techniques.

The question may be raised, of course, as to whether any of this matters very much: after all, the CPI does not determine the actual level of corruption in a given country, and so it could be argued that its rankings should not be given too much attention. In practice, however, Transparency International's CPI rankings do receive very extensive international attention: not only are they highly publicised, but they are also used as an element in decision-making about loans and creditworthiness, as well as underpinning moves – supported by the World Bank, the IMF, the OECD and many western governments – which sponsor a particular, deregulated market-based approach to achieving 'good governance'. As will be argued below, some components of the prevailing understanding of 'good governance' may actually generate additional incentives to engage in corrupt practices. In addition, the CPI has been subjected to extensive analysis by academics seeking to understand the reasons for the emergence of corruption and its greater incidence in some countries as opposed to others: it is to these causal hypotheses that the chapter now turns.

On the causes of corruption: structure and social capital

It would clearly be of great significance for anti-corruption strategies if key causal factors which contribute to the emergence and persistence of corruption could be identified. There have been several recent studies which use large-n approaches to isolate the key explanatory variables, many of them taking the CPI rankings, or else some of the surveys on which they are based, as their starting point for analysis. Essentially, as indicated above, some of the most consistent findings (or at least those which demonstrate the greatest statistical significance) suggest that Spain should offer a fertile environment for corruption to prosper. Amongst the key factors identified are religious tradition, legal code, nature of state structure and economic organisation. Thus La Porta *et al.*, Treisman, Paldam, and Lambsdorff all find a correlation between Protestantism and lower levels of corruption, and point variously to the individualist emphasis in Protestantism on taking personal responsibility for actions (as opposed to the Catholic emphasis on inherent human fallibility); a lower reliance on family ties, with its attendant risk of nepotism, than in hierarchical religions; and the tendency for

Protestant countries to have a more vibrant civil society, with a clearer separation between church and state.[15] In short, the more collectivist tradition of Catholicism appears to offer fecund terrain in which family-linked, favour-driven social mores can all too easily shade into corrupt practices.

In regard to legal codes, it has been argued that the common law tradition of Britain and many of its former colonies is more flexible than the civil law tradition which has predominated throughout most of the rest of Europe and which has historically been closely tied to the interests of the sovereign. Under common law, it is argued, there is less emphasis on hierarchy and high office and a greater stress instead on the importance of procedural rectitude: it is thus easier to prosecute individuals found transgressing the rules, no matter what their social status or standing. That democracies should be seen as less prone to corruption than non-democracies is hardly surprising, given democracy's definitional emphasis on the accountability of decision-makers and citizens' equality before the law. Slightly more puzzling, perhaps, is the idea that federal regimes should be more prone to corruption than unitary ones – although it may simply be the case that federal organisations create more decision-making points which in turn generate additional incentives to find ways of short-circuiting bureaucratic procedures.[16] Finally, the idea that free trade should be associated with lower levels of corruption closely fits the findings of the CPI rankings, and lies at the heart of the emphasis in conceptions of 'good governance' on establishing an appropriate environment for private enterprise.

The majority of these factors are essentially constants, or givens, resistant to any short-term fix or change. Until the post-Franco transition to democracy, Spain met all of the conditions associated with a propensity towards corruption, except federalism. The transition brought about democracy, but also asymmetrical devolution, as well as free trade as Spain moved towards its objective of joining the European Union. The Franco regime was certainly characterised by the existence of routine corruption, which extended from the highest levels of government down to the everyday experience of dealings with officials and bureaucrats.[17] If such day-to-day corruption no longer characterises dealings with civil servants, can we point to the fact that Spain is now a democracy as a major causal factor? At one level the answer is almost certainly 'yes', but it is an answer which does not take us very far. After all, other democracies – notably, Italy – have experienced long periods of systemic corruption. One National Court judge, Javier Gómez de Liaño, even claimed in 1996 that Spain was on a par with Italy in having a gigantic corruption system which affected politics, the justice system, the economy and the world of finance, and against which only magistrates were taking action. If such a claim is plainly an exaggeration, there have in recent years been major corruption scandals not just in Italy and Spain, but also in Belgium, France, Germany and Greece, and concern over standards in public life has been expressed in several other established European democracies.

Clearly neither the fact of democracy, nor the length of time it has been established, act in themselves as effective safeguards against corruption. If there is indeed some causal connection between democracy and lower levels of corruption, we need to account for the variation in apparent levels of corruption between otherwise similar democracies. The kinds of distinction outlined above in regard to religious tradition and legal code fail to explain such variations, since the recent scandals have occurred across a range of countries with different historic traditions and trajectories. One potential response might be to focus on the nature or quality of democracy in question, and ask whether its particular organisation, structure or functioning in a given state provides greater or lesser scope for corruption. Indeed, there is a burgeoning literature on how best to measure the quality of democracy and promote 'good governance', though no widespread consensus exists on what exactly it entails.[18] This chapter does not seek to engage with the wider debate on the quality of democracy, but instead will discuss briefly the related issue of social capital, the presence of which has been seen as offering some protection against corruption.

The vogue concept of social capital, associated most directly with the work of Robert Putnam,[19] has received very considerable attention – with some recent works looking specifically at the links between social capital and corruption.[20] As Putnam acknowledges, the term 'social capital' has a long history and has been used in a number of different senses over time. Currently, though, there is seemingly widespread agreement as to its principal characteristics: stripped to its essentials, social capital refers to the networks of civic engagement which promote social trust and norms of reciprocity. These networks typically include such things as neighbourhood civic associations, schools, churches, sports clubs, co-operatives and so forth. Through a range of different channels – shared information, mutual aid, collective action, solidarity – such networks give rise to mutual support structures, generating positive value for those involved. The supposed link between high levels of social capital and corruption is straightforward: if norms of reciprocity and social trust are well established, it is more difficult for corruption to prosper, whereas when they are lacking the possibilities of engaging in corrupt practices are greatly enhanced. Whilst Putnam accepts that not all social capital has positive benefits, and that it can engender illiberal or exclusionary networks,[21] the great majority of research on social capital has tended to focus on the social benefits it produces: much of the recent literature sees it as a positive asset, something to be aspired to on account of its beneficial impact on social organisation and good governance.

Ideas related to the concept of social capital have been used to distinguish between north and south. For instance, Tanzi distinguishes northern efficiency and respect for rules from southern back-scratching and favours: 'the very features that make a country a less cold and indifferent place are the same that increase the difficulty of enforcing arm's length rules essential for modern efficient markets and governments'.[22] Harrison makes the even more starker claim that:

human development is frustrated in most Hispanic-American countries
. . . by a way of seeing the world that impedes the achievement of
political pluralism, social equity, and dynamic economic progress. And
that way of the world has been driven, without significant deviation, by
the momentum of centuries.[23]

Although highly tendentious, Harrison's comment shares with Putnam's
original work on social capital in Italy the idea that deep-rooted historic and
institutional factors exercise a pervasive and continuing impact on political
structure and organisation. In looking at the emergence of effective democratic politics in northern Italy, as opposed to the south, Putnam focused on
the development of a vigorous and autonomous civil society, characterised
by the existence of voluntary institutions that engendered trust and
co-operation.[24] Such ideas are in some respects similar to Banfield's concept
of 'amoral familism': weak states, poorly developed and inefficient
bureaucracies, and a lack of civic virtue are all related to the creation of the
clientelistic ties typical of Greece, Portugal, Spain and southern Italy.[25] In
contrast to northern European states with high stocks of social capital and
dense networks of associations, these southern states have been
characterised by patronage and '*amiguismo*'.[26]

Even if such characterisations have some validity as a description of social
and political arrangements (as they do, at least historically), a major
question remains over the precise nature and direction of any causal
relationship between such arrangements and social capital, as well as
between social capital and good governance. Social capital has explanatory
power only if it is conceived of as an independent variable, an exogenous
factor which is usually presented as a highly durable 'given'. But it is equally
plausible to invert the causal relationship: if social capital is conceived of as
an endogenous, dependent variable, the question then becomes one of why
it takes the particular shape it does in any given state or context. Following
Coleman,[27] far from acting to establish an immutable, embedded culture,
social capital may instead be a reflection of rational calculations by actors
according to the setting in which they find themselves. Thus, for example,
trust and reciprocity emerge in those markets where the costs of losing them
are very high, or people may join civic associations and networks when the
advantages of doing so are obvious, but not otherwise. Conceived in these
terms, social capital can be analysed in terms of incentive structures and
rational, strategic actions, a perspective which helps avoid reductionist
appeals to social norms or cultural generalities.

Linked to this issue of seeing social capital as an exogenous or an
endogenous variable is the issue of causal direction. Much of the literature
which sees social capital as a positive good also appears to assume that good
governance (associated with participation, accountability, transparency,
inclusiveness, the rule of law and so forth) in large measure reflects high
levels of social capital. But social capital could equally well be seen as
politically neutral, able to be influenced for good or ill according to a range

of other factors. The key issue in this context is whether social capital generates specific outcomes, such as good governance with associated low levels of corruption, or whether particular institutional arrangements generate social capital (good or bad). According to della Porta,[28] there may be 'blessed' and 'unlucky' communities in which a self-sustaining dynamic becomes established between social capital, government performance and trust in government. Depending on whether social capital or government performance is the independent variable, there may be different outcomes (see Figure 3.2). In Figure 3.2, scenarios 1 and 3 generate virtuous circles, in which the good governance or positive social capital become self-sustaining, whereas scenarios 2 and 4 generate vicious circles. Crucially, though, it may be much more of a challenge to break out of the vicious circle in scenario 2 than the one in scenario 4, since institutional reform to promote good governance may be a more practical aspiration than the generation of social capital where it is absent, or moving 'bad' social capital in a positive direction.

Spain provides a potentially valuable test case, precisely because it has been identified as having low levels of social capital,[29] but also had the opportunity to engage in comprehensive institutional redesign following the end of the Franco regime. If social capital (or some similar or related cultural variable) is a key explanatory factor behind the propensity towards corruption, we should expect there to be some likelihood of a corruption problem in Spain, which in turn should remain relatively consistent over time. If, on the other hand, appropriate institutional design and organisation is what generates good governance and low levels of corruption, we should be able to investigate whether and in what ways the institutional reconfiguration of the Spanish state after the Franco regime has contributed to the issue of corruption. In practice, as will be argued below, both social capital and institutional design are important issues in explaining corruption in democratic

Independent variable	Generates	Results in	Feeds back into
1. High level of positive social capital	Good governance, low corruption	Trust in government	Positive social capital
2. Limited social capital	Bad governance, high corruption	Lack of trust in government	Limited social capital
3. 'Good' governance, low corruption	Trust in government	Positive social capital	Good governance, low corruption
4. 'Bad' governance, high corruption	Lack of trust in government	Limited social capital	Bad governance, high corruption

Figure 3.2 Self-sustaining relationships between social capital and governance.

Spain, but the prior problem is that the concept of corruption itself needs to be specified more precisely in order to understand its dimensions and development.

Opportunities and incentives for corruption: from clientelism to cartel parties

A central analytic problem with all the approaches outlined so far in this chapter is that they effectively see corruption in generic terms, as if there were some overall mean or level in any given country which may be susceptible to measurement or explanation. To some extent, such a view of corruption is understandable – but it does mask the fact that, in practice, corruption takes many shapes and forms. It is not my aim here to suggest that we need to construct highly detailed taxonomies of all the different types of corruption possible. But it is important to distinguish between some basic forms of corruption: for instance, there are well-established differences between grand (systemic) and petty (day-to-day routine) corruption, between corruption for personal financial gain and for party political gain, between extortive (enforced) and transactive (voluntary) corruption, between administrative, political and financial corruption. It is also possible to identify forms of corruption which involve no monetary exchange, such as a 'betrayal of the democratic transcript', when political leaders act deliberately to subvert transparency or accountability – a form of what Thompson has termed 'mediated' corruption, which is concerned with the *process* of democratic politics.[30] It is logical that these different forms of corruption will also have different causes, sometimes systemic (the nature of state authority, weak institutions, poorly developed civil society), sometimes contextually specific (mechanisms of accountability, perverse incentives), sometimes simply down to personal venality. The challenge for analysis is to identify how the mix of such factors contributes to the nature and extent of corruption in a given setting.

Democratic Spain's social and political organisation has undoubtedly been influenced by a clientelist tradition which in turn reflects the nature of state development. It could certainly be argued that path dependence has contributed to the continued influence of clientelistic relationships, particularly those involving political parties, and that this has been reflected in a range of activities which some observers see as bordering on corruption if not overtly corrupt. But Spain has also been subject to wider pressures and trends which have affected political processes in all Europe's established democracies. It is possible that such pressures have generated new incentives and opportunity structures for particular forms of corruption. It is helpful in the context of this discussion to distinguish between 'old-style' clientelism, associated with patron–client relationships in predominantly rural societies, and more modern versions linked to political parties.[31] In this latter version, parties act as patrons, but establish a relationship of mutual dependence with their clients (the electorate) on account of the need to win support in the form of votes.[32] Lyrintzis has described this process in the Greek context as 'bureaucratic clientelism', whereby parties use the resources of the state to build up clienteles by granting favours and resources, leading to the systematic infiltration of the state machine by party devotees who are thereby able to maintain control over the allocation of favours.[33]

Whereas Spain has long been associated with 'classic' clientelism, the emergence of bureaucratic clientelism may reflect in part the circumstances under which political parties were established after the Franco Dictatorship. Parties faced a twin challenge in post-Franco Spain: as well as supporting the creation of a democratic culture, they had to establish their own identities within it. However, there was little time to sink roots in society: parties were legalised a matter of months before the elections of June 1977. Electoral success was a more immediate priority than developing a membership base. Votes had to be the first objective; party structures could develop later – although, as it would turn out, mass affiliation to the new parties never took place and levels of party membership in Spain remained below the European average.[34] Spanish parties have extended electoral and clientelistic, rather than participatory, linkages to their supporters: party leaders dominate their organisations and offer 'favours' in return for votes.[35] Some analysts have argued that the lack of a clear *ruptura* between the Franco regime and the new democracy allowed established clientelistic networks to continue operating: certainly, there is evidence that the UCD coalition, under Adolfo Suárez, sought to take advantage of such networks.[36] Indeed, traditional practices of *caciquismo* were observed during the 1977 elections. A local party leader in Segovia, interviewed by Gunther, recognised that 'personal ties were very important in the selection of our candidates'. Characteristics of UCD candidates, especially in rural provinces, included prominent membership of Chambers of Agriculture, the Agricultural Branches of the Francoist Vertical Syndicates, Irrigation Syndicates, or positions in provincial delegations of the various Francoist ministries.[37]

Such concerns were not tied exclusively to the experience of the UCD during the transitional period. Under the PSOE administration, an example of 'favours for votes' concerned the Socialist heartland of Andalusia: under Spanish law, in towns with a large rural proletariat, anyone who could document working on a farm for sixty days in any one year qualified for community employment benefits for the whole year. Official certification was easy to come by if local officials decided not to look too closely at the facts. In return for pledging support to the Socialists, a very vulnerable sector of the population was helped to get through hard times and the PSOE benefited from the clientelistic network which became established.[38] In fact, the Socialist administrations of Felipe González (1982–96) systematically used their control of the state machinery to reward party members and sympathisers by giving them jobs in the public administration. Between 1982 and 1994, more than half a million new state jobs were created.[39] The PSOE also made direct appointments to some 25,000 administrative posts between 1984 and 1987, largely in relation to the new autonomous regions.[40] Given the small number of party members, such patronage appears highly significant, with some 70 per cent of party members being either functionaries or public office holders by the 1990s.[41] In practice, however, the small numbers involved (because of the small size of party membership) suggests that the extent of bureaucratic clientelism in Spain should not be exaggerated. Certainly there is little evidence to indicate that the PSOE engaged in a similar scale of distributing jobs (or promises of jobs) to that of the Christian Democratic and Socialist leaders in southern Italy.

Rather than develop relationships of exchange between party representatives and voters, as in Italian case, the PSOE was more concerned to establish links with business firms and entrepreneurs in order to secure party funding.[42] It is noteworthy that the Filesa/Malesa/Time Export affair, for instance, formed part of a wider pattern of party-related corruption scandals in western Europe which have emerged since the early 1990s: the Agusta-Dassault military contracts affair in Belgium, the Urba and Elf Acquitaine affairs in France, Helmut Kohl and secret CDU accounts in Germany, DC and PSI involvement in a host of scandals in Italy, the funding of both Conservative and Labour parties in the UK.[43] These scandals cut across both ideological and geographical divides, suggesting the likelihood of a common causal factor at work in the organisational structure of west European politics. The argument I seek to outline here is that the shift from 'government' to 'governance', which has taken place in Spain as in other west European democracies, has created new opportunity structures for corruption, especially where political parties are concerned. The transition from 'government' to 'governance' encompasses a shift of policy delivery from traditional bureaucracies to a range of more fragmented service providers.[44] The idea of governance thus covers such developments as the transfer of policy responsibility to so-called third-sector agencies, the creation of quasi-markets by separating purchasers and providers, and – most significant in this context – extensive privatisation and contracting out. Known also as the 'hollowing out of the state', this steady ceding of power both to supra-national and sub-national institutions (the European Union and the Autonomous Communities in the case of Spain), alongside the creation of independent and semi-independent agencies, has given rise to new networks and power relationships in which governments act as just one amongst several players.

The issue of privatisation is important. Rose-Ackerman has commented that 'the process of transferring assets to private ownership is fraught with corrupt opportunities'.[45] The Spanish privatisation process, under the Socialists in particular but also under the Partido Popular, has been decidedly opaque as regards its precise operation, with questions raised about bribes and back-handers in the award of concessions.[46] Indeed, investigations during 2001 into the role of the PP foreign affairs minister, Josep Pique, in the sale a decade earlier of Ertoil to Elf Acquitaine (the so-called Ercros affair) was just one of a string of cases in which accusations have been made about improper activity during state sell-offs. In Spain, as elsewhere, contracting out (or the 'out-sourcing') of state supplies, has also contributed to a sense that the accountability and transparency of government activity have been undermined. Thus many of the changes associated with the shift from government to governance and the hollowing out of the state can be seen to have offered new opportunities for corruption – but not necessarily the incentives which lead to those opportunities being acted upon.

It is undoubtedly the case that a major element in corruption cases is straightforward rent-seeking behaviour by individuals, with the primary incentive being the prospect of personal enrichment. Yet not all corruption can be explained by self-interest or even individual motivation. Institutional needs can also play a key role, and here the position of political parties is critical. The chairman of Transparency International, Peter Eigen, commented in October 2000 that '[t]he current wave of corruption scandals we are witnessing across Europe is not about personal enrichment – it's about the purchase of access to policy-makers, and political parties are the prime target in this game'.[47] Political parties, particularly those in office, have placed growing emphasis on cultivating relationships with the business and financial worlds – and one obvious reason is that they require financial support. Pilar del Castillo has described the role of brokers who mediate between parties and business interests, negotiating the exchange of covert funds for political influence.[48] Spanish parties, like many in western Europe, are state-funded – but, unlike in most other countries, the introduction of state funding took place in parallel with the establishment of the parties themselves at the start of the post-Franco transition. Most therefore had limited financial patrimony on which they could rely. Whilst the principal reason for adopting such a policy was to help ensure the survival of political parties in what was seen as likely to be an increasingly media-dominated, and therefore expensive, political marketplace, parties have none the less struggled to generate sufficient income. Membership has remained low, leading all Spain's major parties into significant debt.

The requirement for extra resources in the context of low levels of membership can certainly be seen as an incentive for parties to engage in corrupt activity: 'The demand for money makes even highly questionable sources attractive to parties, and it is important to find ways of keeping such funds hidden from public view.'[49] Del Castillo states:

> [t]he rules of party finance in Spain prescribe a dominant role for public funding . . . By imposing a strongly statized system and condemning private financing, continuing private financing operates outside the control of the established mechanisms of the law. This system fosters irregularities and corruption that would be less likely to develop in a framework of complete freedom and disclosure.[50]

Moreover, the adoption of state funding has also contributed to Spanish parties resembling what Katz and Mair identified as 'cartel parties', heavily reliant on state subsidies and with a professional core of salaried officials.[51] Cartel parties tend to operate within the interstices between state and civil society, leading to a risk of the distinction between the two spheres becoming blurred as party bureaucracies effectively act as para-state organisations. The shift from government to governance, meanwhile, has further fuzzied the separation between public and private sectors, and given rise to new opportunity structures for political parties to become involved in corruption.

In sum, the argument in this section is that, whilst corruption has clearly been a serious issue in democratic Spain, we should avoid collapsing the various forms it has taken into some global assessment of the overall level of corruption. In regard to political corruption, there have been abuses of power – some linked to the country's clientelist tradition (and involving all major parties), but probably the most damaging involving the misuse of state resources by the PSOE during the GAL scandal. There is little evidence of systemic, routinised bureaucratic corruption in citizens' day-to-day inter-actions with state officials (i.e. having to pay bribes to receive service), as opposed to venal rent-seeking behaviour on the part of a number of high-profile individuals. But the particular nature of political party development in Spain has not only given rise to a certain 'cartelisation', but has also generated incentives to develop ever closer relationships with private interests. In the meantime, the shift from government to governance has created new opportunity structures to exploit such relationships in ways that have contributed to many of the corruption scandals of the last decade. In this regard, Spain stands comparison with most other established European democracies – although, given the nature of corruption, we are unlikely ever to know the full extent of corrupt activity in Spain.

Governance, scandal and cycles of contestation

Although corruption scandals in democratic Spain appeared to reach a peak during the first half of the 1990s, they were hardly unknown before then. Early in the transition, for instance, PSOE politicians found themselves implicated in the West German Flick scandal through having received funds from the SPD. More recently, too, there have been a number of significant scandals, such the Ercros affair involving foreign minister Josep Pique, supposed irregularities within the Ministry of the Environment in regard to the expansion of the Yesa reservoir in Aragón, the resignation of Juan Villalonga as head of Telefónica following allegations of insider trading, the tax avoidance scandal involving the BBVA, and – most notably – the Gescartera case, in which the brokerage company collapsed in 2001 having 'lost' major investment funds belonging to ONCE, the state institution for social protection, amongst others.[52] The Gescartera case led to the resignation of deputy treasury minister, Enrique Giménez-Reyna, whose sister was managing director of the company, and of Pilar Valiente, head of the Stock Exchange Commission, who was accused of passing confidential information to Gescartera.

These latter scandals, which emerged under a PP administration, attracted somewhat less frenzied media attention than did the scandals of the mid-1990s under the PSOE. Indeed, according to *The Economist* it was merely 'all a bit embarrassing' for the government of José María Aznar, which had taken office in 1996 with a pledge to provide 'clean government'.[53] This brings us back to the question of perception raised at the start of this chapter: what is the relationship between the objective circumstances of corruption and the ways in which these reach the public domain? Did Spain really become markedly less corrupt in the space of just five years, as suggested in Transparency International's Corruption Perceptions Index, or is it rather that the issue has come to assume less public salience? Pujas and Rhodes have described the generation of scandal as a process of 'competitive elite mobilisation', which follows a particular pattern: after the revelation of usually small-scale corruption by magistrates, there follow denunciation and an escalation of public outrage via a press campaign which relies primarily on strategic leaks from the legal investigation. With public opinion 'scandalised', politicians are subjected to a media-led campaign which plays upon public indignation, and investigating magistrates are encouraged to continue in their pursuit of corrupt activity.[54]

What has made such a process possible in western Europe is the changing relationship since the end of the Cold War between political parties on the one hand, and between political and other social actors on the other. In contrast to the traditional organisation of political space in democratic Europe during the Cold War era, when there was a clear ideological distinction between left and right around which parties competed for votes, the grounds of contemporary political competition have shifted. Control over political space has been increasingly contested, with political parties facing growing competition from the media and other interests to influence public opinion. The long-established and clearly delineated boundaries between the political, commercial, judicial and reporting worlds have become steadily more porous, characterised by a growing number of high-profile figures moving between these various spheres. Media proprietors have become increasingly powerful political players in their own right, politicians have developed closer ties with the business world, and magistrates (such as Baltasar Garzón) have moved between the judiciary and elected political office.[55]

In place of ideology, parties have increasingly sought to differentiate themselves from their opponents on the basis of their claims to honesty, reliability and effectiveness. The policy platforms which used to characterise and distinguish left and right have increasingly converged, whilst the pressure to demonstrate governmental effectiveness in an increasingly complex and interdependent policy environment has led to an emphasis on technocratic, rather than ideological, prescriptions.[56] The grounds of political competition have thus shifted, and political parties attempt to make growing use of the public concern over corruption an issue over which to attack their opponents. Indeed, as greater emphasis is placed by organisations such as the World Bank and the European Union on 'clean government' as a positive good, so parties have sought to claim the moral high ground in order to appeal to ideologically disoriented voters.

What emerges, then, is a 'cycle of contestation' in which public attention is captured by, and then ultimately tires of, media exposure of politicians' shortcomings.[57] The cycle is characterised by a process in which concern over any given corruption scandal amongst both politicians and the public tends to die down in parallel with the transient nature of media focus on news stories: the media moves on, the public loses interest, and investigations run out of steam.[58] Such a cycle may help explain the seeming reduction in the amount of corruption experienced in Spain after the Partido Popular won power in 1996. Although, as we have seen, corruption scandals continued, they generated far less media attention – a reflection, in part, of over-saturation reducing the potential to generate scandal. Scandals are by their very nature ephemeral. Corruption, on the other hand, is an ever-present risk.

Notes

1 See, for example, J. Sinova and J. Tusell, *El secuestro de la democracia* (Barcelona: Plaza y Janés, 1990); J. Tusell and J. Sinova, *La década socialista* (Madrid: Espasa Calpe, 1992); A. Guerra, *Las Filípicas* (Barcelona: Editorial Planeta, 1992); J. Díaz Herrera and I. Durán, *El saqueo de España* (Madrid: Temas de Hoy, 1996); J. Díaz Herrera and I. Durán, *Pacto de silencio* (Madrid: Temas de Hoy, 1996); J. Díaz Herrera and I. Durán, *El secuestro de la justicia* (Madrid: Temas de Hoy, 1997); A. Nieto, *La 'nueva' organización del desgobierno* (Barcelona: Ariel, 1996); A. Nieto, *Corrupción en la España democrática* (Barcelona: Ariel, 1997); V. Pérez-Díaz, *Spain at the Crossroads* (Cambridge, MA: Harvard University Press, 1999).
2 See J. B. Thompson, *Political Scandal. Power and Visibility in the Media Age* (Cambridge: Polity Press, 2000), pp. 258–9.
3 Cited by AP Worldstream, 6 September 2001. Two years earlier, José María Aznar had announced that corruption in Spain was 'over': see 'De la corrupción', *El País*, 14 October 1999.
4 F. Jiménez, 'Political Scandals and Political Responsibility in Democratic Spain', in P. Heywood (ed.), *Politics and Policy in Democratic Spain* (London: Frank Cass, 1999), pp. 80–99; P. Heywood, 'Spain', in F. F. Ridley and Alan Doig (eds), *Sleaze: Private Interests and Public Reaction* (Oxford: Oxford University Press, 1995), pp. 178–89; P. Heywood, 'Continuity and Change: Analysing Political Corruption in Modern Spain', in W. Little and E. Posada-Carbó (eds), *Political Corruption in Europe and Latin America* (London: Macmillan, 1996), pp. 115–36; P. Heywood, 'From Dictatorship to Democracy:

Changing Forms of Political Corruption in Spain', in D. Della Porta and Y. Mény (eds), *Democracy and Corruption in Europe* (London: Pinter, 1997), pp. 65–84.

5 For a comprehensive analysis of the GAL scandal, see P. Woodworth, *Dirty War, Clean Hands* (Cork: Cork University Press, 2001).

6 J. G. Lambsdorff, 'Framework Document' (Background paper to the 2001 Corruption Perceptions Index) at http://www.transparency.org/cpi/2001/methodology.html, p. 2. A similar point is made in the 2003 Index: http://www.transparency.org/cpi/2003/dnld/framework.pdf, p. 3.

7 M. A. Seligson, 'On the Measurement of Corruption', *apsa-cp* 13/2 (2002), pp. 5–6, 30.

8 Lambsdorff, 'Framework Document', pp. 10–11.

9 M. Manion, 'Anticorruption Reform at the "Dirty" End of the New Corruption Continuum', *apsa-cp* 13/1 (2002), p. 15.

10 It is noteworthy that there were also marked changes in the ratings for Germany which rose from twentieth in the overall list in 2001 (following the Kohl scandal) to sixteenth in 2003, and even more dramatically for Belgium, which rose from twenty-fourth in 2001 to seventeenth in 2003.

11 J. G. Lambsdorff, 'Transparency International 2001 Corruption Perceptions Index', in Transparency International, *Global Corruption Report 2001* (Berlin: Transparency International, 2001), p. 233.

12 See Lambsdorff, 'Framework Document', pp. 4–5.

13 See 'Informe GRECO: de evaluación sobre España', in *Evaluación sobre la corrupción en España*, Documents Pi y Sunyer 15 (Barcelona: Fundació Carles Pi y Sunyer, 2002), p. 27.

14 Lambsdorff, 'Framework Document', p. 8.

15 R. La Porta, F. Lopez-de-Silanes, A. Shleifer and R. W. Vishny, 'Trust in Large Organizations', *American Economic Association Papers and Proceedings* 87/2 (1997); R. La Porta, F. Lopez-de-Silanes, A. Shleifer and R. W. Vishny, 'The Quality of Government', *Journal of Economics, Law and Organisation* 15 (1999); D. Treisman, 'The Causes of Corruption: A Cross-national Study' (unpublished manuscript, Aarhus University, Denmark, 1999); M. Paldam, 'Corruption and Religion. Adding to the Economic Model', *Kyklos* 54/2–3 (2001); Lambsdorff, 'Transparency International 2001'.

16 See J. Gerring and S. C. Thacker, 'Political Institutions and Corruption: The Role of Unitarism and Parliamentarism', *British Journal of Political Science* 34/2 (2004), pp. 295–330.

17 R. Abella, *La vida cotidiana en España bajo el régimen de Franco* (Barcelona: Argos Vergara, 1985); S. G. Payne, *The Franco Regime 1936–1975* (Madison: University of Wisconsin Press, 1987), pp. 451–2.

18 International IDEA, 'State of Democracy Project', at http://www.idea.int/ideas_work/14_political_state.htm (2002); World Bank Group, 'Indicators of Governance and Institutional Quality', at http://www1.worldbank.org/publicsector/indicators.htm (2002).

19 R. D. Putnam, *Making Democracy Work: Civic Traditions in Modern Italy* (Princeton, NJ: Princeton University Press, 1993); R. D. Putnam, *Bowling Alone* (New York: Touchstone, 2000).

20 M. E. Warren, 'Social Capital and Corruption' (unpublished draft paper, 2001); see also papers presented at the APSA Annual Conference on 'Social Capital and Political Corruption – the Causal Link' (Panel 11–11: Boston, MA, 2002).

21 Putnam, *Bowling Alone*, pp. 350–63.

22 V. Tanzi, 'Corruption, Governmental Activities, and Markets', IMF Working Paper WP/94/99, 1994.

23 L. E. Harrison, *Underdevelopment is a State of Mind: The Latin American Case* (Lanham, MD: University Press of America, 1995), p. 168.
24 Putnam, *Making Democracy Work*.
25 E. Banfield, *The Moral Basis of a Backward Society* (Glencoe, IL: The Free Press, 1958).
26 J. Hopkin and A. Mastropaolo, 'From Patronage to Clientelism: Comparing the Italian and Spanish Experiences', in S. Piattoni (ed.), *Clientelism, Interests, and Democratic Representation* (Cambridge: Cambridge University Press, 2001).
27 J. S. Coleman, 'Social Capital in the Creation of Human Capital', *American Journal of Sociology* 94 (1988).
28 D. Della Porta, 'Social Capital, Beliefs in Government, and Political Corruption', in S. J. Pharr and R. D. Putnam (eds), *Disaffected Democracies* (Princeton, NJ: Princeton University Press, 2000), pp. 203–5.
29 M. Torcal and J. R. Montero, 'Facets of Social Capital in New Democracies. The Formation and Consequences of Social Capital in Spain', in J. W. van Deth, M. Maraffi, K. Newton and P. F. Whiteley (eds), *Social Capital and European Democracy* (London: Routledge, 1999).
30 D. F. Thompson, 'Mediated Corruption: The Case of the Keating Five', *American Political Science Review* 87 (1993).
31 E. Gellner and J. Waterbury (eds), *Patrons and Clients in Mediterranean Societies* (London: Duckworth, 1977).
32 M. Caciagli and Fr. M. Belloni, 'The "New" Clientelism in Southern Italy: The Christian Democratic Party in Catania', in S. N. Eisenstadt and R. Lemarchand (eds), *Political Clientelism, Patronage and Development* (London: Sage, 1981), pp. 35–55.
33 C. Lyrintzis, 'Political Parties in Post-Junta Greece: A Case of "Bureaucratic Clientelism"?', *West European Politics* 7 (1984), pp. 103–4.
34 J. F. Tezanos, 'El papel social y politico del PSOE en la España de los años ochenta. Una década de progreso y democracia', in A. Guerra and J. F. Tezanos (eds), *La década del cambio: Diez años de gobierno socialista, 1982–1992* (Madrid: Editorial Sistema, 1992), p. 46.
35 K. Lawson, and P. H. Merkl (eds), *When Parties Fail* (Princeton, NJ: Princeton University Press, 1988), pp. 13–38.
36 Nieto, *Corrupción en España*, p. 21; J. Hopkin, *Party Formation and Democratic Transition in Spain: The Creation and Collapse of the Union of Democratic Centre* (London: Macmillan, 1999).
37 Hopkin, *Party Formation and Democratic Transition*.
38 V. Pérez-Díaz, *The Return of Civil Society: The Emergence of Democratic Spain* (Cambridge, MA: Harvard University Press, 1993), pp. 48–9.
39 M. Beltrán, 'La administración pública', in J. Tusell *et al.*, *España entre dos siglos* (Madrid: Alianza, 1996), p. 269.
40 R. Gillespie, 'The Resurgence of Factionalism in the Spanish Socialist Workers' Party', in D. Bell and E. Shaw (eds), *Conflict and Cohesion in Western European Social Democratic Parties* (London: Pinter, 1994), pp. 50–69; R. Gillespie, 'Spanish Socialism in the 1980s', in T. Gallagher and A. Williams (eds), *Southern European Socialism* (Manchester: Manchester University Press, 1989), pp. 59–85.
41 Gillespie, 'Resurgence of Factionalism', p. 55
42 J. Cazorla, *El clientelismo de partido en España ante la opinion pública. El medio rural, la administración y las empresas* (Barcelona: Institut de Ciències Polítiques i Socials Working Paper 86, 1994).
43 See P. Heywood, V. Pujas and M. Rhodes, 'Political Corruption, Democracy and Governance in Western Europe', in P. Heywood, E. Jones and M. Rhodes

(eds), *Developments in West European Politics* (Basingstoke: Palgrave Macmillan, 2002), pp. 184–200.

44 R. A. W. Rhodes, *The Governance Narrative: Key Findings and Lessons from the ESRC's Whitehall Programme* (London: Public Management and Policy Association, 2000), pp. 5–6.

45 S. Rose-Ackerman, *Corruption and Government* (Cambridge: Cambridge University Press, 1999), p. 35.

46 On the privatisation of Seat and Enasa under the PSOE, see R. S. Chari, 'Spanish Socialists, Privatising the Right Way?', in Heywood, *Politics and Policy in Democratic Spain*, pp. 163–79.

47 Transparency International, 'Bribes to Political Parties an Increasing Threat to Democracy' (Berlin: TI Press Release, 19 October 2000).

48 P. del Castillo, 'Problems in Spanish Party Financing', in H. E. Alexander and R. Shiratori (eds), *Comparative Political Finance Among the Democracies* (Boulder, CO: Westview Press, 1994), pp. 97–104.

49 A. Ware, 'Conclusion', in P. Burnell and A. Ware (eds), *Funding Democratization* (Manchester: Manchester University Press, 1998), p. 235.

50 Del Castillo, 'Problems in Spanish Party Financing', p. 100.

51 R. S. Katz and P. Mair, 'Changing Models of Party Organization and Party Democracy: The Emergence of the Cartel Party', *Party Politics* 1/1 (1995).

52 See 'El PP y la corrupción', *El País*, 12 June 2001; 'Caiga quien caiga', *El País*, 27 August 2001; Miguel Sánchez Morón, 'La corrupción existe, hay que afrontarla', *El País*, 26 February 2002; José A. Segurado, '¿Qué ha pasado?', *El País*, 7 December, 2002.

53 'Spain's Government under Fire', *The Economist*, 30 June 2001.

54 V. Pujas and M. Rhodes, 'Party Finance and Political Scandal in Italy, Spain and France', *West European Politics* 22/3 (1999).

55 For references drawn primarily from the Italian case, see D. Della Porta, 'A Judges' Revolution? Political Corruption and the Judiciary in Italy', *European Journal of Political Research* 39/1–2 (2001) and D. Della Porta and A. Pizzorno, 'The Business Politicians: Reflections from a Study of Political Corruption', in M. Levi and D. Nelken (eds), *The Corruption of Politics and the Politics of Corruption* (Oxford: Blackwell, 1996).

56 P. Heywood, 'Executive Capacity and Legislative Limits', in P. Heywood, E. Jones and M. Rhodes (eds), *Developments in West European Politics*, vol. 2 (London: Palgrave, 2002), pp. 151–67.

57 Heywood *et al.*, 'Political Corruption'.

58 In 1998, the Centro de Investigaciones Sociológicas (CIS) removed two questions on corruption from its public opinion surveys, on the basis that it was no longer an issue of interest to the Spanish public: this followed several years of almost incessant focus on corruption under the PSOE administration. See 'La corrupción deja de interesar', *El País*, 30 January 1998.

4 Using terror against terrorists

The Spanish experience

Paddy Woodworth

Introduction

Since the 'international war on terror' declared by the United States after the September 11th attacks on New York and Washington, we have been reminded almost daily that terrorism is a threat to democracy. No democrat would challenge that statement, but its apparent simplicity begins to unravel as soon as we attempt to define these terms. The experience of recent Spanish history indicates that the threat terrorism poses is more insidious – and ultimately more dangerous – than is often realised.[1] One of its greatest dangers lies in the way in which terrorism tempts democracies to take short-cuts, to break their own best rules. Terrorists begin to win when democracies become less democratic in response to the terrorist threat. Concepts such as tolerance, pluralism and respect for human rights must be numbered among the potential long-term casualties of car-bombs and assassinations.

This chapter will look back on the war against terrorism which Spain has been fighting for many years. In particular, it will examine the state's use of dirty war tactics against ETA in the 1980s, and the consequences for Spanish democracy since then. When contemporary Spanish democracy was born, with the 1978 constitution, the Spanish made the rule of law (Estado de Derecho) the core value of their new society. That value would be sorely tested over the next 20 years. The Spanish experience offers some valuable insights into the ways in which counter-terrorists, as well as terrorists, can undermine democracy.

Before we shift the focus entirely to Spain, however, we need to pause to look briefly at the word 'terrorism' itself.

Defining terrorism – and state terrorism

Our experience of both the Basque and Irish conflicts over the last 30 years, to go no further afield, should surely make us deeply uneasy with this word. It often tells us more about its user's point of view than about the situation he or she is trying to describe. There is more than a grain of truth in a wry comment made by the Irish playwright, Brendan Behan, a former IRA bomber himself. Behan said that 'the man with the small bomb is a terrorist, the man with the big bomb is a statesman'. All weapons of mass destruction could indeed be legitimately considered terrorist from an ethical point of view. The possession of nuclear, chemical and biological weapons implies a willingness to terrorise civilian populations. It is no accident that analysts of the Cold War period referred to the 'balance of terror' between NATO and the Warsaw Pact.

Terrorism, though, is not a word we can easily avoid. It will be used here to describe *the illegitimate use of violence to achieve political goals*. Immediately, however, we must make two crucial qualifications.[2] First, such violence should only be described as terrorist – that is, it is only illegitimate – in a context where the democratic rule of law applies. When opposition groups are denied the liberties of democracy, they may argue convincingly that violence is their only option to achieve change. The African National Congress (ANC) in apartheid South Africa, for example, used political violence, among other strategies, to achieve democratic goals. The ANC was clearly operating in a situation where all democratic freedoms were denied to the vast majority of the population. Such violence can no more be described meaningfully as terrorism than can the violence used by the French Resistance against the Nazis. Conversely, it is equally important to stress that the use of violence for political ends in a democracy is always illegitimate, always terrorist.

Second, many commentators make a further distinction. The use of violence against dictatorships is legitimate when its targets are representatives of the state or members of the security forces, but terrorist when there are civilian casualties. This qualification does, however, impose a moral straitjacket on underground resistance movements, one that is not usually imposed on the conventional armies of democracies. If the ANC's bombing of civilian bars must be described as terrorist, then so, surely, must the bombing of Dresden by the RAF, to say nothing of the Russian bombing of Chechnya in recent years. We are back, in fact, to the question of whether or not we should label the use of all weapons of mass destruction as terrorist per se.We need to look at one more question about the term terrorism before we move on to ETA's violent campaign in pursuit of Basque independence, and the Spanish state's response to that campaign. The question is: can the term terrorist be applied to actions carried out by the security forces? It seems patently clear that it can: leaving a car-bomb on a busy street, assassinating a political leader, shooting up a crowded bar, kidnapping, torturing and 'disappearing' suspects – all these actions terrorise the civilian population for political ends, regardless of who carries them out.

Grant Wardlaw, an Australian specialist in terrorism theory, says that we should 'apply the term terrorism even-handedly to governments, groups and individuals'.[3] From this starting point, another qualification is especially relevant to the Spanish situation we are about to examine. The use of terrorism by a democratic administration is not only ethically wrong and legally criminal: state terrorism is a disease which attacks the roots of the very democracy the administration purports to be defending. Worse still, state terrorism will immunise the revolutionary terrorist groups from criticism within their own community. And this immunisation may persist for many years after such a campaign has been abandoned. That has certainly been the case in Spain, as the consequences of the events which unfolded in the French Basque Country in the mid-1980s illustrate all too well.

The disappearance of Lasa and Zabala

On the night of 16 October 1983, two young Basques decided to go to a village fiesta in the hinterland of Bayonne. Joxean Lasa and Joxe Zabala seem to have led a fairly hectic social life. Like most young Basques, they enjoyed *txikiteando*, a social custom which involves a rapid series of visits to more bars than most of us can count. However, there was another and much grimmer side to the two young men's characters. They were members of ETA, the Basque terrorist group, and had fled across the border from the Spanish Basque Country some months previously, after a botched bank raid.[4] They had spent the Saturday night in question with other radical Basques in Bayonne. At that time it was common knowledge that this town was openly home to hundreds of ETA-supporting refugees. Around mid-night, Lasa and Zabala borrowed car keys from one of their friends, but never arrived at the fiesta. It turned out they had never even taken the car. The two young men had simply disappeared. Or, as the Latin Americans put it, they had 'been disappeared'.

Demonstrators in Bayonne immediately accused the Spanish prime minister Felipe González of being responsible for their murder. But they had no proof whatsoever, not even proof that Lasa and Zabala had been killed. For 11 years, their distraught relatives had no bodies to bury. In fact, however, the bodies had been found, but not identified, only a year after the disappearances. Thanks to the random curiosity of a hunting dog, their remains – broken skeletons and a few bandages – were discovered, buried in quicklime, in Alicante, 800 kilometres from Bayonne. But the local Guardia Civil made no effort to match these remains with missing persons outside that province. A local magistrate wanted the bones disposed of in a common grave, but a diligent pathologist insisted they should be kept in a mortuary drawer.

Ten years later, an equally diligent Alicante policeman was reading news of the GAL investigations in Madrid. What he read made him wonder if there was a connection between this shadowy organisation and the wretched bundle of unidentified bones in the local mortuary. The GAL – Grupos Antiterroristas de Liberación – had been responsible for a series of shootings, bombings and kidnappings in the French Basque Country between 1983 and 1987. They had killed 27 people, at least 9 of whom had no connection with ETA. It had been evident from the outset that elements of the Spanish security forces were involved. In 1991, two middle-ranking police officers, José Amedo and Michel Domínguez, had been convicted of organising attacks on bars in St Jean de Luz and Bayonne.

Every step of the GAL investigations had been obstructed by the Madrid government. Privately assured that they had state backing, the two policemen had pleaded not guilty, and kept their mouths shut, confident that they would receive a quick pardon. After waiting in vain for three years, they volunteered dramatic new evidence to a high-profile investigating magistrate, Baltasar Garzón.[5] Amedo and Domínguez admitted participation in the GAL, and implicated several key members of Spain's former anti-terrorist high command in its activities. The scandal became the story of the year in Spain, as senior policemen were joined in custody by a former deputy interior minister. Opposition politicians accused Felipe González of having masterminded the GAL's dirty war.

The diligent policeman in Alicante knew from the media that the bodies of the GAL's first victims, Lasa and Zabala, had never been found. But he also read that there were rumours that they been buried in quicklime. He sent dental records from the bones in the morgue to a prosecutor in Madrid. The prosecutor consulted Lasa's and Zabala's families and confirmed the identification of the bones. The news sparked a series of angry riots across the Basque County, in which a Basque policeman received ghastly injuries. This was just one small instance of how the GAL's dirty war continued to fuel a cycle of violence, long after the GAL itself had ceased to operate in 1986.[6]

Indeed, the Lasa and Zabala saga was a massive propaganda coup for ETA supporters. ETA had always claimed that little or nothing had changed in the Basque Country since the Franco Dictatorship. The grim revelations from Alicante, more proper to Pinochet's Chile than to a democracy, made that claim sound plausible, even to many people who abhorred ETA's violence. In the words of José Luis Barbería, one of the most experienced and sober observers of the Basque scene, the GAL scandal made 'rage propagate itself like a blind tide, which threatens to bury all the Basques in civil conflict'.[7]

Nevertheless, a great deal had of course changed in the Basque Country, as in all of Spain, since the death of Franco. The outcome of the investigation of the Lasa and Zabala case itself ultimately demonstrated precisely that. On this occasion, the Spanish judiciary delivered remarkable results, aided by a reformist Interior Ministry. In April 2000, 17 years after Lasa and Zabala had disappeared, one of the Guardia's Civil's most charismatic generals, Enrique Rodríguez Galindo, was convicted of their kidnapping and murder. So was the Socialist civil governor of San Sebastian, Julen Elgorriaga. A Madrid court found that the two men had organised an irregular Guardia Civil unit to seize the two ETA members on French soil. They were brought back to a villa in a smart suburb of San Sebastian, where a special dungeon had been prepared. There they were interrogated for several weeks by two *guardias* with a well-deserved reputation as torturers. Finally, in the chillingly euphemistic language of the investigating magistrate, 'General Galindo decided . . . given the lamentable physical state of the two boys . . . that Lasa and Zabala should be taken to Alicante, where they would be made to disappear.'[8]

Galindo and Elgorriaga were sentenced to 60 years in prison, and their appeals have been rejected by Spain's highest courts. The former general remains in jail despite a campaign for pardon by his family, which has the support of many influential figures in the Spanish establishment and media, and a public petition which has attracted 100,000 signatures.[9] It should be said, however, that other high-profile GAL convicts have been treated much more leniently, and that ETA terrorists are generally far more harshly treated for similar crimes.[10] The Lasa and Zabala case proved to be the most dramatic of the GAL investigations, but it is only one of many.

ETA: the spiral of action–repression–action

To put the GAL's dirty war in context, we must now return to the origins of ETA late in the Franco Dictatorship.[11] The acronym ETA stands for Euskadi Ta Askatasuna – the Basque Country and Liberty. This group was born as a clandestine student study circle in the 1950s. Its members were young Basque nationalists impatient with the inaction of the Partido Nacionalista Vasco (PNV) under the Franco regime. Franco's repression of Basque nationalists may not have been quite as bloody as that suffered by the left elsewhere in Spain. But the Generalísimo's determination to eradicate the Basque language, culture and traditions made his Dictatorship particularly suffocating in the region. The Franco regime confirmed, in the lived experience of many Basques, what had previously seemed to be merely nationalist rhetoric: their country now indeed appeared to be occupied by a foreign power.[12]

The PNV focused on survival rather than resistance. It was good at survival: it is one of those groups which are as much a society within a society as a political party. Despite the repression, its members continued to meet through a dense and extensive social network of choirs, mountaineering clubs and, especially, gastronomic societies – the Basques do love their food. Entertaining and sustaining as these activities may have been, they failed to inspire the rising generation of nationalists, some of whom set up ETA in 1959. This group committed itself unambiguously to full independence for the Basque Country. Within a year it had established a military wing, though it was nine years before it carried out its first killing.[13]

During the 1960s, ETA went through intense ideological turmoil, heavily influenced by Marxism and third-world liberation-movement thinking, finally defining itself as 'socialist'. Perhaps more significant, however, was its espousal of a specific model of revolutionary practice in 1965. The so-called 'spiral of action–repression–action' is supposed to work like this: an initial armed action by a revolutionary group produces a reaction of repression by the state. This repression falls on a wider circle than the revolutionary group, alienating sectors of the population from the state. The revolutionary group thus gains popular sympathy, a broader support base, and new members. The revolutionary group is then able to undertake more, and more dramatic armed actions, which in turn provoke wider indiscriminate repression, which duly produces more support for the group. This spiral should ultimately build to a full-scale and victorious popular uprising.[14]

While ETA's spiral has never approached that level, it has provided sufficient grim momentum to sustain the group in action, with generation after generation of new militants and supporters, for more than three decades. For the spiral to function at all, however, the state must respond to revolutionary violence with the kind of illegitimate repression that will win popular sympathy for the revolutionaries. Saturation police presence, indiscriminate arrests, torture of suspects and extrajudicial killings are all essential grist to this particular mill. Under the Franco Dictatorship, the Spanish state responded to the stimulus of ETA's violence like one of Pavlov's dogs.

In 1968 ETA escalated its armed campaign. The group graduated from bombing Francoist war memorials to killing members of Franco's security forces. A young *guardia civil* was shot dead by a charismatic ETA leader, Txabi Etxebarrieta, in a chance encounter. This action by ETA immediately triggered the repression which the group's model predicted – and required. Within 24 hours, Etxebarrieta had himself been shot dead. ETA had its first victim, and its first martyr, in the space of a day. The huge attendance at masses commemorating Etxebarrieta showed that ETA had struck a deep chord in the Basque populace.

The dynamic spiral of action–repression–action continued to function in ETA's favour throughout the late Franco period. Further armed actions were countered by the imposition of states of emergency. An aggressive police force occupied city centres and put check-points on every country road. Torture was commonplace, and the victims often had no connection with ETA. Franco's security forces became the best recruiting sergeants the Basque revolutionaries could desire. The spiral reached a spectacular climax in 1973. Striking in the heart of Madrid, ETA used a sophisticated tunnel-bomb to assassinate Franco's prime minister and intended political heir, Admiral Luis Carrero Blanco. While all the major democratic opposition parties formally condemned the killing, many of their members were at least ambiguous about it in private, and some of them celebrated with champagne.

This raises the question of whether we should consider this assassination and other attacks in this period, as terrorist acts. Referring back to the criteria cited earlier, ETA was operating in a context where all democratic routes to their goals were closed off. Moreover, Carrero Blanco was no innocent civilian but a key representative of the anti-democratic regime.

The killing of Carrero Blanco can certainly be justified in the abstract – if one is not a pacifist. Hindsight shows us, however, that in practice such actions can set a very ominous precedent, and create their own negative momentum. Carrero's assassination had the effect of 'sacramentalising' the use of violence for future generations of young Basques, with disastrous consequences.

The first dirty war against ETA

Carrero Blanco himself left another hidden legacy, which also did much to favour ETA's continued existence. As prime minister, he had found that not even the formidable repressive machinery available to him under Francoist legality could stem the rising tide of militant democratic opposition. Meanwhile, far-right groups, like the Warriors of Christ the King, were springing up and using extra-legal violence against democrats. It appears that Carrero Blanco decided to bring these 'uncontrolled' groups under control. He wanted to use them to fight a dirty war – outside the law but protected by the state – against the opposition, and especially against ETA. The Madrid car-bomb ended Carrero's involvement in this plan, but his lieutenants gradually brought it to fruition.

A sustained campaign of assassinations, bombings and arson got under way in the Basque Country within two years of Carrero's death. An elusive new organisation, which usually called itself the Batallón Vasco-Español (the Basque-Spanish Battalion) targeted ETA members and many ordinary Basque citizens as well. Its death squads were largely made up of mercenaries, directed by members of the security forces.[15]

The Basque-Spanish Battalion operated from 1975 to 1981. This period covers virtually the whole of Spain's supposedly exemplary transition to democracy. It includes Franco's death, the legalisation of opposition parties, the referendum on the 1978 democratic constitution, the approval of the Basque statute of autonomy and the attempted *coup d'état* in the Spanish parliament by Lieutenant-Colonel Antonio Tejero. Given the experience of dirty war throughout this period, it is perhaps not surprising that the transition to democracy looked rather less rosy in the Basque Country than elsewhere in Spain.[16]

ETA escalates terrorist attacks under democracy

During the very same period, it must also be stressed, ETA became more lethally active than ever. In the mid-1970s, the group had averaged about 15 killings a year. In 1978 that figure more than quadrupled, and by 1980 it reached a peak of 91. How can we explain this? Why, in the very years when Spain adopted a democratic constitution, and a majority of Basques voted in favour of Madrid's offer of a statute of autonomy, should ETA have escalated its violent campaign in this way? Why had a total amnesty for ETA prisoners failed to bring a single day's peace? Most critically, why did up to 20 per cent of the Basque electorate still support ETA's political fronts?

It would take far too long to attempt to answer those questions comprehensively here. Briefly, however, I think that three basic factors were involved.[17]

First, ETA's origins, and specific aspects of Basque religion and culture, created a strong tendency to fetishise decisive 'action', and recoil from the messy compromise involved in democratic politics.[18] Second, the Francoist regime, and the transitional Suárez administrations, continued to offer more than enough illegitimate state violence, augmented by the Basque-Spanish Batallion's dirty war, to keep the action–repression–action spiral in operation. Third, and perhaps most problematically, the entire Basque nationalist community, moderate and radical, had refused to endorse the 1978 constitution, at least partly because it did not offer the Basques the right to self-determination.

Ironically, this was also the constitution which laid such great emphasis on replacing the arbitrary rule of the Dictatorship with the Estado de Derecho. Roughly translated this means the rule of law. The concept includes the separation of powers, the judicial oversight of government decisions, and human rights guarantees.[19] All of these principles would either be violated, or come under extreme pressure, during the GAL campaign and the GAL investigations.

The moderate Basque nationalists of the PNV, and former supporters of ETA's 'political-military' wing in Euskadiko Ezkerra, appeared to return to the Spanish constitutional fold in 1980. Both parties endorsed a statute of autonomy within the terms of the constitution they had rejected. Under this statute, the Basque have enjoyed powers of self-government probably unequalled by any region in Europe. However, the radicals who supported ETA's hardline 'military' wing emphatically rejected the new institutions. Grotesquely exaggerated as it may sound, ETA-Militar[20] supporters saw, and see, 'armed struggle' as their last and legitimate resort against what they call 'genocide' – the assimilation of their nation into a state they regard as alien.

This was the intractable conflict which Felipe González's youthful and dynamic Socialist Party (PSOE) inherited when it won its historic absolute majority in 1982. González's administration was the first post-Franco Spanish government with clean hands. By this I mean that, unlike many of the ministers in the transitional administrations, all its members were free from any close association with the Dictatorship. The Socialist Party victory came at a time when Spain was still badly shaken by Tejero's coup attempt only 15 months earlier. The army and other security forces were still dominated by former Francoists. They were still deeply distrustful of democracy, and doubly so of a government they suspected of being Marxist. ETA's continuing campaign was probably the greatest single factor in keeping that distrust on the edge of insurrection. The Socialists were painfully aware of the terrible price exacted from Spain's last left-of-centre government, the 1936 Popular Front, for failing to maintain 'public order'. If ETA continued to kill army officers and policemen, this government could also be short-lived.

Initially, the Socialists expected that ETA would at least offer them a breathing space, a de facto truce during which, perhaps, some new accommodation might have been hammered out. Instead, González and his colleagues got a rude awakening. Only days after he was elected prime minister, ETA killed a general, the commander of the Brunete armoured division. This was one of the Spanish army's elite units, and had come perilously close to participating in Tejero's coup. By the end of the year, ETA had claimed five more victims. The new interior minister, José Barrionuevo, and his deputy, Rafael Vera, found that hardly a week passed without their having to attend a funeral, face to face with officers furiously demanding a harder line against the terrorists.

Coupled with this tremendous pressure at home, the Socialists met with a grave disappointment abroad. As we have seen, the French Basque Country had long been a sanctuary for ETA militants. France was proud of its reputation as a land which gave asylum to opponents of despotic regimes, and had been slow to recognise Suárez's governments as fully democratic. But now, with parties affiliated to the Socialist International in government in both Paris and Madrid, surely the Spanish could expect France to start extraditing suspected terrorists to a fraternal democracy? Here again the Socialists got a very nasty shock. France's interior minister refused to take Barrionuevo's requests for extraditions seriously. He denied that senior ETA members, who were visible to any well-informed observer on the streets of Bayonne, were sheltering on French territory. Paris clearly wanted to do nothing, at this stage, to disturb the delicate status quo in the French Basque Country. González's youthful and inexperienced government found itself between a rock and a very hard place. As the funerals stacked up through early 1983, it seems that elements in the security forces made some members of this government an offer they found impossible to refuse.

The GAL in operation

The Basque-Spanish Battalion's dirty war had petered out, somewhat mysteriously, after Tejero's coup had failed, but its expertise was still available. According to one well-informed figure, Javier Pradera, launching the new dirty war was simply a question of supply and demand. Pradera is a senior journalist with *El País*, and one of ETA's severest critics. He was a close friend, confidante and supporter of the most senior Socialists on many issues, but he believes they made a fatal error at this point. His conjecture is that, in the case of the GAL, the supply came from the security forces, and the demand from the Socialists. During my research for *Dirty War, Clean Hands*, he told me:

Someone in the state apparatus – we don't know exactly who – accepted the offer from these groups who said: 'Give us the money and cover, and we will clean things up for you. If you give us a free hand, we will finish off ETA in a very short space of time. We don't want to do it in an amateur way, like it was done before, and under the fear we would be reprimanded for doing it. We want to do it with the security of knowing that we have the political support of a left-wing and democratic party.' Well, knowing the Socialist leadership as I know them, Pradera said, I think they could have fallen into that trap.[21]

Pradera stressed that he was reconstructing a hypothetical conversation. However, we now know that the pros and cons of launching a new dirty war were being seriously analysed at the highest level by Spanish military intelligence in the early months of the first González administration. A paper drawn up in July, whose authenticity has been confirmed by the Spanish Supreme Court, warned of the dangers of such operations. Rather prophetically, military intelligence showed a keen appreciation that such actions, if traced to the security forces, would be counter-productive and boost popular support for ETA. Nevertheless, it concludes that 'we consider the most advisable form of action to be use of disappearances through kidnapping'.[22]

Just months later, Lasa and Zabala disappeared. Over the next three years, the GAL carried out dozens of attacks. The modus operandi varied. The GAL started off with several kidnappings. Then there was a series of surgically precise executions of significant members of ETA, particularly in the first year of the campaign. Later, there were several car-bombs and a number of random gun and grenade attacks on crowded bars. The concerns of the military intelligence theoreticians seem to have been ignored; their fears about boosting support for ETA were certainly realised.

The GAL's death squads, so far as we know for certain from proven court testimony, were either mercenaries acting on the direction of the Spanish national police or civil guards reporting to their own commanders. There may have been other groups involved. On one occasion, a death squad made up of mercenaries was instructed to shoot 'anyone with beards' in a café in Bayonne. On arrival, they found the bar was crowded with women and children. They withdrew without firing. They were reprimanded by their Spanish police controller, who told them that they were being squeamish. The women in such bars, he said – and presumably the men without beards as well – could all be assumed to be members of ETA. The following night, the mercenaries returned to another bar in Bayonne, which has an entirely glass frontage. Through it, they could see that two girls under five years old were among the customers. 'What about the children?' one of the mercenaries asked. His comrade replied decisively: 'Let's hit the children too. ETA wouldn't worry about something like that. That is how they operate themselves.'[23] This philosopher-king among hit-men was succinctly establishing the moral equivalence between state terrorism and its revolutionary counterpart. The two little girls were both seriously wounded, as the mercenaries raked the bar with shotgun and submachine-gun fire.

Achievements – and consequences – of the GAL

What did the democratic politicians who, actively or passively, approved the GAL hope to achieve from such operations? Did they achieve these goals, and, if so, what was the cost to Spanish democracy? I think we can say that the goals of the dirty war were threefold: keeping the military and police onside with democracy; hitting ETA hard; and pressurising France to crack down on the terrorists in their 'French sanctuary'.

We have seen that the Socialists were under immense pressure from the security forces to take a harder line against ETA. Andrés Cassinello, a senior general whose cynicism about democracy was notorious, said that the GAL was 'an imaginative campaign, successfully conducted'.[24] We can take it that his views were widely shared among his comrades, and that the dirty war did provide a kind of safety valve for the angry frustrations of the military and the police. It is a sad reflection, however, that the leadership of a great democratic party like the PSOE preferred to appease the Francoists within the security forces rather than to purge them.

Did the GAL really hit ETA hard? Several senior leaders of ETA were indeed shot dead by them. Such killings were obviously a short-term blow to the organisation. Nevertheless, ETA maintained its early 1980s killing rate of roughly 40 victims a year throughout the GAL period. In 1987, the year the GAL's guns fell silent, ETA actually pushed that figure up to 54. The elimination of experienced activists may have driven ETA to become more reckless in the use of explosives, and to target civilians rather than the security forces, thus pushing up the numbers killed. Such a change in direction hardly constitutes a democratic success against terrorism.

The cost to Spanish democracy, in any case, was very high indeed. ETA's skilful propagandists turned each GAL victim's funeral into an act of well-publicised and potent political theatre. ETA's claim that its violence was merely a response to the violence of the state is not supported by the statistics, even during the GAL period. But the GAL campaign gave this view popular currency, far outside the ranks of ETA's own political wing, Herri Batasuna. This was borne out by the GAL's only political assassination, which was also its only action on the Spanish side of the border. Santi Brouard was a popular medical doctor and Herri Batasuna's most charismatic leader. He was shot dead in October 1984, as he tended a young child in his Bilbao surgery. His funeral was attended by as many as half a million people, a staggering demonstration of support in a region of less than three million.

GAL operations like the killing of Santi Brouard made the core task of ETA supporters much easier: this was to persuade the first Basque generation that grew up under democracy that the new liberties and institutions were merely a facade for the old Francoist repression.

Targeting the French sanctuary

The Socialist politicians who sponsored the GAL must have been aware of this. But they obviously believed that the death squads were producing positive effects which outweighed the negative fallout. It has been widely noted that the GAL stopped operating once France committed itself to effective and energetic collaboration against ETA suspects. Rafael Vera, a former deputy interior minister indirectly conceded this in an interview he gave me in 1997. 'I believe that, speaking objectively, the dirty war was a help in this respect.'[25] A year after that interview took place, Vera was convicted for participating in the kidnapping of Segundo Marey, the first action publicly claimed by the GAL. It was also significant in that Marey was known to be an innocent man, having been mistaken for an ETA member by GAL mercenaries. Nevertheless, according to evidence given to Judge Garzón,[26] senior Interior Ministry figures decided to keep Marey in illegal detention for ten days. They realised that holding an ordinary French citizen could put more pressure on the French government than holding an ETA member. In fact it seems that from the beginning the death squads were working to an agenda aimed less at decapitating ETA than at persuading Paris to abolish the group's 'French sanctuary'.

The dirty war certainly succeeded in creating an unprecedented climate of terror in the French Basque Country. The GAL is often described as chronically inefficient, given the high proportion of entirely innocent people it killed and wounded. However, it seems more likely, cynical though it may sound, that at least some of these 'mistakes' were deliberate. The threat to French citizens was indeed much more persuasive to the French government, and especially to French public opinion, than the killing of ETA refugees. The price of being the land of asylum simply became too high, even for those French Basques who regarded the ETA diaspora with some benevolence.

From 1987 onwards, the French expelled hundreds of ETA suspects to Spain. This shift in French policy has undoubtedly seriously undermined ETA's infrastructure, and was probably a major factor in the decline in the group's level of armed activity in the 1990s. As we are reminded all too often, however, ETA still retains significant terrorist capacity today. Above all, it has retained a remarkable level of popular support, the sine qua non for an indigenous terrorist group to remain viable, as it were, in a democracy.

ETA owes its deep roots in Basque society to complex causes, as we have seen. But there can be no doubt that the GAL campaign gave those roots vital nurture in the 1980s. Furthermore, the blatant obstruction of the GAL investigations in the 1990s also provided fertile ground for Basque scepticism about Spanish democracy. That democracy, unfortunately, had countenanced the kind of illegitimate repression which is an essential component of ETA's model of an ongoing spiral of violence.

Patxo Unzueta, another *El País* journalist, and an acute critic of ETA (of which he was a leader in the 1960s), wrote that:

> the GAL . . . have been decisive in the generational reproduction of nationalist violence in the Basque Country . . . Even conceding that the GAL were efficient in convincing the French . . . to dismantle the ETA sanctuary installed in their territory, the GAL were much more efficient as a destabilising factor in the democratic system and as a catalyst for a new flow of members to ETA.

'That is the paradox of terrorism', Unzueta continues. 'By itself, it is impotent to overthrow the democratic state. But a mistaken response by that same state can seriously destabilise the system.'[27]

The scandal of the GAL continued to destabilise Spanish democracy long after the GAL ceased to kill people. Throughout the 1990s, Felipe González and many of his colleagues used every political and judicial trick in the book to prevent the truth about the GAL being known. There were times when this policy of obstruction stretched the relationship between executive and judiciary to breaking point. Indeed, there were times when González seemed to attack the very principle of the separation of powers between these two pillars of democracy.[28] To this day, González refuses to acknowledge what the courts have revealed about his administration.

Yet he does not seem to be able to speak about the subject without ambiguity, without implying that the GAL had not been such a bad thing after all. González's famous dictum that 'democracy is defended in the sewers as well as in the salons',[29] is sadly typical of his debased argument in this debate. His stance, and that of most of his party, damaged the credibility of democratic politics, not only in the Basque Country, but throughout Spain.

Manipulating the GAL scandal, muddying the waters

This damage to democracy and the standing of democratic institutions during the period of the GAL investigations was compounded by the conjuncture of several extraordinary circumstances in the early 1990s. The opportunistic manipulation of the GAL scandal by an unholy alliance of forces hostile to González further muddied the waters of this already turbid affair. Legitimate (indeed essential) questions about the government's links to state terrorism became entangled in an obscure plot to blackmail the government. The confusion among the public which this manoeuvre generated gave the PSOE, in turn, an opportunity to paint all critics of the GAL as anti-democratic conspirators. Those sections of the political opposition, the media and the judiciary who had links to this conspiracy, or thought they could exploit it, did Spanish democracy a service almost as poor as those who were trying to cover up the traces of the dirty war.

The complex narrative of this aspect of the legacy of the GAL demands too much space to recount in full here. But some of its salient points will indicate the dangerous opportunities which the dirty war created for unscrupulous forces with no interest in democracy, justice or the rule of law.[30] The context for conspiracy was created by González's extraordinary success in holding on to power, against all expectations, in the 1993 general elections. José María Aznar's revamped Partido Popular had been in the ascendant in the early 1990s. Its leadership was confident that the odour of corruption which had enveloped the PSOE would be sufficient to turn a majority of voters away from the Socialists and towards the PP after 11 years in power.

González, however, here played his last master-stroke as PSOE leader. He ostensibly demonstrated his determination to reform his administration by successfully inviting some of his severest critics to stand as parliamentary candidates for his party. These included Baltasar Garzón, the judge who had investigated Amedo and Domínguez so tenaciously, and another magistrate with strong human rights credentials, Juan Alberto Belloch. The Spanish public, probably also unconvinced by the PP's claim to have shifted from the hard right to the centre-right, decide to give the PSOE one more chance, albeit as a minority government.

The frustration felt by the PP leadership in the aftermath of this election can hardly be overstated. There was undoubtedly a feeling in the party that if normal democratic methods could not drive the PSOE from power after so many years, other means would have to be considered. Even opinion-formers and ideologues not sympathetic to the PP convinced themselves it was their democratic duty to re-establish alternation of power in Spain, even by dubious strategies. This feeling was rife in sectors of the media which had become deeply hostile – viscerally so, in fact – to the Socialists' apparent hegemony in Spanish society. They claimed this was analogous to the position of the Mexican PRI, which had never lost an election in 70 years, despite massive corruption and human rights violations. Two key journalists who held these views were Pedro J. Ramírez, editor of *El Mundo*, and Luis María Anson, editor of *ABC*. Anson subsequently admitted that a cabal of top media figures had decided to put the screws on González to a point which could have 'affected the stability of the state'.[31]

The dramatic fall from grace of the charismatic and maverick banker, Mario Conde in December 1993 seems to have provided an opportunity to move against González that some of his enemies could not resist. When the Bank of Spain deprived Conde of control of his own bank, Banesto, after an emergency audit, he found himself facing very serious fraud charges. He was desperate for a lever against a government and financial establishment he believed had shut him out of its own golden circle. And he found a powerful ally in a senior military intelligence agent, Colonel Juan Alberto Perote, who had also just lost his job.[32]

Perote had left his office with many classified documents, some of which appeared to incriminate not only the administration, but González himself, in the GAL.[33] He showed these documents to Conde, who promptly recommended that they should share the same defence lawyer, Jesús Santaella. This lawyer then took the audacious step of asking for a private meeting with the prime minister. Even more exceptionally, González agreed to receive him. Santaella denies that he attempted to blackmail González, claiming that he was merely sharing information and concern about the circulation of documents prejudicial to state security. But he made outrageous demands on behalf of his clients, including massive financial 'compensation' for Conde.

Some sort of deal may have been struck, but if so it unravelled over the summer of 1995, and documents identical to those taken from the CESID by Perote[34] began to appear on the front pages of *El Mundo*, apparently implicating the government and its top 1980s counter-terrorists more and more directly in the GAL. These leaks often coincided with judicial moves against Perote or Conde. In 1997, *El País* revealed details of a 1994 meeting which linked *El Mundo*'s Pedro J. Ramírez, the key GAL witness José Amedo,[35] and Aznar's future deputy prime minister Francisco Álvarez Cascos. This meeting occurred prior to crucial judicial revelations about the Interior Ministry's links to the GAL. By this time, the idea that the PP was directly involved in conspiratorial moves to unseat González was firmly rooted in the Spanish public mind.[36] And another remarkable turn of events after the 1993 PSOE election victory had contributed to an equally strong belief that the judiciary was also tainted by this conspiracy.

Baltasar Garzón had been returned to the Cortes as one González's MPs in 1993, but he left the administration in controversial circumstances the following year. Returning to his judge's chambers, he found a GAL investigation on his desk, which he pursued with a relentless energy that many observers believed was generated by personal animus against the premier for not making him a minister. These charges have never been substantiated, however. Maverick as he undoubtedly is, Garzón is probably far too much his own man to participate in a conspiracy. Some of the conspirators certainly passed through his hands, and the evidence they left behind was sometimes reliable, sometimes not. Good testimony from bad witnesses was a characteristic of the GAL cases, another distorting mirror in this murky saga.[37]

While the various conspiracies associated with the GAL investigations make the establishment of the facts even more problematic, they do not support the Socialist argument that links between their administration and the dirty war were fabricated by their enemies. The PSOE, as the late novelist and commentator Manuel Vázquez Montalbán pointed out, 'sometimes have fallen back on the childish formula that because the aims of the conspirators are illegitimate, the facts did not exist. Excuse me, Sir, the facts did exist.'[38]

The conspiracies tell us much about the state of Spanish political culture in the 1990s, but the buck for the dirty war still stops at the González cabinet table. No judicial responsibility has been attached to the former prime minister for the dirty war. But the conviction for GAL crimes of his long-term interior minister, and most of his 1980s terrorist high command, make his political responsibility crystal clear.

One cheer for democracy

This account of the GAL would be incomplete without making one positive point: despite all the machinations, obstruction and hypocrisy involved, the GAL investigations do suggest something remarkably healthy in the new Spanish democratic institutions. It is notoriously difficult to subject Interior Ministries and security forces to effective scrutiny in any country. Think of the huge difficulties faced – and not yet overcome – by the likes of the Stalker, Stevens and Saville inquiries into Britain's alleged use of state terror in Northern Ireland. Then compare the achievement of democratic sectors of the Spanish judiciary, aided by courageous investigative journalists and a minority of campaigning politicians and intellectuals. It is a remarkable record, especially in a country that had so recently emerged from a dictatorship. If the GAL was a dark stain on Spanish democracy – and it was – then the relative success of the investigations was an example which much more established democracies would do well to follow. The Spanish courts have shown they have the nerve, when presented with sufficient evidence under due process, to convict very senior counter-terrorist politicians, policemen and generals.

However, several commentators, including senior jurists, have pointed to a flaw in the GAL sentences, which brings us back to the question of the nature of terrorism itself. This was the failure, or refusal, of the courts to recognise that the GAL was a terrorist organisation. In the first Amedo case, in 1991, a Madrid court ruled that the crime of terrorism only existed if the aim was to destroy democracy. Groups like the GAL, which claimed to be defending democracy, could not be defined as terrorist even if, as the court so delicately put it, they used 'reprehensible methods'.[39]

When the Supreme Court convicted the 1980s anti-terrorist high command for the Segundo Marey kidnapping in 1998, the judges explicitly closed this rather extraordinary loophole. Nevertheless, they argued that the defendants were not terrorists, mainly because the kidnappers did not seek to produce 'the alarm or fear specific to terrorism'.[40] This judgement curiously ignores both the calculated impact of the kidnapping on Segundo Marey's fellow citizens, and the communiqué which the GAL left with the victim, which clearly threatened further attacks.[41] In the Lasa and Zabala case two years later, the prosecutor Jesús Santos made a lucid and impassioned case to show that General Galindo and his colleagues were state terrorists. Yet again, the court convicted the defendants of specific and appalling crimes, but resisted calling them terrorists.[42]

It is therefore arguable that, despite the judiciary's relatively laudable record in prosecuting GAL crimes, there was and still is some inhibition about recognising the full enormity of what this organisation represented in a democracy. The courts, it seemed, dared not speak the real name of the GAL's campaign or pursue its relationship to government beyond certain limits.

Positive lessons and uncertain prospects

There is no doubt, though, that there were some other positive consequences of the GAL debacle. Spanish citizens have learned the hard way that democratic governments and their security forces can abuse power in terrible ways. But they have also learned that politicians and counter-terrorists can, to some degree at least, be held accountable. And, given what public opinion has learned from the GAL investigations, it seems unlikely that any democratic government in Madrid will ever re-activate the dirty war option against ETA.

The centre-right Partido Popular may be no more ideologically immune to such a temptation than the Socialists. Perhaps rather less so. But the PP's record in opposition, when it attacked the Socialist Party so relentlessly for its links to death squads, meant that it could hardly espouse a dirty war strategy once in power. More positively, it seems fairly clear that its counter-terrorist strategists have indeed understood the degree to which a dirty war undermines the democratic struggle against political violence. There were shoot-to-kill incidents in the Basque Country after the PP came to power in 1996, and at least one person died in circumstances that suggest an extra-judicial killing. But all the evidence is that such incidents, deplorable as they are, were aberrations, and not part of any officially sanctioned campaign. And we must remember that ETA's persistent targeting of the Partido Popular's vulnerable local councillors must often have made the temptation to go outside the law bitterly attractive.

Some observers argue, however, that the PP's post-2000 strategy of banning Batasuna, and indeed its crusading zeal against Basque nationalism in general, could have counter-productive effects similar to the damage done by the GAL. The jury is still out on this question, and this is not the place to call it in, but it must be said that the banning of any political party in a democracy is very disturbing step, and deserves very careful scrutiny. Moreover, the extraordinarily close co-ordination between the executive and the judiciary in these matters raises very serious concerns that these two powers are still far less separate in Spain than they should be.[43]

Spain's experience of the GAL teaches us a fundamental lesson: when democracy breaks its own rules to fight terrorism, it is democracy that is damaged, and the terrorists who make gains. It may be that this applies as much in the political and judicial fields as in the specific area of counter-terrorist operations.

Notes

1 This chapter is concerned with the domestic terrorism of ETA, and with the Spanish state's response. However, these general principles also apply to international terrorism, where the primacy of the rule of law is also fundamental. See also note 3 below.

2 A third qualification might appear necessary if we are to include Islamist terrorism within the definition of 'the illegitimate use of violence to achieve political goals'. The goals of the Islamist groups associated with al-Qaeda do not seem primarily political, but rather to be based on apocalyptic religious values. (See A. Elorza, 'Religión y violencia', *El País*, 16 April 2004). But it would be a serious mistake for western democracies to accept these irrational elements as the sole cause of Islamist terrorism. There are evident political grievances which feed into Islamist hatred for western democracies. Thinking of Islamic terrorists as entirely outside the political universe also strengthens a dangerous tendency to deny them the human rights which we claim to regard as universal. It is significant that the new Spanish prime minister, José Luis Rodríguez Zapatero, has stressed that his decision to withdraw Spanish troops from Iraq is motivated by his conviction that the international struggle against terrorism can only be waged effectively from a position of 'the most rigorous respect for international law' (*El País*, 18 April 2004).

3 G. Wardlaw, *Political Terrorism*, 2nd edn (Cambridge: Cambridge University Press, 1989), p. 8.

4 For a full account of the Lasa and Zabala case, see P. Woodworth, *Dirty War, Clean Hands* (Cork: Cork University Press, 2001), pp. 71–81, 281–94 and 422–4.

5 This is the same judge who later made world headlines by serving an extradition warrant on General Pinochet, the former Chilean dictator.

6 The GAL claimed the killing of Juan Carlos García Goena in July 1987. Circumstantial evidence indicates, however, that this was a 'freelance' operation by GAL members who wished to embarrass their superiors, rather than part of the GAL's strategic campaign, which ended with the killing of a 60-year-old farmer (Christophe Matxikote) and a 16-year-old girl (Catherine Brion), both without any links to terrorism, in February 1986. For the background to the García Goena killing, see Woodworth, *Dirty War, Clean Hands*, p. 222.

7 *El País*, 22 June 1995.

8 Auto de Procesimiento contra el General Enrique Rodríguez Galindo, Sumario 15/95, Audiencia Nacional, Madrid, 27 May 1996.

9 Elgorriaga was subsequently released, on the grounds of serious illness.

10 The judges who convicted Galindo and Elgorriaga refused to accept that their crimes could be categorised as 'terrorist', despite cogent arguments to this effect from the prosecutor. This decision inevitably led to more favourable penal treatment for the convicts. The reluctance of Spanish magistrates to recognise the terrorist nature of the GAL's operations, especially where senior members of the administration were implicated, is revealing in itself. See Woodworth, *Dirty War, Clean Hands*, p. 424, and the conclusion of this chapter.

11 For accounts of the history of ETA, see A. Elorza (ed.), *La historia de ETA* (Madrid: Temas de Hoy, 2000); J. M. Garmendia, *Historia de ETA* (San Sebastian: Hordago, 1979); F. Letamendia, *Historia del nacionalismo vasco y de*

ETA, 3 vols (San Sebastian: R&B Ediciones, 1994); J. Sullivan, *ETA and Basque Nationalism* (London: Routledge, 1988); Woodworth, *Dirty War, Clean Hands*, chapter 2; J. Zulaika, *Basque Violence: Metaphor and Sacrament* (Reno: University of Nevada Press, 1988).

12 See Garmendia, *Historia de ETA*, p. 39: 'If Sabino Arana [the founding ideologue of Basque nationalism] considered Euskadi to be an occupied country, Francoism made that occupation real and effective' (my translation).

13 Some recent research suggests that a child may have been killed accidentally in an explosives incident in 1961, but that ETA succeeded in hushing up the matter.

14 See Elorza, *Historia de ETA*, pp. 228–9; Sullivan, *ETA and Basque Nationalism*, pp. 41–5.

15 The participation of senior security force figures in this dirty war is particularly clearly demonstrated by the Bar Hendayais case; see Woodworth, *Dirty War, Clean Hands*, pp. 44–6 and 54–6.

16 There were dirty war actions in other parts of Spain against democratic opposition groups. But these attacks were not nearly as frequent or as systematic as those directed against Basque nationalism.

17 These points are expanded in Woodworth, *Dirty War, Clean Hands*, pp. 50–1. More detailed consideration, from diverse points of view, can be found in the histories of ETA also cited in note 11 above.

18 The 'cultural' aspects of ETA's *raison d'être* are extensively dealt with throughout Zulaika, *Basque Violence*.

19 See P. Heywood, *The Government and Politics of Spain* (London: Macmillan, 1995), p. 104.

20 All subsequent references to ETA refer to this group, which became the only ETA after ETA Político-Militar dissolved in the early 1980s.

21 Interview with the author, Madrid, November 1997.

22 This document became known, tendentiously, as the 'Founding Memorandum of the GAL'. It was one of the CESID (Centro Superior de Información de Defensa) documents stolen by Colonel Juan Alberto Perote, and used in the manipulation of the GAL scandal. It first appeared verbatim on the front covers of both *El Mundo* and *El País* on 6 September 1995, the day after a copy had been presented in evidence to judge Baltasar Garzón.

23 Quoted in R. Arques and M. Miralles, *Amedo, El Estado Contra ETA* (Barcelona: Plaza y Janés, 1989), pp. 249–50, based on the mercenaries' own testimony to investigations in Lisbon and Madrid. This book contains the first comprehensive account of the GAL. Despite having been overtaken by events, it remains a key reference for the early investigations of the dirty war.

24 *El País*, 21 December 1994.

25 Interview with the author, Madrid, November 1997.

26 *El País*, 18 July 1995.

27 P. Unzueta, *El terrorismo: ¿Qué es?¿Qué era?* (Barcelona: Ediciones Destino, 1997), pp. 43–5.

28 See especially his interview with *El País*, 29 June 1997.

29 *El País* and *Diario 16*, 30 July 1988.

30 A very detailed account of the financial and judicial machinations that created the conspiracy can be found in E. Ekaizer, *Vendetta* (Barcelona: Plaza y Janés, 1996). I have attempted to synthesise the details of the conspiracy in Woodworth, *Dirty War, Clean Hands*, especially in chapters 19 and 20. A partisan account largely from the point of view of key GAL defendants can be found in E. Bayo, *GAL: punto final* (Barcelona: Plaza y Janés, 1997); for a self-serving account by one of the key conspirators, see J. A. Perote, *Confesiones de Perote* (Barcelona: RBA Libros, 1999).

31 *Tiempo* magazine, 16 February 1998.
32 Perote had been in charge of the elite 'special operations group' of CESID.
33 The Spanish courts never accepted that Perote's documents incriminated González, though many newspaper articles claimed they did. However, the courts did accept some of the documents as legitimate evidence in GAL cases, as we have seen earlier.
34 *El Mundo* editor Pedro J. Jamírez and his journalists have always denied that either Conde or Perote was their source but Ekaizer (*Vendetta*) makes a strong case that they were. For the newspaper's view, see M. Cerdán and A. Rubio, *El orígen del GAL* (Madrid: Temas de Hoy, 1997).
35 This former police inspector and GAL organiser had become a vital but often unreliable and highly selective prosecution witness when the pardon he expected failed to materialize, and substantial Interior Ministry payments to his wife were cut off by the reforming minister Juan Alberto Belloch. Amedo had in effect also attempted to blackmail the government.
36 *El País*, 11 May 1997.
37 There were other questions about the judiciary's independence in the GAL cases. The Socialists made much of the fact that the magistrate investigating the Lasa and Zabala case was brother to a close business associate of Mario Conde's. As we have seen, however, the initial bias of the senior judiciary was actually *against* any thorough investigation of the dirty war. That this bias may have shifted after the PP came to power in 1996 throws up a more serious issue than possible individual malpractice: the decidedly incomplete separation of powers in the Spanish system. See also note 41 below.
38 Interview with the author, Madrid, November 1997.
39 *El País*, 21 September 1991.
40 Sentencia No. 2/1998, Tribunal Supremo, Sala de lo Penal, Causa Especial No. 2530/95, 29 July 1998, pp. 77–9.
41 Other and quite different questions are raised by the Segundo Marey trial. The decision to convict the defendants was taken by a 7–4 majority on the bench. The minority judges made some very strong points against the majority verdict in dissenting statements. While the circumstantial evidence against Rafael Vera and his colleagues was very strong indeed, some of the conclusions drawn by the majority, and even some of their methodology, is certainly open to question. One has to ask whether the pressure of public opinion on the GAL cases was not having a negative effect on the independence of the judiciary. Aznar's deputy prime minister, Francisco Álvarez Cascos, had made an extraordinarily inappropriate statement in 1995 to the effect that the court's judgment was obliged to 'correspond to the verdict of the citizens in the light of the facts which have been established'. Cited in *El País*, 26 July 1998.
42 Nevertheless, it is worth noting that in some cases where no Socialist Party members or security forces officers were indicted, GAL mercenaries were convicted of terrorism.
43 Writing of the Constitutional Court's ruling on the application of the 2001 Ley de Partidos, which excluded almost all radical Basque nationalists from running in the May 2003 local elections, Javier Pérez Royo, wrote bluntly: 'It is shameful that the judges have seen fit to put their names to a text like this. *It is a political decision and not a judicial argument.*' Italics and translation are the author's. Pérez Royo is professor of constitutional law in the University of Seville. *El País*, 17 June 2003.

5   Terrorism and nationalist conflict

The weakness of democracy in the Basque Country

José Manuel Mata[1]

Translated by Alejandro Quiroga

According to most analysts, democracy in the Basque Country is weak and even in crisis. The Basque Country is today convulsed by terrorism, backed by a significant collective, with an anti-system and anti-democratic culture with totalitarian features. Nationalist parties and organisations have created tensions within the political and social arena with a discourse that challenges the state and the rule of law and its institutions – especially since the so-called Lizarra Pact and ETA ceasefire in 1998 and later with the so-called Ibarretxe Plan. In the Basque Country today there is still a biased ethno-political substratum that mistakes being Basque for being nationalist. The Basque citizens are divided because those political forces which consider that just one sector of the population possesses the original features of the Basque people have tried to capture social and political legitimacy. In sum, there has been a breakdown of the consensus necessary to hold a democratic system together.

The framework of Basque autonomy

The CAV (Comunidad Autónoma Vasca, Basque Autonomous Community) has a Statute of Autonomy which was approved in the 1979 referendum by the Basque people. The Statute is the main legal body of a self-governing system, which is, in turn, unique and unlike that of the other Spanish autonomous communities. The CAV's internal political framework is based on a provincial (*foral*) system. This system divides the CAV into three historical territories according to the traditional characteristics of the Basque Country's institutional design, including a specific 'economic agreement' (*concierto económico*) – the latter being one of the sources of legitimacy (if not the most important) of the current autonomous model.

In addition to the executive and legislative powers enjoyed by the Community and the provincial administrations, a Basque Supreme Court of Justice also operates in the CAV. Among the CAV's most important powers are those related to local councils, public order, tax collection, the health system, labour relations, education, culture and the mass media. One of the main pillars of the CAV is the 'economic agreement', a deal which entitles the Basque government to collect all taxes, a share of which it then passes on to the state. The implementation of home rule has also endowed the Basque government with a great deal of symbolic power, such as the official promotion of the Basque anthem and flag, the creation of a Basque police force (*ertzaintza*), the fostering of the Basque language and the legal mechanisms to incorporate Navarre into the CAV. Even though the complete transfer of powers and competences established in the Statute has not been completed, most scholars point out that the Statute of Autonomy has endowed the Basque Country with the highest level of regional self-government in the European Union.[2]

Moreover, the Basque Statute and the Spanish Constitution acknowledge the possibility of transferring exclusive state competences to the Basque government and establish provisions for a further development of the Statute beyond its current limits. By the same token, both the Constitution and the Statute have their own legal mechanisms to be reformed. The Statute is an 'open' norm in all senses. There is no pre-established limit. Theoretically, all competences may be transferred to the Basque government, although technically there could be some limits regarding legal proceedings.

The Statute states that Basques are all those administratively registered in any municipality of the CAV. It also assigns to Basque authorities the task of protecting and fostering the fundamental rights and duties established by the Constitution. In addition, the Statute divides the CAV into three provinces, the Historic Territories of Álava, Guipúzcoa and Vizcaya, and opens the door to an eventual incorporation of Navarre, whenever the Navarrese people choose it.

The historical development of each of the Historic Territories, or Basque provinces, has differed and each has had different cultural and political features and diverse political behaviour. Every province has a specific and relevant set of powers (for example, tax collection) which is co-ordinated by and, at the same time, 'competes' with the CAV government. This peculiarity is included in and legitimised by the Spanish Constitution.

The struggle over the Statute

Nowadays, the Statute is one of the cornerstones of the conflict in the Basque Country. Whereas the nationalist parties consider the Statute useless, the constitutionalist parties underline its validity. There are three main areas in which the Statute is at the core of the conflict. First, Spanish integration into the European Union limited the level of regional autonomy within the state, as well as the state level of autonomy within the Union. Initially, integration led to tensions because of the necessary harmonisation over a range of issues between the Basque and the Spanish governments and Brussels. Second, the Constitutional Court turned down the main articles of the LOAPA, a bill seeking to establish a basic symmetry between all Autonomous Communities. Third, nationalists claim that the basis of the agreement within the Statute has been broken, since not all powers have been transferred to the Basque government. Therefore, they feel entitled to challenge the whole Statute.

As some scholars have correctly pointed out, instruments to facilitate the regional governments' participation in state policies, such as a territorial chamber, and participation at the European level in those areas in which the CAV have exclusive powers, are absent from the current political framework.[3] Nevertheless, the evaluation of the dynamics of devolution varies according to political positions. A thorough and realistic analysis of the transfers and the final completion of the Basque Statute has yet to be undertaken.[4]

When examining the dissensions about the Statute, some authors have argued that the political conflict over devolution lies in the legal nature of the Statute, for it is a law derived from the Constitution and dependent on the state, that is, central government and the Constitutional Court.[5] However, it needs to be stressed here that this is not a conflict between abstract entities but rather a struggle between political parties temporarily in power in both governments (in Madrid and Vitoria).[6]

The PNV and the ambiguity of nationalism

The stamp of nationalism in general, and of the PNV in particular, can be observed in the process of elaboration, drafting, development and implementation of the Statute. In addition to displaying a remarkable capacity to intimidate political opponents during the constituent period and the subsequent negotiations of the Statute, the PNV has followed a path towards self-government that can be characterised as follows: first, 'the steady appeal to History, in an effort to overcome constitutional and historical rationality . . . History is not History, but rather a title aimed at gaining legitimacy.' This is complemented by the 'intensification of an emotional discourse of pre-liberal rationality . . . the rejection of political opponents on the grounds that "they don't understand us"', and a permanent systematic sense of 'victimisation'. The third factor 'is moderate nationalism's ability to put political pressure on rivals because of the existence of ETA and radical nationalism'. Fourth is 'the use of possibilism, justified to the radicals as the means of achieving independence, and radicalism, used as a way of intimidating the central authorities'. Fifth is 'the increasing importance given to provincialist and foralist positions . . . seeking to confirm the provincial personality of the territories in order to keep the door open to an eventual incorporation of Navarre and to avoid problems in Álava'.[7]

Since the approval of the Statute in 1979, the PNV has been the hegemonic governing party in every single legislature. Yet the PNV and the President of the Basque government, Ibarretxe, challenged the Statute in 2000.[8] The PNV nationalists argued that the Statute was merely a means of frustrating further progress. In the process of elaborating the Statute, they claimed, the very spirit and letter of its norms had been betrayed, it had failed institutionally to incorporate those who initially rejected it, and it had forcibly brought the CAV into Spanish jurisdiction.[9]

On the other hand, as mentioned above, the challenge of the Constitution is a key discursive element in ETA's and radical nationalism's rejection of autonomous institutions and the democratic system.[10] Thus the PNV's assumption of the existence of a conflict between two generic entities, Spain and the Basque Country, indirectly endows terrorism with an implicit legitimacy when portrayed as the manifestation of that conflict.

Political conflict has gained a huge virulence and M. Oniandía, one of the leaders of the PSE (Partido Socialista de Euzkadi), has pointed out that:

> the PNV's problem is that Basque society has taken on the nationalists' most rational claims . . . this is a proven reality as shown by the fact that the vast majority of Basque society has assumed the Statute and everybody agrees with the necessity of promoting the Basque language [*euskaldunización*] and completing the devolutionary process . . . Continually stressing the divisions among Basques is not politically operative . . . the only division is between democrats and non-democrats.[11]

Even though Basque public opinion has systematically supported the Statute, a certain disenchantment with its development and the transfer of competences has recently been expressed, which can be attributed to an imbalance between reality and the expectations that the Statute generated at the beginning. Nevertheless, it should not be forgotten that this critical view of the state of self-government may be due to a criticism of parties responsible for governing the state, as well as of those nationalist parties in the Basque government (see Tables 5.1 and 5.2).

In this sense, the Basques' preferences for an alternative state framework can be divided into three groups: those supporting the current autonomous model, those advocating a Spanish federal state, and those opting for an independent Basque state. Since all three options have a similar level of popular support, it is clear that those who advocate independence are in a minority, even though they are a significant minority.

Political forces, provincial phenomena and institutional fragmentation

There are six political parties represented in the Basque parliament.[12] These parties can be placed along three axes: nationalists versus constitutionalists; right versus left; and supporters of ETA's terrorism versus opponents of violence. This polarised party system has created two fronts, and thereby blocked the possibility of reaching agreements on the governance of the

Table 5.1 Basque satisfaction with the Statute of Autonomy

Year	1993 %	1998 %	2000 %	2003 %
Satisfied	31	43	42	30
Partially satisfied	25	30	19	40
Dissatisfied	26	25	27	25
No answer	18	2	12	5
%	100	100	100	100
N	(629)	(1,400)	(1,800)	(1,200)

Table 5.2 Preferences regarding the state framework in the Basque Autonomous Community

Year	1977 %	1982 %	1987 %	1993 %	1997 %	2000 %	2003 %
Centralism	9	7	3	8	5	3	1
Autonomy	29	37	29	30	39	38	32
Federalism	32	18	15	30	26	27	35
Independence	24	17	29	28	22	30	30
Don't know	4	17	19	2	7	2	2
No answer	2	4	5	2	1	–	–
%	100	100	100	100	100	100	100
N	(1,200)	(1,800)	(1,800)	(629)	(1,400)	(1,400)	(1,200)

Basque Country.[13] In addition to the widespread fear generated by terrorist violence, the polarisation of the political arena is projected into cultural and social life, affecting many social relationships altered by violence in an atmosphere of mistrust, tension and disaffection.

Until 1998, nationalists and constitutionalists formed coalition governments in the CAV for most of the periods of office. However, ever since the Lizarra Pact was signed between the nationalists and ETA, the atmosphere of extreme confrontation and the breakdown of dialogue between political parties has led to the systematic formation of minority governments and increasing problems of governance in the Basque Country. Political instability has been aggravated by the fact that the radical nationalist party close to ETA has become the 'referee' in many parliamentary votes, at times blocking bills and projects, and thus virtually paralysing the Basque parliament.

Territoriality is yet another cause of fragmentation. As I pointed out earlier, the Historic Territories, provincial regions and the particular urban networks have different political traditions, the origins and cultural–linguistic roots of their inhabitants are different, the weight of different sectors of production varies and so on. At the political level, there has been a debate on the assignment of competences and the relationship between the provinces and the CAV institutions, as well as on the very nature of the provincial governments' powers (*foralidad*) because of the nationalist attempt to centralise the Basque Country politically.[14]

The marginalisation experienced by the more or less influential political, economic and cultural groups in the different provinces generates tensions among the 'political families', giving rise not only to single-province parties (Unidad Alavesa in Álava and Iniciativa Ciudadana Vasca in Vizcaya), but also to splits, tensions, and different stances and leaderships in all political parties. Clear indicators of this dynamic are the split from the PNV by Eusko Alkartasuna, the transformation of Guipúzcoa into the radical nationalist stronghold, and the tensions among the *vizcaíno* and *guipúzcoano* sectors of the PSE.

What may help to explain this dynamic are the differences between and consequences of fast and slow processes of nation-building.[15] Basque cultural nationalism has not been homogenous and yet it aims at nationalising the entire territory as defined by its ideology. This has led to contradictory strategies and internal crises. Unlike slow nation-building in which formally autonomous political institutions were created throughout the centuries, Basque nation-building has followed the fast track, seeking to create a nation in a territory lacking a previous political base. It is for this reason that centrifugal tendencies emerge based on diverse ideological, cultural and localist claims.

The breakdown of the consensus

Democracy is about sharing and connecting. What is to be shared is related to the existence of three types of consensus. The first one is at the community level. Political society has to share the same values and goals.[16] Even if it is not a sine qua non, the absence of this consensus would lead to an atomised and heterogeneous political culture and democracy would be weak and difficult to implement. Second, procedural consensus establishes the so-called rules of the game (the processes regulating the exercise of power) and, above all, the rules to solve conflicts. In a democratic system the main rule of the game is respecting the will of the majority. Not sharing this rule makes democracy impossible and paves the way for struggle and civil war. Third, political consensus relates to the governments' political actions and includes dissent and opposition as defining elements of democracy.

When analysing the Basque situation, it is possible to detect various breakdowns of the different forms of consensus. Some authors have defined Basque society as a society of consensus and agreements, in which phenomena of social and political privatisation, together with occasional apathy and de-mobilisation, have secularised political confrontation. The population at large, the argument goes, is much more interested in bread-and-butter issues and solving everyday problems than in the parties' political debate. However, an explicitly assumed and expressed basic consensus has not been reached; nor has any agreement concerning the rules of the game and conflict-solving mechanisms.

Exclusion and intolerance towards difference, systematic appeals to the past and to mythological history, territorial tensions, almost endemic violence, hatred for the opponent, and the belief that 'the more one fights the more one politically represents' still persist in the Basque Country. In addition, every political debate on specific policies is conditioned by the possibility of the breakdown of the basic and procedural consensus. This shows that the formation of coalition governments between nationalists and constitutionalists for various periods of office, although an important phenomenon, has not led to any greater integration of political life in Basque society.

The Statute, the Spanish Constitution, the idea of citizenship, territorial cohesion and the Basque language are systematically debated and challenged, and, on many occasions, subjected to a de-legitimating dynamic from the Basque institutions themselves. Any observer can notice this in everyday situations: among groups of friends, in textbooks, in the media, in speeches by opinion-formers at the university, and in the politicians' proposals.

Nationalist strategy: the core of the crisis

Three stages can be identified in the development of the PNV's strategy in the 1990s and in the first years of the new century. The first, identified by both Aierdi and Vitoria as *nacionalismo tranquilo*, originated from the so-called Arriaga spirit of 1988 and signalled a historic turning point in the PNV's perception of the Basque Country. In an attempt to catch up with a changing Basque society, and probably also seeking to enlarge its electoral and sociological base, the PNV modified its discourse.[17] The starting point of the Arriaga spirit was the explicit acknowledgement that not all Basques were nationalists. If the Basque Country was eventually to become nationalist, this should be achieved by persuasion. The goal was to create a basic consensus in which certain nationalist definitions and values of Basqueness would be accepted. The former President of the Basque government, J. A. Ardanza, pointed out:

> The tendency to equate nationalism with Basqueness has had a perverse effect, since non-nationalists mistook Basqueness for nationalism, thus preventing them from accepting the former as something of their own. Nationalism's patrimonial sense has had a slowing-down effect on the integration process, although this has also been used by the more reticent as an excuse not to join in.[18]

At the time, the plan to put an end to violence was based on the following premises: the rejection of any negotiations with ETA, the need to develop the legitimacy and efficacy of the political system, the acknowledgement of the existence of non-nationalist Basques and therefore the need to reach a consensus between nationalists and non-nationalists, and finally the belief that the more unified nationalists and non-nationalists were the weaker ETA's terrorism would be. In the anti-terrorist struggle, these premises crystallised into the Ajuria-Enea Pact, signed by all democratic parties.[19]

As I have pointed out, social and political privatisation affected young people and urban areas above all, weakening the nationalist socialisation networks. More importantly, nationalist discourse failed to retain its hegemonic position in Basque society and nationalism lost its capacity for social control.[20]

The assassination of the PP politician Miguel Ángel Blanco in July 1997 was a turning point. The nationalists understood that fighting against terrorism on a common front together with the constitutionalist parties would increase popular support for the latter. United social mobilisation of the democratic parties against terrorism would box the nationalists into a corner and lead to a loss of political initiative.

In these circumstances, the PNV decided to change its strategy. The new approach involved prioritising unity among nationalists, pushing for further self-government as a means of gaining sovereignty and independence from Spain, strengthening the weakened nationalist networks and, finally, integrating and deactivating ETA and its support in the belief that more self-government and nationalist unity would lead to the weakening and eventual disappearance of terrorism.

The change in the PNV's official discourse began to take shape in 1997. The organisation undertaking the task of giving a greater social legitimacy to this strategic shift was Elkarri. Formed in 1992 in nationalist milieux, this association explicitly seeks a peace agreement through active political involvement. Its main tenet is that peace is only possible through negotiation among the 'parties in dispute' and greater sovereignty concessions. With this aim, Elkarri has adopted an intermediate position between ETA and the democratic political forces in a so-called 'third space'. This new ideological plan took shape in the Elkarri peace talks, the conclusions of which are basically copied from the PNV documents on pacification.

Another basic discursive tenet of the PNV's shift is the so-called Ollora route.[21] It is based on two main arguments. The first is the acknowledgement of the political nature of ETA's conflict and the need to end this conflict through dialogue and political negotiations. And the second is the creation of a nation-building project based on the integration and unification of Basque nationalisms, which would go beyond the Statute to win political sovereignty via self-determination. Regarding the Ollora route, Oniandía pointed out:

> The PNV had to elaborate its own solution to the Basque question via claiming sovereignty, or in its own words, a 'Basque decision

framework'. Once ETA and HB [Herri Batasuna] were taken on board, a [nationalist] front would be formed to negotiate with the central government the acceptance of this formula [of sovereignty] as compensation for peace. This proposal breaks with the policy of reconciling the construction of the nationalist community with the further democratic development of self-government together with other political forces, by prioritising the former project. In this manner, those political forces still supporting self-government and the Constitution were to be ostracised. But . . . far from finding this inconvenient, nationalists understood it as a great virtue, since those pro-Constitution Basque citizens should consider themselves represented by the central government.[22]

This strategy culminated in the talks between ETA and the PNV and Eusko Alkartasuna (or EA), leading to the so-called Lizarra Pact. The reference point for these discussions was the emerging Northern Ireland peace talks, the key issues of which were applied to the Basque Country in an almost mimetic manner. The Pact was signed in September 1998 by 23 groups, associations, trade unions and political parties. Eight of these groups formed part of ETA's orbit, providing support for the organisation and for radical nationalism. None of the constitutionalist parties, trade unions or associations signed the Pact, with the exception of Izquierda Unida (IU), which later opted out of the declaration once it realised the consequences of its implementation.[23]

The Pact expressed the changes that were taking place in Basque nationalism and was endorsed by an ETA ceasefire that lasted just over a year.[24] In a nutshell, the agreement included the following points: the characterisation of the Basque conflict as political; the definition of the Spanish state and ETA as the conflicting parties; a method for the resolution of conflicts based on dialogue and negotiation without pre-conditions; and the identification of three issues on which the conflict was supposedly based: territoriality (the six territories belonging to the Spanish and French states), the Basque people as the decision-making subjects (defined in ethno-cultural as opposed to civic terms), and political sovereignty expressed in the right to self-determination.

This nationalist manoeuvre brought about a change in proposals to solve the terrorist problem. In fact, it aimed to unite all the Basque nationalisms (including ETA and its supporters) as the means of deactivating terrorism and, at the same time, achieving sovereignty based on the hegemony of the PNV in the Basque Country.

Thus the PNV–EA strategy went from gathering support from pro-autonomy Basque citizens to searching for unity among nationalists. This entailed drawing up more radical proposals in an effort to deactivate terrorism and its network. The PNV's official strategy was crystallised in the 2000 pro-sovereignty report and its tenet 'to be in order to decide' (*ser para decidir*). The report's main arguments were similar to those of the Lizarra Pact, though this time the PNV relied on ETA's social bases rather than on ETA itself. Its expressed aims were to unite all territories considered Basque by the nationalists, achieve the right of self-determination, make use of the European Union to achieve nationalist objectives, and create a new legal framework through which sovereignty could be won. The starting point was no longer the plurality of Basque society and its transformation into a more tolerant, open, enriched and multicultural national reality, but rather totally dissolving this plurality into an exclusively nationalist nation.[25]

In the 2001 regional elections, a change of government in the Basque Country was possible for the first time since democracy. The PNV's electoral promises included the right of self-determination and the implementation of a plan to deepen self-government. In an atmosphere of intense confrontation between constitutionalists and nationalists, the votes of many of the radical nationalist social bases critical of ETA swung to the PNV–EA coalition because of their promise to break from the state and fearing the nationalists might lose control of the institutions. After its relatively successful electoral victory, the PNV–EA launched the so-called Ibarretxe Plan on its own.

The Ibarretxe Plan can be considered as a logical projection of the PNV doctrines of the previous years and of Elkarri's proposals to end violence. The novelty of the Plan lies in its institutional character. It comes from the President of the Basque government, it is supported by those parties in power (PNV, EA and IU) and it has led to an unprecedented institutional confrontation with the Spanish government and the two main Spanish parties (PP and PSOE).

The three main pillars of the Plan rest on the assertion that the 'Basque people' have their own identity and right to decide their own future and that this decision must respect the rights of the citizens in the French Basque Country and Navarre.[26] Among other demands, the Plan claims: the judicial, political and administrative acknowledgement of Basque nationality; an open relationship with Navarre and the French Basque territories; full judicial power for Basque legal institutions; exclusive competences in the field of self-organisation, public security, local, provincial and private law, together with language, cultural and sports education (including the right to create national sports teams); infrastructures and natural resources management; autonomous management of political economy, tax and fiscal systems and social security; and direct representation, with the power to sign treaties, in all international institutions and organisations, especially European ones, under the status of an associated power.

Ibarretxe has always stressed that each and every article of his proposal is negotiable. However, among other polemical aspects, his Plan can be criticised for breaking with current legal and political norms, that is, the Statute and the Constitution. Even though Ibarretxe and some legal experts maintain that the project is legal according to a flexible interpretation of Spanish and international law,[27] most analysts consider that it would be necessary to carry out a root-and-branch transformation of the Constitution and the Statute in order to implement the Plan, quite apart from the difficulty of fulfilling the preconditions: getting the approval of the Basque parliament and bringing ETA's terrorism to an end.[28]

Without going into a deeper and more detailed analysis of the contents of the Plan (its first articles betray a worrying differentiation between people and society and between citizenship and nationality), it seems that those problems that it allegedly seeks to solve will continue to exist or even intensify. First of all, as ETA stated, terrorism will persist. If a ceasefire is called, its aim will be to pressurise for the approval and enactment of the Plan, for the demands of ETA and its supporters are different.[29] It may even stimulate radicalism and encourage its deeper penetration into the PNV by reinforcing a sense of nationalist victimisation when it becomes clear that the Plan cannot be implemented.

Second, the Plan provides a new pretext to those justifying the efficacy of violence as the only way to 'wake the PNV up' and force all Spaniards to acknowledge 'the inalienable rights and the historical essences of the Basque People'. Likewise, it exempts terrorists from any responsibility and blames violence on 'Spanish oppression'. The Ibarretxe Plan and the PNV policy, which are opposed to the prosecution of ETA and the MLNV (the broad Basque National Liberation Movement), hamper and may even preclude the political defeat of terrorism. Third, the real goal of the Plan is to establish a pact among nationalists to defeat the constitutionalists once and for all by excluding half of the Basque population. However, even if this happens, it seems that the Plan is unlikely to placate the demands of ETA and most radical nationalism.

Fourth, the Plan is not going to unite Basque society in the pursuit of a common goal. On the contrary, it is going to fragment and divide Basque society further into two halves and this process is already underway. Fifth, the Plan will not foster relations with Navarre and the French Basque Country, in so far as these societies and their institutions demonstrate an overwhelming rejection of independence adventures or being tied to the CAV. Sixth, if the Ibarretxe Plan is implemented one of the territories within the autonomy may opt out of the CAV. For instance, Álava could legally abandon the CAV using the Constitution's First Additional Disposition. Seventh, unless the Plan undergoes profound reform, it will be difficult for a consensus with the constitutionalist parties to be reached *a posteriori*, as in the case of the Statute, because it is nationalist in its bases, methodology and goals. Finally, the Plan is inappropriate at a time of terrorist persecution, fear, uncertainty and confrontation.

Two further issues need to be stressed. First is the demand for 'territoriality' embracing the Autonomous Community of Navarre and the

French Basque Country. The current Statute contemplates the option of signing treaties with Navarre through special channels. It even establishes the possibility of drafting a new Statute should the Navarrese vote in a referendum to join the CAV. Today, however, the vast majority of the Navarrese and their institutions do not want to vote on this issue. In the case of the Basque provinces in the French state, the situation is even clearer. The influence of Basque nationalism is minute and groups close to it seek the formation of their own *départments* and the creation of cross-border economic and cultural, rather than political, relations. The second issue is to do with the proposal to call a referendum on self-determination. Together with the obvious legal provisions, referenda always require a prior minimum consensus, as well as prior guarantees, stipulations and definitions on which the consensus should be based.[30] This is especially true when the question at stake affects the roots of the democratic system and the political basis of the society.

For all these reasons the judgement made by the Canadian Supreme Court over Quebec is apposite. It ruled that the right of self-determination is a matter for all Canadians and that it would be illegal under both Canadian and international law for Quebec unilaterally to declare independence. However, it also stated that the secessionist wish of a part of the population cannot be ignored but that if this wish is to be taken into account and negotiated, it would have to be the result of a referendum in which a 'clear majority' vote affirmatively in response to a 'clear question'.

On the eve of the 2004 general elections, the PP and its government continued to reject any reform of the Statutes and even proposed polemical legal norms backed by prison terms for those who call referenda without being legally authorised to do so. For its part, the PSOE continues to reject the Ibarretxe Plan, but has openly raised the possibility of a reform of the Statutes and the Constitution, above all as the result of pressure from the Catalan President Pasqual Maragall and other leaders, as well as important sections of the party in the Basque Country. The PSOE has offered the PNV a legally valid accord for the reform of the Basque Statute. Izquierda Unida, even though it had approved the Ibarretxe proposal within the Basque government of which it forms part, has presented its own proposal termed 'free adhesion federalism' (*federalismo de libre adhesión*).

ETA has adopted an ambivalent position, accepting the Ibarretxe Plan critically but rejecting it as 'autonomist' at the same time, yet regarding it as a means of exercising the right of self-determination and advancing towards the sovereignty and unity of the Basque Country. So Batasuna has been insistently inviting PNV–EA to reach agreement with all the nationalists with the implicit promise that the terrorist organisation might declare a ceasefire or indeed lay down its arms. Although Ibarretxe refuses to have talks with the representatives of Batasuna until they reject ETA's terrorism, and even though the new PNV President Imaz appears to be more willing to negotiate with the constitutionalist parties, several analysts have suggested that negotiations are probably going to take place between the banned Batasuna and the PNV–EA to reach agreement for an ETA truce, thus complying with the condition of 'absence of violence' that Ibarretxe laid down in order to further his objectives.

In the light of recent events and given the positions adopted by the parties it seems doubtful that the State of the Autonomies can be maintained without any change, so the victory of the Socialists in the March 2004 elections has been crucial in defining the territorial configuration of the Spanish state.

Underlying ethno-political discrimination[31]

There is still today a big potential for discrimination in Basque society which is inherent in nationalist beliefs especially those articulated by the radical nationalists. It should be stressed that a good percentage of the Basque population considers Basque and Spanish identities incompatible (see Table 5.3). Basque nationalism lays out a series of key characteristics concerning belonging to the collective 'we', that is, to the 'Basque people'. The starting point draws upon the PNV founder Sabino Arana's discourse: not all inhabitants of the Basque Country are Basque.[32] If they are legally Basque this is only because of the Constitution and the Statute, but this does not turn them into 'real' Basques, the argument goes.[33]

Nationalists do not publicly and explicitly adopt this discriminatory stance, but rather implicitly through comments and ideological structures that show that there are different levels of Basqueness. ETA's terrorism and the ethnic, at times xenophobic, principles of some nationalist discourses are part of this context. The ensuing problems seriously and directly undermine both the possibility of reaching a basic consensus within Basque society and about the perception Basque society has of itself.

Table 5.3 Basque national identity

Year	1981 %	1987 %	1992 %	1997 %	2000 %	2003 %
Spanish only	5	5	9	5	7	4
More Spanish than Basque	28	4	8	6	7	6
As much Spanish as Basque	–	24	35	36	33	33
More Basque than Spanish	31	25	20	20	18	25
Basque only	28	34	20	26	32	29
Don't know	3	3	4	–	1	–
No answer	5	5	4	7	2	3
%	100	100	100	100	100	100
N	(1,800)	(1,800)	(1,615)	(1,400)	(1,800)	(1,200)

According to nationalists, within the Basque territory there are the 'others': constitutionalists who are accused of being Spanish nationalists. The nationalists rely on a restricted concept of citizenship which challenges the spirit of the Statute. In their eyes, those voting for constitutionalist parties, or having different cultural and political views or a sense of a shared Basque-Spanish identity or a Spanish identity, are Basques only because the current institutional framework imposes it. Thus civic links are broken on behalf of restrictive ethnic bonds.

Nationalist discourse blurs the distinction between being nationalist and being Basque. The essential differential trait of a superior level of Basqueness is considered to be 'the will to be Basque', understood as 'the fight against Spanishness' and 'the defence of the Basque Country'. This will is brought to fruition by knowing the Basque language Euskera. Bringing together these characteristics means sharing a particular vision of the situation in the Basque Country, according to which it has been 'invaded' and 'oppressed' by a foreign army and police, and the people's demands have not yet been met.

Language and the crisis of social relations

Democracy, freedom, armed struggle, terrorism, fascism, nazism, constitutionalism, Euskadi, Euskal Herria (or Basque homeland): nowadays in the Basque Country many words lose their meaning and acquire a different, even opposite, symbolic connotation, depending on who uses them and his/her political perspective. In addition to the use of Euskera as an ethno-political weapon and a potential tool for ethnic and ideological discrimination, Basque nationalists use certain classifications in the Spanish language as devices for assimilation. As P. Bourdieu pointed out, 'nothing classifies us better than our own classifications' and 'political struggle is essentially a struggle of words'.[34]

Nationalist discourse is transmitted through its own socialisation channels that are structured within the nationalist community and it reaches beyond family and friends, the fundamental agencies for the transmission of nationalist codes in general and ETA's supporters in particular. Moreover, it is through the public mass media dependent on the Basque government (EITB) that nationalism reproduces and launches its 'official' discourse to the nationalist part of Basque society. Especially since the Lizarra Pact, nationalism has adopted, transmitted and pervaded society with the sort of language and classifying codes which subsume ideological elements and nationalist beliefs often with essentialist features. For instance, the use of the term Euskal Herria instead of Euskadi signals the transposition of a democratic concept of citizenship at the political-institutional level to an ethno-cultural one.[35] Some other significant examples implicitly showing the radicalisation of political language are those terms taken from the MLNV and ETA's vocabulary (for example. 'repentants', *arrepentidos*) and from the Northern Ireland case ('Unionists'). Many years back, the words Spanish and Spain were turned into stigmas and insults amounting to anti-Basqueness by the nationalists.[36]

The spiral of silence in operation

Today approximately half the population in the Basque Country defines itself as non-nationalist (see Table 5.4), yet the 'spiral of silence' is still operating.[37] The 'spiral of silence' is a sociological process that works as follows: the individual is afraid of isolation and marginalisation, so he or she observes the comments of those surrounding him; if this individual agrees, then he/she will talk, otherwise he/she will remain quiet. This generates a social climate in which dominant ideas are magnified, whilst minority ideas are minimised as senseless. Consequently, the one who stays quiet seems to consent, which in turn reinforces domination, notwithstanding the fact that the majority may actually be the minority and vice versa. As a result, allegedly minority ideas are socially stigmatised and the opportunity of their spreading into society is severely restricted.

In this respect, it should be stressed that the majority of those identifying themselves as both Spanish and Basque and constitutionalist fear talking about politics in public and participating in the political process (see Tables 5.5 and 5.6). This has led to widespread mistrust and fear of voting and asserting certain political options, as well as to enormous difficulties when drawing up electoral lists. The cooling and breakdown of numerous social and kinship relations is evident and has been demonstrated.[38] A direct consequence is that an indeterminate number of people have left the Basque Country as a result of social pressure and terrorist attacks. The fact that a large number of citizens would be willing to leave the Basque Country if offered similar living conditions elsewhere is just another by-product of this situation.[39]

The organisational network and social bases of terrorism[40]

At the beginning of the transition to democracy, ETA saw the need to adapt

Table 5.4 Basque nationalist identification

Year	1987 %	1991 %	1997 %	2000 %	2003 %
Nationalist	48	45	43	42	43
Non-nationalist	41	44	45	54	50
Don't know/No answer	11	11	12	4	7
%	100	100	100	100	100
N	(3,200)	(1,400)	(1,400)	(1,800)	(1,200)

Table 5.5 Fear of active participation in politics

Year	1979 %	1995 %	1998 %	2000 %	2003 %
Very afraid	11	12	26	17	12
Quite afraid	39	39	39	24	36
A bit afraid	40	30	20	36	32
Not afraid	7	10	10	19	18
Don't know/No answer	3	9	5	4	2
%	100	100	100	100	100
N	(1,400)	(1,400)	(1,400)	(1,800)	(1,200)

Table 5.6 Feeling free to talk about politics

Year	1987 %	1995 %	1999 %	2001 %	2003 %
With everybody	40	33	36	25	43
With some people	40	40	41	48	37
With almost no one	7	14	13	18	12
With no one	7	9	8	8	8
Don't know/No answer	6	4	2	1	–
%	100	100	100	100	100
N	(1,800)	(1,400)	(1,400)	(1,200)	(1,200)

its strategy to the new political system. Seeking an independent Basque state, ETA created and developed a number of political and social organisations to implement its tactical and strategic goals in different social milieux. ETA's strategy rests on the attitudes and beliefs that cement the cohesion of its support network. Among them, the following can be underlined: a mythification and support for ETA as unquestionable leader; belonging to a 'community of hate' towards all those considered as representatives of the Spanish state: non-nationalist politicians, police, entrepreneurs, teachers, judges, journalists; self-identification as exclusively Basque and anti-Spanish; the use of Euskera as a political symbol; the rejection of representative democracy in favour of the so-called 'identitarian socialism' – a mixture of a diffuse progressive ideology, decision-making by assembly, self-management and autarky. Members of this network keep their hopes and expectations alive through ETA's terrorist actions and street fighting (*kale borroka*). The feeling of belonging to a broader nationalist community is also fuelled by the PNV–EA government's weakness or failure to enforce its responsibilities at different levels, which has led to 'areas of impunity'. In this manner, a social environment has been created that facilitates the movement's goals spreading and the belief that its methods and objectives are appropriate.

The MLNV itself has a mass media and communications network that is used to articulate the discourses, language and propaganda of radical nationalism. Among the most important are the newspaper *Gara*, the magazine *Herria 2000 Eliza*, several publishers, 'educational' seminars, local magazines and radio stations, and other channels and resources that stretch from the use of new technologies to the production of countless posters, placards and leaflets. Inside the terrorist and MLNV network there are groups devoted to all sorts of actions covering all possible social sectors, such as youth, students, trade unions, ecology, feminism, foreign affairs, education, ideological debates, mass media, prisoner support groups and so on (see Figure 5.1). It is important to note that the relationship between ETA and its network of support is informal, intentionally blurred and hidden in order to take advantage of the democratic legal system. For ETA, the benefits of this method are impunity, the possibility of spreading conflicts to different sectors of society, the legal status of many groups and organisations close to the terrorist group, and the use of institutional flaws and legal gaps.

These groups employ a tactic called the 'accumulation of forces' in which they seek to intensify conflicts through a process of infiltration and proselytism in order to expand, deepen and radicalise the struggle in different social sectors and thus to extend the movement's field of influence. The goal of this tactic is to gain such an accumulation of conflicts (both in quantity and intensity) that it becomes unsustainable for the Spanish state to confront what radical nationalists call the 'Basque people'. A measure of its influence was that in the 2003 local elections, approximately 150,000 blank votes were cast, following the instructions of ETA and its radical circles.

The struggle against terrorism

The PP–PSOE Anti-Terrorist Pact signalled the start of unprecedented political, judicial and police activity against ETA and its support network.[41] It led to the banning of Batasuna and most of the MLNV organisations, the closing-down of newspapers linked to the MLNV, the ban on electoral platforms for political successors of Batasuna, prison reforms, the inclusion of ETA–Batasuna in the list of international terrorist organisations and French and European Union collaboration, among other things.[42] For some years, Judge Baltasar Garzón had prosecuted and banned some of the terrorist network's key organisations. The state powers' anti-terrorist drive may lead to a serious political, economic and social erosion of ETA. Its leaders have attempted to radicalise the PNV and to show the PNV's grassroots that the Basque government is not going to break with Spanish legality. But ETA supporters are facing a dilemma. Either they remain outlawed and choose a dynamic of total confrontation with those that might attract the radical nationalist grassroots (PNV–EA and the Aralar party, which broke from Herri Batasuna), or they call for a new ceasefire in order to influence the Ibarretxe Plan, testing how far the PNV is willing to go.

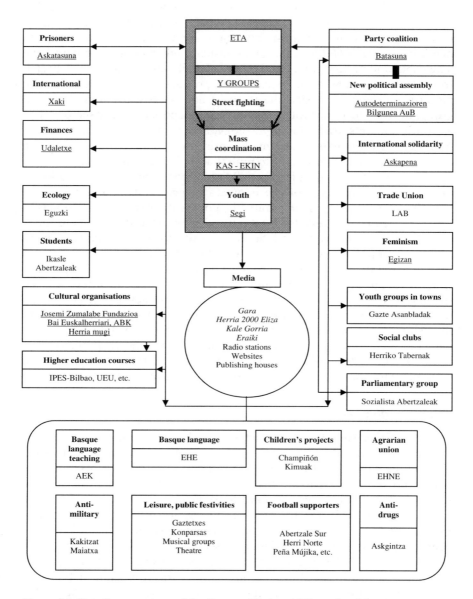

Figure 5.1 Putative structure of the Basque National Liberation Movement
(BNLM)'s basic network 2004: activities and organisations.

Sources: information gathered from legal proceedings and rulings, and media reports.

Note
Activities appear in bold, organisations proscribed by the Spanish state are underlined, the
BNLM's main groups are in the shaded box, and publications are in italics. For further details
of the names and acronyms of organisations, see Mata, *El nacionalismo*.

As an outstanding analyst has recently stated:

> ETA is in an extremely weak situation and its supporters have been unable to respond to its electoral retreat and banning, which means there may be important changes that will turn 2004 into a crucial year. However, it should always be borne in mind that for ETA truce and assassination are not incompatible options, two divergent strategies ... but follow the same path whose final objective is [ETA's] survival as a real power.[43]

Differences with Northern Ireland

At the core of nationalist discourse about ETA's terrorism lies a systematic reference to the Northern Ireland peace process. But there are essential differences between the situation in the Basque Country and that of Northern Ireland.[44] Unlike the Basque Country, there are terrorist groups on both sides of the Northern Irish divide. Unlike ETA, the IRA has recognised that violence has been ineffective. While the IRA abandoned violence because the moderates resisted its maximalist proposals, the Basque nationalists have given up trying to defeat ETA. Their goal is to integrate ETA within a non-violent greater nationalist community. In Northern Ireland, it is widely accepted that the obstacles to a lasting peace are internal. In contrast, Basque nationalism regards such obstacles as external: that is, they derive from the Spanish government's impositions. In Northern Ireland, unlike the Basque Country, the Republicans' right of self-determination is conditioned by the Unionists' own right of self-determination through the principle of Unionist consent or acceptance. Moreover, the plan accepted by the IRA did not centre on sovereignty, but autonomy for both communities and the agreed solution implied the formation of mixed governments including both parties in conflict. Finally, the IRA's rejection of violence was due not to a change of policy by the British and Irish governments but rather to a reconsideration of the limits of its own discourse.

The consequences: persecution, fear and marginalisation

Attacks against the militants and local branches of the constitutionalist parties in many municipalities have prevented them from drawing up electoral lists, leading them to fill the list with militants from outside the Basque Country. Persecution and death threats against all those (teachers, intellectuals, politicians, entrepreneurs, journalists and others) who publicly refused, criticised, condemned, or acted against ETA's nationalist plans from a constitutionalist position have led many of them to leave the Basque Country. Others have taken refuge in what is called 'an internal exile' or live in constant uncertainty and ostracism, especially in small towns and villages where the majority of the population supports the terrorist network in particular or nationalism in general.

In the Batasuna writ of suspension, the judges stated that ETA had committed 3,391 terrorist acts, killing 836 people and injuring 2,367, of whom 1,294 were physically incapacitated, 150 declared unfit for any job, and 41 seriously disabled. In addition, according to data provided by the judiciary and the Agencia Vasco Press, the so-called Y Groups linked to ETA committed 3,954 acts of street violence between 1991 and September 2002. In the summer of 2002, 499 ETA prisoners were in Spanish jails and 99 were in French jails.[45]

In a report on 'violence and persecution' published in early 2003, the pacifist organisation Gesto por la Paz calculated that over 42,000 people were under direct threat and persecution in the CAV and Navarre.[46] This figure does not include grassroots members of the constitutionalist parties, those attending PP and PSOE electoral meetings, and all those whose have never made public that they have received threats. Among those directly threatened by ETA are over 200 teachers and intellectuals, over 1,200 politicians and party militants, approximately 15,000 entrepreneurs, over 24,000 policemen, 350 judges and attorneys, 400 journalists and 800 prison officers. To get an idea of the significance of the figures, we should take into account that the population of the CAV in 2001 was 2,082,587, according to the Basque Institute of Statistics, and that per capita income in the Basque Country was 1 per cent above the European average in 2000.[47]

Threatening telephone calls and letters sent to non-nationalists' homes or those of their relatives, verbal abuse in the street and other public places, threatening graffiti, physical aggression and terrorist attacks all aim at identifying, persecuting and isolating those who do not follow the nationalist code. As a consequence, citizens under threat are forced to avoid company, crowds, travelling to certain places and municipalities, and attending public events and fiestas. They are also forced regularly to change their itineraries, be constantly vigilant, check their vehicles for bombs and even employ bodyguards. All of this, with the exception of assassinations, still produces a timid social reaction. Notwithstanding the rejection of terrorism by the majority of Basque society (see Table 5.7), an important sector of the population turns a blind eye to these crimes and persecutions as if it were an inexorable part of Basque 'normality'. This passive attitude is fostered by a certain institutional neglect and a permissive approach towards violent Basque nationalist networks and actions.[48]

It should not be forgotten that ETA has nationalist political goals. The persistence of terrorism is the main but not the only problem the Basque Country faces. There is a climate of ostracism and an underlying ethnic ideology that turns an important sector of the population into second-class citizens. Likewise, Basque society and its language, symbols and attitudes are impregnated with nationalism, which is reinforced through channels of socialisation contaminated by nationalist values. In addition, the Basque

Table 5.7 Evolution of attitudes towards ETA

Year	1981 %	1983 %	1989 %	1995 %	1998 %	2000 %	2003 %
Total support	8	6	3	1	1	1	–
Critical justification	4	4	5	4	4	6	2
Supporting the ends but not the means	3	2	9	10	12	13	13
Used to support it but now oppose it	12	6	15	13	14	11	18
Indifferent	1	1	3	2	4	2	2
Afraid of it	1	2	4	7	6	3	4
Total rejection	23	41	45	57	53	60	60
Don't know/ No answer	48	38	16	6	6	4	1
%	100	100	100	100	100	100	100
N	(1,800)	(600)	(2,300)	(1,400)	(1,400)	(1,800)	(1,200)

Source: all data from Euskobarómetro, research team at the Departamento de Ciencia Política y de la Administración at the Universidad del País Vasco, www.ehu.es/cpvweb.

language is used as both a political tool and a device for ideological transmission.

After more than 20 years of nationalist governments and control of the most important Basque institutions, a network of institutional dependencies has emerged and the PNV and EA have moved towards a programmatic radicalisation, accompanied by the social radicalisation of their grassroots. This could break Basque society.

Notes

1 The author is grateful to Professor Sebastian Balfour and the Cañada Blanch Centre at the London School of Economics and Political Science for their kindness and their invitation to participate in the series of seminars that gave rise to this book. The Basque Government Departamento de Educación, Universidades e Investigación provided the author with the financial assistance for research and conferencing in the United Kingdom. Much of the quantitative data used in this chapter has been taken from the database of the Equipo Euskobarómetro, the research team of which the author is a member. Some of this data can be accessed on the Departamento de Ciencia Política y de la Administración at the Universidad del País Vasco webpage: www.ehu.es/cpvweb.

2 The 1936 Basque Statute granted the right to form an army and a police force, to issue passports, coinage, etc. However, all these rights were granted in the exceptional situation of the Civil War. Spain's integration into the European Union has led to the transfer of some of these tasks, such as printing money, to European institutions.

3 For example, G. Jaúregui, *Entre la tragedia y la esperanza* (Barcelona: Ariel, 1996), p. 139.

4 Many scholars have pointed out that only two important competencies remain to be transferred.
5 M. Bilbao, *Consensos y conflictos ante el Estatuto de Autonomía* (Oñate: IVAP, 1992), p. 189 and *passim*.
6 Another key element in this dissension is based on the erroneous interpretation that the Basques rejected the Constitution. This argument is based on the fact that only 31 per cent of the Basque electorate voted in favour of the Constitution. Some commentators have gone as far as to deny the evidence of the approval of the referendum for the Statute. For a rigorous analysis of the constitutional referendum results see F. Domínguez, *De la negociación a la tregua ¿El final de ETA?* (Madrid: Taurus, 1998), p. 28 and *passim*.
7 J. Corcuera, *Política y derecho: La construcción de la autonomía vasca* (Madrid: Centro de Estudios Constitucionales, 1991), p. 309 and *passim*.
8 For the PNV see 'Ponencia política del PNV de enero del 2000'; 'Concreción de la ponencia política: Reconocimiento del ser para decidir 2000'; 'Ilusión por hacer, nota de prensa del EBB de 2003'; 'De la ofensiva electoral a la guerra político judicial, EBB 2003'. For Ibarretxe see 'Konponbideak – una iniciativa para la convivencia. 2002–2003'. All documents at wwww.eaj-pnv.com and www.elcorreodigital.com.
9 *El Correo*, 25 October 2000, p. 21 and *DEIA*, 20 October 2000, p.12.
10 Another key discursive element is the conception of the Statute as a constitution 'granted' by Spain. This view is supported by radical nationalists close to ETA and some very influential sectors of the PNV and the EA. The view of one ETA leader in the 1990s on this subject is illuminating see E. Etxebeste, *Veinte años después* (Bilbao: Argitaletxe-Iru, 1994), p. 30 and *passim*.
11 M. Oniandía, 'Entrevista', *El Correo*, 28 June 1994, p. 12. See also M. Oniandía, *Guía para orientarse en el laberinto vasco* (Madrid: Temas de Hoy, 2000).
12 At the time this chapter was drafted, the radical nationalist group close to ETA was still participating in the Basque parliament, despite the sentence passed by the Supreme Court. This is due to the non-fulfilment of judicial orders by the parties forming the Basque government. They have argued that the Basque chamber is sovereign and independent regarding the dissolution of parliamentarian groups.
13 See G. Shabad *et al.*, *El sistema de partidos políticos en España. Génesis y evolución* (Madrid: CIS, 1986); J. J. Linz, *Conflicto en Euskadi* (Madrid: Espasa Calpe, 1986); and F. J. Llera, *The Construction of the Basque Polarized Nationalism* (Barcelona: ICPS Working Papers, no. 64, 1993).
14 For an analysis of the Constitution's First Additional Disposition, related to the *foralidad*, see J. García Roca, 'España asimétrica. Descentralización, territorial y asimetrías autonómicas: una especulación teórica (1)', in *Asimetría y cohesión en el estado autonómico* (Madrid: MAP, 1997), pp. 51–71.
15 J. R. Recalde, *La construcción de las naciones* (Madrid: Siglo XXI, 1982), p. 431 and *passim*.
16 G. Sartori, *Teoría de la democracia. 1. El debate contemporáneo* (Madrid: Alianza, 1988), p. 121 and *passim*.
17 The PNV's historic conception was based on equating Basqueness with nationalism. The party sought to shape the country along the nationalist model, using the nationalist local branches and social networks as its sources of clientelism. See J. C. Vitoria, 'El fracaso del nacionalismo tranquilo. Del espíritu de Arriaga a la vía Ollora', in *100 años de nacionalismo* (Bilbao: El Correo, 1995), p. 79 and *passim*; X. Aierdi, '¿Es un contrasentido un nacionalismo tranquilo?', *Revista Inguruak*, no. 5, pp. 63–96. UPV/EHU, Universidad de Deusto, AVS. Bilbao, 1989.
18 J. A. Ardanza, 'Pacificación y violencia' and 'Euskadi en el estado de las

autonomías'. Conferences at the Fundación Sabino Arana (Bilbao) (Vitoria: Secretaría Presidencia del Gobierno Vasco, 1993), p. 32. See also J. A. Ardanza, 'Debate de política general. Intervención del Lehendakari' (Vitoria: Secretaría General del Gobierno Vasco, 1992), pp. 10–20.

19 J. V. Viloria, 'El fracaso del nacionalismo tranquilo. Del espíritu de Arriaga a la vía Ollora', in *100 años de nacionalismo*, p. 81 *passim*.

20 On top of this should be added the 'divorce' between the PNV and Basque intellectuals in all fields. J. Juaristi, 'Símbolos, cultura, y etnicidad, Los signos de identidad del partido de Arana', in *100 años de nacionalismo*, pp. 43–51.

21 J. M. Ollora, 'El nacionalismo del futuro', in *100 años de nacionalismo*, pp. 91–5. This article opens with an Ingushio proverb showing a very low level of ethnic responsibility: 'The one that thinks of the consequences cannot be brave.'

22 Onaindía, *Guía para orientarse en el laberinto vasco*, p. 109.

23 For details of the Pact see http://www.lizarra-garazi.org.

24 ETA's communiqués bringing the ceasefire to an end blamed the PNV and the EA for the non-fulfilment of the Pact and made them responsible for the consequences of the broken promise.

25 J. L. Zubizarreta, 'Pesada hipoteca', *El Correo*, 17 October 1999. See also I. Zubero, 'El debate sobre el derecho de autodeterminación en Euskadi', in X. Etxeberria Mauleon *et al.*, *Derecho de autodeterminación y realidad vasca* (Vitoria: Servicio de Publicaciones del Gobierno Vasco, 2002), p. 72.

26 J. J. Ibarretxe, 'Konponbideak – Una iniciativa para la convivencia. 2002–2003'. Document at wwww.eaj-pnv.com. The text of the Plan can be found at http://www.nuevoestatutodeeuskadi.com.

27 Nationalists have defended the legality of the Plan according to a flexible interpretation of the Constitution's First Additional Disposition, the Basque Statute's Additional Disposition, its Civil Rights International Pact, and Economic, Social and Cultural International Rights.

28 The current legal system establishes the Spanish Prime Minister as the only person entitled to call a consultative referendum. Second, the Ibarretxe Plan is impossible to implement without previous negotiations and agreements with state institutions. Legally, the process needed for the Ibarretxe Plan to be approved is the following: both the Spanish parliament and senate would have to pass a bill proposing constitutional reform. This bill would require a two-thirds majority in both chambers. This would set in motion the constituent process: parliament and senate would be dissolved, elections would be held for new upper and lower houses, and a referendum would be called in Spain to pass the Ibarretxe Plan and the reform of the Basque Statute. Later the new elected chambers would have to pass the reform with a two-thirds majority in each house. Finally, Basque citizens would be asked to vote in a referendum to approve the new Statute.

29 At the time I am completing this chapter some Spanish media are suggesting ETA might call for a ceasefire in order to facilitate and influence the starting of the Plan.

30 See J. M. Mata, *El nacionalismo vasco radical: discurso, organización y expresiones* (Bilbao: UPV/EHU, 1993), pp. 55–63.

31 Ibid., chapters 2 and 10.

32 'Qué somos' and some other writings by the PNV founder in S. Arana, *Obras escogidas. Antología política* (San Sebastian: Haranburu, 1978). Unlike most political parties, the PNV never publicly abandoned or revised its original xenophobic postulates. Today the use of racist terms such as *maketo*, or defining Basque identity in terms of individuals' origins and surnames, is not 'politically correct', although this does still happen. Nowadays discrimination takes place at the ethnic-linguistic and political levels.

33 Ibarretxe himself made clear this discrimination. In an electoral meeting he told the people present, the majority of them immigrants from other Spanish regions, 'You are Basque like us.' In saying this, Ibarretxe betrayed himself. His words implied 'You are like us, but you are not us.' The ex-PNV president's discriminatory declarations are more frequent and blunter. X. Arzalluz has stated that non-nationalists in the Basque Country would be treated like 'Germans in Majorca', with social but very few political rights. He often mentions the Basque blood type as a sign of distinctiveness. In addition, mythic and quasi-religious references to the Basques as the 'chosen people' and the idea of a Basque *Volkgeist* and its essentialist and anti-democratic implications are evident to any student of Basque nationalist ideology.

34 P. Bourdieu, *Cosas dichas* (Buenos Aires: Gedisa, 1988), pp. 62, 134.

35 The term Euskal Herria was included in the Statute as an alternative name for the Basque Country. Yet it has a cultural ethno-linguistic meaning, for it applies not only to the CAV but to all territories in which the Basque language is still spoken.

36 In the words of V. Klemperer:

> language not only creates and thinks for me, it also leads my emotions, my psychical personality. The more I take a natural and inconsistent approach to language, the more this happens . . . Words may act as very little doses of arsenic: one swallows them without noticing and they seem to have no effects; yet, eventually, they have a toxic effect. If someone says again and again 'fanatic' instead of 'heroic' and 'virtuous', he/she would end up truly believing that a fanatic is a virtuous hero and that without fanaticism one cannot be a hero.

> In *LTI. La lengua del Tercer Reich. Apuntes de un filólogo* (Barcelona: Minúscula, 2001), p. 31.

37 On the spiral of silence see, for example, E. Noelle-Neumann, *La espiral de silencio* (Barcelona: Paidós, 1995); Linz, *Conflicto en Euskadi*, pp. 17, 624–5; J. R. Llera, 'Continuidad y cambio en la política vasca: notas sobre identidades sociales y cultural política', *Reis*, no. 47 (July–September, 1989), p. 129.

38 Nationalists argue that the banning of Batasuna (precluding its supporters from expressing their views via the ballot box) and media linked to ETA, systematic accusations of torture (most of them filed by the judiciary), and the dispersion of ETA prisoners around Spain have increased social problems.

39 According to the spring 2003 Euskobarómetro, 16 per cent of Basques would be willing to leave the Basque Country should they have similar living conditions somewhere else. The situation is worse in Álava and Vizcaya (20 per cent), among immigrants and their sons (23 per cent), and among PP and PSOE voters (40 per cent). Figures are also high among youngsters (26 per cent), students (28 per cent) and those with a university degree (25 per cent).

40 For a further analysis see Mata, *El nacionalismo vasco radical*; J. M. Mata, 'Nationalism and Political Parties in the Autonomous Community of the Basque Country. Strategies and Tensions', *ICPS*, no. 137 (1998); J. M. Mata, 'Batasuna: la estrategia de la insurrección', *El País Domingo*, 18 August 2002, pp. 1–3; J. F. Llera, J. M. Mata and C. L. Irwin, 'ETA: From Secret Army to Social Movement. The Post-Franco Schism of the Basque Nationalist Movement', *Terrorism and Political Violence*, 5/3 (Autumn 1993), pp. 106–34.

41 On several occasions the PSOE has criticised and even challenged the Pact, alluding to the partisan use the PP have made of it and to measures and changes in the penal code carried out by the government that the PSOE believes go against human rights.

42 For the judicial edicts see the following webpages: www.elcorreodigital.org; www.elpais.es; and www.gara.net.
43 K. Aulestia, 'Balance provisional', *El Correo*, 28 December 2003, p. 26.
44 For a further discussion see R. Alonso, *La Paz en Belfast* (Madrid: Alianza, 2000); 'La retirada del IRA', *El País Domingo*, 28 October 2001, pp. 1–3; 'El conflicto interno', *El Correo*, 15 November 2002, p. 32; 'De la retórica al compromiso', *El Correo*, 26 January 2003, p. 40; and 'El buen ejemplo irlandés', *El Correo*, 27 April 2003, p. 34.
45 José Luis Barbería and Paxto Unzueta, *Cómo hemos llegado a esto. La crisis vasca* (Madrid: Taurus, 2003), pp. 304–5.
46 Gesto por la Paz, 'Monográfico. Violencia de persecución', 4 November 2002, www.gesto.org.
47 See the Instituto Vasco de Estadística and the Basque government webpages: www.eustat.es and www.euskadi.net.
48 Politicians, intellectuals, teachers and constitutionalists have formed various civic associations against ETA and the current nationalist strategy, such as Basta ya, Foro de Ermua, and Fundación para la libertad.

6 Convergència i Unió, Catalonia and the new Catalanism

Andrew Dowling

In December 2003 Pasqual Maragall, former mayor of Barcelona, and leader of the Partit Socialista de Catalunya (Catalan Socialist Party), the PSC, became president of the Generalitat and thus of the autonomous government of Catalonia. His investiture as president brought to an end 23 years of continued government by the nationalist coalition Convergència i Unió, CiU. Significantly, the victory of Maragall in 2003 was on the back of a 'defeat'. His party performed worse than in the last Catalan elections in 1999, losing some 180,000 votes and ten seats.[1] Maragall's 'victory' and CiU's defeat were in fact made possible by the substantially improved performance of the smaller progressive forces in Catalonia, both of which doubled their representation. Maragall was thus able to form a rainbow coalition government. Within a month of its formation it was plunged into a crisis that led to the resignation of its chief minister.[2]

This chapter examines how CiU came to be such a remarkably successful formation and analyses its slow, relative decline from the mid-1990s. To unravel the trajectory of CiU we need to look back at the transformation of political Catalanism during the Franco regime, in particular in the declining years of the Dictatorship, and during the transition to and consolidation of parliamentary democracy. CiU transformed political Catalanism and Catalan political culture, yet its rise to power in the 1970s caught many observers by surprise.

CiU is composed of two parties: the liberal and conservative nationalists of Convergència Democràtica de Catalunya (CDC) and the smaller Christian Democratic party of Unió Democràtic de Catalunya (UDC). Since 1979, UDC and CDC have fought every election in coalition. In 2002 the relations between the parties were altered and their official status has subsequently been that of a federation. CiU became the most important nationalist formation in the Spanish state and the most successful representative of stateless nationalism in western Europe. The political dominance of CiU has turned the Catalan question into a central preoccupation of the Spanish state since the transition, though clearly it has a different dimension to the Basque problem. Furthermore, a constant referent in Catalan political debate has been the place of Catalonia in Spain, what is called in Catalan *l'encaix*.[3] The importance of Catalan and Basque nationalisms in Spanish political culture is a reflection of the concern among Spanish elites that Spain might lose these economically advanced territories. Catalonia, after all, is one of the ten richest regions of Europe.

CiU played a pivotal role in the Spanish polity between 1993 and 2000 as a result of the electoral arithmetic of the Spanish state. Jordi Pujol, CiU president for 25 years, was described as almost a 'co-president' of the Spanish government during this period.[4] CiU's support of the Madrid government, first the Spanish Socialists (PSOE) from 1993 to 1996, and after 1996 the conservative Popular Party (PP), helped to ensure free-market orthodoxy in Spain as well as convergence for entry into the euro. At a Catalan level CiU's health and education policies, among others, can hardly be described as progressive, as party leaders claim. Expenditure on social protection in Catalonia is only 17.5 per cent compared to a Spanish average of 19.9 per cent and a European Union average of 27.6 per cent.[5] Though CiU has been consistent in its support for the PP since the mid-1990s, it has often been able to blame the PP for the harshness of its measures of political economy. This external support for all-Spanish governments by CiU can be seen as a revival of the tradition of support for the Madrid government by the conservative representatives of Catalan nationalism during the first third of the twentieth century.[6]

The emergence and consolidation of CiU coincided with transformations in the world economy that favoured the party. In that period Catalan society also experienced profound social and cultural change. In the mid-1970s, Catalonia was still often known as 'Red Catalonia' because of the dominance of left political forces. As one commentator put it in 1977, following the first democratic elections in Spain, 'Catalonia has become a strong bastion of western leftism'.[7] Indeed, there was a genuine concern at the time amongst business leaders and conservatives that Catalonia would be the first west European country since the 1940s to have communists in the government. There was a serious fear as the leader of Catalan business put it in February 1980, that 'Marxists' would turn the Catalan autonomy statute into 'an instrument of class struggle and [a means] of taking power'.[8] The electoral campaign leading to the first autonomous elections of 1980 was characterised by 'Red Scare' tactics on the part of the right, led by Catalan business organisations. This was a response both to the radical position adopted by Catalan social democracy and to the strength of the Catalan communists of the Partit Socialista Unificat de Catalunya (PSUC).[9] CiU was the main beneficiary of this campaign and this was one factor in explaining its surprising victory in 1980.

The years between the death of Franco in 1975 and the second Catalan elections in 1984 were marked by the rising political confidence of the right (increasingly represented by CiU) and the growing disorientation of the radical and social democratic left. Social democratic projects in Europe, from British Labourism to those of Mitterrand, were failing. During this period the market economy became both totemic and seemingly all-victorious. These developments were of particular significance for Catalonia because during the Franco regime and throughout Spain the most important opposition force was the Communist Party. In Catalonia the Communists had displaced the anarchists during the course of the Franco regime as the main organisation of the left. As the transition to democracy demonstrated, CiU thus faced an opponent with a vociferous and highly mobilised base. Yet, at that time, the PSUC was promoting Euro-communism and *pactisme* (the pragmatic Catalan tradition of dialogue and compromise) and, like its Spanish equivalent, the Partido Comunista de España (PCE), was much concerned with the 'fetish' of party legalisation. The PSUC has been seen by some commentators as pivotal in labour demobilisation in the transition years.[10] For all the PSUC's political moderation and commitment to Catalanism, it was undermined by the crisis of Brezhnevism, Poland and Solidarity, as well as the 1979 Soviet invasion of Afghanistan. Thus the most successful opposition force to the Franco regime split and declined.[11] Like the PCE, it was forced to restructure to ensure its political survival from the mid-1980s. This process culminated in the creation of the Red–Green alliance, Iniciativa per Catalunya (IC).

Paradoxically, there was near unanimity amongst Catalan political forces about the future political shape of Catalonia by the end of Franco's Dictatorship. More importantly, the political left felt they dominated Catalanism.[12] Yet, between 1975 and 1984, the CiU skilfully manufactured the perception that, in marked contrast to the final years of Francoism, only they could represent Catalonia. This was aided by the fact that the Catalan socialists were damaged by the policies pursued by the PSOE government following its victory in 1982. The first of these was the LOAPA, a law introduced in response to the attempted coup of 1981, in an attempt to slow down the process of devolution. CiU was able successfully to portray the PSC as part of the governing power in 'Madrid' that was negatively affecting Catalonia. The PSC enjoyed a certain degree of autonomy from the PSOE but its ultimate subordination to the Socialist headquarters made it vulnerable to these attacks.

Catalanist sectors in the PSC were further undermined by Spanish nationalist/anti-Catalanist voices in the PSOE, represented above all by Alfonso Guerra, vice-president of the party and deputy prime minister until 1991. At one point, Guerra had called the Catalan autonomy process a *choteo* or joke and 'farce'.[13] Thus in the 1984 election in Catalonia, which gave an overall majority to the coalition led by Pujol, CiU labelled the PSC as 'Madrid's representative'. In this election CiU received 46 per cent of the vote and, contrary to many simplistic interpretations of Catalan voting behaviour, a third of its votes came from Spanish immigrants. Perhaps surprisingly, CiU's victory (against the Catalan branch of the PSOE) was interpreted in much of the conservative Madrid press as a victory for 'moderation' against 'socialism'. For distinct reasons, then, in the years immediately following the transition, both the PSC and the PSUC lost credibility as Catalan national forces. CiU would successfully rule Catalonia as a majority government until 1995 and would be embroiled in innumerable clashes with the PSOE concerning the devolution of powers to Catalonia and challenges to Catalan legislation from 'Madrid'.

The policies of CiU in power since 1980 also have their own historical continuities. The incremental award of concessions from Madrid was a continuation of the strategy of Pujolism inaugurated in the 1960s and early 1970s. This Pujol-led programme has come to be termed *Fer país*, 'making a country'; that is, its economic, social and cultural reconstruction. *Fer país* has been central to the CiU's programme of Catalan nationalism. Its key project was the modernisation of the Catalan economy. Thus the plans for motorway construction under Franco were supported by the nationalist sector in the 1960s. The Catalanist modernisers and nationalists centred around Pujol and the Banca Catalana were acutely aware that the national project was important because of the economic strength of Catalonia. These two elements have been seen as interconnected, as Catalan prosperity could aid in the dissemination of the discourse of Catalanism, as it had done in the nineteenth century.

The revival of Catalan nationalism occurred during the period that has been termed 'neo-nationalism'.[14] The Pujolist-led projects of *Fer país* and the 'construction' of Catalonia were thus part of the regionalist response to the transformations in the world economy that began to be discerned in the 1970s. Indeed, Pujolist Catalan nationalism has been labelled 'bourgeois regionalism'.[15] Pujol's qualified affirmation of globalisation was clear in his remark in 1999 that 'Globalisation is positive, but it has to be rounded off by maintaining identity.'[16]

An added component of the project of contemporary Catalanism is that of Europeanism. The vision of a 'Catalanised Spain' shared by the conservative Catalan party of the early twentieth century, Lliga Regionalista, was transformed during the Franco regime into that of a 'Europeanised Catalonia'. The Spanish market, once of pivotal importance to the Catalan economy, is of declining importance. In 2003, Spain received only 50 per cent of Catalonia's exports.[17] Catalan business associations have backed pro-EEC and EU organisations from the very beginning. This cultural and political shift can begin to be discerned in the 1950s in the work of Father Josep Armengou, a pivotal influence on Jordi Pujol and Catholic Catalanists, who declared in 1958: 'Catalan nationalists have to be . . . the promoters of European union and in answer to the question, "with Spain or with Europe", Catalonia has no option – "with Europe".'[18]

Since the nineteenth century, 'bourgeois' Catalonia, far more than anywhere else in the Iberian peninsula, has been keen to adopt the latest cultural and political trends from Europe. In its view, Catalonia has acted as a bridge between Spain and Europe.[19] The 'Europeanism' of contemporary Catalanism echoes a long tradition in Catalanist discourse, which has seen

Catalonia as an integrally European culture. It has also been a celebration of Catalan 'modernity', and often contrasted with Castilian/Spanish 'backwardness'.[20] This continues in the present day; for example the CiU's webpage at the end of the twentieth century showed Catalonia as an oasis in a Spanish desert.[21] The party's self-definition has always been of a moderate Catalanism and a reflection of the Catalan bourgeoisie, regarded as the most progressive, modern and European in the Spanish state.

The Catalan bourgeois was given his opportunity when a new business sector emerged during the 1950s centred on financial services and publishing. This group became the backbone of the Catalan nationalist business class during the latter half of the Franco regime. The growth of multinational businesses in the Catalan economy began at that time, when the first hesitant steps in the economic liberalisation of the Spanish economy were taken.[22] This shaped the emerging discourse of Catalan nationalism in the 1960s, which has consistently sought further autonomy but not independence. These trends, as has been seen, were noted by Catalan business, particularly during the mid-1980s. 'Catalan industry is a dependent industry. As an industry it has always been dependent on the Spanish economy and it is becoming more [dependent] on the world economy.'[23] A notable transformation in the Catalan economy has taken place in the service sector, with the tourist industry alone employing around 13 per cent of the Catalan workforce. Catalonia receives 15 million tourists annually, more than two and a half times the Catalan population. Furthermore, the Catalan rural small proprietor sector has dramatically declined to around 3 per cent of the populace.[24] The Catalan economy, service-oriented and ever less reliant on manufacturing, is a paradigmatic late-modern economy.[25]

The origins of CDC, founded in 1974, lay in the Catalan Church, the business and financial strata and the cultural community, sectors that had evaded Francoist repression. The new Catalan business elite identified with its west European counterparts. This liberal and relatively enlightened bourgeoisie believed that a western parliamentary system was a better guarantor of business stability than the often irrational rule of Franco's governing elite. Although Convergència initially described itself as 'social democratic', this was mere rhetoric, as Pujol has himself subsequently acknowledged.[26] In a speech made to Barcelona's business school in 1974, he clearly laid out his conception of an appropriate political structure:

> The most important development of the Catalan economy has almost always been the product of private enterprise, under the existence of a strong political regime, with industrial peace, the expansion of the western economy, tariff protection of the entrepreneur, [who] is the creator of wealth.[27]

Nevertheless, the Catalan business class as a whole remained suspicious of CiU until 1980 because of its rhetoric of social democracy. Subsequently

CiU ensured for itself the support of the business sector. In late 2003, the business vote was split between CiU and the PP, with only 6.7 per cent supporting the PSC in spite of the Socialists' efforts to court Catalan business with pro-business policies.[28]

As we have seen, a series of factors, from the apparent strength of Catalan communism to the ambiguous position of Catalan socialism regarding Catalanism, as well as the peculiarities of the transition in Catalonia, helped CiU attain its dominance. It was able to take advantage of a number of other factors. As we have seen, what has become known as Pujolism was a significant factor in late Francoism. Pujol himself had come to be the best-known embodiment of Catalanism inside and outside Catalonia by the 1970s. During the transition, he met with leading figures, including the king and the leader of the conservatives, Manuel Fraga. It was little noticed in the mid-1970s but CDC was the fastest growing party in Catalonia by 1977 and was the biggest in the region by 1981.[29] It was able to occupy a broad political space stretching from Catalan conservatism to nationalism: the Lliga Regionalista had disappeared and the left nationalist party Esquerra Republicana (ERC) only attained any real strength in the late 1990s.

Although Spanish conservatism has been ambivalent towards CiU for most of the period since the transition, both have shared many of the same values except that of the 'nation'. As Manuel Fraga put in 1982, AP, UCD and CiU were 'the natural majority'.[30] As for Catalan nationalism, CiU was able to profit from the conflict with Madrid over the transference of powers to the Catalan government, the Generalitat, following the victory of the Spanish Socialists in October 1982.[31] During Francoism and the transition the Catalan left had dominated 'popular' Catalanism. After 1980, on the contrary, Catalan identity became 'institutionalised' through the Generalitat. Cultural manifestations of Catalanism provided new employment opportunities for cultural elites and a form of clientelism emerged promoted by CiU. During the first CiU-led government between 1980 and 1984 there emerged the triad 'Pujol–CiU–Catalonia', which would be politically effective for the next 20 years. The Pujolist discourse equated any attack on, or even lack of support for, Pujol or CiU with an attack on Catalonia.

Since the restoration of the Generalitat in 1977, Catalonia has sought to cement and extend its self-government, and this extension and deepening of autonomous power has been central to the political project of Catalanism. This has been represented in recent years by calls from almost all Catalan political forces for the creation of a new Statute of Autonomy. The new statute will be certain to address questions of taxation and other fiscal matters. The 'financial' question has been at the centre of Catalanist debate since the 1960s. According to a leading bank in 1967, 'a draining of capital from Catalonia to the rest of the state would tend to slow the growth of Catalonia, without necessarily producing more rapid growth in any other parts of Spain'.[32] It has been at the heart of power struggles between Madrid and Barcelona. It has also been closely linked to business calls for self-government and is most directly related to Catalan competitiveness.

Indeed, the Generalitat and CiU have acted as a lobby for Catalan business, concerned at what is seen as the financial 'plundering' of Catalonia. Importantly, the 'exploitation' of Catalan wealth has also resonated with the wider public. The Generalitat under CiU has also been able to capitalise on popular perceptions that the Catalans are economically 'exploited' by Madrid. Though they have damaged the reputation of Catalans with the wider Spanish public, the Generalitat also encouraged populist campaigns such as that against high Catalan motorway tolls that affect both business and the populace at large.[33] These popular/populist perceptions were also encapsulated in the early 1990s by ERC who declared that 'Spain is robbing us'.[34]

Catalan nationalism, because it has a linguistic dimension, has kept the question of the Catalan language at the centre of cultural and political debate throughout the twentieth century. It has been central to the question of Catalan identity. The Generalitat has repeatedly clashed with governments in Madrid of varying political hues over the policies and strategies of linguistic 'Catalanisation'. In the Catalan legislature of 1995–9, CiU proposed a language reform law strengthening the use of Catalan (Llei de Política Lingüística) which created its own polemics, particularly with the government in Madrid, although it was supported by almost all parties in the Catalan parliament. According to a Catalan commentator, the language law 'was the most ambitious that could be achieved without provoking a social rupture'.[35] Even so, much of the language law has not been fully implemented, nor have the fines that go with it been seriously applied, a perhaps classic example of Catalan pragmatism.

The language question is of course closely related to that of immigration. Between 1930 and 1970, when large numbers of Spaniards migrated in search of work, Catalonia doubled its population, a dramatic demographic revolution. As early as 1964, Pujol had spoken of the implications of this mass transformation: 'Our central problem as a country is not the language or the social question, nor economic progress, nor is it a political problem: our central problem is immigration, and therefore, integration.'[36] 'Integration' in this sense has meant and means the adoption of the Catalan language by those new arrivals. Immigrant labour has contributed to the economic transformation of Catalonia and has not threatened the employment prospects of native Catalans. Far from it: indigenous Catalans benefited from this enormous influx.

Furthermore, Catalonia has been more secure in the vitality of its language and culture than the Basque Country. Greater Barcelona has been the area most affected by the pattern of migration, but in spite of the arrival of large numbers of Spanish speakers it continued to have a strong presence of Catalan speakers.[37] The fears expressed by Pujol and others in the 1960s that mass immigration would lead to de-Catalanisation have not been borne out. It is true that most first-generation immigrants to Catalonia have not fully integrated in the sense that they have not learnt Catalan. More importantly, though, they have not mobilised against nor become hostile to Catalanism. In spite of controversies over language planning laws, post-transition Catalonia has not experienced a resurgence of the anti-Catalanist popular movement of the 1930s, Lerrouxism.[38] The broad consensus in Catalonia continues to be in striking contrast to the divisions faced in the Basque Country. The question of immigration, however, has re-emerged with renewed vigour since the mid-1990s as in all European countries. The new immigrants are no longer Spanish and this therefore represents a further challenge to Catalan integration policies.

The failure of the PSC and progressive Catalanists to remove CiU from power after 1980 has its parallel in the first quarter of the twentieth century. Conservative Catalanism, then embodied in the Lliga Regionalista, was hegemonic, whilst parliamentary liberal Catalanists were prone to divisions and splits. The emergence of the PSC at the beginning of the twenty-first century under the leadership of Pasqual Maragall transformed the political culture of the diverse forces of the Catalan parliamentary left. After the great disappointment in the elections of 1999, they finally displaced CiU in government in December 2003. Yet almost immediately, in January 2004, the three-party government, the *tripartit* of the PSC, ERC and IC, was plunged into crisis leading to the resignation from the government of the ERC party leader and chief minister, *conseller en cap*, Josep-Lluís Carod Rovira, following a political and politically manipulated scandal concerning a clandestine meeting held by him with the leadership of ETA. The origins of this crisis are to be found in the changes experienced by the *tripartit* parties over the course of the 1990s.

The liberal nationalists of ERC were the striking victors in the election of November 2003 in spite of the split and ideological crisis they suffered in the early 1990s. ERC, as mentioned, did not re-emerge as an important formation in the transition and, owing to its support for CiU in 1980, almost imploded. Over the course of the 1980s, ERC was ineffectual until a new leadership emerged that prioritised the question of political independence. This had some electoral benefits to the party but the party was convulsed by a new crisis as many within it felt it had forgotten its social agenda and that ERC had come to be seen as little more than a campaigning platform for (an improbable) Catalan independence. Since the mid-1990s, ERC has re-launched itself as a pragmatic party supporting Catalan independence.[39] Yet it has also given renewed importance to social questions and has successfully capitalised on CiU's closeness to the PP on 'social' issues. It was noticeable after the municipal elections of May 2003 that ERC was more inclined to enter into electoral agreements with the PSC rather than CiU, and was an early indication of the choice of coalition partner the party would make later that year. The peculiar circumstances of the Spanish general election of March 2004 also resulted in a triumph for ERC, increasing its representation from one to eight seats in Madrid.

For its part, the PSC, following its fifth successive defeat at the hands of Pujol in 1995, had embarked on a thorough revision of its strategy to defeat CiU by seeking to occupy its political space. This would culminate in the choice of Maragall as party leader and a programme of 'Catalanisation' of the party. Officially, the PSC is the Catalan federation of the PSOE and this has enabled nationalists to accuse it of *sucursalisme*, or subordination to the party centre. CiU has successfully marketed itself as the only 'true' Catalan political force. In one poll held before the elections of 1999, only 10 per cent of those polled considered that Maragall and the PSC would defend 'the interests of Catalonia'. The figure for Pujol and CiU was 70 per cent.[40] Maragall sought to challenge these electorally damaging accusations. As one of the leading figures in CiU, Miquel Roca, put it as early as 1977, 'What is the use of voting in Catalonia for a candidature who also stands in Madrid?'[41] The 'Maragall' project of the 'Catalanisation' of the PSC envisaged capturing what has been called the 'dual vote' in Catalonia, meaning sectors of the Catalan electorate that vote CiU in Catalan elections but PSC in the general elections.[42] Just as CiU won every Catalan election after 1980, so the PSC won a majority in Catalonia in every general election between 1977 and 2000. A huge component of the membership and voter base of both the PSC and the PSUC consisted of immigrants. The PSC electorate is mostly made up of those born in other areas of Spain, or, as one writer has put it, 'one might infer that we are faced with a PSC electorate loyal to the PSOE'.[43]

Maragall created a civic organisation, Ciutadans pel Canvi (Citizens for Change), to Catalanise the Catalan socialists. Inspired by Blairism, Maragall also saw the changes in the PSC as indicative of a move beyond the politics of left and right. A consequence of this broad church strategy was a further dilution of the social-democratic content of the PSC and thus a narrowing of its differences with CiU on questions of political economy. Since the transition, divisions within the PSC have also related to its electoral constituency, its 'core vote', made up, on the one hand, of Spanish-speaking workers and, on the other, of liberal-social democratic middle-class and cosmopolitan Catalanists. Like other west European social democrats, this has been a fragile coalition. The PSC won in 2003 by a narrow margin and with a substantial loss of votes. Notably, abstention in the industrial areas surrounding Barcelona was high.[44] This fragility has been heightened by Maragall's courting of the Catalan business lobby. As the president of the most important forum of Catalan business, the Fomento de Trabajo Nacional, declared before the Catalan elections of 2003: 'Business does not fear a Maragall government.'[45] This represents a considerable shift on the part of Catalan business from their negative attitude towards the prospect of a PSC government in 1980.

Maragall's Catalanisation of the PSC was reflected in its policy call for the federalisation of Spain and for a new Statute of Autonomy. The Maragallian paradox has been to combine appeals to the centre-left with appeals to nationalism (traditionally Catalan liberals and leftists prefer the term 'Catalanist'). Since his emergence as party leader, Maragall's Catalanist shift has frequently clashed with sectors of the PSOE. Many commentators have noted that Spanish nationalism has re-emerged with renewed vigour in the early twenty-first century (see Chapter 7), and the Popular Party has attempted to tarnish the PSOE with being 'weak' on Spanish unity. One response in the PSOE has been the 'Jacobin' Declaration of Mérida, which defended the Spanish state and present constitutional arrangements and was a direct response to the so-called Declaration of Barcelona.

The document and agreement that became known as the Declaration of Barcelona of July 1998 was made with the political forces of Basque and Galician nationalism. The core of the text is a call for the recognition of the multinational nature of the Spanish state.[46] This defence of Spanish unity has continued to be made by the same sectors in subsequent years and the comments of PSOE regional barons such as José Bono, who called nationalism 'out of date' during the Catalan elections, were seen as damaging to the PSC. Maragall's incorporation of the 'separatist' ERC in his government and the controversies of January and February 2004 were further seen as damaging to the PSOE in the Spanish general election campaign of early 2004. Indeed, the Socialist leader Rodríguez Zapatero was accused of collaborating with ERC and of being 'soft' on 'separatist' nationalism by the PP, and was the object of strong criticism from sectors within his own party.

Although Spanish socialism was greatly damaged by questions of corruption in the 1990s, the PSC seemed unable to capitalise on the increasing cases of corruption that have been periodically linked to the Generalitat because of the memory of the scandals associated with the PSOE in power.[47] Perhaps the only area in which Maragall differentiated himself from Pujol was that of language. But even here he has called for the polemical Llei de Política Lingüística not to be reformed or abolished but to be applied with more caution, clearly reflecting the sensitivities of his electorate.[48] However, in all other questions, from the 'financial' question to the policy of federalism and the creation of Catalan sporting entities, Maragall and the PSC have followed CiU. The positions adopted by the PSC are then a reflection of the CiU-led Catalanisation of society.

As was made clear at the beginning of the 2003 electoral campaign for the Catalan parliament, nearly all Catalan parties, from CiU to the Greens, call for greater Catalan autonomy. The only party opposed to further quotas of self-government, the conservative Popular Party, obtained around 12 per cent of the vote, and has in recent years tried to obtain greater support by presenting itself as 'Catalanist' through name and leadership changes and by evoking the conservative Catalanism represented in the early twentieth century by Francesc Cambó, one of the founders of the Lliga Regionalista. It would therefore be erroneous to see the relative decline of CiU since the mid-1990s as an indication that Catalan nationalist sentiment has peaked.

Maragall and the PSC had two possibilities to defeat CiU: mobilisation or Catalanisation. The fact that Maragall chose the latter is a confirmation of how much CiU has transformed the terrain of Catalanism in the past 20 years.

Many questions arise concerning the future trajectory of political Catalanism. As noted, it has invested highly in Europeanism as a project that would enable Catalonia to 'by-pass' the Spanish state. CiU and Pujol were firm believers throughout the 1990s that globalisation and European integration were leading to the decline of the nation state. Yet the constitution of the European Union appears certain to consolidate existing nation states and their territorial integrity and seems unlikely to allow for an increased role for the regions.[49] Catalanism is therefore going through a period of ideological renewal in the new post-Pujol period. The first indications of this renewal are the wide-ranging and broadly supported calls for the reform of the Statute of Autonomy promoted by all parties in Catalonia except the PP. These have not stirred up much controversy at a Spanish level because they coincided with the Basque Ibarretxe Plan (see Chapter 5), which many argue might lead to the break-up of Spain.

Indeed, in recent years, the question of the nature of Spain and of Spanish unity has come to be at the forefront of Spanish political debate. As a headline in *El País* noted in 2003: 'PP and PSOE open the [electoral] campaign with a debate on the unity of Spain.'[50] The increased hostility on the part of the PP towards the sovereignty drive of the regional nationalists, whether Basque or Catalan, led Pujol to accuse Aznar of breaking the pact of the transition concerning Spain.[51] CiU has paid the price for its support for the PP. Though it has been experiencing electoral decline since the mid-1990s, it is clear that the votes lost to ERC in 2003 and in the 2004 elections are part of the electorate's punishment of CiU's support for a PP that had hardened its political strategy after obtaining an overall majority in the Spanish general elections of 2000. CiU governed Catalonia from 1995 thanks to support from the PP, and Pujol has recognised that being seen to be allied with the PP has cost CiU electorally yet felt CiU had to do it 'out of responsibility towards Catalonia and the governability of Spain'.[52]

Pujol's decision not to stand again for the post of president of Catalonia and his anointing of Artur Mas as successor was initially interpreted as a radicalisation on the part of CiU towards more nationalist positions. The government of Pujol has zig-zagged since the late 1990s with, on the one hand, its support for the conservative Spanish Popular Party and, on the other, its attempts to prevent its own decline by increasing the tempo of Catalan nationalism. CiU-led Catalan nationalism also increasingly adopted other populist strategies, as seen, for example, in its call for the creation of Catalan sporting entities, particularly a Catalan football team.[53] Mas has performed the classical Pujolian balancing act of nationalist rhetoric and pragmatism. The 1998 regional nationalist Declaration of Barcelona, signed by CiU alongside the more radical Basque and Galician nationalisms and once interpreted as a sea-change in CiU's policies, has effectively been put on ice.

Pujol's retirement as party leader and his choice of Mas as successor have placed CiU in a fluid situation. The decision initially caused a serious deterioration in relations between the partners of the CDC and UDC coalition Within CDC, there emerged two factions to battle over the Pujolist inheritance. Like all successful formations, political office had held the disparate elements within the party together. With the leader of UDC now leading CiU representation in Madrid following the Spanish general election of March 2004, and Mas leading the federation in opposition in Catalonia, CiU faces uncertain times. The real danger may be an unravelling of the coalition if it is excluded from power for long. It is most unlikely that Mas will ever attain the status of Pujol within CiU and be able to overcome these potential crises. There is also the possibility of a pincer movement between the PSC, ERC and the PPC[54] to carve off sectors of the CiU electorate. CiU thus faces a serious challenge over the next few years and its status as a 'catch-all party' could be fatally undermined.

Dividing Catalan politics between a nationalist axis based on CiU/ERC and a 'state-wide' axis with the PP, PSC-PSOE and IC, fails to capture the Catalanism of IC as well as much of the PSC. This state–nationalist division also misses the CiU alliance with the PP on many issues, as well as UDC's greater proximity to some sectors of the PP.[55] Strikingly, only the PP in Catalan politics sees Spain as a nation.

The new governing coalition of Catalonia, made up of the PSC, ERC and IC, is unambiguously a Catalanist coalition and has defined itself in opposition to the Catalanism of the Right (CiU). The Maragall-led coalition will be careful not to alienate important sectors of Catalan society and will have noted how the rainbow coalition, the *Govern de 'progres'*, in the Balearics was removed from power in May 2003 after only one period in office. Yet moderation by the tripartite government may not be enough either, and there is an expectation in Catalan society that it will have to carry out social reforms.

Catalan politics since the death of Franco represents a complex phenomenon and we still require more detailed data on how second-generation Spanish-speaking immigrants may have shifted the PSC towards a more Catalanist position. The election of 1999 saw a part coalition between PSC and IC obtain a higher vote than CiU because of seat distribution, though CiU obtained more seats and kept out Maragall. The year 1999 was also the high point for the socialist vote in Catalonia in the autonomous elections. The election of November 2003 has signified many things and one of them is that the domination of the great forces in Catalan politics, the PSC and CiU, has been seriously challenged for the first time, both forces mustering only 60 per cent of the Catalan vote, a drop from a figure of around 75 per cent for nearly all Catalan elections since 1984.[56] Catalonia, however, continues to experience broad political consensus where the general principles of Catalanism are shared by around 85 per cent of the Catalan electorate.

The unexpected electoral victory of the PSOE in March 2004 means that CiU will, for the first time in its history, lack serious political influence at both a Catalan and a Spanish level. The dramatic political changes experienced in Catalonia since the mid-1990s seem to confirm that since the transition Catalan politics has really been about capturing the space occupied by Convergència i Unió. It is also confirmation of the profound impact that this formation has had on Catalan political culture. Yet one of Catalonia's, Spain's and Europe's most successful political formations may face its greatest challenge in the years to come.

Notes

1 *La Vanguardia*, 18 November 2003.
2 *La Vanguardia*, 29 and 30 January, 1 February 2004; *El Temps*, 3–9 February 2004.
3 X. Filella, 'Els intel·lectuals i la ideologia nacional: darreres tendències', *Revista de Catalunya* 95 (April 1995), pp. 28–40.
4 Francesc Marc Álvaro, *Ara sí que toca! Jordi Pujol, el pujolisme i els successors* (Barcelona: Edicions 62, 2003), p. 41.
5 Vicenç Navarro in *El País* (Edición de Cataluña), 9 April and 23 July 2003.
6 Agustí Colomines i Companys, *El catalanisme i l'Estat. La lluita parlamentària per l'autonomia (1898–1917)* (Barcelona: Publicacions de l'Abadia de Montserrat, 1993).
7 *Avui*, 24 July 1977.
8 *Destino*, 14–20 February 1980, no. 2,210.
9 J. Lorés, *La transició a Catalunya (1977–1984). El pujolisme i els altres* (Barcelona: Empúries, 1985), pp. 36–41.
10 For example Sebastian Balfour, *Dictatorship, Workers and the City. Labour in Greater Barcelona since 1939* (Oxford: Clarendon Press, 1989).
11 The PSUC split led to the formation of the Partit dels Comunistes de Catalunya and the loss of 350,000 votes. Membership of the PSUC dropped from 35,000 in 1978 to 12,000 in 1982.
12 Josep M. Colomer, 'El pensament catalanista en l'època franquista', in *Catalanisme: Història, política i cultura* (Barcelona: L' Avenç, 1986), p. 275.
13 *Treball*, 25–31 January 1979, no. 563.
14 P. Alter, *Nationalism* (London: Edward Arnold, 1989), pp. 97–104 and E. Gellner, *Nationalism* (Oxford: Basil Blackwell, 1983), pp. 110–22. S. Rokkan and D. W. Unwin, 'Centres and Peripheries in Western Europe', in Rokkan and Unwin (eds), *The Politics of Territorial Identity: Studies in European Regionalism* (London: Sage, 1983), p. 3; A. Smith, *National Identity* (Harmondsworth: Penguin, 1991), p. 125.
15 C. Harvie, *The Rise of Regional Europe* (London, Routledge, 1994), p. 53.
16 *Avui*, 20 September 1999.
17 *El País* (Edición Cataluña), 21 July 2003.
18 J. Armengou, typed manuscript, 'Justificació de Catalunya', p. 73, in AFH Pau Mercader, Carpeta 70, Arxiu Nacional de Catalunya.
19 Pau Roig, *La Vanguardia Española*, 29 January 1970. See also H. Raguer,

'Nosaltres i Europa', *Serra d'Or*, August–September 1962 and the Banca Catalana, *Memoria* (Barcelona, 1965), p. 13.

20 This had its echoes in the nineteenth century with the emergence of Catalanism; see Joan Lluís Marfany, *La cultura del catalanisme* (Barcelona: Empúries, 1995), pp. 198–202.

21 *El País* (Edición Cataluña), 9 October 1999.

22 J. Maluquer de Motes i Bernet, *Història econòmica de Catalunya, segles XIX i XX* (Barcelona: Salvat, 1998), pp. 168–72.

23 J. Ros i Hombravella, 'L'economia catalana, demà passat', *Revista de Catalunya*, 3 December 1986, p. 17.

24 S. Giner (ed.), *La societat catalana* (Barcelona: Institut d'Estadística de Catalunya, 1998), p. 538; *Avui*, 27 September 1999.

25 J. Conejos, E. Duch, J. Fontrodona, J. M. Hernández, A. Luzárraga and E. Terré, *Cambio estratégico y clusters en Cataluña* (Barcelona: Gestion 2000, 1997), pp. 115–25.

26 *El País* (Edición Cataluña), 26 May 1999.

27 Jefatura Superior de Policia de Barcelona, untitled report, 12 May 1974, Caja 188, Archivo del Gobierno Civil de Barcelona.

28 *Dossier Econòmic de Catalunya*, 3 December 2003.

29 *El Món*, 19 March 1983, Year 3, no. 14.

30 Ibid., 9 July 1982, Year 2, no. 30.

31 Arcadi Calzada and Carles Llorens, *Reconstrucció nacional* (Barcelona: Edicions Destino, 1995), pp. 68–72.

32 Banco Urquijo, Servicio de Estudios, *Desarrollo económico de Cataluña 1967–1970. Un plan de inversiones para el sector privado* (Barcelona: Banco Urquijo, 1967), p. 479.

33 *El Temps*, 7 and 14 December 1998.

34 The campaign, '*Espanya ens roba*' was led by the wing of the Esquerra that has since abandoned the party.

35 Jordi Bañeres, 'Quinze mesos intensos. L'ús social del català al Principat (gener de 1998–març de 1999)', *Revista de Catalunya*, 140, May 1999, pp. 131–54. For a contrast with the linguistic situation at the beginning of the 1990s, see A. Rafanell and A. Rosich, 'Quin futur hi ha per la llengua catalana?', *Revista de Catalunya* 37 (January 1990), pp. 21–6.

36 *Serra d'Or*, August 1964.

37 See K. Woolard, *Double-Talk: Bilingualism and the Politics of Ethnicity in Catalonia* (Stanford, Stanford University Press, 1989) and J. Termes, 'La immigració a Catalunya: política i cultura', in Termes, *La immigració a Catalunya i altres estudis d'història del nacionalisme català* (Barcelona: Empúries, 1984), pp. 129–83.

38 Lerrouxism was the anti-Catalanist and populist movement that became successful in certain working-class sectors in Barcelona during the early twentieth century.

39 Manel Lucas, *ERC. La llarga marxa: 1977–2004, de la il·legalitat al govern* (Barcelona: Nou Mil·leni. Columna, 2004).

40 *La Vanguardia*, 19 September 1999.

41 *Avui*, 12 June 1977.

42 Santiago Pérez-Nievas and Marta Fraile, 'Is the Nationalist Vote Really Nationalist? Dual Voting in Catalonia 1980–1999', Estudio/Working Paper 2000/147, March 2000.

43 Cited in ibid.

44 *La Vanguardia*, 26 January 2004.

45 Ibid., 9 November 2003.

46 For the full text, see *El Viejo Topo* 122 (October 1998).

47 This also affected Catalan socialism when the former first secretary of the PSC, Josep Maria Sala, was himself imprisoned over the illegal financing of the PSOE in a scandal known as Filesa. The Catalan weekly, *El Triangle*, has been a consistent critic of the close relationship between business and CiU in recent years, a somewhat lone voice in a rather timid media in terms of investigative journalism.

48 *El País* (Edición Cataluña), 24 September 1999.

49 *Avui*, 13 August 2003.

50 *El País* (Edición Cataluña), 19 January 2003.

51 Ibid., 22 January 2003.

52 *La Vanguardia*, 9 October 2002.

53 *El Temps*, 19 October and 21 December 1998.

54 The PP in Catalonia has re-named itself the Partit Popular de Catalunya (Popular Party of Catalonia).

55 Both the PP and UDC, for example, are part of the same Christian Democrat international movement.

56 *La Vanguardia*, 19 November 2003.

7   From National-Catholic nostalgia to constitutional patriotism

Conservative Spanish nationalism since the early 1990s

Xosé-Manoel Núñez Seixas[1]

What is the current status of Spanish nationalism, at the beginning of the twenty-first century? One of the least researched areas of Spanish politics is the ideological, political and social weight of Spanish nationalism. The purported non-existence of Spanish nationalism is a common belief echoed by prominent intellectuals, politicians and the mass media. Even among most Spanish public opinion shapers, and for a large part of the Spanish academic community, Spanish nationalism is virtually absent, a pheno-menon that dissolved with the end of Francoism and the birth of the democratic monarchy. Yet this is just one side of the issue. Most Spaniards, including many intellectuals and influential public figures, have no difficulty claiming Spain is a multicultural and historical *nation*. To its defenders, this affirmation seems to fall entirely outside the category of *nationalism*.

This illustrates the ambiguity surrounding Spanish nationalism when one attempts to identify it as an object of study. Spanish state nationalism may express itself in a diffuse form, as a component of public policy and the state's institutional agency. Like every state nationalism that develops within the frontiers of a political community and has existed in a recognised form since the pre-modern period, Spanish nationalism does not always function as such; nor does it adopt the form of a political organisation or a social movement associated with a visible nationalist creed. On the contrary, it may be identified as a political ideology permeating the agency of diverse socio-political actors, as well as a social sentiment of identity, as an imagined community shared by a majority of the Spanish population. The presence of state nationalism may be diluted, but it is persistent. Its intensity varies according to the presence of external and internal opponents. It may even be an idea underlying everyday phenomena, aptly labelled by Michael Billig as banal nationalism.[2]

My aim in this chapter is to provide an overview of the present trends and competing discourses that coexist within conservative-leaning Spanish nationalism, or rather of the various discourses of Spanish patriotic affir-mation within the right-wing political spectrum. An attempt will be made, therefore, to establish a basic typology. However, the trends that are analysed below have to be understood as ideal typical constructions. In fact, the object of my analysis, Spanish nationalist discourse, constitutes an often confusing set of very different ideological elements that are present to some extent in the views expressed by a range of actors.[3]

The indelible Francoist stigma

The monopolisation of Spanish nationalist discourse by Francoism and the anti-democratic right had a significant impact on the entire spectrum of Spanish nationalism, particularly when it was forced to present a democratically legitimised face during the last years of Francoism and the democratic transition. At that time any explicit affirmation of Spanish patriotism was automatically delegitimised and identified with the defence of the old National-Catholic tenets. This was particularly noticeable among liberal and left-wing milieux, and during the first phase of the transition it manifested itself somewhat chaotically in the problems that most democratic parties experienced concerning public use of the term 'Spain'.[4] State nationalism seemed to lack all coherence in its social and organisational expression, at least until the mid-1990s. However, though organisationally and politically less visible, Spanish nationalism continued to exist, both on the right and on the left of the political spectrum. Like every nationalist ideology, whether stateless or not, it displays a broad internal diversity. Different political and social actors with a plethora of worldviews and ideological programmes support the common cause of turning Spain into the sole sovereign entity with collective political rights. As with stateless nationalisms, civic tenets and ethnocultural elements combine to form complex and elaborate ideologies.[5]

The 1978 Constitution was ambiguous when it came to defining the nation. On the one hand, it stated that Spain is the sole existing nation and should enjoy 'indivisible unity' as the 'common and indivisible Fatherland of all Spaniards'. Hence, Spain was the sole collective entity to have full sovereignty. On the other hand, it also recognised nationalities and regions. The difference between a nationality and a nation was not clearly established in the constitutional text, though during the parliamentary debates the meaning of 'nationality' was reduced in practice to that of a cultural and linguistic community without sovereignty.[6] By mentioning the existence of nationalities, the Constitution intended to satisfy peripheral nationalist demands that the new territorial structure of the state recognise the qualitative historical and cultural peculiarities of their territories. The State of the Autonomous Communities was accepted by the main substate nationalist parties as a first step towards the consolidation of regional self-government. In contrast, for most Spanish parties the model established by the Constitution was the final stage of the decentralisation process.[7]

Nevertheless, some were not at all convinced of the long-term effectiveness of the autonomy system. The leader of Alianza Popular (AP), Manuel

Fraga, strongly criticised 'Part VIII' of the Constitution, and four AP parliamentary representatives voted against the Constitution. AP subsequently opposed the term 'historical nationalities' and was reluctant to accept full bilingualism in those autonomous communities that had their own language. AP bitterly opposed further political decentralisation until 1982, emphasising instead the idea of 'Spain's unity' and healthy regionalism to avoid 'anarchy and disorder' in the periphery. This attitude was to endure throughout the 1980s.[8]

However, the new territorial framework drawn up by the 1978 Constitution meant that Spanish nationalist discourse had to be reinvented. Explicit Spanish nationalism disappeared from the statements and speeches of most political parties and leaders, with the exception of the far right and some AP spokesmen. This denial of the 'nationalism' label allowed progressive intellectuals from the mid-1980s to brandish a pervasive but frequently used argument to oppose substate nationalist claims. Their strategy basically consisted of censuring all forms of explicit nationalism, repudiating and criticising them as potentially totalitarian and exclusive.[9] Since the defence of the territorial integrity of the Spanish nation by left-wing leaders and intellectuals was never defined as nationalism but as 'patriotism', or later on 'loyalty to the Constitution', what had been a form of political renunciation in the 1960s and 1970s became a politically persuasive tool during the 1980s and 1990s.[10] Only substate nationalists used the term 'nationalism' to define themselves, though they gave a very different meaning to that concept.

However, since the mid-1990s conservatives have increasingly held high the banner of 'explicit' Spanish patriotism, which in some cases is equated with 'good nationalism' or with a vaguely defined 'supranationalism'.[11] But patriotism is also used as a synonym for 'personal virtue', a means of enhancing respect for liberty as well as pride in the best liberal traditions of Spanish history.[12] In the twenty-first century, Spanish conservatives seem to have 'reappropriated' Spanish nationalist discourse, and to some extent they also claim to have reinvented it. Nevertheless, as will be explained, the limits of this discursive renovation are quite evident, particularly regarding the tortuous relationship of contemporary conservative patriotism with Spain's recent past.

Since the 1990s, Spanish patriotic discourse has run through the public sphere particularly the mass media, books and pamphlets. The rearticulation of Spanish nationalism springs from confrontations with the stateless nationalisms. During the late 1980s the ongoing debates about the existence of a 'regional problem' led to a recurrence of the disputes among exiled Spanish Republicans in the 1950s, now reformulated and updated: does a 'Spanish problem' exist? This has given rise to a myriad of booklets and newspaper articles whose main concern is to uphold the existence of Spain as a nation, while opposing and stigmatising minority nationalisms.[13] What took place during this debate was a slow process of adaptation of the main ideological currents of Spanish nationalism and patriotic discourse to the new circumstances of democratic Spain.

Since 1978 Spanish nationalist discourse has had to face three simultaneous challenges. The first entailed adapting to the new political/institutional framework set up by the 1978 Constitution and the State of the Autonomous Communities. The renewal of Spanish nationalist discourse had to take into account the institutional plurality brought about by the pressure exerted by the stateless nationalisms, as well as adjust to political decentralisation and the renewal of regional cultural diversity. However, the extent of its tolerance is not clearly defined.

The second challenge was to reinvent a new political and historical legitimacy, side-stepping the heritage of Francoism and the legacy of recent historical memories, and starting anew at the most basic symbolic level. Nevertheless, this new legitimacy could not derive from an explicit condemnation of Francoism because that would mean that Spain would be refounded around an 'anti-fascist consensus', the road taken by other post-war European state nationalisms.[14] The need to 'forget' the Civil War and the Franco regime in order to maintain coexistence with the transition's main actors has made it difficult for many of Spain's democratic nationalists to unite around common issues.[15] Thus, even though left-wing parties and organisations have continued to venerate their leaders and their past, including exile and the Civil War, the Socialist government (1982–96) focused on celebrating events such as the quincentenary of the discovery of America (1992), or the bicentenary of the death of the Enlightenment king, Charles III. The recent past, that is the Civil War and the Franco Dictatorship, was left in oblivion. This was combined with a selective appropriation of the particular collective memories of regionalisms and substate nationalisms by adopting as symbols those intellectuals and political leaders who had not advocated independence. There was renewed interest in the liberal left-wing nationalist/patriotic tradition, from nineteenth-century republicanism to former president of the Second Republic Manuel Azaña. However, the historical pessimism of these and other authors, along with the thesis of the two Spains and of 'Spain's problem', it was believed, had to be evaded. A change began only in 1996, and became more evident in 1999, when the Socialist Party 'rediscovered' the memory of the Civil War in order to use it as an electoral weapon against the conservatives.[16]

The reluctance of the PP explicitly to condemn the 1936 *coup d'état* and the Francoist regime (until the parliamentary bill of November 2002), as well as its continued resistance to the idea of removing Francoist symbols from streets and squares, have also contributed to the re-emergence of recent historical memory as a barrier between the right-wing and left-wing variants of Spanish patriotic discourse. This dynamic had been intensified by the PSOE's search for commonalities with organisations further to the left and with substate nationalist parties, all of which cultivate memories of the

Civil War, anti-Francoist resistance and exile as their foundational and relegitimising myths.[17] A sort of 'common republican' identity is only feasible in places where the peripheral nationalist challenge and terrorist violence are so intense that Spanish parties must seek to overcome the past, even if this is done by agreeing temporarily to forget the Dictatorship.[18]

The 'guilty conscience' has tended to encourage the emergence of two parallel and frequently overlapping tendencies within Spanish nationalist discourse. One is to look back in history for respectable forerunners to Spanish liberal nationalism, preferably in the period prior to 1931. The second is to emphasise universal values (individual rights, etc.) as a new basis on which to legitimise Spanish patriotism by adopting the concept of 'constitutional patriotism' and trying to adapt it to the Iberian context. In practice this has resulted in the emergence of a kind of 'constitutional nationalism' whose similarities with Habermas's concept are more superficial than real.

The theoretical foundations for Spanish 'constitutional nationalism' are based on the legacy of philosopher José Ortega y Gasset, combined with a continued reaction against minority nationalisms. Ortega y Gasset's reflections on the national question in his 1921 book, *España invertebrada*, are a mixture of historical determinism – the idea that Castile had been the forging power of Spanish unity under the monarchy and that the Iberian kingdoms united around Castile's hegemony as an unavoidable outcome of this process – and a search for a 'common project' for all the Spanish peoples. This first took shape during the discovery of America, enabling Spain's various ethnic groups to coalesce into a 'superior unity'.[19] For constitutional nationalists, this emphasis on a 'common project' oriented towards the future had the advantage of being tremendously flexible and malleable. A new common goal was defined: reconquering democracy and modernising Spain through membership in the European Union; the first step was taken with the framing of the 1978 Constitution. Nevertheless, Ortega y Gasset's historical determinism remained as the often hidden and implicit basis of the discourse of constitutional nationalism.[20]

The third challenge facing Spanish nationalism comes from the minority nationalisms. The latter have set no limit to their constant demands for increased self-government, and reiterate their determination to achieve political goals that clearly go beyond the 1978 Constitution, as stated in the Barcelona Declaration (June 1998) by the main Basque, Catalan and Galician nationalist parties, and particularly in the radical strategy pursued by Basque nationalism since 1998 aimed at achieving a status of shared sovereignty with Spain. The persistence of certain ethnocentric tenets in the discourse and praxis of minority nationalisms, along with continuing Basque terrorist violence, has encouraged the re-emergence of Spanish patriotic discourse in constant reaction to stateless nationalisms and particularly to Basque nationalism.[21]

Conservative nationalism: the search for an (unfulfilled) renovation

Within this ideological camp, two main tendencies may be distinguished: (a) the persistence of National-Catholicism on the far right, now a rather marginal phenomenon in Spanish politics, and (b) the slow, multifaceted evolution of the democratic right. Within the latter, three variants will be analysed: a very minor current, which may be labelled as 'neo-foralist nationalism'; an important variant in some regions, which may be termed 'regionalist nationalism'; and the majority trend nowadays within this camp, 'Spanish neo-regenerationism', which may currently be considered as the conservative variant of constitutional nationalism.

National-Catholic nostalgia

During the transition to and the consolidation of democracy, explicit Spanish nationalism visibly persisted among the far-right parties and organisations on ideological and symbolic levels. The transparency of this discourse, mostly inherited from Francoist principles, has led researchers more fully to identify and analyse its nationalist characteristics. Most parties within the Spanish extreme right, from Fuerza Nueva to the Frente Nacional, as well as the remnants of the single party of the Dictatorship, stayed loyal to the legacy of National-Catholicism. For some of its most prominent leaders, such as Blas Piñar, this ideology promoted a mystical identification of Spain with the Catholic faith.[22] The persistence of National-Catholicism went hand in hand with an idealised nostalgia for the premodern Spanish Empire, along with an emphasis on cultural imperialism towards Latin America, opposition to 'Europe' and membership of the European Economic Community, and a strong 'anti-separatism' that identified Spain's historical enemy as Basque and Catalan nationalism. During the transition this took the form of a repeated condemnation of political 'blackmailing' by minority nationalisms, depicted as traitors and ambitious provincial elites serving the interests of Spain's foreign enemies: 'Europe' as a whole.[23] Moreover, the new territorial structure set up under the State of the Autonomous Communities was regarded as a complete waste of money and a falsification of Spain's traditions.

This basic interpretation has remained throughout the 1990s, particularly among some late-Francoist intellectuals who advocated the return to a form of authoritarian rule under a more or less technocratic appearance, though devoid of religious and traditional codes. Thus the former Francoist minister and neo-conservative intellectual Gonzalo Fernández de la Mora spoke in 2000 of how Spain had entered a process of 'denationalisation' since the restoration of democracy. This denationalising process was due to the impact of three factors: the influence of certain minority-led peripheral nationalisms as a result of the 1978 Constitution, the transfer of sovereignty to the European Union, and the 'demographic denationalisation' caused by the arrival of inassimilable Muslim and Amerindian immigrants. All this has led to the fragmentation of Spain, a country that should be considered the product of a positive historical evolution due to the constructive efforts of the Visigoth kings, the Reconquest of Spain from the Muslims, the national unification decreed by the Catholic kings in the fifteenth century and the colonial venture as seen at its high point: the colonisation of America.[24]

Certain extreme-right organisations emerged during the first half of the 1990s in an attempt to overcome the electoral weakness of their elders. They emphasised a more statist, radical and explicitly non-religious nationalism. Their intellectual roots can be found in the fascist thinkers of the 1930s, such as Ramiro Ledesma Ramos. This ultranationalist discourse recently raised the ghost of a new *other*, a threat that should be fought in order to preserve the purity of the Spanish nation: non-European immigrants (whose presence has increased in Spain since the mid-1980s). Nevertheless, the relatively moderate number of immigrants until very recently, along with the electoral hegemony of the Popular Party over the right, has made it difficult for this kind of discourse to gain any broad support. Old National-Catholicism is still present in the ideological discourse of some young leaders of the Spanish far right. In contrast, the most sophisticated and elaborate theories of the Spanish neo-Nazis are characterised by openness towards other Iberian nationalisms, fuelled by a desire to win adherents for their racial and Pan-European project under the banner of 'European ethnicism'. However, this programme seems to have got nowhere.[25]

The slow evolution of the democratic right wing

Francoism interrupted the tradition of liberal-democratic Spanish national-ism after 1936, and also left the democratic right with some obvious problems of legitimacy. But because they have difficulty coping with the recent past, particularly over openly rejecting the legacy of the Francoist regime, conservatives find it hard to invoke that liberal tradition convin-cingly. The National-Catholic worldview, though confined to a less visible and mostly academic historiographical expression, has not entirely dis-appeared from the spectrum of right-wing Spanish nationalism, particularly among older leaders such as Manuel Fraga and more conservative currents.[26] Intellectuals close to the PP still insist that Spain's historical roots lie in the struggle of the Christian kingdoms against the Muslims in the Middle Ages, while also emphasising the role played by the unifying agency of the Spanish monarchy – which is taken to be part of the essence of the nation – and the intrinsic Catholic nature of the Spanish nation, whose moment of glory was the discovery and conquest of America.[27] This perspective holds that the substate nationalisms are principally a product of foreign conspiracies to weaken Spain's power and to erase its glorious contribution to the history of mankind.[28] Although these attitudes are still present today, Spanish conservatives do not openly display them. A small current tends towards neo-foralism, while the majority may be labelled as 'constitutional nationalists'.

A minority current: neo-foralist Spanish nationalism

A very small variant, represented by several isolated members of the Spanish right, recognises the multinational character of the Spanish state. Their preferred formula for accommodating national plurality within a single state would be to resurrect the old concepts that inspired the 'composite monarchy' of the Habsburgs in the sixteenth and seventeenth centuries in the belief that regional liberties and *fueros* (or local historical rights) could be transplanted today into a 'composite state' based on the traditional divided sovereignty. The mechanism for implementing this solution would be a reinterpretation and reform of the 1978 Constitution through the possibilities offered by its 'additional provision', which opens the way for renewing and deepening the *fueros* of the Basque provinces and Navarre.

The solitary, though intellectually influential, representative of this current is former UCD minister Miguel Herrero de Miñón, one of the members of the parliamentary committee that framed the text of the 1978 Constitution.[29] However, his proposals, which have received a positive response from several sectors of Basque nationalism, have had no real influence on conservative policy-makers. Instead, they stirred up bitter reaction from both right- and left-wing ideologues of 'constitutional nationalism', who consider Herrero de Miñón's thesis a return to the *ancien régime*.

The 'regionalist' variant

The political praxis of the conservatives in Galicia and the Balearic Islands, regions that the party has governed since the early 1980s, has been one of implementing a moderate policy of defence of the peripheral language and culture, along with a policy of promoting the regional 'autonomous' identity. This has sometimes clashed with the more centralist positions of the central organs of the Spanish conservative party. The process of 'regionalisation' has been a strategic tool used to combat the rise of left and substate nationalisms in regions where there is a distinct culture and language. But the rapid integration of regionalist local elites, and the need to maintain regional power in a context marked by territorial competition, led both regional branches to reinforce their regionalist tenets during the 1980s. The term 'historical nationality' was first accepted in 1991 by Galicia's PP branch.[30] Under Fraga's charismatic leadership, the Galician PP has gradually proposed a new formula seeking to combine Spanish constitutional loyalty with a reinforced regional identity. This 'self-identification' includes pride in being Galician and loving the 'dignified' language and traditions of the region, combined with the promotion of folklore, popular culture and the 'recognition of our own personality', from which a right to 'a real self-government and administration' emerges.[31] Support for the regional culture often adopts a banal and populist tone but there are also theoretical initiatives to adopt and 'reconvert' the historical legacy of peripheral nationalism into a form of 'healthy regionalism' that does not damage the integrity of Spain as a nation. Nevertheless, a clear distinction is made between this 'healthy' concept and self-determination, which is fiercely rejected.[32] An autonomous identity is legitimised through references to regional history and especially by means of a suitable reinterpretation and appropriation of certain peripheral historical traditions, emphasising their non-separatist aspects. Thus, the moderate leader of conservative Catalanism before 1936, Francesc Cambó, who stressed the Catalan objective of 'regenerating' Spain is often quoted. Organic intellectuals of the Galician PP have even claimed that the whole tradition of Galician nationalism prior to 1950 may be subsumed within the regionalist doctrine of the conservatives.[33]

Likewise, several conservative presidents of regional governments have become staunch defenders of the principle of subsidiarity and the need for a vigorous decentralisation. A good example of this has been the 'single administration' formula proposed by Fraga, which envisages full devolution to the regional administrations and the elimination of any overlapping of central and regional spheres of government. The government in Madrid would retain power in areas considered of essential interest to Spain's social, economic and political cohesion. Fraga argues that this would serve to deepen the State of the Autonomous Communities while also freezing the growing demands for self-government among substate nationalists. The final stage is the full implementation of autonomy as outlined in the Constitution.[34]

The consolidation since the mid-1980s of this regionalist alternative has been decisive in persuading the conservatives to accept the autonomy model established in the 1978 Constitution. At the same time, they see Spain as a unitary sovereign nation that includes different cultures, languages and regional institutions. Decentralisation therefore means the reinforcement of Spanishness from the bottom up, making the 'provinces' fully responsible for their own part of a joint project.[35] The PP advocates complete uniformity of competencies for all autonomous communities, though it acknowledges the existence of 'linguistic and geographical' as well as juridical peculiarities in certain regions. And the PP's discourse obviously denies the nationalities any possibility of becoming sovereign, rejecting any idea of the 'divided sovereignty' demanded by minority nationalist parties. In fact, the regionalist praxis of some PP branches has faded considerably since 2000 as the new 'constitutional nationalism' has taken shape.

The new right-wing 'constitutional nationalism'

This current insistently waves liberalism and civic principles as its flag. There are at least two main discourses that intertwine intricately, so much so that one may have arisen in response to the other.

First, it should be stressed that this tendency emerged from a highly *reactive nationalism*. That is, it represents *a continuous reaction against peripheral nationalism* and shares this with left-wing patriotic discourse. Right-wing nationalism, and particularly the PP's political strategy in the Basque Country and Catalonia, has taken advantage of the confrontations with substate nationalists and exploited the linguistic conflict. During the 1980s and 1990s a number of books and leaflets, as well as articles in journals and newspapers, insisted on the 'discriminatory' nature of the cultural and linguistic policies implemented by Catalan and Basque nationalists, warning that Castilian would become a persecuted language in these regions. This was presented as the first step in the Balkanisation and deconstruction of the Spanish nation. A debate also arose concerning individual versus collective rights. Nonetheless, what was really at stake in most cases was the allegedly traditional and natural supremacy of Castilian. This type of nostalgia reveals how for much of the Spanish right Castilian is a defining cultural marker of Spanish national identity, a common tie uniting all Spaniards of any regional origin, and a distinctive contribution to universal culture.[36]

These authors presented substate nationalism as a step on the road to totalitarianism, since it would impose a monolithic culture on all citizens under its authority. This view initially arose because of the Catalan government's linguistic policies.[37] Similar reactions continued during the early 1990s, though less prominently or frequently, and more recently they have been voiced in the Basque Country.[38] Since 1993 there has been a noticeable increase in the frequency of these types of books, some of them written by prestigious ex-left-wing intellectuals. This group has grown as articles in the press and remarks in the media – particularly on radio broadcasts – were directed against the main Spanish parties (first the PSOE and later the PP) for their dependency on the parliamentary support of Catalan and Basque nationalists to maintain a majority in the Spanish parliament between 1993 and 2000.

An additional factor encouraging the proliferation of this 'reactive literature' has undoubtedly been the persistence and intensification of Basque terrorism since the mid-1990s, as well as the strategic radicalisation of Basque nationalist parties since 1998. Well-written essays by academics and journalists (such as Jon Juaristi, Fernando Savater or José Mª Calleja) devoted to combating Basque nationalism ideologically have become best-sellers. Most of this new wave of 'reactive' literature has not been concerned with theorising the Spanish nation. Instead, it censured radical Basque nationalism, stressing its anti-democratic and violent side. But its criticism has extended since 1998–9 to mainstream democratic Basque nationalism, blaming it for the persistence of violence and accusing it of anti-democratic tenets. In the end, however, this has become an authentic 'vindication' of Spanish *patriotism*. Many of the most important proponents of a new formulation of Spanish patriotic discourse from right and left come from either Catalonia or, in particular, the Basque Country. Conversely, the increasing demands for sovereignty and self-determination emanating from some of the most important nationalist parties of the periphery led the conservatives to ascribe an absolute and unchangeable character to the 1978 Constitution.

Moreover, this tendency has been characterised by a constant call for the renovation of historical legitimacy. Since the mid-1980s, Spanish right-wing intellectuals have undertaken the task of reinterpreting the history of Spain by presenting it as an example of 'unity within diversity', which would inevitably lead to the constitutional formula of 1978. According to this view, Spain had been a mosaic of different peoples and cultures since Roman times, unified either by the historical destiny of sharing a common space and a common project, or by the will of constituting a political unit since the early Middle Ages, during the Christian kingdoms' struggle against the Muslims, who are usually excluded from the legacy of 'Spanishness' along with Jews, deported in 1492. The traditional notion of 'unity in diversity' proposed by Spanish traditionalist thinkers since the late nineteenth century, such as Menéndez y Pelayo, has been renewed and resurrected in a novel form: the 'different Spains' (*las Españas*), in spite of their variegated cultures and peculiarities, have always been part of a greater national community whose supreme manifestation would be the present State of the Autonomous Communities. According to this teleological conception of history, Spain is a *true* outcome of historical experience, and its objective 'body' has adopted different forms over time. In contrast, the stateless nationalisms are said to be based on historical fantasy and non-scientific literary imagination, the invention of second-rate intellectuals.[39]

The new conservatives define Spain as a single, though multicultural and decentralised, nation. They accept the State of the Autonomous Communities in its present shape without leaving room for further evolution in a 'federalising' direction, as the left proposes. Any further symbolic recognition of Spain's cultural and ethnoterritorial plurality would be considered an unwarranted capitulation that might threaten the very integrity of Spain. According to José María Aznar, the Spanish people should instead be renationalised and become 'normal' within a European context. Moreover, Spain should not make further concessions to peripheral nationalisms, since their demands have proven impossible to satisfy.[40] The real fear is neither for the continuity of the state structure nor for the existence of the states within the European Union, which continue to be considered the main actors of European life,[41] but for the survival of the nation. According to European MP and former leader of the Catalan branch of the PP, Aleix Vidal-Quadras, the Spanish state will not survive if it ceases to be a nation. The Spanish 'national fact', however, is not to be confused with exalted nationalism, which is exclusive to the periphery.[42]

This illustrates the main contradiction of this position. Nationalism as such is reputed to be obsolete and pre-modern, an expression of tribal ties and totalitarian dreams of homogeneous ethnic identity. Of course all substate nationalisms are subsumed within the category of ethnic nationalisms, as distinguished from political nationalism, which is a sort of purely civic and healthy form of patriotism represented by nation-states such as Spain.[43] Liberal individualism and individual rights are held to be above any form of collective rights. Spanish state nationalism and all the state nationalisms that emerged and developed in the nineteenth century are deemed to produce positive results, such as economic modernisation, consolidation of the liberal revolution, etc.: 'the apostles of the new States have invoked progress, ambition and the future'. According to Vidal-Quadras, the Spanish national community constitutes a given reality forged by a common history whose existence is unquestionable. The concept of a Spanish nation means 'a common project, a common spiritual substance, a common language, a common cultural matrix and a common History, all fully compatible with cultural and linguistic plurality . . . in the State of the Autonomous Communities'. The acceptance of cultural and linguistic plurality presupposes the existence of a widespread social sentiment of cohesion around a common objective. Certainly this concept of a 'plural Spanish nation', later redefined by the same author as a 'nation-project' providing a corporal existence for the state, is legitimised by its efficiency in protecting the liberty, dignity and material/cultural advancement of its citizens, free from 'any mystic or primordial essences'. But Vidal-Quadras also proposes retaining the strength of 'emotional cohesion sustained by historical, religious, linguistic or ethnic facts, as expressed in the use of symbols and nationalising liturgy', though the latter should be void of any 'instinctive tribal identity'.[44] In his opinion, the fact that the territorial and historical existence of Spain was considered a given fact in the 1978 Constitution does not undermine its democratic legitimacy.[45]

Other conservative leaders and MPs express this more radically, particularly since 1998–9. History is considered to be a 'more authentic' basis for the national legitimisation of Spain than ethnocultural and linguistic features. According to a member of the team that drafted the Constitution and currently a conservative MP, it is an 'axiomatic fact' that 'the Spanish nation, subject and object of the constitutional pact, is a reality that exists prior to the Constitution', shaped from an ontological point of view since Roman times, and from an intellectual point of view since the Middle Ages.[46] Moreover, Spain is an ancient nation, 'a secular reality' which, like many other old European nations, is based on 'deeper and more solid elements, and thus less emotional ones than the purely ethnic links that define so many of the aspiring nations that are so frequent nowadays in Europe'.[47] Brilliant polemicists, such as the journalist Federico Jiménez Losantos, have recently undertaken the task of 'rewriting' a nationalist history of Spain going all the way back to pre-Roman times. History and a kind of shared memory of common coexistence thus constitute the real basis for the legitimacy of Spain; but for those who defend the 'objectively defined fact' that Spain is a nation, this does not mean that they are nationalists.[48]

Nevertheless, it must be noted that right-wing Spanish nationalism also attempted to carry out a limited reformulation of its reading of history. By the early 1990s it had undertaken to 'recover' and reinterpret the historical legacy of Republican reformism that arose in the first third of the twentieth century. Through a convenient reinterpretation, conservative intellectuals were able to invoke the memory and the 'patriotic' intellectual legacy of Republican President Manuel Azaña.[49] Aznar, the PP's leader from 1989 to 2003, also partly joined this tendency, arguing that Spain is a historical reality forged in the fifteenth century and unified by the agency of the monarchy and the existence of a common project, best expressed in the 'generous' Spanish conquest of America. This historical tradition should sustain the legitimacy of the Spanish nation, which pre-dates the liberal Spanish constitutions: Spain is 'one of the most ancient nations of Europe'. In spite of the fact that there was a long period lacking in 'normality' after 1812, the 1978 Constitution consecrated the idea of a Spanish nation based upon principles of democracy, cultural plurality and progress.[50] From this point of view, Spain's full participation in the European project involves putting an end to the traditional 'isolationism' of Spanish history and returning it to the normality it had lost.

Since the beginning of the Popular Party's second government in March 2000, its absolute majority inspired the conservative intellectual and political elites towards a more decisive public emphasis on the existence of a historically based Spanish nation. But this historicism has been conveniently incorporated within an apparently more sophisticated ideological construct adopted from the repertory of the Spanish left. This can be seen in the PP's programme on 'The Constitutional Patriotism of the Twenty-First Century', approved during its fourteenth Party Conference (January 2002) and penned by two prominent Catalan and Basque PP leaders, former Minister Josep Piqué and San Sebastian town councillor, María San Gil. The concept of constitutional patriotism, developed by German philosophers Sternberger and Habermas, was incorporated into the political vocabulary of the Spanish left during the early 1990s,[51] and has now been reappropriated by the PP in a contradictory way. First, it has been reinterpreted not as the complete refounding of the political community on the basis of purely civic values, but as a new cover for a more primordial attachment: a 'political updating of a form of loyalty to Spain – that integrating and plural Spain of the 1978 Constitution – with deep roots in our history'. Spain is once again defined as a 'plural nation', with its values embodied in the Constitution. This plural nation also expresses its collective pride in the fact that it successfully concluded the democratic transition. The 1978 Constitution is implicitly and purposefully presented as a kind of historical achievement of the entire national community, and therefore as a patrimony that should be preserved in its pure and original form, which in practice means setting it in stone.[52] Hence, the real challenge for Spanish identity consists in looking towards the 'future' while relying on a solid historical base. The idea of Spain ought to be accepted by Spaniards 'naturally, without historical complexes', since:

> Spain is a great country, a nation shaped through the centuries . . . A plural nation with an identity that is not ethnically based, but politically, historically and culturally based, which developed through its contribution to universal History and Culture, its own constituting plurality, and its historical project rooted in two worlds, Europe and America.[53]

Hence, Spain is a product of history and culture. The new 'modern' character of the present concept of the Spanish nation is clear, as well as its 'indissoluble' character and the impossibility of tolerating any secession. By drawing a further line between the 'exclusive nationalists' of the periphery, particularly Basques, and constitutional patriotism, defenders of the latter conclude that 'we are not nationalists'. Thus, the concept of 'constitutional patriotism' is used as a general label to increase respect for values such as liberty, tolerance and pluralism, while also creating new confidence in the Spanish national project. This is presented as the reshaping of a nation that should now play an important role in Europe, Latin America and the Mediterranean.[54]

However, since 2002 other conservative thinkers have explicitly stressed that the new meaning of constitutional patriotism makes it synonymous with political (civic) nationalism. Contrary to the most common interpretation of the concept within the intellectual ranks of the left, this new meaning emphasises not only the civic values embodied in the Constitution but also the Fatherland of the Constitution, as well as Spanish history, symbols and culture. The 'emotional limits' of the concept of pure constitutional patriotism based on exclusively civic and contractual terms should be overcome by increasing recourse to history, symbols and a new liturgy.[55] Moreover, some Basque intellectuals insist on the fact that ETA's violence and substate radical ethnonationalism have contributed to relegitimise the new Spanish patriotism. Since Spanish patriots are persecuted and physically threatened, particularly in the Basque Country, or at least attacked in the public sphere of other regions, a defence of the Spanish nation becomes a defence of freedom, of pluralism and of European values. Specifically, 'ETA clearly shows citizens . . . that Spain means democracy and that the anti-Spain [movement] means totalitarianism, crime and persecution'.[56] Spanish patriotism would therefore be an incarnation of political and civic nationalism, mostly void of ethnocultural elements but retaining the Spanish language as a cultural marker that impregnates the political nation. Spanish patriotism would act as a precondition for the positive development of democracy. The national cohesion of Spain constitutes a prerequisite for long-term democratic consolidation.[57] In other words, conservative Spanish nationalism does not seek to become 'constitutional patriotism' in a purely civic sense, but a full-fledged 'constitutional nationalism' without complexes.

This emphasis on a new democratic patriotism runs in tandem with an insistence on building and expanding common symbols. This requires shaping and fostering a new patriotic liturgy. The former UCD minister José Manuel Otero Novás already argued in 1998 that it was urgent for the state to reinforce patriotic liturgy in order to strengthen Spanish national feelings and regenerate Spain by emphasising the commemoration of the Día de la Hispanidad (12 October). Conservatives have shown themselves to be particularly interested in promoting the public use of the Spanish flag, national anthem and coat of arms. Proof of this lies in the attempt by the officially sponsored Centre of Political and Constitutional Studies to outline the historical origins and evolution of the Spanish flag, coat of arms and national anthem, which are considered to be the most visible expression of 'democratic patriotism . . . that provide a certain level of cohesion and values for people to be able to learn to live with one other'. Since 2000, the PP's in-house intellectuals have likewise proclaimed the need to retrieve and support collective ceremonies, events and even sports that strengthen the cohesion of different social strata, 'by giving them a communitarian sense of common coexistence' within Spain. In fact, recent disputes between the Spanish conservative government and substate nationalists have centred on Madrid's attempt to regulate use of these symbols by law, requiring the national anthem to be played when the king attends a ceremony. Further proof of this attempt at restoring the public use of 'nationalising' symbols was seen in September 2002, when the government put up a huge Spanish flag in the central Plaza de Colón in Madrid. This included a practice maintained by the conservatives of regularly holding public ceremonies for the Spanish army to pay homage to the flag. The explicit aim of this measure was to make the place a site for 'constitutional' patriotic liturgy, particularly on national holidays.[58]

This new insistence on reinforcing common Spanish symbols is combined with a no less emphatic revival of Spain's 'glorious' past. The recent history of Spain should not be presented as a series of exceptional collective failures, but as a new beginning exemplified in the democratic transition. This period is regarded as a success story that has contributed decisively to overcoming the dark periods of Spanish decadence and intolerance, and it has to be presented as a positive contrast to the 'tragic' confrontation that took place during the Civil War.[59] Paradoxically, this means forgetting the recent past. Conservative thinkers have repeatedly stressed the expediency of putting aside such 'shameful' episodes of the past as the Civil War and the Franco Dictatorship for the sake of Spain's unity. Recent historical memory should not play any significant part in the recovery of a new national pride. In addition, the Franco Dictatorship is said to have emerged from a war between two totalitarian worldviews, Fascism and Bolshevism, *both* born out of Marxism. So the Spanish Civil War should not be considered a Spanish failure, but rather the expression of a European conflict. In spite of the fact that a renewed historical interest in the memory of the victims of Francoism re-emerged at the end of the 1990s among broad sectors of Spanish public opinion, the official discourse of conservative patriotism emphasised that Francoism belongs to the *forgotten* past. According to Edurne Uriarte, most Spaniards *do not remember* that distant period at all. Rather, they are increasingly proud of the collective enterprise known as the successful Spanish transition to democracy and pay little attention to 'isolated' disputes concerning the rather remarkable survival of Francoist monuments, street names and historical sites.[60]

Moreover, the pessimistic view of Spain's history since the sixteenth century as a decadent empire and an inefficient modern state should be abandoned since it constitutes a relic of an outdated view predominant in Spanish 'leftist' historiography since the fin-de-siècle disaster of 1898.[61] A new national project needs a new historical narrative. However, historiographically speaking, the reconstruction of a renewed Spanish historical memory remains heavily dependent on the old discursive patterns inherited from Spanish traditionalist and National-Catholic historiography. Proof of this may be found in the official support given since 1996 to the revival of the Spanish empire's historical personalities of the Golden Age, such as the Habsburg emperors Charles I and Philip II, or the 'Catholic' Queen Isabel. Some biographies of these historical figures, written by historians of the Royal Academy of History, have found an unexpectedly broad audience.[62] These works have an extremely traditional focus and their express purpose is not to provide the public with the benefits of recent advances in historiography but to present the old themes of imperial Spain, shining a positive light on the personalities that symbolise Spain's unity and greatness in the past and for the future.[63]

This rekindled interest in the Golden Age of Spanish history goes hand in hand with what might be termed a benevolent interpretation of the conquest and colonisation of America by the Spanish monarchs. This is seen in the PP Ministry of Education's clear preference between 1998 and 2004 for a classical narrative and chronology of the history of Spain in primary and secondary schools. This reform of the history curriculum, according to the PP government, should include more 'common' elements in all regions, thus contributing to the reshaping of a shared consciousness of the historical unity of Spain.[64] The conservative government also demonstrated a strong partiality for institutions that remain loyal to the most traditional tenets of nineteenth-century nationalist historiography. This is the case with the Royal Academy of History, which has taken up the task of rewriting a historical legitimisation of the Spanish nation by appealing to the classic 'golden periods' of Spanish history.[65]

Besides restoring the traditional historical narrative of Spain's past as a teleological process leading to Spain's political unity in the pre-modern period, the conservatives warmly support rewriting the history of Spanish liberalism in the pre-Civil War period. This has focused on the implicitly stigmatised period of the Second Republic,[66] but especially on the real policy-maker of the Restoration and architect of the Constitution of 1876, the staunch conservative leader Antonio Cánovas del Castillo.[67] Given that the Restoration governments had embarked on a process of redefining Spanishness on the basis of a liberal and secularised national project, a recovery of its positive values is now taking place, including its supposed national stability. This stability flowed from the basic consensus established between the two main political parties concerning the state structure, which, according to this interpretation, ought to be imitated by present-day conservatives and Socialists for the sake of Spain's constitutional unity.[68] However, the pessimistic view of the political system held by the writers of the so-called 1898 Generation and later on by the 1914 Generation blocked that project, so the argument goes, and gave the following decades an unfair interpretation of what the restored monarchy might have achieved in terms of national cohesion. This view would have been essentially maintained after 1939 by exiled Spanish liberals such as historians Américo Castro and Claudio Sánchez Albornoz. But now the time has come, according to this view, to revise that *distorted* image.[69]

This new historical memory is officially presented as patriotic memory. But, as has been mentioned, whenever possible it consciously avoids mentioning Francoism and the Civil War. The conservative-leaning patriotic discourse on historical memories rejects the Franco Dictatorship in a rather generic way while hardly mentioning uncomfortable matters such as state-led repression and Republican exile. In November 2002 the PP finally condemned the Dictatorship in the Spanish parliament and promised to rehabilitate the memory of the victims of Francoism. This was intended to stop the 'endless' discussions about the past by means of a political agreement that would avoid public debate on the lingering responsibilities for the Civil War. This 'concession' was bitterly criticised by some ideological spokespersons of the conservatives.[70]

In contrast certain journalists and some of the media (including the second channel of Spanish state TV) have supported a younger generation of non-professional revisionist historians such as former communist Pío Moa.[71] Moa's writings insist on how the left, the Republicans and substate nationalists all 'shared responsibility' for the outbreak of the Civil War. In the final run-up to the war, Moa argues, the Republicans and left-wing parties were the ones to provoke the conflict by forcing the right defensively to 'counteract' the communist and separatist threat through a pre-emptive *coup d'état*. This revisionist theory has had an unexpected appeal among broad sectors of conservative public opinion, as voiced in newspapers, internet fora, and so on. But this is not as new a development as it may seem. Aside from the profuse writings of older authors who claim to be heirs of Francoism, such as Ricardo de la Cierva, the aim of 'revisiting' the history of the Spanish Civil War had already been articulated by certain conservative thinkers and historians at the end of the 1990s. They presented the Spanish conflict as a consequence of the 'totalitarian infection' of Spanish political forces, which frustrated Manuel Azaña's modernising attempts to make Spain a fully integrated nation.[72] But political and intellectual circles close to the PP have reinterpreted Moa's revisionism in the light of present political circumstances.[73] They argue that the left made a historical mistake in supporting 'Russian Bolshevism' and regional separatism in 1936. This error is said to persist today in a similar way: nowadays the left has made the mistake of not being clearly identified with a well-defined national project, which could lead Spain to a new disaster.[74] A revised history should show the correct way to defend Spain's unity to the present-day Spanish left.

Furthermore, the persistence of this discourse within right-wing political forces also reveals the limits of the term 'constitutional patriotism'. In contrast to Habermas, Spanish conservatives talk about it without previously undertaking a rigorous *Vergangenheitsbewältigung*, a criticism of the recent past, or an explicit rejection of Francoism and the refoundation of the national community upon a broad anti-fascist consensus. The absence of this element makes the PP's constitutional patriotism a hybrid product, with limited credibility among other political forces. In other words, it appears to be old wine in a new bottle.

The future of Spanish identities and Spanish 'patriotic' discourse

To what extent are these national identity discourses shared by the citizens in contemporary Spain? It seems that a delicate balance exists between Spanish state nationalism and the stateless nationalisms. It could even be said that Spain constitutes a paradoxical example of the failure of both state and minority nationalisms. Neither Spanish nationalism nor Catalan, Basque or Galician nationalism has been able to impose itself as the hegemonic doctrine and exclusive identity of the territories they target.[75] 'Classical' instruments of nation-building since the nineteenth century, such as education, symbolism and public ceremonies, are now being questioned by more pragmatic forces that in a global society influence citizens but evade the controls imposed by public policies.

Thus a Spanish paradox has emerged. On the one hand, Francoist state policies were unable to uproot alternative nationalisms at the grassroots level and were incapable of extinguishing the use of regional languages. Likewise, the democratic state has been unsuccessful in convincing all the citizens of the Basque Country, Catalonia and Galicia of the new *national* legitimacy of the Spanish political community. On the other hand, the Basque and Catalan regional governments have also been relatively unsuccessful in promoting the new exclusive *national loyalties*, in spite of the resources and power at their disposal. Even in the Basque Country and Catalonia, a peculiar form of 'dual patriotism' predominates: among their citizens there coexists a variable identification with the peripheral nationality and a feeling of solidarity or identification with Spain as a whole. Opinion polls demonstrate that those who feel Basque/Catalan/Galician, etc. *and* Spanish constitute a variable majority of the population.[76]

Feelings of Spanish identity express themselves in a contradictory but very effective way as far as social spread is concerned. On the one hand, certain traditional vehicles for Spanish national cohesion, especially anything that refers to formal *national* symbolism – the bicoloured flag, the national anthem – are weaker than in other countries. And the concepts of 'Spanish nationalism' and 'patriotism' are still associated with right-wing positions by a majority of citizens.[77] On the other hand, some surveys have recently suggested that most Spaniards, including many in the periphery, also share some degree of emotional identification with certain *formal* Spanish symbols. So most Spaniards feel 'emotional' when they hear their national anthem. The level of identification peaks when *informal symbols* that have no Francoist memories attached to them are at stake, such as Spain's national sports teams when competing abroad.[78] Nonetheless, with the possible exception of the monarchy, it is still difficult to find common symbols within democratic Spain that have an emotive force capable of overcoming the conflict of national identities.

There is not one Spanish nationalism, but several Spanish nationalist discourses. Most of them accept the 1978 constitutional agreement as the legitimate basis for maintaining political unity in Spain and for advocating Spain's national existence. Leaving aside the undeniable democratic contents of the 1978 Constitution, the democratic agreement was not considered the founding moment of a new political community. On the contrary, it supposedly gave new political content to a pre-existing *nation*, whose existence as a demos was taken for granted and remained unquestioned by most of the framers of the Constitution as the result of an explicitly cultural and historicist determinism. However, the defenders of Spanish constitutional nationalism insist on its ostensibly civic nature. Conservative intellectuals add to this another legitimising argument: Spain is already established, both historically and culturally, and therefore Spanish patriotism flows 'in a single and natural direction', resisting 'the dual harassment of falsehood and ignorance' as well as 'the underrating of its symbols'. Patriotism is considered to be 'the nationalism of the great nations consecrated by history and by the present'.[79]

In contrast, minority nationalisms are accused of being essentialist and potentially anti-democratic. Although appeals to language, history and territory are more visible in minority nationalisms, it would be unfair to ascribe only essentialist traits to all of them: first, because Spanish 'patriotic' discourses, with the possible exception of the predominant discourse within the (post-)communist left, also include an appeal to supposedly objective elements such as history, culture and even language, which are reputed to be the basic founding elements of the Spanish nation, though they are relegitimised through the acceptance of an internal and limited cultural plurality; and, second, because minority nationalisms are not exclusively cultural, nor entirely ethnically based. Instead they are a mixture of civic and ethnocultural ideological elements, like almost all nationalist discourses.[80]

Conservative Spanish nationalism has by and large accepted cultural pluralism and has apparently abandoned the claim to full ethnocultural and linguistic homogeneity. Nevertheless, the extent of its tolerance towards the practice of ethnoterritorial pluralism and multiculturalism is unclear. For many Spanish 'patriots', particularly those living outside bilingual regions, multilingualism is a social reality that is difficult to accept beyond the limits imposed by the Constitution and the widespread belief that Castilian is, and should remain, the dominant and common language. Its superiority is held to derive from history and in the future it is intended to be the weapon of new digital technologies, forging a common linguistic market with Latin-America and the Hispanic community of the United States.[81] Thus the policies of 'positive linguistic discrimination' implemented by some regional governments are hardly acceptable to Spanish conservatives.[82] The same applies to the use of regional symbols in several domains, such as flags and anthems.

Finally, it must be noted that Spanish nationalism has to face a completely new challenge: the integration of African, Muslim and Eastern European immigrants. The recent surge in the rate of immigration to Spain has created a completely new preoccupation for most Spaniards. Hence multiculturalism, as a multidimensional experience and as political praxis, will alter the basic profile of Spanish nationalism in the twenty-first century, as it will affect peripheral nationalist claims to sovereignty. Spanish identity is being reshaped in 'laboratories' such as the Northern African enclaves of Ceuta and Melilla, where Spanish 'patriotism' has taken up many ethnically exclusive features dating back to the sixteenth century, such as the expression of Spanishness as a positive ethnocultural stereotype in contradistinction with Muslims and Jews.[83] In fact, a new concern has emerged among some conservative intellectuals committed to the reinforcement of Spain as a cohesive nation: the danger that multiculturalism and the integration of new waves of immigrants allegedly pose to Spanish identity.[84] How far immigration will affect the patriotic discourses of the Spanish right wing, particularly after its unexpected electoral defeat in March 2004, remains to be seen.

Notes

1 Funding for this research has been provided by the Spanish Ministry of Education, Research Project BHA 2002–01073.
2 M. Billig, *Banal Nationalism* (London: Sage, 1995).
3 For an attempt at formulating a typology, see X. M. Núñez, 'What is Spanish Nationalism today? From Legitimacy Crisis to Unfulfilled Renovation (1975–2000)', *Ethnic and Racial Studies* 24/5, pp. 719–52.
4 J. de Santiago Güervós, *El léxico político de la Transición española* (Salamanca: Universidad de Salamanca, 1992) pp. 192–251.
5 See W. Kymlicka, 'Nacionalismo minoritario dentro de las democracias liberales', in S. García and S. Lukes (eds), *Ciudadanía: justicia social, identidad y participación* (Madrid: Siglo XXI, 1999), pp. 127–57 and D. Brown, *Contemporary Nationalism. Civic, Ethnocultural and Multicultural Politics* (London and New York: Routledge, 2000), pp. 50–69.
6 See X. Bastida, *La nación española y el nacionalismo constitucional* (Barcelona: Ariel, 1998).
7 By Spanish parties, I am referring to those parties that span the entire territory of Spain.
8 See M. Fraga Iribarne, *Ideas para la reconstrucción de una España con futuro* (Barcelona: Planeta, 1980), pp. 136–7 and M. Fraga Iribarne, 'La Constitución española de 1978: su elaboración, la actitud de los partidos políticos y la experiencia tras un año largo de vigencia', in *España 1975–1980. Conflictos y logros de la democracia* (Madrid: José Porrúa Turanzas Eds., 1982), pp. 140–52; M. Fernández Lagunilla, 'Stéreotypes discursifs de la droite contemporaine espagnole autour de "la Nación"', in *'Nation' et nationalisme en Espagne du franquisme à la démocratie. Vocabulaire et politique* (Paris: Institut National de la Langue Française/École Normale Supérieure de Saint-Cloud, 1986), pp. 65–88.
9 J. L. González Quirós, *Una apología del patriotismo* (Madrid: Taurus, 2002), pp. 138–40.
10 The use of the term 'patriotism' instead of 'nationalism' in order to define one's own nationalism can be considered as a rhetorical distinction with rather weak scientific foundations. See Billig, *Banal Nationalism*, pp. 55–9.
11 E. de Diego Villagrán, *La España posible* (Madrid: Fundación Cánovas del Castillo, 1999), p. 125; P. Muñoz, *España en horas bajas. La guerra de los nacionalismos* (Madrid: Brand Editorial, 2000), p. 402.
12 See González Quirós, *Una apología*; M. A. Quintanilla, 'A propósito del patriotismo. Autoestima o autocondena, límites de la conciencia histórica', *Nueva Revista* 85 (2003), pp. 9–14.
13 A reflection on this 'resurrection' of the debates on the 'Spanish problem' is found in J. L. Cebrián, 'El problema de España', *Claves de Razón Práctica* 70 (1997), pp. 2–11.
14 See B. Strath (ed.), *Myth and Memory in the Construction of Community. Historical Patterns in Europe and Beyond* (New York and Brussels: Peter Lang/ Presses Interuniversitaires Européennes, 2000).
15 J. I. Lacasta Zabalza, *España uniforme* (Pamplona: Pamiela, 1998), pp. 334–52; P. Aguilar and C. Humlebaek, 'Collective Memory and National Identity in the Spanish Democracy: The Legacies of Francoism and the Civil War', *History and Memory* 14/1–2 (2002), pp. 121–64.
16 C. Humlebaek, 'Usos políticos del pasado reciente durante los años de gobierno del PP', *Historia del Presente* 3 (2004), pp. 157–67.

17 Of course, this does not change the fact that the memory cultivated by the Basque, Catalan or Galician nationalists concerning their own direct and united opposition to fascism is still a *construct* that functions well as a relegitimising myth but whose correlation with reality is far from accurate.

18 Nonetheless, this truce is fragile, as is clearly seen in the internal division within the Basque branch of the PSOE over the legitimacy of its regional alliance with the PP.

19 X. Bastida, 'La búsqueda del Grial: la teoría de la nación en Ortega', *Revista de Estudios Políticos* 96 (1997), pp. 43–76.

20 This hidden historical and to a certain extent cultural determinism is certainly not an exclusive feature of Spanish state nationalism. The blend of historicist and organic features and civic content is also characteristic of other European state nationalisms. In fact, a pure civic patriotism, embodied in a constitution devoid of appeals to emotional, historical or cultural links, has yet to appear anywhere. As several authors emphasise, democratic theory usually avoids any normative discussion of the historical background of the nation-building processes that led to the present nation-states, by taking for granted that a minimum cultural homogeneity already exists. See M. Canovan, *Nationhood and Political Theory* (Cheltenham: Edward Elgar, 1996), pp. 83–96 and R. Dahl, *Democracy and its Critics* (New Haven: Yale University Press, 1989), p. 209.

21 De Diego, *España posible*, pp. 141–58.

22 B. Piñar, *Hacia un estado nacional* (Madrid: Fuerza Nueva Editorial, 1980).

23 See J. L. Rodríguez Jiménez, *Reaccionarios y golpistas. La extrema derecha en España: del tardofranquismo a la consolidación de la democracia (1967–1982)* (Madrid: CSIC, 1994), pp. 44–7 and X. Casals, *La tentación neofascista en España* (Barcelona: Plaza y Janés, 1998).

24 G. Fernández de la Mora, 'La desnacionalización de España', *Razón Española* 118 (2003), pp. 149–62.

25 X. Casals, *Neonazis en España* (Barcelona: Grijalbo, 1995), pp. 139–55.

26 Fraga Iribarne, *Ideas*, pp. 132–3.

27 The vindication of Spain's conquest of America is one of those areas where conservatives still remain attached to traditional paradigms of historical interpretations. Former ministers like J. M. Otero Novás (*Defensa de la nación española. Frente a la exacerbación de los nacionalismos y ante la duda europea* (n.p. [Toledo]: Fénix, 1998), pp. 32–9 claim that the view of the Spanish conquest of America as genocide is merely a product of a foreign conspiracy inspired by Spain's historical enemies.

28 J. Blanco Ande, *El estado, la nación, el pueblo y la patria* (Madrid: San Martín, 1985).

29 M. Herrero de Miñón, *Derechos históricos y Constitución* (Madrid: Taurus, 1998).

30 For the Galician case, see N. Lagares Díaz, *Génesis y desarrollo del Partido Popular de Galicia* (Madrid: Tecnos, 1999), pp. 281–305.

31 F. Puy, *Ensaios acerca da nosa autoidentificación* (Santiago de Compostela: Fundación Alfredo Brañas, 1991).

32 M. Fraga Iribarne, *Da acción ó pensamento* (Vigo: Ir Indo, 1993) and M. Fraga Iribarne, *A contribución de Brañas á identificación dunha política galega* (Santiago de Compostela: Fundación Alfredo Brañas, 1999).

33 X. Rodríguez Arana and A. Sampedro Millares, *O galeguismo* (Santiago de Compostela: FOESGA, 1998).

34 See M. Fraga Iribarne, *Administración única. Una peropuesta desde Galicia* (Barcelona: Planeta, 1993); M. Fraga Iribarne, *Impulso autonómico* (Barcelona: Planeta, 1994); X. Rodríguez Arana, *La administración única en el marco*

constitucional (n.p.: Fundación Instituto Gallego de Estudios Autonómicos y Comunitarios, 1993).

35 E. Zaplana, *El acierto de España. La vertebración de una nación plural* (Madrid: Temas de Hoy, 2001).

36 See G. Salvador, *Lengua española y lenguas de España* (Barcelona: Ariel, 1987). Likewise, A. López, *El rumor de los desarraigados* (Barcelona: Anagrama, 1985).

37 See F. Jiménez Losantos, *Lo que queda de España. Con un prólogo sentimental y un epílogo balcánico*, second and expanded edition (Madrid: Temas de Hoy, 1995); A. Vidal Quadras, *Cuestión de fondo* (Barcelona: Montesinos, 1993).

38 M. Jardón, *La 'normalización lingüística', una anormalidad democrática* (Madrid: Siglo XXI, 1993); E. Uriarte, *España, patriotismo y nación* (Madrid: Espasa-Calpe, 2003), pp. 48–51.

39 Among authors who defend this viewpoint are philosophers such as Gustavo Bueno (*El mito de la cultura* (Barcelona: Prensa Ibérica, 1996)) and historians like Antonio Domínguez Ortiz (*España, tres milenios de historia* (Madrid: Marcial Pons, 2000)). For a critical evaluation, see E. Manzano Moreno and J. S. Pérez Garzón, 'A Difficult Nation? History and Nationalism in Contemporary Spain', *History and Memory* 14/1–2 (2002), pp. 259–84.

40 Uriarte, *España*, pp. 226–7.

41 A. Muñoz Alonso, 'El nuevo papel del Estado', *Veintiuno. Revista de Pensamiento y Cultura* 54 (2002), pp. 35–40.

42 A. Vidal Quadras, 'Nacionalismos identitarios en la España finisecular: diagnóstico y posibles terapias´, in F. Molina Aparicio (ed.), *Aula de cultura de El Correo*, Vol. XIV (Bilbao: El Correo, 1997), pp. 28–48.

43 A. Vidal Quadras, 'Derecha, izquierda y nación constitucional', in T. Fernández and J.-J. Laborda (eds), *España ¿cabemos todos?* (Madrid: Alianza, 2002), pp. 292–5; E. Uriarte, 'Nación española y nacionalismo español', *Revista de Occidente* 248 (2002), pp. 109–32; Uriarte, *España, pp.* 54–5.

44 This is reminiscent of the concept of 'thin national culture' defined by W. Kymlicka (*States, Nations and Cultures* (Amsterdam: Van Gorcum, 1997), p. 40), though not explicitly conceived in such terms by Spanish polemicists.

45 See A. Vidal Quadras, *Amarás a tu tribu. Un libro inoportuno y necesario en recuerdo de España* (Barcelona: Planeta, 1998), pp. 33, 143, 162–3 and 194–6; A. Vidal Quadras, 'Nación y pacto constitucional', in R. L. Acuña (ed.), *La porfía de los nacionalismos* (Madrid: Universidad Complutense, 1998), pp. 73–92 (particularly, pp. 83–4) and Vidal Quadras, 'Derecha, izquierda y nación constitucional', p. 294.

46 G. Cisneros Laborda, 'La España en la que cabemos todos', in Fernández and Laborda, *España ¿cabemos todos?*, pp. 103–24 (particularly, pp. 104 and 112).

47 A. Muñoz Alonso, *El fracaso del nacionalismo* (Barcelona: Plaza y Janés, 2000), p. 35.

48 F. Jiménez Losantos, *Los nuestros. Cien vidas en la historia de España* (Barcelona: Planeta, 1999).

49 F. Jiménez Losantos, *La última salida de Manuel Azaña* (Barcelona: Planeta, 1994).

50 J. Mª Aznar, *España, la segunda transición* (Madrid: Espasa-Calpe, 1994); J. Mª Azar, 'Discurso', *Revista de Occidente* 229 (2000), pp. 109–21.

51 J. C. Velasco Arroyo, 'Los contextos del patriotismo constitucional', *Cuadernos de Alzate* 24 (2001), pp. 63–78.

52 For an analysis of the Conservative use of the Constitution as an unalterable 'historical fact', see H. R. Song, 'Cap a una "España unida". La produció del patriotisme constitucional', in *Les mentides del PP* (Barcelona: Angle Editorial, 2003), pp. 34–49.

53 J. Piqué and Mª San Gil, 'El patriotismo constitucional del siglo XXI', political program of the Fourteenth PP Party Conference, Madrid, 25–7 January 2002, available at www.ppvizcaya.com/pages/patrio.html.
54 Ibid.
55 Some left-wing intellectuals have also insisted on this. See J. Aguado, 'Los límites del neopatriotismo', *Claves de Razón Práctica* 122 (2002), pp. 41–6.
56 Uriarte, *España*, p. 124.
57 Ibid., pp. 18–19, 58–9 and 117–20.
58 Otero Novás, *Defensa*, p. 287; Centro de Estudios Políticos y Constitucionales (CEPC) (ed.), *Símbolos de España* (Madrid: CEPC, 1999), n.p.; De Diego, *España posible*, pp. 123–4; Esther Esteban's interview with Federico Trillo in *El Mundo*, 14 October 2003.
59 González Quirós, *Una apología*, pp. 179–210.
60 De Diego, *España posible*, pp. 110–11; Uriarte, *España*, pp. 159–62.
61 Uriarte, *España*, pp. 166–8; De Diego, *España posible*, pp. 101–7.
62 See, for example, M. Fernández Alvarez, *Carlos V, el César y el hombre* (Madrid: Espasa Calpe, 1999) and M. Fernández Alvarez, *Isabel la Católica* (Madrid: Espasa-Calpe, 2003).
63 A. Sáez Arance, 'Auf der Suche nach einem neuen "demokratischen Zentralismus"?, Nationalkonservativer Geschichtsrevisionismus im Spanien der Jahrhundertwende', unpublished paper (2003).
64 See a good analysis in J. Mª Ortiz de Orruño (ed.), *Historia y sistema educativo* (Madrid: Marcial Pons, 1998) and J. S. Pérez Garzón *et al.*, *La gestión de la memoria. La historia de España al servicio del poder* (Barcelona: Crítica, 2000).
65 Real Academia de la Historia, *España. Reflexiones sobre el ser de España* (Madrid: Real Academia de la Historia, 1997) and Real Academia de la Historia, *España como nación* (Barcelona: Planeta, 2000).
66 See, for instance, the interpretation of the latter-day Francoist historian F. Suárez Fernández, *Azaña y la guerra del 36* (Madrid: Rialp, 2000).
67 A. Bullón de Mendoza and L. E. Togores Sánchez (eds), *Cánovas y su época* (Madrid: Fundación Cánovas del Castillo, 1999).
68 A. Pérez de Armiñán y de la Serna, 'El consenso constitucional y el estado autonómico', *Nueva Revista* 56 (1998), pp. 8–12.
69 De Diego, *España posible*, pp. 120–1.
70 M. Álvarez Tardío, 'Pactar un olvido colectivo o denunciarlo. El control público de la memoria histórica', *Nueva Revista* 85 (2003), pp. 15–26.
71 See P. Moa, *La Segunda República y el maniqueísmo histórico. El derrumbe de la Segunda República y la Guerra civil* (Madrid: Encuentro, 2001); P. Moa, *Mitos de la guerra civil* (Madrid: La Esfera de los Libros, 2002) and P. Moa, *Contra la mentira: Guerra civil, izquierda, nacionalistas y jacobinismo* (Madrid: LibrosLibres, 2003).
72 De Diego, *España posible*, p. 115; A. Bullón de Mendoza and L. E. Togores Sánchez (eds), *Revisión de la Guerra Civil* (Madrid: Actas 2002).
73 See, for instance, J. M. Marco, 'Las raíces de la izquierda española', *El Mundo*, 10 February 2004, pp. 4–5, as well as P. Moa, 'La idea de España en la II República', in J. Mª Lassalle (ed.), *España, un hecho* (Madrid: FAES, 2003), pp. 199–230.
74 See P. Fernández Barbadillo's review of Pío Moa in 'Los mitos de la guerra civil', *Veintiuno. Revista de Pensamiento y Cultura* 57 (2003), pp. 159–61, as well as Antonio Sánchez Martínez, 'Pío Moa, sus censores y la historia de España', *El Catoblepas. Revista Crítica del Presente*, 14 (April 2003), available at http://www.nodulo.org/ec/2003/no14p14.htm. Some left-leaning intellectuals have repeatedly asserted that the left has 'renounced' the idea of Spain as a nation. See, for instance, C. Alonso de los Ríos, *La izquierda y la nación. Una traición*

políticamente correcta (Barcelona: Planeta, 1999) and G. Bueno, 'La izquierda ante España', in Lassalle (ed.), *España*, pp. 231–68.

75 See J. J. Linz, 'Los nacionalismos en España: una perspectiva comparativa', in E. d'Aura and J. Casassas (eds), *El estado moderno en Italia y España* (Barcelona: CNRS/Universitat de Barcelona, 1993), pp. 79–87, as well as X. M. Núñez, 'A State of Many Nations: The Construction of a Plural Spanish Society since 1976', in D. Juteau and Ch. Harzig (eds), *The Social Construction of Diversity: Recasting the Master Narrative of Industrial Nations* (New York/ Oxford: Berghahn, 2003), pp. 284–307.

76 See F. Moral, *Identidad regional y nacionalismo en el Estado de las Autonomías*, (Madrid: CIS, 1998).

77 CIS survey, December 2000, quoted in Uriarte, *España*, p. 190.

78 Moral, *Identidad regional*, pp. 52–3.

79 B. Pendás García, 'Sobre patria, nación y otras logomaquias', *Veintiuno. Revista de Pensamiento y Cultura* 54 (2002), pp. 31–4.

80 There are important political and intellectual segments of Catalan, Basque or Galician nationalism that insist on the need to build inclusive civic nations. On the Catalan case, see a recent analysis by M. Guibernau, *Catalan Nationalism. Francoism, Transition and Democracy* (London: Routledge, 2004).

81 See Mª Andrés, 'El imperio de las palabras', *Nueva Revista* 74 (2001), pp. 91–6; J. R. Lodares, *El paraíso políglota* (Madrid: Taurus, 1999); J. R. Lodares, *Lengua y patria* (Madrid: Taurus, 2002); González Quirós, *Una apología*, pp. 173–4.

82 Language policies are not applied with uniform criteria wherever the PP or the PSOE governs. In Galicia, Navarre, the Valencian region and the Balearic Islands the antidote promoted by the PP's 'regional patriotism' consists in supporting a populist and folkloristic cultural policy.

83 Ch. Stallaert, *Etnogénesis y etnicidad en España. Una aproximación histórico-antropológica al casticismo* (Barcelona: Proyecto A, 1998), pp. 127–64.

84 Uriarte, *España*, p. 184.

8 The reinvention of Spanish conservatism

The Popular Party since 1989

Sebastian Balfour

Introduction

No critical examination of the Popular Party (PP) can deny its considerable achievements since it was founded in 1989 under the leadership of José María Aznar. The party overcame the bitter internal divisions of the 1980s, modernised its image, created a formidable PR team and policy unit, and won a qualified majority in the 1996 elections and an absolute majority in 2000. The PP government's most important achievement during its two terms of office was macro-economic. It oversaw Spain's incorporation into the EMU and fulfilled the conditions of the EU Growth and Stability Pact.

The success of the PP is part of the broader process of the consolidation of Spanish democracy through the stabilisation in the 1990s of a party system and party competition sharing many of the characteristics of Western European democracies.[1] At national level, two catch-all parties of centre-left and centre-right now dominate a relatively closed, bipolar system of competition and at least until recently have shared an unacknowledged consensus on a range of policy issues.

The transformation of the democratic right in Spain into a governing party was the result more of its search for office than a change in its internal ideology or a generational renovation, though these were important. As a party seeking office and then maintaining power, the PP has faced similar problems of self-definition to the Spanish Socialist Party (PSOE). For both, it entailed moving towards the political centre, normally the key to electoral success, on a range of policy issues, while endeavouring to maintain the vote of their traditional supporters. For the PP it also meant reinventing Spanish conservatism. To do so, it needed to disassociate itself, explicitly or implicitly, from Francoism.

The new attempt at repositioning as a catch-all party in the 1990s was the result of considerable internal argument, won by a new and pragmatic generation of leaders. The key to their success was the prolonged occupation of the opposition benches. Opposition is of course a school for power. The Spanish statesman of the early twentieth century, Antonio Maura, put it in his characteristically succinct way: 'Parties break down in power and remake themselves in opposition.'[2] For almost 20 years, the conservatives remained in opposition. They fought six general elections and until 1993 failed to go beyond a ceiling of 25 per cent of the votes. Only on their seventh bid for power in 1996 did they win enough votes to form a minority government.

The PP's journey towards the centre meant shedding inherited right-wing ideologies. The process of realignment was a painful one, fraught with factionalism, confrontation and conspiracy. But the internal disputes were as much concerned with personalities as with policies. One of the problems facing any study of the PP is its hermeticism. While there are some accounts of the internal wrangling from disillusioned actors, access to information became very limited once the party achieved unity and imposed a strict internal discipline.[3] This was even truer of the PP during its eight years in power. The party presented a united front that was hardly ever breached from within, despite differences among its ideological and political 'families'. Thus some of the analysis that follows is based on surmise rather than hard facts or explicit documents. This account focuses on the origins of the party, party organisation, ideology and positioning, and the policies of the first and second administrations between 1996 and 2004. It is not intended to be a history of the party and its two governments. A number of issues, such as the oil spillage of the tanker *Prestige*, the mini-war with Morocco and the problem of Gibraltar, will not be examined at any length. Some of these, such as the European Union, corruption, Gibraltar and the PP government's handling of the Basque and nationalist questions, are discussed in other chapters of this book.

The origins of the Popular Party

The PP has both family and ideological roots in Francoism. Apart from Manuel Fraga, ex-minister of Franco and founder of PP's predecessor, Alianza Popular (AP), the majority of its leaders are sons, daughters or grandchildren of leading members of the Francoist political elites. Its political roots lie in the variegated reformist elements of the Francoist state that sought to take part in the new democracy. It is hardly surprising that it took a relatively long time for the new conservative party to materialise out of the alliance of political families as it first emerged. Without the democratic traditions from which the new party could draw its politics, fragments from a range of conservative ideologies grouped around individual politicians to form factions needing to test their ideas in electoral contests and submit them to internal debates to forge common ideas and objectives.[4]

During the transition, the fundamental cleavage within the AP concerned the extent of democratic reform and devolution. Half of AP's deputies refused to vote in favour of the Constitution in 1978, largely because of the autonomy it granted to the regions. The Basque branch of AP campaigned against the Gernika Statute of 1979 giving the Basque Country a substantial measure of autonomy as part of the process of devolution. Another cleavage regarded AP's internal structure: whether it should be open to debate and competition or a disciplined and hierarchical party dependent on the leadership.[5] A further problem for the AP lay in maintaining the alliance with a range of parties with differing agendas, as well as electoral coalitions with right-wing regional parties. This required considerable negotiations, programmatic concessions and the over-representation of minority parties within AP, a dilemma that plagued the party during the early to mid-1980s.

A fragile balance among the internal elites was finally achieved at some cost. But Fraga's search to merge the parties of the electoral coalition into a single party called Partido Popular was blocked because they wished to retain their identity as parties. The Christian Democrats in particular were keen not to be merged in a party of the right in which they would no longer be able to exercise the same pressure for centre politics.[6] In any case, the Church was not offering AP the kind of support the party thought it deserved in the light of its anti-abortionist stand, just as there were sectors of the bankers and employers who were in sympathy with the now economically liberal Socialist government.[7]

The sudden disintegration of the UCD between 1980 and 1982 (partly engineered by a pincer movement between the AP and the Socialists, as Hopkin's chapter argues) offered the coalition renewed hope that it might achieve its aspiration of forming a Gaullist-type 'natural majority of the centre right' led by Fraga.[8] An even more influential foreign model for Fraga and his close followers was Thatcherism, with its mix of populism, economic liberalism and conservative morality. But the 1982 and 1986 elections were won emphatically by the PSOE. Although the AP was now the main opposition party, it became clear that its electoral ceiling would remain at 25 per cent of the popular vote unless it moved towards the centre.[9] Although Fraga was prepared to contemplate repositioning the party, many of his internal critics were also convinced he needed to be replaced because he was too tainted by his Francoist past. Some of the financial and business leaders closest to the party urged Fraga to resign in December 1984.[10]

The AP's two main coalition partners walked out after the 1986 elections, and Fraga, overwhelmed by internal divisions and party debts and conscious of his failure to attract the centre vote, finally resigned as party leader. A bitter battle for his succession began, from which a new party model emerged that formed the basis of the Popular Party of the 1990s.[11] The crucial issue in the contest for the leadership of AP was not so much party policy as a conflict between two different party models. The divisions therefore cut across political or ideological differences. One model represented a continuation of Fraga's populism and search for a 'natural majority'. The other, backed by Opus Dei members of the party, sought to restructure the party into a disciplined organisation, eschewing populist leadership and coalition politics.[12] The first faction, led by the young Andalusian senator Hernández Mancha and endorsed by Fraga, won a resounding success in a special congress in 1987.

Opposition within the opposition was as much a school of political power as the spell in opposition of the party as a whole. Internal opposition forged close relations with the new generation of middle-ranking AP leaders who had supported the rival faction. It gave them the opportunity to build networks of support in the media and in business and financial circles unhappy with the direction of AP. One of the most ambitious and active amongst these leaders was José María Aznar. He had been a younger member of the so-called Valladolid clan, and when he was elected President of Castilla y León in 1985 he filled the top layer of the new administration with his closest advisers and friends, an old tradition of Spanish politics. Aznar's role in the opposition to Hernández Mancha was strengthened by his efficient presidency of one of only three autonomous governments controlled by AP. He cannot be described as charismatic by any standards but he had demonstrated considerable political skill and won the respect of liberal conservatives for his cost-cutting and anti-interventionist measures. As a relatively young politician he also had no Francoist past.

With party support fast eroding, Hernández Mancha resigned in December. The ninth AP Congress of January 1989 (nicknamed the Refoundation Congress) voted in Fraga as President and approved a fundamental reform of the party's statutes, reducing internal democracy and strengthening party hierarchy and cohesion. The congress also voted to change the AP's name to the Popular Party, thus stressing its new organisational identity but also conforming to the generic European Christian Democratic family. In the same motion, the party was defined as liberal, conservative and Christian Democratic in acknowledgement of the existence within its own ranks of different ideological tendencies.[13] The ascendancy of Aznar's team within the PP was consolidated by a modest swing towards the party in the general elections of October 1989. Having initiated the reorganisation of the party, Fraga then ceded the presidency of the PP to Aznar after his victory in the Galician elections the following December and redirected his considerable energies towards his new post as President of the Galician government, though he continued to play a key role in the party.

Party organisation, ideology and positioning

Under the leadership of Aznar, the PP was further reorganised into a cohesive and highly specialised and hierarchical organisation. He created a compact opposition team drawn largely from those party members of his own generation who had collaborated with him in the campaign to transform the party. The unwieldy system of elite representation within the party constructed by Fraga was comprehensively dismantled. Aznar and his closest collaborators intensified the reforms which Fraga had initiated after the 1989 Party Congress. They constructed a centralised, presidentialist party, concentrating all the party's resources into the hands of the leadership and awarding the leader of the party an extraordinary range of powers, including the ability to co-opt political figures from inside and outside the party into the leadership.[14] Tough negotiations brought almost all the local party bosses from the traditional cacique mould more or less into line with headquarters, while the provincial party apparatuses were overhauled. In January 1989, 26 of the party's provincial committees had been taken over by management committees appointed by headquarters because of internal problems; two years later, under Aznar's presidency, all but two had been put back into the hands of local officials.[15]

The whole operation of institutionalising the party along presidentialist lines gave rise to innumerable and bitter conflicts, but Aznar always ensured he had the decisive support of Fraga and his still powerful party faction.[16] The party's social constituencies also played an important role in creating internal unity and discipline. Of these, the backing given to Aznar's team by the main employers' organisation was crucial. The CEOE was keen to establish policy convergence with the PP leadership and avoid the sort of divisions plaguing the relationship between the Socialist government and its main social partner, the Unión General de Trabajadores.

The redefinition of the PP's ideology under Aznar, like the internal reorganisation of the party, has its roots in the trauma of the years spent in opposition. It can be argued that it was driven more by electoral strategy than a need for political definition, as some commentators have claimed.[17] Aznar's own trajectory is an example of the pragmatic readjustment of political positioning in the search for power typical of his generation of conservatives. He was the grandson and son of close friends and collaborators of Franco. As a 16-year-old, he had written a letter in his local paper attacking the official Francoist movement and declaring his membership of the independent Falangists, the 'authentic incarnation', in his own words, of José Antonio, the founder of the fascist Falange.[18] Ten years later, he joined the AP branch of La Rioja, where he was working as a tax inspector, and immediately began to contribute to the local conservative paper *Nueva Rioja*, attacking the UCD government, criticising the Constitution for its ambiguity and alternately calling for a vote for the right and, five days later, for 'belligerent abstention' in the 1979 elections.[19] By 1991, on the contrary, he was seeking to define the PP as a centre party heir to the UCD.[20]

Aznar's ideological journey was typical of the young generation from middle- and upper-class Francoist families who joined AP in the 1970s and formed the core of its ruling elite in the 1990s.[21] Their university experience and professional training had alienated them from the inefficient corporatism and bloated ceremony of the old regime within which they had grown up.[22] Quite a number were steeped from their youth in the messianic values of the Opus Dei, perhaps the most powerful of the Francoist families, with its mix of economic liberalism, profound religiosity and ultra-conservative morality (and indeed several remain members of the secret organisation along with government advisers). Undoubtedly, Opus Dei exercises considerable influence within the PP but does not appear to be an organised faction. In fact from the early 1990s it became ever more difficult to demarcate the different tendencies amongst the PP elites as party discipline was strengthened. Thus a transmogrified *opusdeísmo* survives in some of the policies of the government, while other features of the old regime also endure in the PP not as ideology but as mentalities and cultures.

This may explain in part the remarkable care the PP has taken to avoid any reference to the Dictatorship, far beyond any concern to avoid upsetting the dwindling band of nostalgic voters. With customary obliqueness, Aznar claimed in an interview: 'we need time before we start looking at our history without excessive passions, with the normality with which others do it'.[23] Nevertheless, when it formed its second government in 2000, based this time on an absolute majority, the PP awarded the Fundación Francisco Franco one of the highest annual state subsidies to non-profit-making private organisations in Spain, despite the fact that the Foundation openly promotes the values of the Dictator.[24] The Foundation, whose president is Franco's daughter, blocked access for years to all but the most fervent supporters of the Dictator. Despite the PP's purely formal disavowal of the Dictatorship in a parliamentary bill in November 2002, Francoism is the skeleton in the PP cupboard.

In their public pronouncements, on the contrary, the PP leaders and their organic intellectuals searched for roots in the Spanish history of an earlier period that they hoped would give greater respectability to their political strategies. The model they have repeatedly conjured up is the two-party political system set up in 1875 by Cánovas, the elder statesman of late nineteenth-century Spain, based on a largely fictitious electoral contest between conservatives and liberals, who negotiated between themselves the share of power and spoils. One of PP's intellectuals called for a policy of 'neocanovismo' through a pact between PP and PSOE to ensure the stability of the state against the 'disintegrative' demands of regional nationalism. Another historical figure, the Catalan politician Francesc Cambó, has been presented as a model for relations between Catalan and Spanish conservatives.[25] Cambó's ambition in the first quarter of the twentieth century was to regenerate Spain from the modernised stronghold of Catalonia. Given the enormous potential for PP of the conservative vote in Catalonia, it was a means of reminding Catalan conservatives that there was a long tradition of mutual support between them and their Spanish counterparts based on recognition of common national interests.

The PP also sought to mobilise the symbolic value of conservative and liberal writers in both Spain and Europe as markers of identity, from Ortega to Popper and Dahrendorf, and then to the neo-liberals most in vogue in the 1990s such as Hayek and Fukuyama.[26] Even the Republican Prime Minister (and later President) Manuel Azaña made a brief appearance in this litany of models. Aznar gave a speech at the launch in 1997 of Azaña's stolen diaries of 1932–3. He expressed sympathy with Azaña's dilemmas, though he cannot have been in agreement with his policies. In any case Aznar denuded his references of any context, so that Azaña appeared to have existed in a historical limbo. He talked about Azaña's tragedy but failed to mention that it was the Spanish right, including its parliamentary confederation, that was directly responsible for the demise of the Republic, except to say cagily that there had been 'certain kinds of errors'.[27]

In fact some of PP's in-house intellectuals have sustained the Francoist demonisation of the Republic. Thus it was 'maximalist' compared to the 'tolerance' and 'openness to dialogue' of Cánovas and Alfonso XIII (who had been happy to support the military coup that overthrew the Canovite system).[28] It was probably felt to be politically incorrect for the PP to find any continuity with the parliamentary confederation of the right in the 1930s, the Confederación de Derechas Autónomas (CEDA), which, in the opinion of many historians, did much to undermine Spanish democracy under the Second Republic, so references to CEDA are extremely rare in the PP-related literature, even though it cannot be ignored as one of the precursors of contemporary Spanish conservatism.

It is no coincidence that the most intensive search for centre positioning on the part of the PP occurred when it appeared to be making least progress in the opinion polls. Two periods stand out in particular. The first was in the early 1990s after the new executive had taken over the party following the moderate results of the 1989 elections. Aznar's speech of April 1991 defined the PP as a party of the centre whose task was to recapture the spirit of the transition to democracy and to launch 'a common project of democratic renovation', an unambiguous appeal to the many people who had once voted for the UCD and were now PSOE voters.[29] In the run-up to the 1993 and 1996 elections, the PP made frequent reference to its vocation as a centre party.

The most decided push to capture the centre votes was during PP's minority government of 1996–2000, when for a while the opinion polls suggested the PSOE were overtaking the PP by almost five points.[30] The hardliners in the PP team were shunted off to other jobs and ministers and PP intellectuals fell over themselves in the effort to locate the PP at the centre. One of these intellectuals, with Fraga's enthusiastic backing, went as far as to identify PP's policies with the 'third way' of Blair and Giddens.[31] In turn, the Secretary-General of the PP in 1999, Javier Arenas, likened Aznar's 'reformist centre' to that of Schröder, Blair and Clinton.

What is not clear is what was meant by the centre. Arenas rejected all the traditional definitions of the political centre. 'It is not the exclusive option of a party, nor equidistance between right and left, nor the intermediate zone between liberalism and extreme socialism. It is an attitude of openness contrary to sectarianism.'[32] This and many other statements suggest the PP conceived of its shift to the political centre as a matter of presentation rather than policy. In other words, the self-definitions as a centre party or a party of the centre-right were driven essentially by electoral needs.[33] The relative absence of references to the political centre after the PP won an absolute majority in 2000 merely confirms this hypothesis.

It should be clear that throughout the process of political realignment the PP's organic intellectuals played an important role in redefining the PP's politics. Because of the party's hermeticism, and the relative lack of defectors from its ranks, it is difficult to estimate the extent to which they have influenced the direction of policies. Aznar likes to give himself a prominent role in the reinvention of Spanish conservatism. But he was influenced by a number of intellectuals, in particular those attached to the neo-liberal wing of the AP, who gave him considerable support in his electoral campaigns in the 1980s. According to one of its intellectuals, Aznar began his political career as an 'intuitive conservative' but 'fell into our hands and we gave him the veneer'.[34] 'He was like a sponge', wrote another sympathetic intellectual, 'permeable to the influences of the milieu.'[35] Conservative think-tanks, of which the most influential was the Fundación para el Análisis y los Estudios Sociales (FAES), whose president is now Aznar himself, helped to shape the PP's strategy, gave advice on documents and speeches, and sought to clothe the new policies with political respectability.[36]

The Popular Party in opposition and in power

During the six years or so during which it was in opposition the newly formed PP adopted an increasingly belligerent stance towards the Socialist government. The AP had used aggressive tactics in its efforts to block parliamentary bills during the first Socialist government, in particular its use of the procedure to refer bills to the Constitutional Court on the dubious grounds that they were against the Constitution.[37] The tense climate these tactics gave rise to in parliament was intensified by the PP's campaign against the minority Socialist government of 1993–6 over two issues in particular: the GAL scandal and the cases of corruption involving PSOE members.

The most important weapon in these campaigns was the media. It seems likely that the war waged against the Socialist administration was a concerted campaign among media that had hitherto competed for conservative consumers, in conjunction with PP politicians and friendly or paid sources in the civil service and the CESID, the Spanish equivalent of MI5. The result was that two antagonistic media blocks emerged with very different explanations of political events, replete with accusations of conspiracy and corruption. Political tensions were augmented by the PP's attack on the state-controlled national television and radio for bias and on the government's supposed incompetent management and failure to ensure plurality in the private media sector.[38] Thus also the campaigns of the 1996 general elections were marked by an unrivalled degree of acrimony and personal smear.[39]

Yet when the PP formed its first government in 1996, many of its policies merely continued those of the PSOE administration. Moreover, the Aznar government revealed a degree of moderation and pragmatism that confounded the predictions of its opponents that it was Francoism by the back door. This would be in marked contrast to the second PP government of 2000–4, during which the deeply conservative agenda of the party rose to the surface. To form a legislative majority after the 1996 elections, the PP had to negotiate the parliamentary support of two immensely problematic allies, the Catalan Convergència i Unió and the Basque Partido Nacionalista Vasco. They may have shared some consensus over socio-economic policies but they were profoundly divided over the status of nation, state and region. Each separately demanded a high devolutionary payoff for their backing. Disinclined to concede the full range of competencies envisaged in the Constitution for the autonomous governments, the PP soon found itself devolving more than any previous government, including the transfer of 30 per cent of tax revenues. Yet the party agreed to other measures, such as reforming the Senate to make it more representative of the regional vote, which it subsequently failed to fulfil and probably had no intention of fulfilling in the first place.

The need to keep the Basque and Catalan conservative parties on board the parliamentary alliance also drove the PP administration to adopt moderate and pragmatic policies in both communities. The hard man of Catalan PP conservatives and the party's president in Barcelona, Vidal Quadras, was replaced by a more accommodating Catalan, Fernández Díaz. In the Basque Country the government carried out measures agreed in the parliamentary pact with the PNV, conceding further devolution to the region and bringing to an end for a brief period the traditional confrontation between the Spanish right and the Basque nationalists.[40]

The new government had also to win over centre voters and to do so it felt obliged not just to dilute its agenda but also to present a moderate image. The PR search for the centre vote was orchestrated by Aznar's Secretary of State for Communications, Miguel Angel Rodríguez, the Spanish equivalent of Blair's Alistair Campbell. The new legislature was nicknamed the 'second transition', the title of a book appearing under Aznar's name in 1994, as if the Socialist government had failed to consolidate democracy. In fact the PP government owed an enormous debt to the Socialists who had persuaded and fought with the left to accept privatisation and deregulation in a way no conservative government could have done. A well-organised, hard-nosed campaign was launched to dominate the media and to exclude the more critical voices from the supply of information.

Far from applying the norms it had criticised the PSOE government for ignoring, the PP encouraged the creation of a powerful pro-PP multimedia group headed by the privatised Telefónica in which sole ownership rose from the previously agreed limit of 25 per cent to 49 per cent. Further legal and technological efforts were made to undermine the pro-Socialist media giant PRISA. The PP attempted to block PRISA's initiative to launch digital television and passed a law prohibiting the digital retransmission of football matches until the pro-PP media group was set up.[41] And in the media controlled by the government, such as the national television and radio networks, or in those close to the PP, reports and interviews with PP politicians were carefully choreographed for maximum effect. The complaisant interviewers, the prepared questions and answers, the lack of contrasting opinions and the absence of information in the public domain represented a continued deficit in Spanish democracy.

Similarly, the PP filled the civil service where and when it could with its own appointees, who were usually party members and often family and friends. Nepotism and cronyism was an old tradition in Spanish politics to which the Socialists had equally adhered in 1982. In the case of the PP government, the rhythm of appointments was hampered by the time-lag of contractual obligations to those selected by the previous government. But gradually the top echelons of state administration, from Justice to the Foreign Office, were filled with PP members and sympathisers.[42] The symbiosis between the party and the state meant that there were few independent voices either in the formulation of policy or in the interface between state administration and the public.

Nevertheless, in the early stages of its first administration, the PP leadership appointed a number of independents as government ministers and state officials as part of a further effort to win the centre vote. It hoped thus to cultivate an image of efficiency free of ideology, balancing the core PP cabinet with technocrats without any clear political affiliation. In several key policy areas, the government sought to maintain some continuity with Socialist government efforts to reach agreement with employers and unions over employment policies, collective bargaining, pensions and welfare benefits in general.[43] In keeping with its cultivation of a moderate image, the government refused to give way to the pressure of the Church for the repeal of the Socialist measures legalising abortion.[44]

The PP administration's more radical agenda was evident in its economic policies and in education and health. It carried through a raft of measures intended to liberalise the economy through privatisation and deregulation. They coincided with a period of unprecedented growth in the international markets from which Spain in particular was able to benefit. Macro-economic stability and growth enabled Spain to fulfil the Maastricht criteria in 1998 and join the European Monetary Union.[45] But privatisation under the PP did not lead to correspondingly greater competition. Many of the public services sold on the market became part of a few major monopolies through a rapid process of mergers and takeovers, with the result that, by the end of the PP's first administration, capital had not diversified to any great extent, in particular in the banking, energy and telecommunications sectors (though the EU Commission's minimum liberalisation framework had been complied with).[46] It was no coincidence that most of the companies that benefited were closely connected to the PP, wrapping business and politics ever closer.[47] The PP's economic policies could not therefore be described as neo-liberal, since they were aimed not so much at creating a fully competitive environment but at raising money, reducing government expenditure, and rewarding powerful benefactors.

As if to keep the traditionalist constituency happy, the moderation of PP's social policies was balanced by more radical policies in education. The new Minister of Education, Esperanza Aguirre, was given the freedom to deliver a full agenda of counter-reforms, especially in secondary education. In her project, private schools were to continue to receive state subsidies and ethics were to be reintroduced as a compulsory alternative to religion. Without sounding out opinion, she delivered an ambitious programme for the reform of the teaching of humanities throughout Spain with a detailed syllabus criticised by many teachers for rewarding encyclopaedic knowledge over intellectual skills.[48] Two of the PP's crucial allies in parliament, the Catalan Convergència i Unió (CiU) and the Basque PNV, joined forces with the opposition to block the passage of the bill because they claimed it sought to impose a Spanish nationalist and centralised model of education on their regions.

The PP's health policies also envisaged a radical reform of the health system but this was more in tune with the previous government's agenda than its educational policies. A range of medicines were formally struck off the national health list (despite the fact that the PP had fought a hard campaign during the last PSOE administration against a similar measure). The national health system in Spain was further decentralised, and foundation hospitals were created with the powers to subcontract to private firms. Finally, tax subsidies were offered to encourage people to buy private health insurance.[49] Health spending in Spain had still not caught up with the European average, but under the PP government it fell even further, representing just 5.8 per cent of GDP, compared to the 7.2 per cent of the average for the European Union. Social spending as a whole was estimated to have fallen to 19.2 per cent of GDP while it was some 27 per cent in the European Union.[50]

The PP's success in the 2000 elections was due in part to its relative moderation and pragmatism, indeed the caution it displayed as it felt its way into the policy networks during its first term of office. The government could claim to be responsible for a number of policy successes, such as economic growth and stability, monetary convergence with the European Union, and the ETA ceasefire, even though some of these factors responded to dynamics outside the PP's control. The unity of the government and party, fuelled by a determination to overcome the divisions of the 1980s, contrasted with the disunity and disarray of the PSOE. And, at least during its first period in office, the PP clearly took opinion polls seriously. As we have seen, the brief period mid-way in its 1996–2000 administration when the PSOE rose above the PP in the opinion polls led the government to market a political identity even closer to the centre. These factors helped to reassure some centre voters disillusioned with the PSOE that the PP was no longer a traditional party of the right (though the abstention of a million PSOE voters played a more important role in the PP's electoral victory).[51]

Another striking example of the PP's pragmatism was its espousal of gender issues post-1989. Survey data had suggested that women were more likely to vote for the Socialists, not least because the PSOE had taken on board some of the feminist demands. In response the PP not only incorporated into its programme some of the more politically neutral social claims affecting women, such as family protection, but also encouraged greater participation by women in the party at all levels. While only 12 per cent of the Executive Committee of AP in 1979 had been women, the percentage rose to 22 per cent 20 years later. In the 1977–9 parliament, only 6 per cent of AP's MPs were women. By 2000, this figure had risen to 25 per cent.[52] Four ministers of the PP's first administration in 1996 and three in that of 2000 were women. The increased presence of women within the party was part of the PP's process of modernisation post-1989 and part of its effort to seek office. But it also generated further demands for gender-related policies and created a new political culture within a party that had once been a largely male preserve.

The PP's search to become a catch-all party was also helped by changes in the social and economic profile and in the values of the electorate. Sections of the urban youth, and the increasingly taxed middle and skilled working classes began to shift towards the PP. The most remarkable change was that amongst the working class. In 1982 only 9 per cent voted PP while by the mid-1990s this figure had risen to 27 per cent.[53] The consolidation of this new electoral profile, added to the positive approval ratings of its first administration, gave the PP a clear majority in the general elections of 2000, allowing it to form a government able to formulate policy without the constraints of legislative bargaining and compromise. While the relative victory of the PP in the 1996 polls was to some extent the result of the erosion of support for the PSOE, the 2000 victory reflected a more positive evaluation of the PP on the part of many voters.

Just as the solid majority enjoyed by the Socialist administration of 1982–93 gave it the platform to move towards more liberal economic policies, so the new PP government of 2000 was able to shift the centre of gravity in its policy-making from centre to right. Among the first legislative proposals was the toughening of the immigration law drawn up during the last days of the first PP administration, and the transfer of overall responsibility for immigration from the Ministry of Labour to that of the Interior. Between 1996 and 2004 the number of immigrants in Spain rose from half a million to around 2.5 million, of which 853,000 were illegal. The first outbreak of racist violence against the immigrant community occurred shortly before the PP's electoral victory of 2000. The new government's proposed regulations went far beyond EU directives, curtailing the rights of illegal immigrants and criminalising their activities in Spain. Nevertheless, the government was forced to re-draft its proposals several times after objections by the Supreme Tribunal and the opposition.

Another policy area reflecting the underlying right-wing agenda of the PP was education. Backed by an unassailable majority in parliament, the new Minister of Education, Pilar del Castillo, introduced in 2003 a far more radical raft of reforms for schools and universities than her predecessor in the 1996 cabinet. Some of the curriculum changes she envisaged were designed to shape the values of new generations of Spaniards along traditionalist lines. For example, religion became a compulsory subject in both primary and secondary state schools. Pupils had to choose between classes of catechism and religious instruction taught by teachers approved by the Vatican according to a curriculum defined by the religious authorities, and classes about religion (entitled *El Hecho Religioso* or 'The Religious Fact') taught by state teachers.[54] The status of religious education was raised to that of the most important subjects in the curriculum. In her initial proposal, subsequently withdrawn because of mass protest, the grades from these courses counted towards end-of-year results and university entrance. This one measure overturned educational policy since the transition to democracy by making religion a compulsory subject in state schools, as it had been under the Dictatorship, despite the ruling by the Supreme Tribunal in 1998 that schools had to provide alternatives. The measure was all the more significant because the Spanish Constitution envisaged the separation of church and state. This is an area where arguably the least progress has been made in fulfilling the constitutional provisions. Far from abiding by these principles, the PP sought to maintain the status of the Catholic Church as a para-state body.[55]

The PP's contradictory stance towards the Constitution is nowhere more transparent than in its call for 'constitutional patriotism'. In a policy document adopted at its Fourteenth Congress in January 2002, the party suddenly came up with this quasi-oxymoron, originally borrowed from the German left and toyed with by Spanish Socialists in the 1990s, to define above all its stance on the problematic issue of nationalism (see Chapter 7 for a more extended analysis). That the PP should identify itself with such a progressive term took everyone by surprise. It was yet another demonstration of the shrewdness with which the PP sought to steal the thunder of the left in its discourse, another discursive effort to occupy the centre of Spanish politics. But buried in the text is an implicit caricature of regional nationalisms as exclusive nationalisms.[56] And in some of its policies and pronouncements, on the contrary, the PP has revealed its attachment to traditional Spanish patriotism and dogmas that hardly conform to the spirit of the Constitution. The continued privileged status of the Catholic Church, to take only one example, is in breach of Article 16 of the document the PP has made the very test and definition of Spanish patriotism.

It can also be argued that beneath the surface of this progressive discourse there lies an agenda that suits the more conservative strategy of the PP. The document seeks to set the Constitution in stone, overlooking the historically conditioned circumstances in which it was negotiated. The Constitution was the result of a skilful and laborious process of compromise between political parties at a time when the shape of democracy was not yet clearly defined and the threat of reaction hung in the air. One of the unacknowledged prices of the transition that appeared necessary at the time was the immunity of the officials (including the torturers) of the Franco Dictatorship, a regime from which the families of the present leaders of the PP had benefited enormously. The Constitution was part of this process of closure of the recent past.

In those areas where agreement could not be reached in the negotiations, the wording was left deliberately ambiguous, with the implicit understanding that the issue would eventually be resolved as democracy unfolded. Of these areas, the most important was the definition of nation, state and region. To find a balance between Spanish and regional nationalisms, both of which defined themselves as nations, the latter were awarded, after much wrangling, the ambiguous designation of 'nationalities'. In its 'Constitutional Patriotism' document, the PP rejected Spanish neo-nationalism and acknowledged the plurality of the Spanish nation. But it implicitly denied the possibility of further negotiating the relationship between the regions and the state. Thus any reconsideration of the existing statutes of autonomy represented a challenge to the *patries*.

It is easy to comprehend the logic of this view in the case of the Basque nationalists who wish to move outside the Constitution in order for Euskadi to achieve the status of an associated nation. However, the Constitution offers only a limited degree of power to those 'nationalities' willing to remain within Spain under its terms. Despite the remarkable breadth of competency devolution, the historic regions enjoy only limited self-government. The state devolved the administration of many functions but retained the power to define national policy. Hedged by state controls and without a representative chamber at national level, the regions can formulate only a limited range of policies and make no contribution to policy-making at a national and European level.[57] In the context of tense discussions over sovereignty and competency, the appeal to constitutional patriotism was thus not only the assertion of the hegemony of the state and the concept of a united Spain on which it is based but also a rejection of the possibility of further devolution or the renegotiation of existing statutes, as the Catalan CiU was demanding. The adoption of the document did not therefore signal a policy drift towards the centre so much as a strategy to deal with growing demands for greater devolution. Yet what was astonishing was the self-discipline with which the PP delegates adopted the document, many of whom must have felt shocked by the sudden abandonment of traditional Spanish patriotism.

Another policy area where it was argued that the PP government failed to respect the Constitution was the manner in which it joined the United States-dominated coalition in the unilateral and pre-emptive war against Iraq. Constitutional norms require the government to seek the approval of parliament before entering war. Aznar took the decision without formal parliamentary debate, arguing that Spanish support for the war was diplomatic and that the troops sent to Iraq were engaged only in post-war peacekeeping efforts. While the claim of the constitutional legitimacy of his decision rested on a strict interpretation of the wording of the document, there were grounds for arguing that the government was going against the spirit of the Constitution.

More importantly, the decision to back the war coalition went against the wishes of the overwhelming majority of the Spanish people as expressed in all the opinion polls. It also overturned a tacit consensus between left and right in Spain over foreign policy: the centrality of the United Nations in matters of peace and international law, the maintenance of good relations with the Arab world, and the need for the European Union to forge a united foreign and security policy. Aznar had made a passionate defence of the role of the UN during the first Gulf War in 1990, criticising the PSOE government for failing to achieve sufficient backing from the public for its highly limited role in the UN-backed action against Iraq. He had insisted that 'the exercise of government responsibility in a situation like this demands the permanent search for the widest possible political agreement and the highest level of support of public opinion'.[58]

In the absence of documentation, the reasons why the government took such a momentous decision over the war in Iraq in 2003 are difficult to determine. There may have been some opposition within the government and the party to the stand adopted by the leadership, but on the rare occasions when this opposition was expressed or reflected publicly, it merely registered disquiet about the war or about the risk of too close an alignment with the Bush administration.[59] In support of their action, Aznar and his ministers always flagged the war against terrorism and the assertion of international security, downplaying the fact that what was really at stake was the legality in international law of the US-led campaign against the Saddam regime in defiance of the United Nations.

Amongst the many possible motives for Spanish support for the US strategy, three stand out. The first is Aznar's own experience of Basque terrorism. Just before he formed his first government, Aznar survived unhurt an assassination attempt by Basque terrorists. Since his youth ETA has been killing conservative politicians he closely identified with. The terrorist attack in New York on 11 September 2001 strengthened his conviction that a concerted effort was needed to stamp out terrorism worldwide. From information provided by the CIA, he was well aware of the networks linking several terrorist groups and providing secret bank accounts. His position on Basque terrorism was similar to that of the US administration on 'Muslim terrorism'. The only effective strategy, in this view, was international action and direct or indirect repression against those political forces as well as the social milieu that provided support for terrorists if judicial measures were insufficient. As he repeatedly claimed, any transigeance merely strengthened terrorism. Joining the war coalition was part of a 'vision of the role of Spain in the defence of a civilised world order'.[60] Such arguments, however, ignored the complexities of terrorism worldwide. In the case of Iraq, Spain and the other members of the war coalition failed to acknowledge the absence of any proof of links between Muslim fundamentalism and the Saddam regime. In his pronouncements over the Iraq war, Aznar appeared to share the Manichaean, almost evangelical concept of good against evil that characterised some of the statements of Bush and Blair.

The second reason lay in the close relationship that was being built between the Aznar and the Bush administrations. US intelligence had been providing useful information about ETA activities abroad and the US Secretary of State Colin Powell had brokered an agreement between Spain and Morocco over their dispute about the island of Perejil. Deepening the transatlantic bond was seen by Spanish conservatives as crucial to Spain's defence and security, as Aznar argued in a speech in parliament on 26 March 2003.[61] Indeed, it appears that Aznar was very much at the centre of the British, Spanish and Italian initiative to back the US strategy over Iraq. The first statement of support, the Letter of Eight, was apparently drawn up in Aznar's office in January 2003 and a draft was sent to the Bush administration for approval, without the knowledge of France, Germany or the European Union, before it was published on the 30th of the month.[62]

Close ties between Spanish conservatives and US administrations had existed ever since the United States rescued Franco from his international isolation in the Cold War. In contrast, Spain's relations with France had often been tense, and the reluctance of the Mitterand government to cooperate with Spanish efforts to crack down on ETA safe havens across the French border had soured relations. Thus a third and more speculative reason for Spain's decision to support the US strategy over Iraq lies in Aznar's instinctive sympathy with the US administration and antipathy towards the French and German governments, strengthened by his ideological inclinations. It is possible he had hoped Spain might also benefit from the split within the European Union. A new alignment critical of the Franco-German axis within the Union backed by the United States might have provided opportunities for Spain to flex its muscles in the negotiations over the Constitution, voting rights in an enlarged Europe and the distribution of EU funds. Yet even before the PP lost the elections in March 2004, the differences within Europe over Iraq were largely resolved and neither Italy nor Britain demonstrated support for the PP government's plea to retain the power to block decisions in the European Union that it had won in the Nice Treaty. The only new alignment that emerged over the

Constitution was a Spanish–Polish axis, hardly the stuff of international power that the PP claimed to have forged.

Purely in electoral terms, the PP's decision was an audacious move but it may have been based on the calculation that the backing it gave to the Iraq war of 2003, however unpopular, would not depress electoral support for the PP unduly because voters were more concerned about domestic issues. Indeed, the elections of 25 May of the same year in the majority of municipalities and regions registered only a slight fall in the PP vote. Nevertheless, as a public opinion survey revealed in April 2003, the misgivings of many Spaniards about the PP's foreign policy, in particular its new international alignment, would not be easily dispelled and, among the centre electorate, might weigh against the government in the future.[63] Revelations later that year exposing levels of spin, exaggeration and inaccuracy on the part of the government that exceeded those in claims critical of the British government, could not have reassured voters.[64] Nor were Aznar or the Minister of Defence, Federico Trillo, ever required to appear before a committee to justify their decisions, as many members of Blair's cabinet were. Even if the special conditions of the Hutton enquiry are taken into account, the British parliamentary system showed a greater power of democratic accountability than its Spanish counterpart.

Indeed the way in which the PP government handled the issue of the Iraq war and the post-war involvement of Spanish troops contributed to the continuing erosion of democratic legitimacy in Spain. In addition to the progressive side-lining of parliament, the level of democratic debate continued to slip. It was above all the PP that was responsible for the spiral of rhetorical vilification in which other parties progressively found themselves caught, with the result that parliamentary debates often degenerated into a discourse of mutual defamation similar to the worst diatribes against wartime enemies. A largely bemused public watched as party leaders jousted with vicious invective and recrimination in the atrophied language of adversarial politics.

The bomb outrage of 11 March 2004, just three days before the general elections, overturned the majority the PP had enjoyed in most opinion polls. The PP's vote fell from the 44.52 per cent it had won in the 2000 elections to 37.64 per cent, while the PSOE's votes rose from 34.16 per cent to 42.64 per cent over the same period. A subsequent survey suggested that the atrocity had brought the issue of international terrorism, and by implication the government's involvement in the intervention in Iraq, to the forefront of voters' minds.[65] The government's insistence until the eve of the elections that ETA was probably to blame, despite mounting evidence that the bombing was the work of international terrorists, undermined some of its support and mobilised the left vote. A likely assumption is that the PP's currency would have been immeasurably strengthened had ETA been responsible. The survey revealed that 16 per cent of PP voters believed the government had handled the issue badly. More importantly, the PSOE was the main beneficiary of an almost 10 per cent increase in voter turn-out, a massive affirmation of democracy against terrorist intimidation.

It would be wrong, however, to attribute the electoral swing solely to the Madrid events. What the vast majority of the opinion polls prior to the election had failed to pick up was the unpopularity of specific policies of the government that had nothing to do with the atrocity. Thus, for example, the swing away from the PP was particularly strong in the Basque Country and Catalonia (confirming an earlier trend in the Catalan regional elections of 2003). It was a measure of the alienation of some traditional conservative voters in those regions from government policies towards their regions. But the swing in Catalonia was also a swing to the left because the Catalan conservatives, the CiU, unidentifiable with either the handling of the Madrid bombings or support for the war in Iraq, registered a fall of over 8 per cent of votes.

Conclusion

Perhaps the most striking feature of the PP has been its internal cohesion. The different ideological families within the party, from Christian Democrats to neo-liberals to neo-conservatives, have been able to maintain a consensus since 1990, even if some of the policies adopted by the government have made one or other of them uncomfortable. It should once again be stressed, however, that these families are not organised. Rather, they are tendencies made up of an assortment of ideas and policy prescriptions from which actors make choices depending on the prevailing political conditions. Another party constituency that the headquarters has managed to preside over is the strongholds based on the control of regional and local government. Outside the party, conservative business and financial elites, church leaders and the media group bosses generally supported the government. The party leadership took care to try to reward, represent or placate these power networks in government appointments, state contracts or policies. However, in a modern, plural and highly segmented society, this support is unlikely to be the basis of a contemporary version of the 1930s historic bloc of the Spanish right, as a recent book argues.[66]

The internal cohesion of the PP has also been driven by the experience of political marginalisation in the past and by the highly centralised party apparatus which frowns on internal dissidence and the open debate of differences. The absence of internal democracy was patent in the way Aznar's replacement as the prime ministerial candidate, Mariano Rajoy, was selected. The PP's method of deciding on its candidate became a simple choice by the party leader at a moment chosen by him followed by a congress to ratify his decision without any consideration of alternative candidates. This method was adopted in the special circumstances of 1989 when the party was facing an internal crisis. That it should have become the norm is a measure of the concentration of power at the top and the lack of pressure from the PP's rank and file for greater participation in decision-making.

This is one of the expressions of the persistence in the party of authoritarian and right-wing habits and mentalities. The relative absence of internal democracy is matched by an incomplete assimilation of parliamentary democracy. Rather than a chamber for debating policy, parliament became a forum for denouncing the opposition and scoring media points. Of the 56 investigative committees requested in parliament in the course of the PP's eight years in power, only three were constituted, not one of which dealt with the environmental calamity of the tanker *Prestige*.[67] Parliament was also sidelined in the formulation of policy, in particular over the Iraq issue. The constitutional norms equip the Prime Minister with the power to pass decrees under certain criteria without submitting them to parliament. Both Felipe González and Aznar used this option, the first during the early administration of the PSOE government in order to bypass the parliamentary obstruction of bills at a time of democratic consolidation. In very different circumstances, Aznar felt little compunction to win parliamentary approval for his policies or to explain them to the chamber, in particular after the PP won an absolute majority in 2000. His final annual state-of-the-nation speech to parliament on 1 July 2003 was a bland statement that gave little explanation of the problems the government had faced since the previous year.

The right-wing tendencies of the PP also surfaced, as we have seen, in its second term of office over policies such as immigration, education and the relationship between centre and periphery. The discourse of constitutional patriotism was balanced by a re-affirmation of the unity of the Spanish nation and a traditionalist interpretation of its history. The confidence derived from the absolute majority in the 2000 elections and the continuing favourable tendency in the opinion polls led the PP to shift its emphasis from centre-right to right, even though it continued to couch its electoral appeal in terms of a catch-all party. Nevertheless, the PP has shown a high degree of pragmatism and ideological flexibility when circumstances have demanded it. In this sense, the PP is as democratic and as moderate as the electorate forces it to be.

It should be clear from the above analysis that the PP is not old wine in a new bottle, as some commentators have suggested.[68] It has undergone considerable repackaging since 1977, but in the process of democratic politics it has become as transformed by contact with the political environment as the Socialists were. Thus many of the policies it originally adopted for electoral purposes became assimilated into party culture. The PP is no more and no less coherent than other conservative parties striving to win elections or stay in power. This is also true of social democracy of course. The ideological distinctiveness of parties in Western Europe has become eroded by the decline of traditional party constituencies because of changing demography and the acceleration of social mobility.[69] At the same time, the margins for formulating distinct policies on the part of parties of left and right have narrowed considerably. The increasing internationalisation and interdependence of the world economy, combined with the growth of supra-state bodies such as the European Union, have eroded the autonomy of government policy formation. There has thus been considerable convergence in some policy areas between conservative and social democratic parties, as there was between the PSOE and the PP governments between 1993 and 2000.

Indeed, for all its contradictions and democratic deficits, the PP government was not such a strange animal as its critics make out. Like the Blair government, it sought to be the 'natural party of government' through its mix of policies and through its catch-all discourse. Yet its strength, like that of its Labour counterpart, lay above all in the weakness of the opposition. The renewal of the PSOE mandate is likely to force the PP to reexamine its electoral appeal and seek to recreate the more consensual policies and political style of its period of minority government between 1996 and 2000. The PP's future also rests on the ability of the new PSOE government to meet the expectations of an electorate mobilised by the atrocity in Madrid.

Notes

1 Juan J. Linz, and José Ramón Montero, 'The Party Systems of Spain. Old Cleavages and New Challenges', in Lauri Karvonen, and Stein Kuhnle, *Party Systems and Voter Alignments Revisited* (London: Routledge, 2001), pp. 150–96.
2 'Los partidos se desbaratan en el poder y se rehacen en la oposición', statement to *El Heraldo de Madrid*, 25 February, 1907 in María Jesús González, *El universo conservador de Antonio Maura. Biografía y proyecto de Estado* (Madrid: Biblioteca Nueva, 1997), p. 118.
3 Of the analyses of the earlier period of the party's fortunes, probably the best is Lourdes López Nieto, *Alianza Popular: estructura y evolución electoral de un partido conservador (1976–1982)* (Madrid: CIS, 1988).
4 The taste among Spanish political commentators for identifying groups, clans, factions and conspiracies within the political parties usually failed to acknowledge that the frontiers between them were very porous.
5 Rogelio Baón, *Historia del Partido Popular*, vol. 1: *Del Franquismo a la Refundación* (Madrid: Ibersaf, 2001), p. 383.
6 Ibid., pp. 385 and 518.
7 Pedro Carlos González Cuevas, *Historia de las derechas españolas. De la ilustración a nuestros días* (Madrid: Biblioteca Nueva, 2000), p. 470.
8 José Ramón Montero, 'More than Conservative, Less than Neoconservative: Alianza Popular in Spain', in Brian Girvin (ed.), *The Transformation of Contemporary Conservatism* (London: Sage, 1988), pp. 145–63.
9 Baón, *Historia*, p. 518.
10 Fernando Jáuregui, *La derecha después de Fraga* (Madrid: El País, 1987), pp. 155–6.
11 Manuel Fraga Iribarne, *En busca del tiempo servido* (Madrid: Planeta, 1987), pp. 445–6.
12 Baón, *Historia*, pp. 771–2.

13 Ibid., pp. 876–7.

14 Frédérique Chadel, 'Penser le changement dans les partis politiques. Le processus d'institutionalisation au Partido Popular', *BCN Political Sciences Debates* 2 (2003), pp. 75–122.

15 Galicia remained the most recalcitrant of the regional and local party apparatuses. For details see Nieves Lagares, *El PP de Galicia* (Madrid, Tecnos, 1999).

16 Carlos Barrera, *Historia del proceso democrático en España. Tardofranquismo, transición y democracia* (Madrid: Fragua, 2002), p. 230.

17 For example González Cuevas, *Historia*.

18 *Diario SP*, 1 June 1969. His Falangist roots have been largely covered up in his hagiographies. Of those consulted for this chapter, only one of the more outspoken of these biographies mentions the fact: Raimundo Castro, *El sucesor* (Madrid: Espasa Calpe, 1995).

19 'El deber de votar' and 'La lección de la historia', *Nueva Rioja*, 18 and 23 February 1979.

20 José María Aznar, *El partido del centro. Conferencia del Presidente del Partido Popular en el Club Siglo XX, Madrid, 25 de abril de 1991* (Madrid: Partido Popular, 1991), p. 12.

21 It should be noted, however, that some contemporary PP leaders such as Josep Piqué had been part of the anti-Francoist opposition in their youth, and others had been recruited from the UCD when it disintegrated.

22 In an interview with conservative journalists in 1994, Aznar made a rare though very indirect criticism of the Franco era for 'that Spanish necrophilia, that ritual of paraphernalia and cult of the dead that exists in Spain': Pilar Ferrer and Luisa Palma, *Retratos del interior* (Madrid: Temas de Hoy, 1994), p. 95.

23 Victoria Prego, *José María Aznar. Un presidente para la modernidad (1996–)* (Madrid: Unidad Editorial, 2002), p. 106.

24 The Foundation continued to receive large sums of money from the government in subsequent years, making it the most subsidised institution of its kind in Spain. For the 2003 award, see *El Periódico de Catalunya*, 25 August 2003.

25 José María Aznar, *España. La segunda transición* (Madrid: Espasa Calpe, 1995), pp. 226–70.

26 Aznar, *Libertad y solidaridad* (Barcelona: Planeta, 1991), pp. 16–17, 27.

27 Aznar, in *Nueva Revista* 55 (1998), p. 173.

28 Miguel Platón, 'España ya no es diferente', *Nueva Revista* 72 (November–December 2000).

29 Aznar, *Libertad*, p. 12.

30 José Ignacio Wert, 'Opinión pública. Encuestas y elecciones 1996–1999', in Javier Tusell (ed.), *El gobierno de Aznar. Balance de una gestión, 1996–2000* (Barcelona: Crítica, 2000), pp. 221–2.

31 Jaime Rodríguez-Arana, *Por qué el centro? Hacia la libertad solidaria* (Santiago de Compostela: Forum Galicia de Estudios Sociales, 1999), p. 18 and 'El nuevo centro', *Nueva Revista* 59 (October 1998).

32 Javier Arenas, *La Vanguardia*, 14 April 1999.

33 Javier Tusell, 'Introducción', in Tusell, *El gobierno*, pp. 30–1, 33–4.

34 In an interview with Enrique de Diego: 'Pero cayó en nuestras manos y le dimos el barniz', in Castro, *El sucesor*, pp. 86–8.

35 Arrondo De Miguel Rodríguez, *Retrato de Aznar con paisaje de fondo* (Madrid: La Esfera de los Libros, 2002), p. 146.

36 The editor and president of the Foundation's journal *Nueva Revista*, Antonio Fontán Pérez, ex-president of the Partido Liberal, an admirer and probably member of Opus Dei, played a highly influential role in shaping the Valladolid clan. In 2002, the conservative think-tanks were merged into the FAES under

the patronage of almost all the ministers and numerous ex-ministers of the PP government and allocated a budget of 5 million euros. Aznar himself became its president. Tusell argues that FAES is a stronghold of the PP's neo-conservatism. Only 12 of its 48 patrons come from the centre or Christian Democratic branch of the PP: *El Aznarato. El gobierno del Partido Popular 1996–2003* (Madrid: Aguilar, 2004), p. 282.

37 Baón, director of Fraga's cabinet until 1989, recognised that the challenges were without foundation: *Historia*, pp. 544–5.

38 Miguel Angel Águilar, 'Los medios de comunicación', in Tusell, *El gobierno*, pp. 182–96; Barrera, *Historia*, pp. 244–5.

39 Sebastian Balfour, '"Bitter Victory, Sweet Defeat". The March Elections in Spain', *Government and Opposition* 31/3 (Summer 1996), pp. 276–7.

40 José Luis de la Granja and Santiago de Pablo, 'La encrucijada vasca: entre Ermua y Estella', in Tusell, *El gobierno*, pp. 155–6.

41 Aguilar in Tusell, *El gobierno*, pp. 196–203; Victoria Prego, *Presidentes* (Barcelona: Asi Fue, 2000), pp. 349–54; Enric Marín i Otto and Joan Manuel Tresserras, 'Els mitjans de comunicació com a engranatge del poder', in n.a., *Les mentides del PP* (Barcelona: Angle Editorial, 2003), pp. 66–85.

42 The PSOE claimed that some 3,000 civil servants were replaced by supporters of the new PP government after it took office in 1997 (*El País*, 31 March 2004).

43 Álvaro Soto Carmona, 'Política social. Relaciones con los sindicatos', in Tusell, *El gobierno*, pp. 76–93.

44 Antonia María Ruíz Jiménez, 'Conservative Parties and Feminist Demands Viewed in an International Perspective: Making Sense of the Partido Popular in Spain', Estudio/Working Paper, Instituto Juan March de Estudios e Investigaciones, 2003/185, p. 23.

45 Juan Carlos Jiménez, 'Balance económico de un fin de siglo', in Tusell, *El gobierno*, pp. 55–69; Sáez Lozano, in *Nueva Revista* 55 (February 1998).

46 Jacint Jordana and David Sancho, 'Policy Networks and the Opening up of the Market: The Case of Telecommunications Liberalisation in Spain', Estudio/Working Paper, Instituto Juan March de Estudios e Investigaciones, 2003/188, pp. 1–34.

47 Jiménez in Tusell, *El gobierno*, pp. 68–9; Angel Fernández Ordóñez, 'Vergüenza e hipocresía', *El País*, 18 July 2003.

48 Francisco Michavila, 'Política educativa', in Tusell, *El gobierno*, pp. 126–7.

49 Soto Carmona in Tusell, *El gobierno*, pp. 89–91.

50 Vicenç Navarro, 'La desconvergencia social en Europa', *El País* 16 September 2003.

51 Antonia Martínez and Mónica Méndez, 'Las campañas de los partidos', in Ismael Crespo Martínez (ed.), *Las campañas electorales y sus efectos en la decisión del voto*, vol. 2: *La campaña electoral en 2000: partidos, medios de comunicación y electores* (Valencia: Tirant lo Blanch, 2004), pp. 73–133.

52 Ruiz Jiménez, 'Conservative Parties', p. 23.

53 Juan J. Linz and José Ramón Montero, 'The party systems of Spain: old cleavages and new challenges', *Estudio/Working Paper*, Instituto Juan March de Estudios e Investigaciones, 1999/138.

54 'Disposición adicional segunda', in *Proyecto de Ley Orgánica de Calidad de la Educación*, 2003, p. 64.

55 Aznar himself has frequently stressed the centrality of Catholicism in the identity of Spaniards. Recently he extended the concept to Europe. In the September 2003 Ambrosetti Forum of world leaders, he argued for the inclusion of the concept of Christian heritage in the European Constitution (*El País*, 6 September 2003).

56 Josep Piqué y María San Gil, 'El patriotismo constitucional del siglo XXI', Comisión no. 2, XIV Congreso Nacional, 2002, p. 5.
57 For a recent discussion of the issue see Carles Viver Pi-Sunyer, 'Finalmente, una amplia autonomía de baja calidad', *El País*, 6 September 2003.
58 Aznar, *Libertad*, pp. 118–19. The PP government's claim that the 2003 Iraq war had the backing of the United Nations rested on a highly distorted reading of Resolution 1,438. For further details see Soledad Gallego-Díaz, 'La presencia', *El País*, 25 August 2003. For Aznar's claims, see, for example, his declaration of 20 August 2003 in *La Vanguardia* (on the same day).
59 Only one PP deputy appears to have openly expressed his discomfort at the government's decision (Jesús López Medel) and one of the founders of the AP, Pastor Ridruejo, criticised the move in *El Mundo*, 28 March 2003. On the other hand, according to the ex-Minister of Labour in the first PP administration, Manuel Pimentel, 'many people were against it but didn't dare express [their opposition]' (interview in *El País*, 14 July 2003).
60 As quoted in *El País*, 10 March 2003. Once in opposition, Aznar reiterated the same unidimensional view of terrorism when in an article in *ABC* he characterised the new Socialist government's decision to withdraw Spanish troops from Iraq as the 'appeasement' of international terrorism, implicitly drawing a parallel with Chamberlain in 1938: 'Desistimiento irresponsable', 26 April 2004.
61 *El Mundo*, 27 March 2003.
62 *FT.com*, 27 May 2003.
63 Javier Noya, 'La España post-Sadam y su opinión pública', Real Instituto Elcano, 29 April 2003.
64 See, for example, the article 'Un agujero en la hemeroteca de Aznar', *El País*, 24 July 2003 about the claim that the Saddam regime posed a nuclear threat. See also 'Defensa aseguró' in ibid., 18 August 2003. It also became clear that the Spanish intelligence services had reported that there was no evidence linking Saddam to al-Qaeda and yet, with this information in hand, Aznar claimed in a parliamentary speech that there was. The government also ignored the report of the intelligence services (CIN) that the regime merely wished to continue developing its WMD programme, thereby implicitly discarding the notion that it had such a programme in place (ibid., 23 June, 25 August and 5 September 2003).
65 *El País*, 4 April 2004.
66 Marín i Otto and Tresserras, 'Els mitjans', p. 76.
67 *La Vanguardia*, 30 March 2004.
68 For example, Vicenç Navarro, 'Ideología y política en España', *El País*, 24 February 2004.
69 David Broughton, 'The Social Bases of Western European Conservative Parties', in Girvin (ed.), *The Transformation*, p. 221, n. 1.

9 The Socialist Party in government and in opposition

Mónica Méndez-Lago[1]

Introduction

The electoral defeat of the Partido Socialista Obrero Español (PSOE) in 1996, after 14 years in power, confronted the party with two main challenges. The first was to replace Felipe González, who had served as Secretary-General of the party for 23 years and as Prime Minister during the whole of the PSOE's period of office. The fact that the PSOE had four different leaders between June 1997, when González decided not to stand again as Secretary-General and July 2000, when the current leader was elected, illustrates how formidable this challenge was. The second was to relaunch party organisation and undertake a process of programmatic renewal in order to regain office.

The difficulties experienced by the PSOE in accomplishing these two goals can be explained in terms of the party's recent history, that is, by the way the party rebuilt its organisation at the time of the transition to democracy and during its time in government. In this chapter I argue that the choices made about its organisational structure and the way the party organisation functioned during the late 1970s and early 1980s acted as heavy burdens for the party when it tried to change some of its organisational features after it lost office in the mid-1990s. These choices, therefore, amounted to a sort of 'genetic imprint'[2] that conditioned the subsequent development of the party.

Maintaining a high degree of internal cohesion and control became the main priority of the party shortly after it reconstructed its organisation. This strategy was based on two pillars: the leadership of González and the intense concentration of power in the hands of the party leaders, González himself and Alfonso Guerra. This proved to be an advantage at the end of the 1970s and the early 1980s, in a context of uncertainty regarding the stability of democracy and intense competition from other political parties. These organisational features did not seem to be a problem for the party during the rest of the decade, when there was hardly any competition from other parties, but they produced diminishing returns as the political context changed at the end of the 1980s, becoming clearly unsuitable for in the increasingly competitive political environment of the 1990s.

The general context in which the PSOE reconstructed its organisation must also be taken into account when considering the alternative courses of action it might have adopted. It was a context in which social democratic parties were having increasing difficulty distinguishing themselves from their liberal and conservative competitors. Developing strategies that kept the essence of their traditional policies while at the same time adapting to the new economic constraints was also an increasingly difficult task. Even though there is a certain degree of variation in the economic and political contexts that characterise different political systems, there seems to be some consensus that the emerging post-industrial international order and the changes in social and political structures have generated problems for the left parties everywhere. During the span of time studied in the chapter, additional constraints emerged on the domestic policies that social democratic parties can offer, such as European integration and globalisation. This is not the place to examine the extent to which these economic conditions are restricting the room for manoeuvre for social democratic parties or whether it is in fact the ways in which political leaders think of the processes of globalisation that matter rather than the conditions themselves.[3]

Context also helps us to understand organisational choices. The PSOE reconstructed its organisation in an era of widespread mass media in which parties had few incentives to develop mass parties.[4] Other factors, such as the availability of public finance for political parties, help to explain why this context was not conducive to the development of large membership organisations. Voters could be mobilised by means other than building a large organisation, which entailed substantial investment both in material and human resources. This is not to say that a party that developed in this new environment did not need members, but the type of party organisation, even if we are talking of a social democratic party, was likely to be different from its counterparts in other Western democracies, which were characterised by a more stable political evolution since the nineteenth century when they generally built large membership organisations.

With this in mind, the following pages explore the development of the PSOE since its reconstruction in the mid-1970s and conclude by examining the main problems it faced during its time in opposition since it lost power in 1996 until it returned to office in April 2004.

The re-foundation of the PSOE in the 1970s

The PSOE virtually disappeared as an organisation during Franco's Dictatorship. Suffering severe repression by the regime, its clandestine executive went into exile in the 1950s. As a result, the PSOE gradually lost its presence in Spain, except for a few groups scattered in different regions. The reconstruction of the party organisation began in the late 1960s and early 1970s when parties were still illegal, but gathered pace once the transition had started in the mid-1970s. Unlike the Communist Party, the

PSOE had a new leadership headed by González as Secretary-General and Guerra as Deputy Secretary-General but very little organisational presence in Spain. Except for a few regions where it was already active at that time, the PSOE had to build its party organisation from scratch.[5]

The PSOE reconstructed its organisation on a territorial basis. According to the statutes approved at the Twenty-Seventh Party Congress in December 1976, the PSOE has a federal structure composed of four territorial layers: the local branch, the provincial,[6] regional and national levels. The main governing bodies are the Federal Congress, the party's highest decision-making body, which elects the Federal Executive Committee, the most important day-to-day decision-making party body and, since 1984, part of the Federal Committee,[7] whose tasks are to control the Federal Executive Committee and deliberate on the main political decisions of the party.[8]

The PSOE is a centrally created (or reconstructed) party at least in its post-Francoist form. In most cases, regional federations were created as a second step in the reconstruction of the party after the provincial branches had been set up. The central authorities of the party closely controlled this process, in particular Guerra, then Secretary of Organisation. The characteristics of this process varied across provinces and the resulting provincial branches were a varying mix of remnants of the PSOE from the Republic (in those areas where they had remained active), plus new members that had joined during the Dictatorship, together with socialists from other parties such as the Federation of Socialist Parties.

During the late 1970s and early 1980s the federalisation of the party is mentioned in the party documents as one of the first priorities for the Secretary of Organisation. The term *federalisation* in this context referred to the creation of regional federations while their provincial equivalents were retained. The process started around 1979 as an attempt to adjust the party structures to the organisation of the state approved in the 1978 Constitution.[9] Already at that time there was some internal debate over the difference between a federation of parties and a federal party. The leaders of the PSOE insisted that the party was federal in its structure and functioning, but not a federation or confederation of parties. They expressed their fear that federalisation would entail a lack of a unified message across the Spanish territory:

> We cannot permit our political project to fragment in the same way that the interests of the right are fragmented . . . If we do, we will lose what is perhaps our major advantage in the medium term, i.e., the fact that we are the only political party that is capable of giving backbone to the whole state, that is, the only party that is able to govern this country.[10]

The control of the process of territorial expansion by the federal authorities of the party facilitated the subsequent centralisation of resources and decision-making capacity. Juliá[11] claims it is extremely important to take into account that the reconstruction of the party and the command of the dominant coalition took place *before* regional or local elites had time to develop. The party's federal (central) authorities were in control of this process and managed to commandeer resources that would otherwise have made regional/provincial leaders more powerful. Provisions were made so that the Federal Executive Committee had the power to decide on political alliances and to veto candidates in the lists for public office.[12]

During the first stage of the PSOE's reconstruction, from the beginning of transition to the 1982 elections, the organisational strategy was governed by the need to grow numerically and to improve its territorial spread. Since the departure point was an organisation with virtually no members, the goal of organisational growth was a fairly obvious one that all intra-party actors shared. Party strategists and organisers also believed it was important *to convey* an image of a strong organisation, given that the other main party of the left, the Communists, had a strong membership base. Thus membership growth was an important concern, at least to reach a certain minimum threshold in order to provide candidates for office and have the basic capacity to organise election campaigns. Candidates had to be found not only for parliamentary but also for regional and local elections. As Table 9.1 indicates, there are many local governments in Spain and it is difficult for a party organisation to muster candidates in all of them. The 'coverage' of the PSOE clearly improved over the 1980s.

The PSOE kept its historically strong ties with the Socialist union, the Unión General de Trabajadores (UGT). The period from the transition to democracy to the electoral victory in 1982 was characterised by close co-operation between the two organisations. An example of this collaboration is the stipulation in the party statutes that PSOE members should also join

Table 9.1 Total number of candidatures and percentage out of the total number of municipalities

	1979	1983	1987	1991
PSOE	3,368 (41.4)	5,588 (68.6)	5,969 (73.3)	6,522 (80.1)
AP–PP	991 (12.3)	5,618 (69.0)	5,200 (63.8)	6,343 (77.9)
UCD–CDS	6,150 (75.5)	1,003 (12.3)	3,150 (38.7)	2,253 (27.7)
PCE–IU	1,525 (18.7)	1,666 (20.5)	1,466 (18.0)	1,561 (19.2)
CiU	385 (4.7)	683 (8.4)	841 (10.3)	863 (10.6)
PNV	186 (2.3)	229 (2.8)	209 (2.6)	217 (2.7)
Others	6,935	5,147	5,277	5,115
Total	19,540	19,934	22,112	22,874

Source: Lourdes López Nieto, 'Local Elections in the Spanish Political System: 1979–1991', in *Local Elections in Europe* (Barcelona: Institut de Ciències Polítiques i Socials, 1994).

Note
The figures in parentheses show the percentage out of the whole number of municipalities (around 8,000 for the whole period) and have been added to the original table in López Nieto.[13]

the UGT. Co-operation was facilitated by the fact that the goals of the PSOE and the UGT were compatible and complementary: both wanted to secure the process of democratisation and, at the same time, dominate their respective arenas of competition. Both organisations helped each other in the electoral processes that took place in both the corporate and the partisan arena of action. Thus, the PSOE and the UGT managed to collaborate at a historical stage when the 'political exchange' was becoming difficult to deliver.[14]

Clearly the PSOE was not a new party. On the contrary, its historical legacy was intelligently managed during this phase: the leaders succeeded in maintaining a link with the past of their hundred-year-old organisation, while at the same time offering new ideas and, more importantly, new leaders. The PSOE provided a combination characterised by 'symbolic continuity and political discontinuity'.[15]

Apart from the establishment of democracy, the other main goal of the PSOE was to maximise its electoral support. In the resolutions of the Twenty-Seventh Party Congress, the PSOE stated that it 'should get as many votes as possible in order to advance on the parliamentary road to socialism, which should be combined with a strategy of mass mobilisation'.[16] Although the PSOE had always been in favour of combining these two strategies, achieving a parliamentary majority as a goal was formulated in a more explicit way as its likelihood increased. This occurred after the 1977 general elections when the PSOE became the main party in the opposition and the dominant political force on the left.

After 1977 the PSOE explicitly presented itself as the alternative to the Unión del Centro Democrático (UCD) in government (*alternativa de poder*).[17] This was important because it influenced other aspects of the party, such as the choice of the social groups in the electorate it would seek to mobilise, as well as its image and discourse. In order to win a parliamentary majority the PSOE needed to appeal to broad sections of the electorate, and this also had consequences for the type of organisational strategy needed to achieve it. The discourse and electoral strategy of the PSOE became more moderate. Thus, while in 1976 the PSOE defined itself as 'a class party and therefore of the masses, Marxist and democratic'[18] and the general tone of the resolutions was based on a strict definition of working class, over time the definition of what working class constituted gradually changed to suit the electoral aspirations of the party. Only three years later, in 1979, the definition was looser and avoided making reference to the working *class* in an attempt to reach *all* workers. For instance, the handbook for the 1979 general election campaign instructs campaigners to 'insist on explaining what it is that the PSOE understands by workers, i.e., anyone who earns a salary'.[19] This is an example of the ideological pragmatism that has characterised the party since its reconstruction in the 1970s.

At this time two 'souls' co-existed within the PSOE: one that sustained a more radical strategy (class party, radical programme, a Marxist definition of the party) and a moderate one that appealed to the middle class and those sectors of the electorate that had voted UCD in 1977. However, the capacity to combine both discourses depending on the situation and the type of public had certain limitations that became clear in the 1979 elections. The results of the 1979 elections were considered a failure by the PSOE[20] since there was virtually no improvement over the 1977 elections. The UCD won the elections with 35 per cent of the vote, while the PSOE obtained 30.5 per cent, only managing to improve slightly on the 29.3 per cent it had obtained in 1977.

This caused widespread frustration within the party, exacerbated by the impression that a decisive part of the electorate was influenced by the UCD leader's televised message on the last day of the campaign undermining the PSOE's moderate image. In his speech Suárez insisted on the perils of voting for a party that defined itself as Marxist and had such a radical programme.[21] By so doing, the UCD was able to take advantage of the contradiction between the PSOE's radical party platform and its moderate image and style.[22]

The stagnation of the PSOE's vote at the 1979 elections provoked different opinions regarding the strategy the party should follow. According to the PSOE's left (the *críticos*), the party had been punished by abstention in traditional Socialist strongholds as a result of its conciliatory attitude during the 'consensus' period. On the other hand, the party leadership considered it proof that the co-existence of the two styles, radical and moderate, made it virtually impossible for the party to obtain enough votes to win the elections.[23] Thus a majority in the party argued that it had to moderate its image further to win an election. An analysis of a survey commissioned by the PSOE[24] argued that defining the PSOE as a class party failed to take into account the importance of new social sectors and could lead to a serious decline in electoral support. It concluded: 'The PSOE has chances to improve its vote both to its left and to its right, but quantitatively speaking the latter yields by far a greater probability of growth.'

The Marxist definition of the party and the strict definition of the working class were perceived as the main impediment to further electoral growth. In fact, Felipe González had already announced his intention to ask the party to remove the term 'Marxist' from the PSOE programme in May 1978. This provoked serious upheaval within the party that remained unresolved until the Twenty-Eighth Party Congress of May 1979, which was dominated precisely by the conflict over the Marxist definition of the party.[25] The conflict emerged between the group of *oficialistas*, sometimes referred to as *felipistas*, and their critics (*críticos*). The *oficialistas* were more numerous in the Executive Committee of the PSOE but some of the *críticos* were also members of this governing body. The *críticos* were opposed to what they thought of as the party's electoralist line that implied changing the party's identity as a workers' party. They preferred a strategy of left-wing unity to that of achieving an electoral majority by becoming a catch-all party. They were against diluting the working-class character of the party and renouncing the term Marxism to define the party's programme. They also denounced the erosion of internal democracy and the increasing concentration of power in the hands of González and Guerra,[26] arguing for the right to form internal organised tendencies.[27]

The *críticos* advocated a strategy of mass mobilisation similar to that which the party had formally adopted in 1976 but had not put into practice. They considered that abandoning a strategy of mass mobilisation so as to follow the *politics of consensus* during the making of the Constitution had carried a heavy price for the goals of the party. It was time to put more effort into mobilising the working class.[28]

The delegates to the Twenty-Eighth Party Congress, directly chosen by the local branches, backed the *críticos* but at the same time expressed their wish to keep González as the PSOE's General Secretary. González refused to stand for re-election since this meant defending the contents of the Political Resolution with which he did not agree, as he mentioned in the closing speech. The *críticos* had not prepared an alternative candidate because they probably never thought that González would decline to stand, so a Steering Committee was appointed to run the party until an Extraordinary Congress was convened.

The main results of the Extraordinary Congress three months later were the re-election of González as the Secretary-General of the party and Guerra as the Vice-Secretary-General, and a compromise solution by which the PSOE disregarded Marxism as one of its defining traits but admitted its utility as an instrument of analysis. Together with ideological moderation, this Congress introduced reforms to facilitate central control in an organisation that had grown very quickly and was becoming increasingly difficult to govern. This control was achieved by a series of statutory reforms that enhanced the ability of central party authorities to influence the composition of regional and provincial delegations to Party Congresses and the way they voted in Congress. The connection between programmatic moderation and internal organisation was clear. The reforms that gave leaders more control and room for manoeuvre also facilitated ideological moderation designed to attract larger sectors of the electorate.

Apart from the consequences that this victory had in the internal party arena, it was important in that it unified the goals of the party around a cohesive leadership and a primary objective, to become the party in power while preserving the 'autonomy of the socialist project': that is, the PSOE rejected the formation of broad alliances with other political forces in order to become the governmental alternative to the UCD. While the (defeated) *críticos* were more eager to reach pacts with political forces to the left of the PSOE, the largest sector, including its leaders, wanted the PSOE to attract enough voters to carry out its own electoral programme independently.[29]

From the end of the 1970s and during the 1980s internal control and discipline prevailed over any other organisational concern. The extent and nature of the investment in different aspects of its organisation – electoral campaigns, increasing membership and the links with the UGT – were subordinated to keeping the party cohesive and united. Party structures enhancing central control over the growth of the organisation were maintained or created anew, and the territorial-hierarchical principle was preferred over other potential forms of organisation (for instance, along functional lines), that might undermine this central control.

Several reasons have been given to account for these options. First, the memories of past fratricidal struggles, particularly during the Second Republic, when the bitter internal conflict among different party factions had contributed to the breakdown not only of the PSOE but of democracy itself.[30] Second, the electoral defeat of March 1979 was attributed to the internal divisions in the party over strategy and policies. Finally, the PSOE saw in the UCD government coalition an example of how damaging internal factions could be for a party. This concern is illustrated by the insistence of various party documents on the need to portray the image of a united party, in marked contrast to that of internal crisis exemplified by the Communists and the UCD governmental coalition.

It was not only a matter of organisational norms and rules; the practices followed in the day-to-day party functioning and at Party Congresses also revealed an increasing concern with limiting the possibilities of disorder within the party. Internal struggles were perceived to have high electoral costs, a perception that was reinforced by the bad results obtained by other main political parties, such as the PCE and the UCD which were both undergoing severe internal crises. As in other political systems in Spain there is a premium on party unity, and the PSOE leaders were well aware of it.

The PSOE in government

In 1982 the PSOE won the elections with a reformist programme with no reference to a 'qualitative break' with capitalism. The main commitments of the PSOE's programme were the modernisation of Spain and the consolidation of democracy. The government's priorities were to conclude the process of political decentralisation of the state, to introduce reforms protecting civil rights, and to consolidate Spanish foreign relations after a long period of isolation, particularly focused on integration into the European Community.[31]

Its central concern, however, was to confront the difficulties the Spanish economy was facing: the economy was growing at only 1.2 per cent, inflation was around 14 per cent, the unemployment rate was 17 per cent, the public deficit 5.5 per cent, and there was a high external deficit. As soon as it came in office, the Socialist government left aside the 'expansionist-oriented' electoral programme which sought to use state investment to stimulate economic growth, create employment and restructure industry, and adopted instead an economic adjustment plan advocated by the social democratic sectors of the party.[32] According to several sources, the previous experience of the French socialists had much to do with the ease, or on other occasions, the resignation, with which this was accepted.[33] The Socialist government introduced a strict programme of economic adjustment and structural reforms from 1982 to 1985, including devaluation, a reduction of the money supply, industrial restructuring and greater labour market flexibility.[34] Its objectives were to reduce inflation by limiting wages and cutting state expenditure. It included an industrial restructuring programme to eliminate inefficient industries and re-direct resources towards other industries. The government also engaged in a process of renovating the fiscal system to help with this readjustment period, involving a tax increase, particularly increases in tax revenues[35] and the creation of a more progressive system, as well as the design of measures to fight fiscal fraud.

By 1985 inflation was down to 8 per cent, and the external deficit had turned into a surplus, but the costs were a higher unemployment rate, which had gone up to nearly three million. This was potentially very damaging for the Socialists because they had made combating unemployment and creating jobs the focus of their 1982 programme. Expansionist measures were adopted; incentives for consumption through a reduction in tax revenue and incentives for investment were implemented. This shift in policy coincided with the worldwide economic recovery. Profits rose and foreign investment in Spain increased dramatically, particularly after Spain's entry into the European Community on 1 January 1986. However, the promise of creating 800,000 jobs made in the 1982 programme was not fulfilled and unemployment remained a worry for the government and a serious political and economic problem.

Another important problem confronting the government during these years was the NATO referendum. The PSOE had been a fierce advocate of non-entry at the end of the 1970s and early 1980s when the UCD government led by Leopoldo Calvo-Sotelo agreed to join NATO. When this effectively took place, in the autumn of 1981, the PSOE organised an anti-NATO campaign and the resolutions of the Twenty-Ninth PSOE Party Congress held in the same year called for withdrawal from NATO.[36] The terms of the debate were substantially changed when the time came to maintain their promise. The question was no longer whether to enter NATO or not, but instead whether to leave NATO or remain,[37] but even accepting the status quo (remaining in NATO) involved a shift of the PSOE's official position. In the 1982 general elections the PSOE included in its manifesto the commitment to hold a referendum on the issue and the promise to freeze the entry into the integrated military command of NATO until citizens had expressed their opinion.

Although this proved to be a very divisive question inside the PSOE, Maravall points out that 'the party was not very difficult to convince',[38] particularly compared to the difficulty in convincing Spanish society at large. The definition of the new position on the NATO issue ended in an intermediary solution that entailed remaining within NATO without integrating into its military command, banning nuclear weapons on Spanish territory, and reducing the number of US troops based in Spain.[39] The change of policy took place officially at the Thirtieth Party Congress (1984). There was hardly any debate at the Congress about the U-turn[40] but together with the referendum campaign it was a dramatic experience for the party and for a large part of the electorate. The policies of other parties as well as the political atmosphere turned the referendum into a sort of popular vote of confidence in González. It was held in March 1986 and the results were a narrow victory for the option of remaining in NATO.

The most important features of the second term of the PSOE in government (1986–9) were the continuity in political objectives related to the social, economic and political modernisation of Spain, and the rise of political tension, particularly within the labour movement. The term coincided with a period of economic growth as part of the worldwide economic upturn. There was an important increase in foreign capital investment in Spain. GDP grew at a rate of over 5 per cent and significant numbers of new jobs were created. However, the labour movement complained that the benefits of this growth did not reach workers, while an atmosphere of making a fast buck pervaded Spain.

In 1987 Solchaga, then Minister of Economics, recommended employers to negotiate wage increases of around 5 per cent. This was rejected by the unions, who after the years of economic restructuring refused to internalise the cost of moderation in a context of economic growth and increasing profits. Labour protest intensified and the government failed to convince the union confederations of the need to negotiate. The result of the increasing confrontation was the general strike of December 1988. The strike was significant not only as a protest against the economic policy of the government, but because it channelled protest against the Socialists' style of politics, which were seen as distant, even authoritarian.[41]

The conditions that had facilitated the close links between the two organisations gradually vanished while the PSOE was in office, culminating in the UGT's support for the general strike. The confrontation between the UGT and the Socialist government deeply undermined party–union ties. The compulsory membership of both organisations (respected by less than 50 per cent of the party membership), was finally abolished at the Thirty-Second Party Congress (November 1990). The article that regulated double membership in the party statutes was replaced by the obligation to be active in *any* social movement. The party's lack of independence from the government blocked any of its attempts to maintain strong links with the UGT.

The general strike also had important indirect consequences in the definition of preferences of intra-party actors. Tension within the party increased among the different sectors that had divergent ideas regarding both socio-economic policy and internal party matters. These internal struggles intensified after rumours emerged a few months after the general strike that González intended to resign, since this implied that a successor had to be elected.

The success of the general strike marked a turning point in the social and economic policies of the PSOE. With this move, the government concentrated on regaining, and maintaining, the support of its 'core' constituencies in an attempt to avoid the electoral dilemma faced by other social democratic parties in their efforts to satisfy the demands of their traditional electoral base, the working class, and those of the middle classes.[42] Owing to the exceptional circumstances in which the PSOE entered office, this dilemma had not been so visible before the end of the 1980s. Changes in socio-economic policy included an increase in social expenditure from 17 per cent to 20 per cent of GDP, a rise in the number of people covered by unemployment benefit, whose coverage went from 34 per cent to 67 per cent between 1993 and 1994, and the creation of non-contributory pensions.[43] All of this occurred during an economic expansion lasting until 1992, when a serious crisis hit the Spanish economy.[44]

The party as an organisation

The PSOE's landslide victory in the 1982 general elections marked a new phase in the development of the party. This success was followed by victory in most local and regional governments in the 1983 elections. Being in government at the different territorial levels had a clear impact on the PSOE as an organisation. First, it had the immediate effect of emptying the party organisation of cadres who took on governmental responsibilities and abandoned, at least temporarily, their tasks in the party organisation. This void was deepened by the lack of a clear idea of the role the PSOE (qua organisation) should have when the party was in government: whether it was required simply to back the government and explain its policies, or whether it had other roles similar to those performed in the pre-governmental phase. It ended up playing the role of loyal follower, but this loyalty was not the result of intense debate but rather the consequence of its internal discipline.

Once in power the PSOE enjoyed a huge number of resources with which to influence society. Apart from developing policies with some ease, given that it had an absolute majority of seats during the first three terms in office, power meant making appointments and exercising patronage. In short, it opened a pool of resources that went far beyond the existing *and* the potential party's organisational resources, and diminished the need and the 'profitability' of investing in party organisation. Moreover, as I have already argued, the institutional, political and social context in which the PSOE operated did not provide incentives for building a mass membership party. The existence of public finance for political parties meant that recruiting new members was not of great importance financially. Nor was having a large membership base essential for election purposes in an era of television and mass media campaigns.

Thus the PSOE needed members to fill all the positions at the different governmental and administrative levels, but they were less needed for vote-seeking purposes, particularly if enlarging the membership base meant losing control of how the party organisation behaved in relation to the government. Except for the initial attempts during its early years in office to find candidates for local elections or the membership drives designed to convert electoral support into organisational resources, as Figure 9.1 shows, there was a decreasing emphasis on recruiting and maintaining members. This does not mean that the PSOE did not cease to grow during these years, as Figure 9.2 shows, but the party organisation made fewer efforts to recruit.[45]

The main organisational novelty of the 1980s was the expansion of the regional federations and the increase in power of their leaders, the regional *barons*. This outcome was facilitated by the process of political decentralisation that had started during the transition to democracy and led to the development of a highly decentralised state, the Estado de las Autonomías.[46] In spite of the varying degrees of autonomy, the most important effect on party organisation and strategy was that there were seventeen new political arenas, with their own parliaments and governments. For most of the 1980s, the PSOE was in power in a majority of these Autonomous Communities.

The decentralisation of the state affected the internal functioning of the party. Regional party leaders, who at the time the party was reconstructed were tightly controlled by its central authorities, began exploiting their

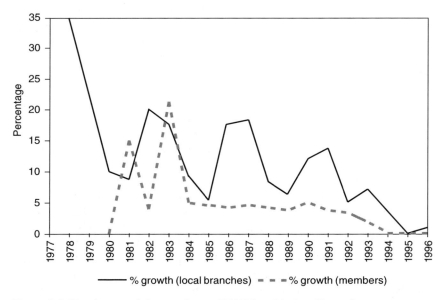

Figure 9.1 Yearly growth in members of PSOE and in local branches.

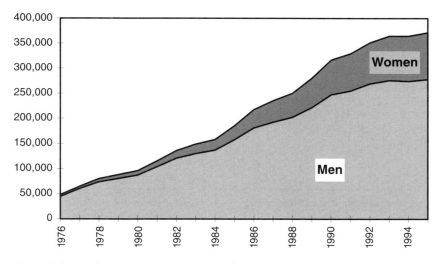

Figure 9.2 Number of members of PSOE (male and female), 1977–96.

command of votes and patronage, and sometimes large Party Congress delegations, in order to assert some autonomy from the federal party authorities.[47] One result of this transformation was reflected in the composition of federal party bodies. As Table 9.2 shows, in the 1980s the Federal Executive Committee started including regional party leaders among its members. As a consequence, regional leaders would also gradually gain influence in central decision-making in spite of attempts by the federal party authorities to keep them under control. However, as we shall see later, the internal power acquired by regional leaders would not become evident until the 1990s.

During its time in government, the PSOE rules underwent minor adjustments facilitating the representation of minorities in internal governing bodies, but very little was done to transform party structures or practices in order to increase rank-and-file participation in decision-making. An exception could be made in the case of women, who increased their presence in the decision-making bodies of the party and in the electoral lists at different governmental levels through the introduction of a quota system in the late 1980s.[48] This innovation did not help to change a general image of stagnation and lack of dynamism in the way the party organisation functioned. This cannot be attributed merely to the exercise of office but also to the PSOE's incapacity for more than a decade to adapt its party organisation to these circumstances. The interest in the PSOE qua organisation gradually declined during these years.

The composition of the party's governing bodies remained very stable during these years. For example, as Table 9.3 shows, the most important

Table 9.2 Federal Executive Committee (FEC)

Composition	Government members	Women	Regional PSOE General Secretaries and Presidents	Heads of regional government
1976	–	5.3	0	0
1979	–	8.3	0	0
1981	0 (3)	12.0	2	0
1984	0 (1)	23.5	0	0
1988	1	21.7	3	1
1990	0 (1)	21.2	4	2
1994	3	30.6	9	4
1997	–	42.4	3	1
2000	–	34.6	6	3

Source: adapted from Mónica Méndez-Lago, *La estrategia organizativa del Partido Socialista Obrero Español 1975–96* (Madrid: Centro de Investigaciones Sociológicas, 2000).

Table 9.3 Degree of renewal (Federal Executive Committee, FEC)

	Size	Old members*	% perm**	% perm2***
27th (Dec. 1976)	19			
Extraordinary Committee (Sept. 1979)	24	9	47.4	37.5
29th (Oct. 1981)	25	17	70.8	68.0
30th (Dec. 1984)	17	17	68.0	100.0
31st (Jan. 1988)	23	13	76.5	56.5
32nd (Nov. 1990)	31	20	87.0	64.5
33rd (March 1994)	36	17	54.8	47.2
34th (June 1997)	33	11	30.3	33.3
35th (July 2000)	25	4	12.1	16.0

Source: adapted from Méndez-Lago, *La estrategia organizativa del Partido Socialista Obrero Español*.

Notes
* 'Old members' represent the number of members of the FEC who were already members in the previous term.
** '%Perm': percentage of old Executive Committee members who are re-elected.
*** '%Perm2': percentage of new Executive Committee who already belonged to the previous one.

party body, the Federal Executive Committee, had low rates of renewal. Columns 4 and 5 represent two different ways of measuring the extent of renewal; while '%perm' represents the percentage of members of the *old* Executive Committee that are re-elected, 'perm2%' is the percentage of the newly elected Executive Committee that already belonged to the previous one. The former way of measuring renewal is usually the only index reported. However, given the variation in the size of the Executive, it is misleading to use only this indicator, since it hides cases of non-renewal (see, for example, the 1984 Executive Committee). In addition, it seems useful to use both, to pinpoint cases in which new people joined the Executive without diminishing the presence of the previously dominant group. According to the information I obtained in interviews with several party officials this also seemed to be the pattern at lower territorial levels. Other indicators of a process of stagnation were, for example, the long periods that elapsed between congresses (three or four years).

The electoral success the PSOE enjoyed at the different governmental levels during the 1980s discouraged their taking risks by changing the organisational structure, rules or practices. The lack of competitiveness in the party system for most of the 1980s contributed to a stabilisation of these characteristics: there were few external challenges to act as catalyst for change and there were also few intra-party incentives to initiate reforms. This situation changed by the end of the decade when the Socialists came under stress, on the one hand because of several political scandals that came to light and, on the other, because of increasing competitiveness of the electoral arena.

The 1990s: an increasingly competitive environment

From the 1990s the PSOE faced a more competitive environment in the electoral arena. Already in the 1989 general elections the fear had arisen that the PSOE would lose its absolute majority in the Chamber of Deputies. The results of the elections confirmed these suspicions, given that the PSOE was one seat short of an absolute majority. However, its closest competitor, the old Alianza Popular, now called the Popular Party, with a new leader Jose María Aznar, failed to increase its share of the vote and was still far from being an alternative government. Izquierda Unida (IU) or United Left nearly doubled its share of the votes and became the third state-wide party, with 17 deputies in the Chamber of Deputies.

The public image of both the party and the government was eroding owing to the emergence of several corruption cases exposed mainly by the press, followed by judicial investigations (see Chapter 3). The consequences of this deterioration on the Socialists' electoral fortunes are difficult to assess, but it seems clear that it helped to spread an atmosphere of political cynicism and distrust of politicians, especially towards the Socialists.

Another distinctive feature of the early 1990s was the emergence of important struggles within the PSOE. There were two main groups: one organised around Guerra and the party apparatus, and the heterogeneous group referred to as *renovadores,* who advocated a transformation of the party discourse and the functioning of party organisation. The Thirty-Second Party Congress (1990) was preceded by an overt expression of discontent by a section of the party over the control of the party apparatus exercised by Guerra and the excessive concentration of power within the PSOE. This Party Congress mainly focused on internal questions related to intra-party disputes over power and control. The result of this Congress was concisely described by one of the best-known *renovadores*, the then Minister of Economics, Carlos Solchaga, who declared: 'we [the *renovadores*] have lost the Congress'.[49] However, this provisional defeat did not quench the internal struggle which escalated until the 1993 elections were held, and continued afterwards.

Until 1991, when Guerra ceased to be Deputy Prime Minister, the co-ordination of the different arenas in which the PSOE participated was ensured by the presence of González and Guerra in all of them. González was simultaneously Prime Minister and PSOE General Secretary, and Guerra Deputy Prime Minister and Deputy General Secretary. The division of roles between the two, through which González was able to concentrate his energies on the government and Guerra on party organisation, led to serious problems of co-ordination between the party in government and the party organisation once Guerra was out of government. As a result of this, as we shall see later, González would try to gain control of the party in the Thirty-Third Congress (1994).

The PSOE started to suffer from a general governmental wear and tear. By 1992, when the Socialists celebrated a decade in power, the sense of crisis, both political and economic, was widespread among Spaniards.[50] Intra-party disputes, the fatigue of González and his doubts on whether to stand as candidate in the following general elections, the economic crisis, the opposition of the labour movement and the aggressiveness of part of the press were the main defining characteristics of the atmosphere in which this anniversary was celebrated. The deep intra-party divisions hampered any response to the now clear external challenges.

For the first time since the Socialists' accession to power, there was a widespread feeling that the Partido Popular *could* win the 1993 general elections. After an aggressive campaign in which González mobilised leftist voters who had abstained in previous elections, the PSOE lost its absolute majority but managed to increase its share of votes as a percentage of the electorate; that is, it managed to mobilise a larger number of voters. The elections confirmed trends in electoral behaviour that had appeared in the previous ballot. Although the PSOE maintained roughly the same amount of votes as in 1982, the characteristics of its voters had changed dramatically. Young, urban and well-educated voters had been abandoning the PSOE since 1982, increasing the relative weight of old, rural and less-educated voters.[51]

The results of the 1993 elections were interpreted by both the press and the voters as a personal victory for González,[52] who in his speech of thanks insisted that he had 'understood the message' implied in those results regarding the need to 'change the change'.[53] The PSOE's loss of its absolute majority led it to seek agreement with other political forces to maintain office. Although sections of the PSOE favoured agreements with IU, there were several aspects of its programme that were unacceptable to González, such as its rejection of the PSOE's economic policy or its criticism of the Maastricht Treaty. The agreement reached by the PSOE to govern with the support of the Catalan Nationalists (CiU) did not satisfy a sector of the party, who saw this as a further confirmation of the PSOE's shift to the right.

According to Maravall, the best way to define the Socialists' last term of office (from 1993 to 1996) is to say that public attention was diverted from policies to politics.[54] Its most relevant feature was the harsh environment that characterised Spanish politics. A good part of the media displayed even greater bitterness towards the government than in the previous term. This atmosphere was worsened by the scandals that continued to emerge, adding to the cases that were still unsolved in various courts of justice. Thus while the Filesa affair regarding the illicit financing of the PSOE was still under investigation, other corruption scandals came to light. The attention of the media and public opinion was so absorbed by political corruption and scandals that little attention was paid to the actual policies carried out by the Socialists. However, the government engaged in more reforms than it had done in previous years, introducing labour reforms that had been postponed, reforming housing legislation and adopting greater budgetary discipline.[55]

Within the PSOE the internal struggles continued, particularly until the Thirty-Third Party Congress held in March 1994, in which the *renovadores* achieved greater representation among delegates than the *guerristas*, or supporters of Guerra, so the previous imbalance was redressed by providing the government with greater control over party organisation. Slowly it became clear that González had decided to abandon his neutral position and to side with the *renovadores*. At the Congress the *guerristas* lost important positions of power within the party but still managed to come to an agreement with the *renovadores* to keep Guerra as Deputy General Secretary and some *guerristas* in an Executive Committee dominated by *renovadores*. In spite of this agreement, the wounds were not completely healed and the PSOE remained divided.

Until that Congress the position of *guerristas* in the party had been enhanced by the fact that many of them devoted a lot of their energies to internal party matters. This tendency became more acute after a rule was established that made it incompatible to hold an executive public office and be a secretary in the Executive Committee in charge of one of the areas of activity.[56] As full-time participants, they had command both of information and communications resources that other party leaders and regular party members lacked.

The internal divisions increased the power and influence of regional *barons*. The mutual 'non-intervention' relations or, in some important issues, the submission of regional federations to the Federal Executive were replaced by the active participation of the federal party bodies, particularly in the Federal Executive Committee (see Table 9.1). The internal struggle concentrated the time and energies of intra-party actors, engaged in an ongoing fight for control over the party organisation. It also enhanced the character of the party organisation as the arena in which the struggle for power occurred at the expense of its instrumental value; that is, existing organisational resources were being used to favour the positions of one internal group over the other, rather than for attaining external goals.

The effect of all of these problems on the electoral arena became clear in June 1994, when the Popular Party obtained its first victory over the Socialists at the European elections. In the following year the PP also won the local and regional elections and made substantial progress in regions where it had previously made little headway, such as Catalonia and the Basque Country. The margin of victory of the PP over the PSOE in the general elections of March 1996 was smaller than expected from the different surveys that had been published all through the 1993–6 term. The Socialists, who again focused their campaign around González, managed to mobilise a substantial number of undecided voters, the majority of whom voted for the PSOE in order to block the PP.[57]

The PSOE in opposition

The structures and practices set in place during the reconstruction of the party and consolidated during the PSOE's period in office worked against the organisational and programmatic renewal of the party when it lost office. This was evident in the problems the party experienced trying to replace the leader of the party and adapt to its new role. In addition to the vested interests and internal obstacles to change, the narrowness of the PP's victory in 1996 did not act as a strong external incentive for change. Thus, although there had already been much debate on the need to start a process of internal party democratisation, to recruit new members and revitalise a languishing party organisation, it was difficult to get the party organisation moving in that direction.

Adapting to its new role in the opposition was also difficult for the PSOE because it had to defend its policies and performance while in office, on the one hand, and, on the other, it had to distance itself from the worst memories of corruption cases. This proved difficult especially because different courts of justice were still examining some of these cases when it was already in the opposition.

The debate before the Thirty-Fourth Party Congress (June 1997) was dominated by the issue of whether Guerra should be re-elected as Deputy-Secretary-General instead of focusing on proposals to turn the party into an effective opposition to the new government. It was the first Congress the party held when out of office, but it was dominated by 'old' questions. Although he was not challenged as Guerra was, González was in a less comfortable situation than in the past. He was still considered a very charismatic leader, but he was also linked to the past. As Almunia points out, *guerristas* preferred Felipe González to any other *renovador* while he was a non-contested leader among *renovadores*.[58] However, the continued presence at the helm of the party of veterans of the previous government, including González and most of the party leadership, made it difficult to put aside the internal struggles of the past and launch an effective opposition to the party in power.

The question was solved by González himself when he decided not to stand as candidate for the post of Secretary-General and communicated this without previous warning in his opening speech to the Congress. The suddenness of this decision made it difficult to choose a leader that had the support of the party elite, delegates and members. González pointed out the person who would replace him as Secretary-General, Joaquín Almunia, who had served as minister in some PSOE governments and was known to be one of the 'founders' of the *renovadores*. The difficult question of replacing González had been solved by a solution concocted by a handful of party leaders, headed by González himself, in a less than transparent process.

Less than a year later, in April 1998, Joaquín Almunia decided to apply the mechanism of primary elections for the selection of the prime ministerial candidate. Winning these internal elections would provide him with the legitimacy he lacked because of the circumstances in which he was elected. Short-term strategic considerations were not the only reason behind holding primary elections. Almunia himself had declared that the new candidate for Prime Minister could not be elected by just the party elite, and that he or she would be elected in a process in which the party membership would participate.[59]

However, the unexpected outcome of these primary elections was the victory by a clear margin (55 per cent to 44 per cent) of Josep Borrell, a left-winger who had served as minister with González. This first shock was followed by yet another unexpected outcome. About a year after having won the primaries, Borrell resigned. Although he formally resigned as a result of the revelation of corrupt behaviour by several functionaries that he had appointed while he served as minister, the lack of clear support by the party elite was also an important factor that led him to that decision. The co-existence of Almunia and Borrell in the highest positions of the leadership had been plagued by tensions, appeased only after the regional barons reached an agreement to act as 'referees' in internal party conflicts in the absence of strong central leadership. After Borrell's resignation, Almunia stood as candidate for the general election of 2000.[60]

In spite of all the party's problems, the primary elections generated a wave of solidarity among members and sympathisers of the PSOE. It was seen as a mechanism that broke with the closed and hierarchical character of party decisions that had characterised the party during the previous decade. However, the PSOE failed to take advantage of this solidarity because of the internal conflict generated by the co-existence of Borrell and Almunia. This showed that internal issues prevailed over external incentives. In other words, internal power struggles hindered the much needed process of organisational and ideological renewal necessary to win elections.

The importance of the role played by the 'regional' barons in the conflict between Borrell and Almunia should be stressed. They also filled the void left by Borrell when he resigned. The new balance of power between the centre and the periphery inside the party asserted itself when the leadership was vulnerable in the early 1990s because of internal divisions and external challenges, and later on at the end of the 1990s when there was no central leadership at all.

One of the consequences of this new balance of power was that the party discourse became more heterogeneous across the territory and party federations diverged in several policy domains. This was used by the PP to attack the Socialists and argue that they were no longer a 'national' party, presenting themselves as the only political party able to put forward a unified political project for the whole country and to defend the same policies in every region.[61] This issue thus became an electoral liability for the PSOE, which failed to turn this diversity into an asset.

In short, the party behaved erratically at the end of the 1990s. Among the more erratic of its decisions was a rapprochement with the IU just before the 2000 general elections. There had been severe disagreements between the PSOE and the IU when the Socialists were in government. In the months before the 2000 elections the PSOE, led by Joaquín Almunia, agreed with the IU on a limited joint programme and decided to present single candidatures in several electoral districts where the quasi-majoritarian effects of the proportional electoral system were particularly adverse for the IU. Finally this latter part of the agreement was applied only to the Senate elections not to those of the lower chamber, the original intention of the Socialists. The rapprochement between the two organisations, after their difficult relationship during the PSOE government, was facilitated by the new leadership of both organisations, Almunia instead of González and Francisco Frutos instead of Julio Anguita.

The disastrous results for the PSOE in the 2000 general elections finally acted as a catalyst for its transformation. If the 1996 results were characterised as a 'sweet defeat', those in 2000 were indeed bitter. The Popular Party obtained an absolute majority of seats in the lower chamber, Congreso de los Diputados, while the PSOE suffered its worst result since 1979. Almunia resigned immediately afterwards. The replacement of González and the question of leadership thus remained an open issue that would have to be tackled in the next Party Congress in July 2000.

On the ideological and programmatic front, the huge defeat meant bad news for those who were in favour of left-oriented policies, given that the PSOE had contested the elections in alliance with the IU coalition. During the election campaign the status of the agreement was not prominent. There were few joint appearances of the leaders of the PSOE and the IU and the pact was practically left out of the PSOE's discourse. Thus it is not that clear whether the failure of this pact should be attributed to the strategy itself or to the way it was decided upon and carried out. It is also unclear to what extent the defeat of the PSOE and the margin of the PP's victory could be attributed to the agreement.[62] Whatever the case, the identification between the agreement and the dire electoral results was not a good precedent for future collaboration between the two political forces.

On the leadership front, moves before the Congress reflected again the difficulties of the PSOE in distancing itself from the past and starting a new post-González era. The candidate best placed to win the election to become Secretary-General, and the one that had the support of most of the party elite, was José Bono, who was at the time president of the Autonomous Community, Castilla La Mancha. Although he had never participated in any González government, both belonged to the same political generation in the eyes of public opinion. In short, Bono was not a new face.

Two of the other candidates for the post of Secretary-General were women: Rosa Díez, a popular Basque politician who had been candidate in one of the first primaries in the regional Basque PSOE, and Matilde Fernández, who had served as minister with González but belonged to the *guerristas*. Finally, the fourth contender was José Luis Rodríguez Zapatero, who had been an MP since 1986. During the PSOE's period in office he had been a backbencher, unknown to the public and even to the party. In the speech in which he presented his candidacy he concentrated on renewal, on imbuing the party with a new impetus necessary to win power. Indeed, ideological considerations were practically absent from the debate. It was more a question of generations: whether it was time that the generation that had carried out the transition to democracy and had held government positions either at the national or at the regional level during the 1980s and 1990s should give way to a new generation.[63]

Bono's narrow defeat by Zapatero (41.7 per cent of the vote to Bono's 40.8 per cent) was facilitated by the composition of the delegations and by the change of rules in the way delegates voted in party conferences in the mid-1990s. The block vote by regional delegations was removed and replaced by secret individual ballot. The new rules also hindered the control of regional delegations by the party leaders. Thus in spite of the support that central and regional-level party elites had expressed for Bono, a majority of delegates supported the candidate representing change, or at least a change of generation.

The mandate of Rodríguez Zapatero

Zapatero faced two important challenges when he became Secretary-General. First, he had to pacify the party and consolidate his leadership, proving that he was able to put an end to the González era, and, second, he had to carry out an effective opposition to the PP government and engineer a strategy that allowed the Socialists to win power.

He has proved fairly successful in achieving the first aim. Although the PSOE has not entirely revitalised party organisation, it has left behind the deep and bitter internal divisions between *guerristas* and *renovadores*. Most of the important leaders of both groups are not in the political front line any more and the labels have not really survived into the new generation. It is true that when an internal conflict breaks out the allegiances of its participants can be traced back to the earlier divisions, and then the two labels help to understand complicated combinations of interests, loyalties and choices. However, they no longer play any role in day-to-day party politics.

The developments that took place in the regional parliament of Madrid after the 2003 regional elections showed the difficulties the PSOE faced in distancing itself from the past whenever a corruption case arose implicating one of its members. This type of event reveals the vulnerability of the progress the party has made since 1996[64] and is a good illustration of the weight of the past, or rather the burden of the past. It was the first scandal for years connecting the PSOE with corruption but it proved damaging for the party because it recalled bad memories of its recent past. After the 'Madrid affair' PSOE lost the narrow advantage it enjoyed over the PP in opinion polls during the first part of 2003.

As soon as Zapatero was re-elected Secretary-General, he declared his intention to carry out an effective but constructive opposition. He promised a 'quiet change' (*el cambio tranquilo*). As a result of this style of non-confrontation, the PSOE reached pacts with the PP in several policy domains such as the reform of the judiciary and the fight against terrorism. Opposition style became more aggressive when the PP approved a large-scale reform in the educational system and, in particular, when it backed the war against Iraq.

In spite of this change in style, it is still doubtful that Zapatero managed to portray an image of an effective opposition force, or at least it was not perceived as such by the majority of Spaniards, as shown in the opinion polls (see Figure 9.3). The evaluation of the role of the PSOE in the opposition improved considerably when he was elected Secretary-General, reaching a peak six months after his election. Since then there had been ups and downs, but no significant improvement. This reveals the difficulties the new leadership found in becoming a credible alternative to the governing PP and in elaborating a party manifesto with policies that would allow the party to get back into office.

This was the context in which the PSOE, with Zapatero as Prime Ministerial candidate, confronted the 2004 general elections. Opinion polls in the months before the elections forecast a victory for the PP, now with Mariano Rajoy as candidate for Prime Minister instead of Aznar, but the margin of victory was uncertain. Opinion polls also reflected that the majority of the Spanish electorate wanted a change in the party in government (34 per cent preferred the PSOE, while 32 per cent supported the PP),[65] but a majority thought the PP would win the elections (63.4 per cent). As election day approached the margin of victory for the PP narrowed

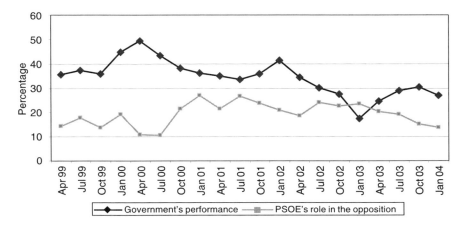

Figure 9.3 Evolution of public opinion regarding the performance of the PP in government and the role of the PSOE in opposition.

but it was always ahead of the PSOE.[66] In short, polls revealed that there was a mood for change, but this did not translate into victory for the PSOE; at least the polls published a week before election day did not anticipate such a move.

The scenario in which elections took place was transformed by the brutal terrorist attacks by al-Qaeda in Madrid on 11 March. The PSOE won the elections and obtained 164 out of 350 seats, regaining power after eight years in opposition. It is impossible to know what the results would have been like had the attack not taken place, and thus it is also difficult to ascertain its impact on voter behaviour. However, all evidence points in one direction: the way the PP government handled the situation after the attack helped increase mobilisation. Turnout was more than 8 per cent higher than in the 2000 general elections. The PP's insistence that ETA was responsible and its reluctance to release information that pointed to any other possibility mobilised an increasing number of voters, first to go out into the streets to demand information, and second to vote. Most of these voters were located on the left to centre of the ideological spectrum. Although more research is needed on this issue,[67] it is a plausible hypothesis that the terrorist attack and the subsequent events acted as a catalyst for change; that is, they were the last straw that helped mobilise voters already very critical of the PP government who would otherwise have voted for other parties rather than the PSOE, or abstained.[68]

Concluding remarks

The development of the PSOE since its reconstruction in the mid-1970s is a good example of the weight of 'genetic' models in shaping party organisation and the way the party faces new challenges. The choices made during the reconstruction of the party in the last half of the 1970s and consolidated during the 1980s weighed heavily on the party when it lost office. It is difficult to open up an organisation once it has been working for 20 years under the same set of (restrictive) rules. These rules increased internal cohesion and discipline and helped the move towards ideological moderation at the end of the 1970s. It also made the party dependent on the leadership of González. In short, these organisational traits were useful for the party on its way to power. Thus the kind of organisational strategy devised at a time when intra-party and inter-party competition was high was sustained during the 1980s when it was low. The failure to monitor party leaders and the type of organisation that resulted from these rules undermined the PSOE's ability to face the new challenges of the early 1990s.

The development of the PSOE confirms Panebianco's claim that parties slow down their organisational development once they attain power.[69] To be more precise, the party organisation continued to develop but at a decreasing speed and intensity. The PSOE represents an extreme example of the effect of governmental power on parties: extreme because the PSOE had only a short period of time after its reconstruction to develop its organisation before it assumed office. Although attaining power was a catalyst for membership growth, it also hindered the internal dynamism of party organisation and shaped its growth in a way that had diminishing returns over time. Reliance on the resources made available by government constrained the party's organisational capacity to react to new environments, particularly once it lost most of those resources (in the 1996 general elections and the 1995 regional and local elections).

The ideological evolution of the Socialists reveals an intense pragmatism that has made the party moderate its policy stances whenever it was necessary to broaden electoral support in order to attain office. This was evident in the move towards ideological moderation made at the end of the 1970s, when it became clear that this transformation was necessary if the PSOE wanted to win elections and become a governmental party without needing the support of any other party. During the 1980s the PSOE focused on carrying out policies to modernise Spain, managing to combine the support of the working class and large sectors of the middle classes. In the 1980s, unlike its social democratic counterparts in Europe, the PSOE did not face the electoral dilemma of having to choose between enlarging its support among the middle classes, jeopardising its core constituency, the working class, or keeping the support of the latter at the risk of losing its dominant position in the party system.

However, this dilemma became evident to the PSOE from the early 1990s, when it became increasingly difficult to keep the support of both the working and the middle classes. By the end of its term in office the PSOE had lost the middle ground of electoral competition, which began to be dominated by the PP. When it went into the opposition the PSOE had difficulty regaining this space while keeping the support of its core constituency. Although the IU is a small party, competition from the left also made things difficult for the PSOE, which had to take care of both the left and the middle ground when developing policy stances to gather enough support to win office.

This chapter has also shown the difficulties the PSOE faced in choosing a new leader who had the support of the party organisation, as well as the difficulties encountered by Zapatero in carrying out an effective opposition to the government of the Popular Party. The unexpected victory of the PSOE in the 2004 general elections opened up a new phase both in Spanish politics and in the development of the party.

Notes

1 A previous version of this chapter was presented in a seminar at the Cañada Blanch Centre (London School of Economics). I would thank all participants for useful comments and suggestions. I would also like to thank Sebastian Balfour for his comments and help in improving this chapter.
2 See A. Panebianco, *Political Parties: Organization and Power* (Cambridge: Cambridge University Press, 1988).
3 See J. Hopkin, 'Ideological Change in European Social Democracy: Assessing Possible Explanations', paper presented for the Political Studies Association-UK, Fiftieth Annual Conference, April 2000.
4 Maurice Duverger, *Political Parties: Their Organization and Activity in the Modern State* (New York: Methuen, 1959).
5 For a detailed account of this process, see Richard Gillespie, *The Spanish Socialist Party. A History of Factionalism* (Oxford: Oxford University Press, 1989).
6 Except in a few regional federations where the *comarca,* a sub-regional division different from the province, is taken as the basis of organisation. This is the case of the Federación Valenciana, the Catalan PSC and Galicia.
7 The other part is elected by the regional federations.
8 The names in Spanish: Congreso Federal, Comisión Ejecutiva Federal and Comité Federal.
9 Joaquín Almunia, personal interview, 14 June 1996.
10 PSOE, internal bulletin, May 1980.
11 Santos Juliá, *Los Socialistas en la política española 1879–1982* (Madrid: Taurus, 1997).
12 PSOE Party Statutes 1976, article 24. This provision remained in the Party Statutes for the whole period studied.
13 It is also important to take into account the distribution of population according to types of municipalities: 86.2 per cent of municipalities have 5,000 inhabitants or less, and represent only 16.8 per cent of the total Spanish population. Conversely, only 0.8 per cent of municipalities represent around 42 per cent of the population, in cities of more than 100,000 inhabitants (see Irene Delgado Sotillos, *Comportamiento electoral municipal* (Madrid: Centro de Investigaciones Sociológicas, 1997), p. 165). For example, Castilla León chooses half of all local representatives, since it contains nearly 28 per cent of all Spanish municipalities, but only 7 per cent of the population.
14 See Alessandro Pizzorno, 'Political Exchange and Collective Identity in Industrial Conflict', in C. Crouch and A. Pizzorno (eds), *The Resurgence of*

Class Conflict in Western Europe since 1968, vol. 2 (London: Holmes and Meier, 1978), pp. 277–98.

15 Expression used by Javier Pradera, 'Las pasiones del poder. El PSOE tras diez años de gobierno (1982–1992)', *Claves de razón práctica* 36 (1992), pp. 32–43.

16 Congress resolutions, Twenty-Seventh Party Congress, December 1976.

17 'From the elections of 15 June [1977] the party defined a strategy to become the governmental alternative. The place we occupied in the political scene and the results of the elections pointed us in this direction' (González, opening speech of the Twenty-Eighth Party Congress, May 1979).

18 Management report of the Federal Executive Committee, Twenty-Seventh Party Congress, 1976, p. 4.

19 PSOE campaign guide, 1979, p. 55.

20 'It is true that these elections [1979] did not confirm the expectations our party had' (González, opening speech of the Twenty-Eighth Party Congress, May 1979).

21 See Joaquín García Morillo, 'El desarrollo de la campaña', in Jorge De Esteban and Luis López Guerra (eds), *Las elecciones legislativas del 1 de marzo de 1979* (Madrid: Centro de Investigaciones Sociológicas, 1979), pp. 189–293 and José Félix Tezanos, 'El espacio político y sociológico del socialismo español', in *Sistema* 32 (1979), pp. 51–75.

22 Gunther cites some interviews with leaders of the UCD in which they chose this incoherence as one of the main campaign lines of the UCD against the PSOE. See Richard Gunther, 'Democratization and Party Building. The Role of Party Elites in the Spanish Transition', in Robert P. Clark and Michael H. Hatzel, *Spain in the 1980s* (Cambridge, MA: Ballinger Publishing Company, 1987), pp. 35–65.

23 'In one and a half years of political struggle we have not been able to integrate other sectors of society in our political project' (González, opening speech of the Twenty-Eighth Party Congress, May 1979).

24 José Félix Tezanos, 'Análisis sociológico del voto socialista en las elecciones de 1979', *Sistema* 31 (1979), pp. 106–21.

25 For a detailed account of the development of this Party Congress see Paul Preston, *The Triumph of Democracy in Spain* (London: Methuen, 1986), pp. 153–7 and Gillespie, *The Spanish Socialist Party*, pp. 348–56.

26 The *críticos* particularly denounced the lack of consultation before the signing of the Moncloa Pact and the intervention of the party leadership over the composition of party electoral lists.

27 Among the critics there were important personalities with a long tradition in the party such as Luis Gómez Llorente, Pablo Castellano and Francisco Bustelo.

28 Resolutions of the Twenty-Eighth Congress (1979), p. 4.

29 José Maria Maravall, 'From Opposition to Government. Politics and Policies of the PSOE', in Maravall *et al.*, *Socialist Parties in Europe* (Barcelona: Institut de Ciències Polítiques i Socials, 1991), pp. 10–11.

30 Craig also shares the same point of view: 'minimising dissent within the party was crucial for the PSOE's rise to power in the context of a post transition policy which associated fractious parties with democratic breakdown': see Patricia Craig, 'Democratization and the Emergence of the Spanish Party System: Dominant Parties and Democratic Transition', paper presented at the conference 'Party Politics in the Year 2000', Manchester 13–15 January 1995, p. 1.

31 Maravall, 'From Opposition to Government', pp. 20–2.

32 See Donald Share, *Dilemmas of Social Democracy. The Spanish Socialist Workers Party in the 1980s* (New York: Greenwood Press, 1989) and Carles Boix, *Political Parties, Growth, and Equality. Conservative and Social*

Democratic Strategies in the World Economy (New York: Cambridge University Press, 1998), pp. 148–50.

33 See, for example, the references to this question in the interviews of the Ministers of Economics, Miguel Boyer (1982–5) and Carlos Solchaga (1985–93) in Tom Burns, *Conversaciones sobre el socialismo* (Barcelona: Plaza y Janés, 1996).

34 Maravall, 'From Opposition to Government', p. 24.

35 The level of fiscal pressure as a percentage of the GDP increased from 18.4 in 1975 to 28.8 in 1985 and 34.4. in 1990. José María Maravall, *Regimes, Politics and Markets. Democratization and Economic Change in Southern and Eastern Europe* (Oxford: Oxford University Press, 1997).

36 The theme of the campaign was 'OTAN, de entrada no'. The campaign was also viewed as an opportunity to mobilise the party and the electorate for the next general elections (see Share, *Dilemmas of Social Democracy*, p. 80).

37 For a detailed account of the development of the position of the PSOE vis-à-vis NATO see José María Maravall, *Accountability and Manipulation*, Estudio/ Working Paper 1996/92, Madrid: Instituto Juan March de Estudios e Investigaciones; and Consuelo Del Val, *Opinión pública y publicada. Los españoles y el referéndum de la OTAN* (Madrid: Centro de Investigaciones Sociológicas, 1996).

38 Maravall, *Accountability and Manipulation*, p. 15.

39 Share, *Dilemmas of Social Democracy*, p. 82.

40 José María Maravall (personal interview 28 December 1995) credits the UGT with being one of the causes limiting the debate. The UGT asked the party not to deepen the debate on the issue in exchange for not positioning itself publicly against remaining in NATO.

41 According to the data of López Pintor, a third of those surveyed concluded that the most important motive for the strike was support for the unions' demands, while around 38 per cent said that strikers were intimidated by the pickets and another 20 per cent decided that the strike was in opposition to the way the Socialists were governing the country. See Rafael López Pintor, 'El sistema político español', in Miguel Juárez (ed.), *V informe sociológico sobre la situación social en España* (Madrid: Fundación Foessa, 1994), p. 591.

42 For a discussion of this dilemma see A. Przeworski and J. Sprague, *Paper Stones: The History of Electoral Socialism* (Chicago: University of Chicago Press, 1986), p. 55. For a broader perspective, including considerations of its reflection in internal party relations, see T. Koelble, 'Social Democracy between Structure and Choice', *Comparative Politics* 24/3 (1991) and T. Koelble, 'Recasting Social Democracy in Europe: A Nested Games Explanation of Strategic Adjustment in Political Parties', *Politics and Society* 20/1 (1992), pp. 51–70.

43 Most of the economic indicators are taken from an extensive report on the 1982–92 period published by *El País* on the occasion of the tenth anniversary of the 1982 elections.

44 The year 1992 was marked by the Olympic Games, which were held in Barcelona, and the World Exhibition 'Expo' in Seville.

45 See Mónica Méndez-Lago, *La estrategia organizativa del Partido Socialista Obrero Español, 1975–96* (Madrid: Centro de Investigaciones Sociológicas, 2000), chapter 5, for a detailed analysis of the membership strategy of the PSOE.

46 These differences of powers and responsibilities would be blurred later on as a result of the transfer of powers that took place at the end of the 1990s. For an analysis of the process of decentralisation and the characteristics of the Estado de las Autonomías, see Eliseo Aja, *El Estado Autonómico: federalismo y hechos diferenciales* (Madrid: Alianza Editorial, 2003).

47 See Méndez Lago, *La estrategia organizativa*, chapter 4, for an analysis of the consequences the process of decentralisation had on the way the PSOE was structured and functioned.
48 This change was introduced at the Thirty-First Party Congress. See PSOE Statutes 1988, article 9.k.
49 *El País*, 11 November 1990.
50 López Pintor, 'El sistema', signals the spring of 1992 as the turning point in what had previously been a largely favourable evaluation of the political and economic situation. Nearly one out of every two citizens considered that both political and economic conditions were bad.
51 Several authors argue that the change in the support structure of the Socialists underwent a process of 'proletarianisation' owing to the withdrawal of middle-class and blue-collar support, so that the weight of dependants or unskilled workers was higher. They agree that this was a partial result of the policies carried out by the Socialist government, particularly from 1989 onwards, prioritising pensions, health and unemployment coverage. See Juan Jesús González, 'Clases, ciudadanos y clases de ciudadanos. El ciclo electoral del post-socialismo (1986–94)', *Revista Española de Investigaciones Sociológicas* 74 (1996), pp. 45–76 and Boix, *Political Parties*.
52 As shown by the responses obtained in a post-election survey carried out in 1993 to the following question (López Pintor, 'El sistema', p. 607): 'In your opinion, what did people support in the 6 June elections, Felipe González or the PSOE?':

	Total (per cent)	PSOE (per cent)	PP (per cent)
Felipe González	73	73	75
PSOE	16	18	14
Both	6	5	6

53 The sentence 'For a change of the change' (*El cambio del cambio*) refers to the PSOE slogan in 1982 'por el cambio'.
54 An expression used by Maravall in several passages of his 1997 book.
55 Maravall, *Regimes, Politics and Markets*, p. 193.
56 PSOE Statutes 1984, article 38.
57 Belén Barreiro and Ignacio Sánchez-Cuenca, 'Análisis del cambio de voto hacia el PSOE en las elecciones de 1993', *Revista de Investigaciones Sociológicas* 82 (1998), pp. 191–211.
58 Joaquín Almunia, *Memorias políticas* (Madrid: Aguilar, 2001), p. 343.
59 Personal interview by the author with Joaquín Almunia, 14 June 1996. He was asked to give his opinion about the way the party handled the doubts of Felipe González to stand as candidate for Prime Minister in the months before the 1996 general elections. On that occasion several party leaders gathered to 'choose' potential alternatives to Felipe González.
60 For an analysis of the primary elections see the work of Carles Boix, 'Las elecciones primarias en el PSOE. Ventajas, ambigüedades y riesgos', *Claves* 83 (1998), pp. 34–8; Jonathan Hopkin, 'Bringing the Members Back In? Democratizing Candidate Selection in Britain and Spain', *Party Politics* 7/3 (2001), pp. 343–61; and Ramón Vargas Machuca, 'A vueltas con las primarias del PSOE', *Claves* 86 (1998), pp. 11–21.
61 The PP used this as an issue against the PSOE during the 2000 general election campaign, to make it appear territorially fragmented. The more the 'territorial' and, particularly, the Basque question becomes central in the political agenda, the more damaging this image can be for the PSOE. For more details on how this issue was used by the PP in the 2000 campaign see Antonia Martínez and

Mónica Méndez, 'La campaña de los partidos', in Ismael Crespo (ed.), *Las campañas electorales y sus efectos en la decisión del voto: la campaña electoral de 2000: partidos, medios de comunicación y electores* (Valencia: Tirant lo Blanch, 2003). This issue continues to be used by the PP to discredit the PSOE. The following statement of Aznar to the press is a good example: 'The problem isn't whether the nationalist parties should or should not be in the Cortes. The problem is whether national parties are ceasing to be national. Until now, there were two. Today there is only one, because it can't be said that the PSOE continues to be one', *El País*, 15 January 2004.

62 There is a certain consensus among researchers and political analysts that the pact did have a clear effect in mobilising the supporters of the PP and thus probably helped it to get the absolute majority of seats in the Congreso de los Diputados. For this thesis, see José Ignacio Wert, '12–M: ¿Lluvia o diluvio? Una interpretación de las elecciones generales', *Claves de Razón Práctica* 101 (2000), pp. 20–30.

63 For example, Rosa González started the speech in which she presented her candidacy for the position of Secretary-General stating 'I was not in Suresnes' ('Yo no estuve en Suresnes') (cited in Gonzalo López-Alba, *El relevo. Crónica viva del camino hacia el iI suresnes del PSOE* (Madrid: Taurus, 2003), p. 122.

64 Two of the regional MPs that had been elected in the regional elections of May 2003 refused to vote for the candidate of the PSOE/IU when electing the president of the regional parliament, thus making it impossible for the PSOE and the IU to form a coalition to govern the Autonomous Community of Madrid. The connection of this affair with corruption stems from the alleged connections of the two MPs with important real estate businessmen, who were in turn allegedly connected with PP leaders.

65 *Centro de Investigaciones Sociológicas*, Study 2555.

66 Even one of the most favourable surveys for the PSOE, published by *La Vanguardia* (7 March 2004), placed the PP ahead.

67 For a preliminary analysis see B. Barreiro, '14-M: elecciones a la sombra del terrorismo', *Claves de Razón Práctica* 141 (2004), pp. 14–22.

68 To the question 'Do you think that the PSOE have won the elections or that the PP has lost them?', 59.7 per cent respondents thought the latter, while 26.4 per cent thought the former: *El País* (4 April 2004).

69 Panebianco, *Political Parties*.

10 Between ambition and insecurity

Spanish politics and the Mediterranean

Richard Gillespie

The Mediterranean has become an important element in Spanish political life under the democracy established in the late 1970s. This applies to domestic politics, where the presence of a fast-growing immigrant population inevitably focuses attention on Morocco in particular. It also applies to the profile of Spain's external relations, within which the Mediterranean,[1] far from simply representing an international regional environment for Spain, has become a prominent feature of its European policy and also, in a more ambivalent way, of Spanish global ambitions. Yet the degree of priority afforded to the Mediterranean by Spain has differed over time, partly as a result of changes of government in Madrid and partly owing to challenges emanating from the South that have demanded more or less Spanish attention at different moments in time, owing to their variable potential to affect Spain's own stability and interests. Moreover, within the Mediterranean the degree of attention given by Spain has varied from country to country and from sub-region to sub-region, bilateral relations generally being cultivated more assiduously with countries of the Maghreb (Morocco, Algeria, Tunisia, Libya, Mauritania) than with most eastern Mediterranean countries.

This chapter will draw attention to the growing importance of the Mediterranean to Spain and the evolving pattern of Spanish interests in the area, while also seeking to analyse the influence of changes of government (from the Partido Socialista Obrero Español or PSOE to the Partido Popular or PP and back) upon shifts in Mediterranean policy. To what extent has this policy and its degree of prioritisation been affected by elite alternation in Spain? Has the country's Mediterranean policy become a 'policy of state', involving relatively little divergence between the parties? Perhaps it is changes in external circumstances that explain shifts in Spanish approaches to the Mediterranean, rather than the transformation of the Spanish ingredients? Finally, in addition to changes that appear to have mainly internal or external origins, what is the significance of transversal factors such as international terrorism and migration? To answer such questions, one needs to focus on Spanish policy over a period long enough to embrace several changes of government. For present purposes, in fact, we can address these questions while restricting the focus mainly to the last decade, given that Spain has seen two government alternations during that period,[2] as well as dramatic changes in the global context.

Beginning with an overview of the evolving significance of the Mediterranean for Spain, the chapter will proceed to discuss the external, domestic and transversal factors involved in this evolution. The traditional analytical procedure of differentiating between 'external' and 'internal' factors is still useful, though not always easy to maintain in the era of globalisation; thus there must be a separate discussion of transversal factors such as northward migration to Spain from the Maghreb and the challenge of international terrorism. Finally, as part of the conclusions, the chapter will comment on the degree of success of Spanish Mediterranean policy in recent years.

Patterns in Spanish diplomacy in the Mediterranean

The salient characteristic of Spanish Mediterranean policy in the early years of democracy was an effort to transform a very limited set of bilateral relationships into a regional policy. In the course of this, earlier tendencies to exploit Moroccan–Algerian rivalry in North Africa and give formal support to the Palestinian cause in the Middle East evolved towards a more comprehensive and even-handed set of diplomatic practices and postures. In this way, by the 1980s Spain was treating the Mediterranean as a coherent region. A decade later, through playing a central role in the launch of the Euro-Mediterranean Partnership (EMP), Spain then helped to commit the European Union to a region-building project. Spanish initiative here continues to be recognised implicitly in the international practice of referring to the EMP alternatively as the 'Barcelona Process'.[3] We are thus dealing with a part of the world where Spain has demonstrated considerable ambition as part of its post-Franco international re-emergence, even if the rhetoric used by the country's representatives, often decorated with perfunctory references to the work of Braudel,[4] has yet to be matched by a commensurate investment of resources. While relatively large sums of money have been involved in cooperation packages granted to certain countries of the Maghreb, these have consisted mainly of the offer of credit on advantageous terms, in some cases resulting in debt–equity swaps later on as Mediterranean partners have struggled to meet mounting debt commitments; meanwhile the level of Spanish aid has been disappointing, as has the failure to expand the country's diplomatic representation in the area.

During the Franco period, one could not really talk of there being a Mediterranean policy – more a discourse of friendship towards the Arab world (itself a romantic notion), at times purely rhetorical, at others reflecting a flurry of diplomatic activity aimed at overcoming international isolation or guaranteeing energy supplies in view of Spain's acute dependence on imported oil. Relatively little interest was shown in the eastern Mediterranean, where there were no relations with Israel; rather the main focus was the Maghreb, where there was a traditional 'fixation' with Morocco[5] and what some have described as a 'pendular' policy in response to regional rivalry between Morocco and Algeria. This referred to a Spanish tendency, when faced with difficult attitudes on the part of one southern partner, to court the other in order to apply pressure for a return to more accommodating attitudes. Of course, the transparency of such tactics hardly endeared Spain to either partner in the long run.

Departures from this pattern began to be made under the Suárez governments in the late 1970s, but became more explicit, deliberate and sustained after the election of the Socialist government in 1982. Central features of the new *política mediterránea global* developed under González included:

- A desire to become more actively involved throughout the whole Mediterranean basin, not least because of the impact of events in the eastern Mediterranean on the riparian states along its western shores. This implied the adoption of a more even-handed position on the Middle East conflict. Recognition of Israel in 1986 was required in any case for Spanish entry into the European Community, an event that also prompted Spain to adopt a foreign policy stance for the first time on issues such as the divided Cyprus.
- In the case of the Maghreb, a commitment to develop improved relations with all its countries simultaneously and even, after their proclamation of the Arab Maghreb Union in 1989, to encourage a process of regional integration among them.
- A policy of diversifying Spain's relations with these countries in particular, in order to overcome a traditionally very narrow basis of exchanges (energy imports from Algeria and Libya, phosphate imports and fishing access in the case of Morocco, and so on). The idea was to diversify the composition of trade, promote Spanish investment and engage in cooperation with the Maghreb countries in a whole range of policy sectors, thereby creating relationships of interdependence. Particularly in the case of Morocco, it was hoped that the creation of a 'cushion of interests' (*colchón de intereses*) would deter the southern neighbour from pressing further its irridentist ambitions in relation to the remaining Spanish territorial possessions in North Africa,[6] and would permit the containment of sectoral disputes in order to prevent them becoming generalised and politicised.

In addition to this new policy design, associated with foreign minister Fernando Morán (1982–5) and other diplomats with experience of Morocco, the Mediterranean policy devised by the Socialists looked increasingly to multilateral frameworks to reinforce Spanish diplomatic efforts to address some of the causes of instability in the area. A variety of Spanish initiatives designed to strengthen or complement EC/EU Mediterranean policy eventually helped bring the EMP into existence in 1995; and Spain played a role too in persuading both NATO and the Western European Union to take Mediterranean initiatives.

This policy was presented by the Socialists as a 'policy of state' (*política de estado*), reflecting national interests, and thus aimed at removing partisan preferences from the foreign policy agenda. The PSOE itself gradually abandoned its own more ideologically driven postures, moving towards pragmatic advocacy of diplomatic compromise in relation to the Middle East and the Western Sahara, while coming to terms with Spanish membership of NATO. However, the fact that José Luis Rodríguez Zapatero's nominee for foreign minister was again advocating a *política de estado* the day after the 2004 general election[7] indicates the persistence of party divergence over foreign policy. Restricting analysis just to the major parties (those capable of forming governments), it is necessary to look then at the extent to which governmental alternation between the PSOE and the PP affected Spain's Mediterranean policy.

At no time did the PP in government expressly break with or implicitly question the Mediterranean strategy developed by the Socialists; indeed, the claim of officialdom was that continuity had prevailed. Yet there did seem to be a relegation of the Mediterranean down the table of priorities of Spanish external relations in the late 1990s and loss of momentum behind the *política global*, or effort to build strong relations on a comprehensive basis. With the exception of Turkey (where excellent prospects for arms sales was to give way to much broader commercial opportunities), Spanish diplomatic effort became less active. By the time of the second Aznar government (2000–4) the traditional preoccupation with the western Mediterranean and even the 'fixation' with Morocco seemed to return. During the crisis with Morocco, which lasted from mid-2001 to early 2003, there was even a suggestion of the PP dipping into the Francoist diplomatic repertoire by resurrecting the old 'pendular' tactic of drawing closer to Algeria when faced with an uncooperative Morocco. Hence, Aznar's fêting of President Abdelaziz Bouteflika at the Euro-Mediterranean conference of foreign ministers in Valencia in April 2002, the planning of a second gas pipeline linking Spain directly with Algeria (unlike the earlier western Mediterranean pipeline, routed through Morocco) and the signing of a Spanish–Algerian friendship treaty in October 2002, upgrading the range of bilateral relations to the level achieved earlier with Morocco and Tunisia.

In fact, as will be argued below, some of the apparent 'shifts' in Spanish policy under Aznar were more apparent than real. While the transition from PSOE to PP did bring changes in the content of policy and the manner of its conduct, there was also substantial strategic continuity, particularly during the first Aznar government, as one might have expected in the absence of a new Mediterranean vision. To some extent, it was shifts in overall foreign policy ambitions that indirectly affected the Mediterranean policy. At the same time, the international, transnational and domestic constraints on the development of foreign policy changed over time and need to be factored in to analysis. With the PP less well endowed than the PSOE with leaders noted for Mediterranean sensibilities or experience, a greater deal of improvisation and *reactive* diplomacy became a hallmark of Mediterranean relations under Aznar. At the same time, the increasing importance of northward migration to Spain during these years meant that the Mediterranean could not be neglected or ignored for long in the course of concentrating on new priority areas. Immigrants from Morocco and elsewhere brought the Mediterranean into Spanish domestic politics, as well as making the question of relations with their countries of origin an unavoidable topic for diplomatic attention.

New environment, new challenges

While the Socialists' foreign policy record was widely seen as successful, there were plentiful reasons in the external environment for their Partido Popular successors to aspire to more than mere policy continuity. Spain had consolidated an influential middle-ranking position for itself within the EU context (partly through a pro-active Mediterranean policy), but had not managed to attach itself to the leading group of member states.[8] This task seemed rather more daunting when seen in the perspective of the forthcoming eastern enlargement. At the same time, the country's modernisation and economic growth also encouraged a focus on wider horizons, as did the reality of an increasingly global economy and the dynamism of both business and defence links to the United States. In this context, a more pronounced Atlanticism came to feature in the foreign policy orientations of the PP,[9] seen as key to future Spanish membership of the Group of 8. Here there was a concentration of effort not only on drawing closer to Washington but also around exploiting historical and cultural links in order to establish a major Spanish multinational presence in Latin America. Meanwhile, Madrid's efforts to establish a more globally comprehensive reach for Spanish external relations[10] were seen in diplomatic activity and commercial promotion aimed at selected countries of central and eastern Europe and Asia (with decidedly modest results).

Thus, without taking a deliberate decision to downgrade the Mediterranean effort, the Aznar administration inevitably deprived the latter of much of its energy purely because it attempted to do more elsewhere without there being a significant increase in diplomatic resources. The only Mediterranean policy innovation made during the first Aznar government was the use of debt–equity swaps in relations with countries of the Maghreb,[11] yet these were already being mooted within government ministries under González. At the same time, there is a sense in which Madrid was obliged to ease off the accelerator (if not transfer to the back seat of the Mediterranean vehicle) as a result of renewed conflict in the Middle East. If the Oslo Accords had been a crucial facilitator of the launch of the EMP, the gradual breakdown of the Middle East peace process

(MEPP) from 1996 brought great difficulties and moments of crisis into the Barcelona Process, and particularly its multilateral dimension. Neither Spain, France nor any other European country was able to compensate for the extent to which the return to violence in the Near East undermined a project involving both Israelis and Arabs. Indeed, it was hardly in any country's interest to appear responsible for the EMP as it stumbled and lost momentum. Spain did what little it could to help revive the MEPP – offering Madrid (as in 1992) as the venue for another international peace conference – but soon was to discover the limitations of European initiatives to end this conflict.[12]

In the longer run, however, the damage wrought to the Barcelona Process by the revival of Israeli–Palestinian violence did lead to fresh Mediterranean initiatives on the part of Spain. With 'sub-regional' cooperation being encouraged by the European Commission as a means of side-stepping the Middle East problem, Spanish attention was stimulated once more in the western Mediterranean and acquired a new vigour following the shock of 9/11 amid perceptions of an urgent need to act to avoid a Huntington-style 'clash of civilisations' scenario. Along with efforts to establish security cooperation among the states of the western Mediterranean and Spanish enlistment in the US 'war on terror', Spain followed Sweden in seeing the need to add flesh to the initially skeletal cultural component of the EMP; this was to be done through reinforcing Euro-Mediterranean cultural cooperation projects and establishing a foundation to ensure a more sustained approach to 'dialogue between cultures'. Spain had the oppor-tunity to introduce the new initiative itself owing to the coincidence of its third EU presidency (during the first half of 2002) with a new mood among European and Mediterranean partner countries, anxious to address at least some of the underlying causes behind al-Qaeda terrorism and not merely see this challenge as a war. Thus, after meeting European resistance to initial Spanish lobbying for the creation of a new Euro-Mediterranean bank, Madrid's big idea for the Valencia Conference (where it was approved) was the creation of a Euro-Mediterranean Foundation for dialogue between cultures.[13]

Mediterranean activism on the part of Spain was also dictated at this time by developments in the external environment closer to home, across the straits of Gibraltar. The death of King Hassan II in July 1999 brought hopes in Madrid of improved relations with Morocco under Mohamed VI. The Spanish authorities made every effort to create the right environment in which a privileged relationship might be established during the young king's visit to Spain in September 2000, offering him the rare privilege of addressing the Cortes and also planning a special reception for him in Granada (the historical capital of *al-Andalus*) – only to be dismayed when signals came back from Rabat indicating that more modest and less public arrangements were preferred.[14] Thereafter, the growing importance of Morocco on the Spanish policy agenda became a reflection of the deterioration in the bilateral relationship, its milestones being formed by the termination of fisheries negotiations between Brussels and Rabat in April 2001 (with both Spain and Morocco blaming the other for the exclusion of Spanish vessels from Atlantic fishing grounds off Morocco and Western Sahara), the sudden withdrawal of the Moroccan ambassador from Madrid the following October and the successive Moroccan and Spanish occupations of Parsley Island (near Ceuta) the following July. Though the reasons for the crisis in Spanish–Moroccan relations are too complex to be fully addressed here,[15] two of the motives behind greater Moroccan assertiveness vis-à-vis Spain were, first, the conviction that growing international support for Moroccan annexation of Western Sahara was leaving Spain more isolated as the only major European obstacle to final victory, and, second, the apparent breakthrough in British–Spanish talks on the future of Gibraltar in 2001–2, which encouraged Rabat to see here a possible model for achieving sovereignty over Ceuta and Melilla. It is arguable that Morocco, under a new king surrounded by mostly new advisers, misread the signs in both of these (linked) cases and that feelings of grievance towards Spain resulted from the dashing of artificially raised hopes – though this would be far from the whole story.

Whatever the full interpretation of this episode of deterioration, crisis and attempts to rebuild the Hispano-Moroccan relationship, it did help to bring the Mediterranean back into the picture of Spanish external relations – not only because Morocco again loomed large but also because diversification of Spanish relations in the Maghreb again acquired urgency. On the surface, there seemed to be a return to the old Francoist policy of Madrid dealing with Moroccan pressure tactics by moving closer to Algiers, and this was indeed how many Moroccans viewed developments at this time.[16] Yet, while there may have been some reactive impulse behind Aznar's courtship of Bouteflika, the circumstantial evidence (as well as the claims of Spanish diplomats) points to Spanish initiatives reflecting the 'global' Mediterranean strategy pursued by the Socialists earlier. To misconstrue the triangular Spain–Morocco–Algeria dynamics to suggest a change of allies by Madrid would be to ignore the extent to which Mediterranean policy, regardless of government, is largely delegated to the Ministry of Foreign Affairs, with the Moncloa (Prime Minister's Office) only involved when a major crisis blows up or a prime ministerial visit is being prepared. With greater North Africa expertise present in the Ministry than in the Moncloa, the more sensible strategy of working simultaneously for improved relations with all Maghrebi countries continued and, moreover, had an opportunity to prosper once more, now that the Algerian conflict of the 1990s was largely over and attempts to 'normalise' political life through permitting a degree of pluralism were under way. Algeria remained very important as a source of Spanish natural gas imports, and there was also some Spanish multinational interest in infrastructural projects. Besides, cooperation between Madrid and Algiers was facilitated now by a more pragmatic Algerian attitude towards the Western Sahara issue and by the North African country finally reaching agreement with the European Union on a Euro-Mediterranean association agreement (signed at the Valencia Conference).

This interpretation is also supported by the general pattern of Mediterranean activity during the final years of the Aznar government, which saw broader Spanish efforts to revive western Mediterranean cooperation through the 5 + 5 grouping (France, Portugal, Spain, Italy, Malta + Mauritania, Morocco, Algeria, Tunisia, Libya) and individual attention to the various countries of the wider Maghreb, including Libya. In September 2003, Aznar became the first European prime minister post-Lockerbie to visit Tripoli to encourage Libya to join the EMP following the lifting of UN sanctions; four months earlier, the oil company Repsol YPF had announced the investment of €75 million in exploration with the National Oil Company of Libya. The old, simplistic and never successful pendular strategy had in fact long been buried. Even during the period of poor relations with Morocco, economic relations had remained largely unaffected and it is worth noting too that Spain refrained from trying to use its presidency of the EU Council in 2002 as an opportunity to apply pressure to Morocco (for example, by thwarting the changes sought by Rabat to its association agreement, or by blocking the idea of an improved 'neighbourhood' status for Morocco vis-à-vis the EU).

Domestic politics and the Mediterranean

Spain's Mediterranean policy under Aznar was also affected by the social and electoral base of the PP, its standing in domestic political life, its ideological orientations, public opinion and the personality of the prime minister. By 1996 the PP had become a credible electoral option via a strategy of presenting itself as a party of the 'centre' while continuing to appeal to conservatives as the only alternative to the left. Yet while many of its policies were moderate, the right-wing origins of the party were frequently in evidence, with traditional Africanista sentiments being echoed by party representatives, harbouring old colonial attitudes towards Moroccans in particular.[17] At the same time, the traditional economic interests supporting the PP were taken into account in the party's early determination to retain access to fishing grounds controlled by Morocco (among others, important to fishermen from the PP fiefdom of Galicia). Moreover, by physically obstructing the transport of Moroccan produce arriving by sea, agricultural producers of Mediterranean products had some success in campaigning for continued national protection against southern competition. The PP's undiluted support for the virtues of capitalism meanwhile led to a new emphasis on the economic aspects of foreign policy, an orientation that had some bearing on its foreign policy priorities, given that investment markets in North Africa were seen as highly problematic.

However, the PP did not invariably seek to serve its conservative constituency. Lacking a competitor on the far right, needing to compete with the PSOE for the centre vote and lacking an absolute majority in parliament during its first government (1996–2000), the PP pursued moderate, conciliatory policies in several areas. It was reliant on parliamentary support from other parties, above all the Catalan nationalists (CiU) of Jordi Pujol who had long defended the idea of Spain projecting influence in the Mediterranean. It was because of the PP's need to deal with other parliamentary parties (and owing also to tactical miscalculations) that, at the end of the first Aznar administration, Spain saw the introduction of the most progressive immigration law[18] in the European Union – this at a time of fast-rising immigration, much of it outside legal channels. The achievement of an absolute PP majority in March 2000 led to the immediate reversal of the law and further restrictions thereafter, combined with a clear official preference being shown for Latin American and eastern European migrants over southern migrants, seen as harder to integrate for cultural reasons. Besides pandering to popular prejudice, the PP government was concerned that Spain might see the entry of the far right into domestic politics, especially after the outburst of violence against Moroccan immigrants in El Ejido in February 2000. Spurred too by increases in the number of immigrants trying to reach the shores of Spain undetected, by boat, there were impatient government demands that Morocco do more to regulate the passage of its citizens and sub-Saharan Africans en route to Spain.

Certainly for immigration policy the year 2000 was a much more decisive turning point than 1996. The ideology and social base of the PP found reflection in a new intransigence (and ultimately in militarism) in dealing with Morocco in 2001–2, before the depth of the bilateral crisis led finally to a return to a more conciliatory approach on both sides. With public concern about law and order becoming salient at this time, Aznar on occasion had no compunction about trying to associate rising crime rates with 'illegal' immigrants, thus feeding strong xenophobic currents in Spanish society, where prejudices are strongest against Arabs and *moros*.[19] At the same time, hard-line tendencies were questioned occasionally by other voices. Within the foreign ministry, for example, Miquel Nadal, while secretary of state for foreign affairs, made the case for making commercial concessions to Moroccan produce in order to help stabilise the southern neighbour's economy and in the interests of reviving the ailing EMP;[20] and there were also moderating EU influences, which during the Spanish presidency blocked the Blair–Aznar proposals to punish third countries that failed to regulate migration to Europe adequately.

The PP proved highly attentive to public opinion polls, with the major exception of its policy of going to war in Iraq in support of the US-led coalition. Majority opposition to this policy failed to deter Aznar, who must have felt vindicated when subsequent local and regional elections brought the PP considerable success in spring 2003. His Iraq policy reflected the centrality of Aznar's strategy of alignment with the United States, further encouraged by a sense of enhanced national opportunity to be derived from it in the aftermath of 9/11. Concern that Spanish military involvement in Iraq would have adverse consequences for relations with Arab countries proved exaggerated, at least at the level of intergovernmental relations, given that many Arab regimes were using the 'war against terror' themselves to clamp down on radical Islamist movements at home. In contrast, there is evidence that the Spanish authorities have felt constrained by the strength of societal sympathy for Polisario (the national liberation front of the Saharans), at least to the extent of accepting that a simple pro-Moroccan solution to the problem of Western Sahara (as advocated by France) was unacceptable and of maintaining that the future lay in a UN-negotiated compromise acceptable to all parties to the dispute. Another case in which active civil society campaigning and press interest may have led the government to take action in an atypical way was in 2003 when representations were made to Morocco over the imprisonment of journalist Ali Lmrabet.[21]

One must note too here the effect on relations with Mediterranean partners of the personalities representing Spain. The first two foreign ministers, Abel Matutes and Josep Piqué, were both linked to the world of business, but the latter showed decidedly more commitment to Mediterranean diplomacy than the former. Matutes was a less assiduous visitor to Morocco than his socialist predecessors; while still industry minister and government spokesman in the Aznar government, even Piqué travelled there more regularly.[22] The third foreign minister, Ana Palacio, appointed shortly before the Moroccan occupation of Parsley Island, was arguably the most pragmatic of the three, lacking new ideas for the Mediterranean but temperamentally well suited to the task of rebuilding bridges with the southern neighbour.

The same cannot be said for the personality of prime minister Aznar, which proved a seriously negative factor in the deterioration of bilateral relations with Morocco in 2001–2. Both the Moroccan press and the country's diplomats make unfavourable comparisons between him and González insofar as dealings with Morocco were concerned. Despite their contrasting political orientations, an effective personal chemistry had existed between Felipe González and King Hassan, perhaps owing something to the former's Andalusian origins and Mediterranean interest. In the case of Aznar and the young King Mohamed VI, not only was this absent (and worse still for Spain, present between Mohamed VI and the French president, Jacques Chirac), but there were negative perceptions of the 'other' as well. Aznar is said to have been disappointed in the new Moroccan ruler, seen as a weak and inconsistent king, still something of a playboy, not entirely devoted to the development of his country. During the sensitive EU–Morocco fishing negotiation of 2000–1, the Spanish prime minister believed that he had been given Mohamed's personal assurance that Spanish interests would be safeguarded, and he was furious when it became clear that there would be no renewal of the agreement (at least not on terms acceptable to Spain).[23] Thereafter came the oft-cited Aznar declaration that the failure of the negotiation would have 'consequences' for Morocco.[24] Although the government does not in fact seem to have delivered on its threat of reprisal, either in the bilateral or multilateral context, the pejorative discourse (incorporating negative references to immigrants as well) certainly helped to poison relations between Madrid and Rabat. The Moroccan perception was of an arrogant, totally unsympathetic Castilian leader, trying to bully his southern interlocutors into compliance, an image fuelled by the recourse to military force to remove the Moroccan gendarmes from Parsley Island in July 2002. Such impressions need to be seen against a backcloth of prejudice and misunderstanding on both sides, rooted in history[25] but still reflected in press coverage on both sides. Within this broader context, however, the personality of leading individuals, above and beyond the institutions they represent, has had a bearing on the climate in which diplomatic initiatives have been developed. The replacement of Aznar by Zapatero following the March 2004 election was warmly welcomed by the Moroccan press, which referred to the superior relations that had existed in the González era, the presence of Mediterranean experts in the new Socialist team and the good disposition of the new prime minister.[26]

Transversal influences on Mediterranean policy

All these domestic factors have influenced the content of Spanish Mediterranean policy and particularly that relating to Morocco, the closest non-European Mediterranean partner in geographical, historical and – in some respects – cultural terms. Unlike some other Mediterranean countries, Morocco was not one that could simply be prioritised or deprioritised by Spain: it was one that – even when Madrid was trying to reduce its reliance on cooperation with Rabat – forced its attention on Spanish policy-makers because of the way in which external–domestic divisions were eroding. Migratory movements, within the space of a decade, had become a major political issue by the late 1990s, and by 2004 Moroccans accounted for more than one-fifth of the growing immigrant population of 2.5 million).[27] The second PP government's determination to draw a firm line between legal and illegal immigrants, its increasingly tough measures against those without papers (which failed to deter their growth) and the lack of government investment in social integration measures even for legal immigrants, all had negative import for official (and societal) Spanish–Moroccan relations, as did Madrid's insistence that Morocco could do much more to police illegal migration. To this claim, Moroccan officials replied that they were doing as much as their resources permitted – a refrain that ignored the relevance of other factors such as official and police corruption.

Spanish official declarations on illegal Moroccan immigration gave the impression of Moroccans as poor, desperate and prone to crime, and thus a real threat to the lives as well as the livelihoods of Spaniards.[28] To the extent that there was also a positive government discourse on immigration, citing the real needs of the economy and the problem represented by an ageing indigenous population for the sustainability of the country's welfare system, this always seemed to relate to immigration in general and never to the qualities of Moroccan workers in particular.

The other transversal factor that forced the Mediterranean back more onto the Spanish foreign policy agenda was the new phenomenon of global yet decentralised terrorism, associated with al-Qaeda. As mentioned earlier, 9/11 brought responses in the domains of both security policy and cultural dialogue as Spain pressed for greater coordination between interior ministries and initiatives to avoid polarisation between Islamic countries and the West. The feeling of being attacked by the same enemy began to draw Spain and Morocco closer following the successive Casablanca and Madrid bombings in May 2003 and March 2004. At least this was the impression given by official declarations on both sides; how much substance there was to this remains unclear. After the horrific devastation in Madrid, some reports suggested that the Spanish security services had proved disastrously distrustful of Moroccan intelligence reports on the threat from extremist Moroccan elements in Spain.[29]

It is too early to assess the full political fallout from the bombs in Madrid, their international repercussions and the Socialists' return to power under Zapatero in 2004. With policy towards Iraq changing and a new political team taking charge, there were new opportunities for a more vigorous Mediterranean policy to be pursued by Spain, seeking to influence the southern dimension of the new EU Neighbourhood Policy. Morocco showed real enthusiasm for this new European project, while many other Mediterranean countries remained sceptical. One of the key questions for the future will be whether new Spanish policies towards immigration (putting resources into social integration and regularising 'illegals' for whom there is work) will help make this area one of sustained cooperation with Morocco, with material assistance from the European Union. The concern must be that, whatever the outlook for immigration in general, the attitudes of Spain's indigenous population towards Moroccan residents will grow even more distrustful following the way in which their nationality has been associated with authorship of the Madrid bombings through the arrest of Moroccan suspects.

A Spanish success story?

Spain has enjoyed some celebrated Mediterranean successes, from hosting the Middle East Peace Conference in Madrid in 1992 to the Barcelona Conference of 1995. Although it was never the sole protagonist, Spain appeared on these occasions to play a constructive, influential international role in a way that would have been unimaginable during the Franco era.

From 1996, a variety of factors conspired to, first, relegate and, later, re-promote the Mediterranean on the Spanish policy agenda during the Aznar governments. The latter were devoid of a new strategic vision, but a degree of continuity with the González era was provided by the diplomatic service, whose members at least deserve some credit for the achievements of the Valencia Conference, after the preceding EMP foreign ministers' meetings had registered little progress. There have been some far less publicised success stories too. Economic links with Turkey have expanded to exceed the growing links with Morocco, and could prove extremely valuable to Spain in the future.[30] But the bottom line for Spain in the Mediterranean has always been security.[31] It has been the national interest in a stable Mediter-ranean, and a variety of security considerations, that have driven Spanish Mediterranean policy – not so much the prospect of conquering markets, which has always seemed more of a lure in other parts of the world. In this regard, the key bilateral interlocutor for Spain is still Morocco. While the 'global' Mediterranean strategy remains an essential complement to this bilateral relationship, Spain has in fact become more reliant on cooperation with Morocco through the growth in immigration from the South. Other relationships have developed but Morocco, as González has always insisted, continues to require special attention, both as a neighbour and as the only country seriously making claims to sovereignty over Spanish territory.[32]

The serious setback to Spain's relations with Morocco represented by the events of 2001–2 had been repaired only at a superficial level by the end of the Aznar administration, albeit with some expansion of dialogue as part of the process of reconciliation.[33] In relation to the strategy of developing a *colchón de intereses*, however, the dispute denoted only a partial failure: on the one hand, the preceding effort in the 1980s and 1990s to increase and diversify Hispano-Moroccan relations did not prevent the use of force during the struggle over Parsley Island; from Madrid's perspective these efforts had not dissuaded Morocco from applying pressure to advance its territorial objectives, and neither did they deter Spain from sending troops to evict the Moroccan occupiers. On the other hand, while the crisis in bilateral relations adversely affected university exchange schemes, Spanish develop-ment projects in northern Morocco and inter-cultural activities, the suc-cession of diplomatic hostilities did not affect economic relations between the two countries, for trade and investment continued undisturbed.[34]

What of the rise of the new transnational terrorism that has come to overshadow the security threat from ETA? Does this reflect adversely on the policies developed by Spain in relation to the Mediterranean? To the extent that al-Qaeda violence is linked to injustices in the Middle East, it is evident that no single European country has the ability to effectively deliver or even promote solutions. On the other hand, Spain under the PP did attract explicit al-Qaeda condemnation through its military involvement in Iraq. To the extent that the new terrorist variety is linked to economic injustice, Spain could certainly be faulted for not helping to address the growing North–South divide across the Mediterranean.[35] Despite its own economic strides since the 1980s, the spread of prosperity to a growing proportion of the Spanish population and the achievement of becoming a net exporter of capital under Aznar,[36] Spain's contribution to aiding poorer countries to develop is among the weakest in the EU-15.[37] Moreover, in terms of international cooperation to counter the activity of transnational terrorist organisations at the level of police and security measures, it is fairly clear that more could have been done (whether enough, is another question), had it not been for the lack of trust and respect between the Spanish and Moroccan authorities, so palpable during the dispute of 2001–3.[38]

Such is the balance of an attempt to weigh up the achievements and short-comings of Spain's own initiatives. For a more rounded view, it is also pertinent to compare Spanish performance with that of other countries, especially the Mediterranean member states of the European Union. Of course, every achievement involving the European Union is collective up to a point and requires coalitions to be built in support of initiatives, yet Spain must be credited with rather more achievement within the EMP than any other potential Mediterranean champion thus far. Although, at the bilateral level, France under Chirac enjoyed generally better relations in the Maghreb than did Spain under Aznar, at the multilateral level neither France nor Italy have achieved the kinds of steps forward taken under different Spanish governments at the Barcelona and Valencia conferences and directly associated with Spanish initiative (although with important preparatory work done by the European Commission as well).

Fresh opportunities arose with the arrival of a new government in Spain in spring 2004, coinciding with closer integration being offered to southern Mediterranean countries as part of the European Union's new Neighbour-hood strategy. These developments came at a time of new challenges too, most dramatically that from groups inspired by al-Qaeda but also from the eastern enlargement of the EU, which had already started to divert foreign investment from Spain to central and eastern Europe; this enlargement seems likely to make it harder for the southern European countries to ensure that more EU resources will be committed to the Mediterranean in the face of competing demands on funds required to narrow the east–west gulf within Europe. If, as announced, the PSOE under Zapatero reverts to an emphasis on Spanish alignment with strong European partners, and places less reliance on Atlanticism, this could favour the articulation of a more effective EU Mediterranean/Middle East policy, especially if Spain and France can overcome their latent rivalry and push together within the European Union in this direction. However, the issue of Spain's retention of a major share of European cohesion funding is bound to be an issue in any bid to boost European spending on Mediterranean policy. It is also possible that, in part owing to the difficulty it has had in dealing with Morocco, Spain will play a less conservative role and start to promote regime change in a more decisive way as part of its future Mediterranean policy.[39] This would be necessary anyway in order to bring central and eastern European countries on board for a reinforced European Mediterranean policy, and it would be in line too with the new EU Neighbourhood Policy's emphasis on political conditionality.

With the eastern enlargement now a reality and with the United States ambitiously developing a new strategy for the 'Greater Middle East', Spanish Mediterranean policy in the future will need to be coherent with a global outlook and not simply, as twenty years ago, triangulated with European policy. It will need to be accompanied, however, by the careful cultivation of a more constructive relationship with its immediate southern neighbour. This challenge, which is one for Spanish society as much as the Spanish state, remains one of the most difficult ones that the country faces.

Notes

This chapter is based partly on research funded by the Economic and Social Research Council of the UK on 'The Spanish–Moroccan Security Relationship and the Euro-Mediterranean Context' (ref. RES-000-22-0432).

1 Here we follow the practice of Spanish policy-makers in using the term 'Mediterranean' to refer just to the countries along the southern and eastern shores of the Mediterranean Sea.
2 Discussion of the significance of regime change from dictatorship to democracy formed part of my book *Spain and the Mediterranean: Developing a European Policy towards the South* (Basingstoke: Macmillan, 2000); so too did analysis of the degree of change resulting from successive government changes, from UCD to PSOE to PP. However, that work only reflected the early stages of PP government, whereas now one can take stock of the entire period of government under Aznar. For a useful set of essays on the twentieth-century historical background, see Raanan Rein (ed.), *Spain and the Mediterranean since 1898* (London: Frank Cass, 1999).
3 In fact, this attempt to build a partnership between the EU countries and their Mediterranean neighbours involves a degree of ambiguity as to which international region is being built: on the one hand, a Euro-Mediterranean entity, primarily through a free trade area; on the other hand, a more geographically based Mediterranean entity through efforts at horizontal integration, albeit with a very significant EU/non-EU divide in the Mediterranean basin.
4 Fernand Braudel, *The Mediterranean and the Mediterranean World in the Age of Phillip II*, 2 vols. (New York: Harper and Row, 1972).
5 Fernando Morán, *Una poltica exterior para España* (Barcelona: Planeta, 1980), p. 196.
6 Successive transfers of North African territory since 1956 had left Spain by the late 1970s with just the small cities of Ceuta and Melilla, as well as a number of rocks and small islands off the Mediterranean coast of Morocco.
7 Miguel Angel Moratinos, 'Una nueva política exterior para España', Real Instituto Elcano, ARI (Análisis del Real Instituto), 37 (13 March 2004). The PSOE argument would be that the search for consensus had broken down as a result of the PP's policy of unconditional alignment with the United States, particularly following the election of George W. Bush, leading to fundamental party divergence over Iraq. Earlier, the PP's clearest pursuit of an ideological foreign policy was seen in the first Aznar government's hostility towards the Castro regime in Cuba.

8 Richard Gillespie, 'Spain and the Mediterranean: Southern Sensitivity, European Aspirations', *Mediterranean Politics* 1/2 (1996).

9 Richard Gillespie, 'Lidiando con la ambición: la política exterior y de seguridad de España al inicio del muevo milenio', in *Anuario Internacional CIDOB 2001* (Barcelona: Centre d'Informació i Documentació a Barcelona, 2002); Paul Heywood, 'Desperately Seeking Influence: Spain and the War in Iraq', *EPS* 3/1 (2003).

10 Elvira Sánchez Mateos, 'Camino viejo y sendero nuevo: ¿España, hacia una política exterior global?', in *Anuario Internacional CIDOB 2000* (Barcelona: Centre d'Informació i Documentació a Barcelona, 2001).

11 Jesús A. Núñez Villaverde, 'The Mediterranean: A Firm Priority of Spanish Foreign Policy', in Richard Gillespie and Richard Youngs (eds), *Spain: The European and International Challenges* (London: Frank Cass, 2001).

12 Of course Spain did provide two of the leading EU representatives dealing with the Middle East: Javier Solana (EU high representative for the Common Foreign and Security Policy) and Miguel Angel Moratinos (special envoy to the Middle East).

13 Richard Gillespie, 'Reshaping the Agenda? The Internal Politics of the Barcelona Process in the Aftermath of September 11', in Annette Jünemann (ed.), *Euro-Mediterranean Relations After September 11* (London: Frank Cass, 2003).

14 Spanish speculation about the reasons for this rebuff pointed to Moroccan anxiety that the new king might be faced with Spanish demonstrations of opposition to Morocco's occupation of Western Sahara, even involving some members of the Spanish parliament.

15 For Spanish and Moroccan views of the episode, see Miguel Hernando de Larramendi, 'España-Marruecos: una vecindad compleja' and Mustapha Sehimi, 'Marruecos-España: ¿qué normalización?', both in *Afkar/Ideas* 1 (2003).

16 Personal interviews with several Moroccan diplomats, 2003–4.

17 The original Africanistas were the people involved in the Spanish colonial presence in Morocco. Although both enlightened and militaristic currents emerged among them, there was a shared sense of superiority in relation to the North African population. See Sebastian Balfour, *Deadly Embrace: Morocco and the Road to the Spanish Civil War* (Oxford: Oxford University Press, 2002), *passim*.

18 'Progressive' mainly in terms of the rights it conferred on even 'illegal' immigrants.

19 See the regular polls conducted by the Centro de Investigaciones Sociológicas on 'Immigration and Racism'.

20 Miguel Nadal, '¿Mare Nostrum?', *El País*, 26 July 2001. Eventually Aznar's government did support partial EU agricultural concessions to Morocco in October 2003, mainly relating to tomatoes.

21 The circumstances surrounding this rare example of Spain taking up a human rights case with Morocco were unusual though: Lmrabet had a Spanish partner; and Colin Powell seems to have made representations to Mohamed VI a few days before Aznar did.

22 *El País*, 13 August and 15 November 1999.

23 Interview with senior Spanish Foreign Ministry official, December 2003.

24 *El País*, 18 May 2001.

25 See Balfour, *Deadly Embrace*, chapter 7 on 'The Moorish Other'; and Domingo del Pino, 'España y el Magreb: Percepciones mutuas de geometría variable', *Cuadernos de Estrategia* 106 (Madrid: Ministerio de Defensa, 2000), special issue on the Maghreb.

26 See, for example, 'Une aubaine pour les relations hispano-marocaines', *La Vie*

Économique (Casablanca), 23 March 2004, which refers to the 'arrogance' of Aznar.

27 *El País*, 11 April 2004.

28 In fact, as Aboubakr Jamaï, editor of the Moroccan weekly *Le Journal*, commented (during a seminar at the Bertelsmann Foundation, Berlin, November 2003), the amount of money that Moroccans need to pay to mafias in order to be transported to Spain by boat means that it is by no means the poorest people who emigrate: rather those who have qualifications or work experience.

29 *L'Économiste* (Casablanca), 19 March 2004.

30 Interview with Xavier Albarracin i Corredor, Consorci de Promoció Comercial de Catalunya (COPCA), Barcelona, 14 November 2003. See too Núñez, 'The Mediterranean', pp. 138–9.

31 Richard Gillespie, 'Spain's Pursuit of Security in the Western Mediterranean', *European Security* 11/2 (2002).

32 One of González's earliest marks on Spanish foreign policy was the institution of annual summit meetings with neighbours France, Portugal and Morocco, though with the latter he had the same difficulty as Aznar in ensuring that such meetings would actually be held each year, given the potential for specific disagreements to contaminate relations in general.

33 During 2003, a working group was established to discuss the issue of territorial waters, for the first time, but Ceuta and Melilla remained taboo subjects (Hernando de Larramendi, 'España-Marruecos', p. 51).

34 Ministerio de Economía, trade and investment data, available at: http://www. mcx.es/POLCOMER/ESTUDIOS/sectex/sectext.htm and http://www. mcx.es/sgcomex/Estadisticas.htm.

35 Iñigo Moré, 'The Economic Step Between Neighbours: The Case of Spain-Morocco', *Mediterranean Politics* 9/3 (2004).

36 William Chislett, 'España se mueve', *Metro* (Madrid), 3 February 2004.

37 The PSOE election pledge in 2004 was to increase this from 0.25 per cent of GDP to 0.5 per cent by the end of the legislature and thereafter to 0.7 per cent by 2012 if re-elected (*El País*, 10 February 2004).

38 Bernabé López García, 'Hipótesis, exégesis y certezas', *El País*, 24 March 2004; *El Mundo*, 23 March 2004.

39 On the lack of Spanish support for democracy promotion in the past, see Bernabé López García and Miguel Hernando de Larramendi, 'Spain and North Africa: Towards a "Dynamic Stability"', in Richard Gillespie and Richard Youngs (eds), *The European Union and Democracy Promotion: The Case of North Africa* (London: Frank Cass, 2002).

11 Spain in the new European Union

In search of a new role and identity

Mary Farrell

Introduction

Throughout the years since its accession to the European Union (EU), Spain was both an ardent supporter of integration and a major beneficiary of its largesse, largely through the Structural and Cohesion Funds. Entry to the European club was in fact a high point of the long post-Franco transition period, marking the culmination of the reformist aspirations of the previous decade. Membership was to consolidate a process of political and economic modernisation envisaged in the principles and aspirations of the Spanish Constitution approved in 1978.

The newly created social democratic state was constructed in part around the notion of the myth of Europe, which epitomised everything that was modern. Among those who shared the myth was the belief that Spain must rejoin Europe, which was critical to the reinvention of a democratic consciousness.[1] Even before accession to the EU, national political elites identified the national interest with European interests.[2] This particular perception of Spain's interest was reflected in the linkage between national identity and European identity. Subsequently, political discourse centred upon bringing together national identity and European common interests to legitimise domestic policy and the requisite adaptation to European institutional frameworks. Both the Socialist-led government and its successor the Partido Popular (PP) government of José María Aznar made references to such legitimising discourse.

However, cleavages emerged in the hitherto solid support for European integration during the 1990s. The cleavage in Spain's position with regard to that of its European partners was especially evident during 2003 as the United States declared war on Iraq. As the US-UK alliance opted for military action against the regime of Saddam Hussein in opposition to the United Nations and many Western governments, Aznar threw his support overwhelmingly behind the alliance. He did so without the support of the other political parties in Spain or that of popular opinion.

Other sources of tension emerged during the period of the Aznar government (1996–2004), particularly over European Union issues.[3] Increasingly the Spanish government showed itself to be at odds with aspects of EU policy and politics. In the discussions prior to and after the European Convention, the government was less than enthusiastic about the entire process of the Convention and the draft constitutional treaty produced under the chairmanship of Valéry Giscard d'Estaing.

Aside from the Convention and its outcome, the other major aspect of European integration to give cause for concern was the eastern enlargement of the European Union. The accession of ten new member states from eastern and southern Europe shifts the focus of policy eastwards and moves the central heartland of Europe away from the western flank, leaving the Iberian peninsula on the periphery.

This is the background against which tensions emerged in Spain–EU relations. These tensions and cleavages may in one sense be seen as temporary in the relations between the European Union and one of its member states, aggravated by singular circumstances in international politics and geo-strategic forces. But, at a more fundamental level, the differences between Spanish policy and political aspirations constitute a new point of departure with more far-reaching implications for how Spain defines its role within the European Union and in the wider world.[4]

This chapter goes beyond the question of whether Aznar was a new European or an Atlanticist to consider the broader context within which national policies and strategies must be developed in the EU-25. The argument of this chapter is that recent tensions in Spain–EU relations extend beyond personalities and contemporary events in international politics, and go to the heart of Spain's search for identity in the new European Union.

The argument is developed over the following sections, beginning with a review of politics and EU relations under Aznar during the 1996–2003 period. Abroad, the prime minister sought to develop an international presence for Spain on the global stage, and the chapter looks at some of the reasons for this shift of emphasis in Spanish policy. The chapter considers what particular challenges are likely to arise for Spain with the accession of ten smaller and much poorer countries, as the new member states undoubtedly constitute a competitive challenge for Spanish economic interests, with lower labour costs and other indirect costs that attract foreign direct investment away from countries such as Spain.

At home, the unity of the Spanish state has come under increasing pressure from the regional communities, particularly since the beginning of the 1990s. One possible result of the escalating demands for greater regional autonomy is that the national Constitution, regarded as the bedrock of the democratic state and the linchpin of national unity in the post-transition phase of the new state, might have to be rewritten, at least in part. However, throughout the term of office of the PP government, the central government was very firmly opposed to any discussion on constitutional reform, despite frequent internal tensions between the regional and central levels of government, with claims for greater autonomy in the Basque country and Catalonia straining the system of national unity to an unprecedented extent in the post-transition democratic state.[5]

It is evident that these new claims for regional autonomy do more than challenge the framework accepted under the 1978 Constitution. Demands for greater autonomy challenge the nature and role of the state itself. And there appears to be very little scope for the state to take its case to Europe and to rely on the European Union for a solution to the problem of national unity in the same way that it did in the past. While Spain may be the problem, it is no longer clear that Europe is the solution. For the European Union remains a community of nation-states, and so Spain must resolve the internal tensions in some form of domestic reconciliation of the national and regional interests.

The EU-25 faces a new set of internal and external challenges distinctive in nature from those of the past. It may be that Spain is one of the first countries to begin to understand that the preferences, interests and motivations in a community of twenty-five states are likely to be significantly different to those of the Community of twelve countries that it joined in 1986. In this new context, Spain has to search for a new role and shape a distinct identity in a larger community where it may not be able to wield influence or to establish alliances and extract benefits in the same way. The next section looks at Spain–EU relations between 1996–2003.

From 1996 to 2003: Spain and the European Union

The Socialist government had guided the country into the European Community on the strength of certain anticipated benefits – the modernisation of the economic system and greater access to the larger European market; modernisation of the political and institutional system, using the European model of democracy as the basis for the creation and consolidation of the new national democracy; and the opportunity to integrate Spain within international society.[6] All of these outcomes were realised over the first decade of EU membership.

Later on, this same desire for modernisation through Europe prompted the government to seek early entry to monetary union, with the support of the central bank and the financial system in general. Given the historical failure to control inflation, there were good reasons for embracing the monetary integration model with its requirements for fiscal rectitude and the insistence upon financial stability.

However, the economic crisis of the early 1990s and difficulties experienced with the European Exchange Rate Mechanism (ERM) in 1992 produced a heightened sense of uncertainty over the course of monetary integration. When the decision was made at the Edinburgh summit of the European Council (December 1992) to go ahead with the planned single currency, the moment was also right for the then Spanish prime minister,

Felipe González, to negotiate a financial support package for the four poorest member states (Spain, Portugal, Greece and Ireland) to assist them in preparing for monetary union.

By then Spaniards had become more critical of the European Union and more demanding in terms of expectations and benefits.[7] It was no longer sufficient to rely on Europe as the moderniser, nor was it acceptable to define the national interests in terms of European interests. When the PP replaced the Socialist Party in government, the new and more critical national perspective on Europe hardened. Aznar's understanding of Spain's place in Europe and the world was distinct from that of the Socialists under González.

No longer content with the myth of Europe as moderniser, or with the idea that the national interest was the European interest, Aznar was more pragmatic and expected Europe to deliver greater material and political benefits for Spain. As one political analyst has noted, the prime minister's vision of Europe was Gaullist in nature. He regarded the sovereignty of the nation-state as fundamental, while the integration process should be conducted on the basis of respect for national autonomy.[8] European integration should always respect national identities. For Aznar, the identity of Spain was that of a leading nation in Europe and in the world.

Although the PP had a different viewpoint on European integration than the Socialist Party, favouring a more intergovernmental European Union, the government continued with the policies of its predecessor. Hence, the national authorities threw their support behind monetary integration, and pursued policies in line with the requirements of the Maastricht Convergence Criteria, and the subsequent Growth and Stability Pact. In parallel, the privatisation programme gained momentum and the political discourse favoured economic liberalisation and labour market reform.

Not surprisingly, the PP government supported the Lisbon Declaration (2000), in particular the development of a knowledge-based economy, the modernisation of the European social model, and the limitation of government activity in the management of the economic system. Monetary union remained a key priority during the PP term of office, with a consensus among the political and financial elites that Spain needed the discipline of a single currency monetary regime in order to reduce inflation, historically an intractable problem for the authorities.

The acceptance of the stringent requirements on monetary union and the adoption of economic liberalisation policies were not simply a reflection of Spanish policy convergence towards the European model. The particular set of policies was an extension of domestic interest preferences. The PP government held the view that Europe should be a community based around greater economic liberalisation, a viewpoint that it shared with the British government under Blair. On the question of EU enlargement, the country was ambivalent, with fears over the possible adverse effects on sectors and markets and concern about future profits and growth.

Nonetheless, Spain was unable to exert a strong voice in the EU deliberations and failed to provide leadership among its partners in the community. Despite Aznar's more assertive style, the government did not deliver any substantive proposals regarding European integration. Instead, there was a vacuum in the contribution of the PP to the European integration process. In the words of Closa, 'if anything characterises the Popular Party's European policy, and above all the policy inspired by prime minister Aznar, it is the absence of any Europeanist discourse or appeal to European objectives either to legitimise Spanish aims or in the form of a project in its own right'.[9] The prime minister did not provide any ideas or vision for a future Europe, unlike the other European leaders, so there was no national debate or discussion around how a future Europe might develop.

In search of international influence

Aznar's support for the United States in the war against Iraq was surprising for many people, given the long-standing support for European integration (and hence for the European stance in international relations). It seemed an unlikely alliance that brought together the United States, Britain and Spain, placing the country in opposition to the rest of the European Union (EU-15) and the vast majority of states across the Arab world, as well as the United Nations and its Security Council.

The issue of terrorism was both a personal concern of the prime minister, and a political priority of the PP government from the time it took office in 1996. When the United States launched what it called the international fight against terrorism, the Aznar government saw the opportunity to ally itself with a powerful partner, nurturing the hope that this might help to provide an effective and permanent solution to the national problem in the international arena.[10]

During Spain's presidency of the European Union in the first half of 2002, terrorism was top of the list of priorities for the presidential term of office.[11] In effect, the PP government was pursuing its political agenda on two fronts simultaneously: at EU level and through the Atlantic alliance. But there was more to the strategy than the opportunistic support for America's war with Iraq. By fixing upon the American global strategy, and distancing himself from 'old Europe', Aznar was breaking the internal consensus that had been established since the transition to democracy. It was a conscious decision to follow the hegemon, and thereby to raise the international presence of Spain.

However, the prime minister's decision to follow the hegemon had consequences for relations with traditional allies within the European Union, and in particular with France and Germany. Unlike his predecessor, Felipe González, Aznar never established close personal relations with his counterparts in the two core countries of the European Union. Regarded as haughty and arrogant, Aznar alienated his fellow statesmen within the European Union by his insistence upon the defence of national interest and a policy of aggressive nationalism – notably in the negotiations over Spain's share of the Structural and Cohesion Funds in the enlarged community, and then during the negotiations over the draft Constitution which promised to cut the number of votes that Spain had been originally allocated through the Nice Treaty. His support for the Iraq war was seen as dividing the European Union, and weakening internal unity precisely at a time when it was most needed.

From the beginning, both France and Germany opposed the US war against Iraq. Both countries were firmly committed to the multilateralist tradition in international relations, and held to the view that any action against Iraq should be conducted within the framework of international law and with the approval of the United Nations Security Council. The failure to get a Security Council resolution showed up the limitations of European Union influence, and in particular the precarious nature of collective will among the member states in international matters. When the eastern European countries joined with Spain, Italy and Britain to sign the letter of support for the United States, the conflicting positions within the European Union were seized upon as representative of the divisions between 'old' and 'new' Europe.

These were not mere differences over the Iraq war, but real divisions over issues long central to national policy in the core countries. France, as Spain's nearest neighbour, had collaborated closely with its southern counterpart in matters of security and domestic terrorism. But the French government did not share Aznar's vision of a Europe dependent upon the United States to provide a security framework for the region. France had always stood back from the security community that had been developed under NATO, and now the former Soviet states were joining both the European Union and NATO. Its position that security problems and security policy should be dealt with at the European level through common agreement was being challenged.

Germany largely shared the French view that there should be a common European Union position on security but it also realised the difficulties in building a consensus. It was, however, anxious to see the enlargement proceed smoothly, believing that once inside the European Union the new member states would support the core EU countries. As the largest contributor to the EU budget, Germany had attempted to wield its influence over Spain during the accession negotiations when the latter sought to protect its share of the Structural Funds, and subsequently threatened to cut the flow of EU funds to Spain in retaliation for supporting the United States.

However, it was in the economic arena that differences between Germany and Spain loomed large. Germany did not share the Spanish prime minister's fervour over economic liberalisation to quite the same extent, and the government was still trying to withstand pressures to move ahead with economic reform and structural changes. When it became evident that Germany would breach the conditions of the Growth and Stability Pact (an agreement for which it was largely responsible), other countries that had managed to keep their public spending under control (particularly Spain) were critical of the differential treatment given to the European Union's largest country.

Spain set itself at odds with Germany and France over the enlargement negotiations, and then with the deliberations of the European Convention and the subsequent negotiations within the Intergovernmental Council over the draft Constitution. The alliance with Poland during this period was in effect a temporary one, useful to both countries as a way of combining their strengths to secure their individual national interests. Certainly, the two countries had common interests – keeping the voting rights won at Nice and supporting the transatlantic security alliance. But these would ultimately turn out to be temporary concerns, and neither country seemed able to develop more long-term strategies for cooperation. In fact, Poland had already been identified as a possible competitor in the battle to retain foreign direct investment.

With the British prime minister, Aznar found a natural ally – one who shared his view on security policy and the role of the United States in protecting Europe. They both believed in a more intergovernmental European Union, and were firmly wedded to economic liberalisation as the preferred strategy for economic growth and stability. The Spanish prime minister supported the vision for Europe set out in the Lisbon strategy, agreed at the 2000 summit meeting of EU leaders, but it was a vision that accorded more closely with the economic model of Anglo-Saxon capitalism already well established in Britain than to the mixed economy of continental capitalism. However, the alliance forged with Britain was also conducted to the detriment of the traditional relations with France and Germany.

While Aznar's stance on the war with Iraq placed him at odds with domestic public opinion and the other political parties in the country, some have identified a historical parallel in the agreement made in 1959 between General Franco and the US president Dwight Eisenhower for the establishment of American military bases in the country.[12] Despite its peripheral position in western Europe, Spain's location has always had a geo-strategic importance for the security of Europe, and the Eisenhower visit was significant in its support for the Franco regime, while it also brought the promise of financial support to a country that was starved of economic resources.[13] However, the contemporary regime needed no international stamp of approval, nor was it devoid of economic resources.

New Europe, new challenges

Spain had become a major beneficiary under the EU Structural and Cohesion Funds over the years. But the country also chalked up some contributions and achievements of its own. It had succeeded in securing the commitment of the other member states to a programme for the Mediterranean Region at the Barcelona summit in 1995; and it entered the single currency in the first round, after an impressive adjustment to its public finances and inflation rates. Yet despite this positive record on European integration, and despite its size as the second-largest country in the EU-15, Spain never succeeded in being part of the European core. In the community largely dominated by the Franco-German alliance, sometimes with Britain as a third partner, Spain was always marginalised. Under the PP government, it failed to secure a more influential position at the heart of Europe. Hence Aznar's search for a greater international presence led him outside the EU-15.

Although the new Europe has yet to be defined with clarity, certain challenges emerge to strike at the heart of Spanish national interests and preferences within European integration. These are grouped around three categories: enlargement, decision-making and power-sharing, and the broad issue of security (including immigration and defence). Enlargement is one of the greatest challenges, representing the most complicated phase in the history of the EU with the greatest potential to destabilise the community that has been created.

The entry of ten new countries with an average income about 45 per cent of the European average will have the effect of lowering the EU average income, and thus affect the continued eligibility of Spain for receipts under the Structural Funds. Currently, Spanish GDP per capita is about 86 per cent of the European average. In the EU-25, this figure will go up to 90 per cent. According to one study, if current eligibility criteria for Objective 1 receipts are maintained, only three of the ten Spanish regions that now receive support will continue to do so in 2007.[14] Spain would also lose the assistance received from the Cohesion Funds. Additionally, Spain will have to compete for trade and foreign direct investment, with Spanish imports likely to increase more than exports. Over the long term, structural adjustment will be needed in the manufacturing sector, while in the context of enlargement and liberalisation of the internal EU market Spanish industry is likely to lose domestic market share.

In the area of decision-making and power-sharing, the difficulties became apparent after the Nice summit. At the summit meeting, Spain was allocated twenty-seven votes in the Council of Ministers, while Germany, France, Italy and Britain were each granted twenty-nine. This division of votes treated Spain as one of the large states. Then, in 2003, the European Convention sought to change the voting system and to allocate votes more directly in line with population size in each of the member states, with a proposal for decision-making on the basis of a double majority, representing 60 per cent of the total EU population. For Spain, this represented a clear deterioration of the position proposed at Nice. For Aznar, it challenged the country's entitlement to membership of the club comprising the large countries.

There is an important issue of image and perception underlying the Convention proposal. Spain is still regarded by the other EU-15 member states as a medium-sized country, yet it fought hard in the 2003 Inter-governmental Council to retain the voting power on the Council of Ministers that had been agreed under the Nice Treaty – placing it close to the European Union's four big countries: Germany, France, Britain and Italy. More than ever before, the identity of Spain in the European Union is being contested – inside the country itself as the political authorities seek to define the role and influence of their country in the larger Union, and (albeit indirectly or unintentionally) by the other member states through the current reformulation of the European Union's institutional and political framework.

This contestation of Spain's identity within the European Union emerged quite clearly in the proceedings of the European Convention. The Spanish representatives supported, or proposed such ideas as the concept of a union of citizens (*not peoples*) and states; the guarantee of territorial integrity; clarifying the division of competences, and the development of a space for freedom and security; an effective mechanism for the control of subsidiarity by national parliamentarians; and the solidarity clause in the face of terrorist attacks and catastrophes.

But the big focus remained on institutional matters: the Council of Ministers votes, the number of Commissioners, and the number of seats in the European Parliament. Hence the tough bargaining by Spain in the lead-up to the Inter-governmental Council prompted the Commission to suggest enlarging the future Commission so that each member state would retain one Commissioner, with bigger countries (including Spain and Poland) having two; also, to give Spain and Poland more seats in the European Parliament; an offer of additional aid; and a suggestion to adjust the 'qualified majority' thresholds to make it easier for the two countries to block legislation.

Spain shares many characteristics in common with Poland, including similar levels of population. Having previously regarded Poland as its principal competitor in the enlarged European Union, with little political or economic interaction between the two countries, the IGC negotiations saw Spain move towards a rapprochement based upon the need to face the challenges of enlargement. Under the PP government, there were shared concerns that bound the two countries, and potential benefits to be gained from joining forces, in particular the priority to retain votes in the Council of Ministers; also, the preference for keeping NATO central to European security; and, given a shared cultural tradition rooted in Catholicism, the desire to see the Christian roots of Europe granted explicit recognition in the Constitution.

Not everything in the new European draft constitutional treaty was regarded as unacceptable to the PP government. Indeed, some areas of the proposal struck a chord with the PP and other national interests that

favoured the intergovernmental vision of Europe. For instance, the document contained no references to a federal Community, while the references
to the values of respect for human dignity, liberty, democracy, rule of law
and human rights accorded with the values espoused by the PP, at least as
expressed in the political rhetoric of the party.

The proposal for a European Union foreign minister was acceptable to
Spain, but it had reservations about the proposed minister being both a
member of the European Commission and also presiding over the Council
of Foreign Ministers. On the issue of security, the Spanish position was that
EU security and defence policy should be subject to unanimity, and respect
the NATO obligations of the member states. Member states that wanted to
go further should sign a clause of mutual defence within the EU framework
and work closely within NATO.

One provision in the draft constitutional treaty with key importance for
domestic political relations was that concerning territorial integrity. The
implication of this provision is that the European Union must respect the
essential functions of the state, including those that have the objective of
guaranteeing the territorial integrity of the state, public order and internal
security. Implicit in this is the endorsement of the national state as the
primary sovereign political entity in the European political system. While
the draft constitutional treaty recognises regional autonomy and gives the
Committee of the Regions the right of appeal to the European Court of
Justice, the overall effect is more favourable to the state than to the sub-
national political levels of decision-making, since the Constitution does not
in any respect change the fundamental nature of the European Union as a
community of nation-states.

The third broad area of challenge in the new Europe is that of security. As
already indicated above, the Aznar government did not support the idea of a
European common security and defence policy, independent of the NATO
structure. Nor did it wish to see greater supranationality in this policy area.
Defined very much by the domestic context and especially the situation in
the Basque Country, security emerged as a key priority in the concerns of
the national government.

In contrast to the first two presidencies of the European Union held by
Spain, the third presidency in the first half of 2002 presented a programme
that was strongly oriented to issues of security, including the fight against
international terrorism. The approach, based upon the appeal to the
international arena, was a departure from the defining attitudes of the post-
accession years, when the national interest was viewed as being synonymous
with the European interest and the priorities were more broadly developed
to encompass modernisation, democratic values, social progress and
development.

The extent of policy convergence towards the United States position
during the Aznar government may be gauged by the tone and content of his
address to the Spanish defence forces in October 2003.[15] Referring to

terrorism as a powerful factor of insecurity at the beginning of the twenty-first century, he emphasised the paramount role of the United States as a guarantor of the security order. He urged the defence forces to be ready to use preventative actions to fight against terrorist groups that could use weapons of mass destruction, and for Spain to be ready to face such challenges.

Although Aznar did not make specific reference in his speech to ETA, the defence minister, Federico Trillo-Figuero, did so in a statement of support for the prime minister's position, declaring that 'without preventative actions, Spain cannot win the battle against ETA'.[16] The position on security (and defence) reflected the importance of such actions to deal with the problem of terrorism in all its forms, whether at the domestic or international level. According to this view, security is not circumscribed by area or limited by geographic boundaries.

The doctrine of preventative action that dominated Spanish security policy during the latter years of the Aznar government was very much at odds with the European approach. It was also at odds with the position outlined by the European Union High Representative for External Relations, Javier Solana, in a paper on security prepared in mid-2003. The Solana defence doctrine *did* recognise the need to act before a crisis emerges. But it also stressed the importance of a multifaceted approach, using not only military means but also political, economic and intelligence means to address the underlying political causes. In practice, Spanish security policy under Aznar was shaped by much more narrowly defined national priorities around the long-standing question of Basque separatism and the activities of ETA, which the government regarded as a threat to the stability of the state itself and to national unity in general.

Since security policy was interpreted so narrowly, constructive policy actions in areas such as immigration were limited. In recent years, Spain, like other European countries, has experienced large inflows of migrants, particularly from North Africa, the Arab countries bordering the Mediterranean and Latin America. The country's location, at the western edge of Europe and in close proximity to North Africa, makes it a natural point of entry for many people. While immigration policy has tightened in an effort to stem the inflow of migrants, the policy remains ad hoc. Moreover, the PP government's position was that immigration should be addressed by the European Union as a whole, and that in this area at least there had to be a common immigration policy for all the European member states.

The economic case for a more liberal immigration policy in Spain is strong, despite the continued levels of unemployment above the European average. Spain has an ageing population, with a declining birth rate that is no longer capable of maintaining the overall population rate. It also has a public social spending level that remains below the European average, so that immigration can be a force in filling jobs, contributing to the government revenue for the future, and lowering the dependency ratio.

Internal tensions: from regional autonomy to constitutional challenges

Any examination of Spain's position in the future European Union must take account of the internal political dynamics, and the relations between the central and regional levels of government. Since the establishment of the seventeen regional autonomous communities in 1978, these relations have been subject to continual adaptation, with gradual and periodic transfers of autonomy from the national to the regional level.[17]

The semi-federal system of government agreed under the Constitution effectively evolved through the bilateral negotiations between the central government and each region, with the levels of autonomy to be devolved for each region being decided by negotiation and agreement between the two parties. The result was a differentiated model of autonomy, with the two regions of the Basque country and Catalonia having the greatest level of autonomy while the other regions negotiated varying levels of autonomy in each case.

In time, the decentralisation model began to exhibit tensions as regions sought greater autonomy beyond what was originally granted. Also, the regions began to compete in a process of catch-up, with the least decentralised regions aiming to match the other regions with greater autonomy.[18] This competition between the regions began to escalate in the 1990s, especially after the decision by the central government to allow regions greater financial and fiscal responsibility. European monetary union imposed certain obligations upon the government, particularly with regard to deficit levels and public spending, so it was imperative for the central authorities to reach an agreement with the regional governments over decentralised levels of public spending.

From the early 1990s, spiralling levels of regional government debt threatened to jeopardise the Spanish obligations under the Maastricht Convergence Criteria and the Growth and Stability Pact. The regional financing arrangement agreed by the central government for the period 1997–2001 allowed regional governments to retain control over a larger share of the revenues collected in the region, in an attempt to establish fiscal co-responsibility.[19] This financing agreement also highlighted for perhaps the first time how European integration was changing the relations between the state and the regional governments, and re-ordering those relations in ways that might not otherwise occur.

European integration continues to exert an influence on state–region relations, sometimes in a positive way but at other times exacerbating tensions between the two levels of government. In the Spanish case, the strong regional identities are expressed in the desire for greater local autonomy and a preference for less control by the central government over regional affairs. Any consideration of Spain's position in the European Union must therefore take account of the internal dynamics between state and region, and of how European integration might affect the somewhat delicate balance between the regional autonomous community and the central government.

A recent escalation in demands for additional regional autonomy has led some analysts to question whether the existing constitutional arrangements can accommodate these aspirations, and 'whether we can all fit within the one-state model'.[20] The Basque government's proposal for sovereignty and association status with Spain has been rejected by the Spanish state, and the European Commission has also given its considered opinion against the proposal. However, it will not disappear so easily from the political discussions within the region nor between the region and the central government.

Regional self-determination is a growing force within many of the Spanish regions. In Catalonia the leader of the Catalan Socialists, Pasqual Maragall, proposed formal inter-regional collaboration within the EU framework. Critical of the centripetal tendencies in the map of Spain, which tend not to take account of such socio-spatial configurations as the Cantabrian axis, the Ebro axis, or the Mediterranean, Maragall put forward a proposal for a Euro-region model for the twelve million people within the area embracing Catalonia, Aragon, the Balearic Islands, Valencia, and the French regions of the South Pyrenees and Languedoc-Roussillon. Later, the left-nationalist coalition government of Catalonia led by Maragall called for the renegotiation of the region's Statute of Autonomy.

It is clear that tensions between the state and the regional autonomous communities have not been resolved by either the arrangements set out in the 1978 Constitution, or the subsequent amendments to the semi-federal model that extended the original grant of autonomy, or indeed by the development of financial co-responsibility. The state cannot continue to rely upon the European Union and the financial transfers under the Structural Funds to alleviate the state–region tensions. Yet it is evident that the state–region dynamics do affect the domestic political stability and order, and through it the position of Spain in the European Union. Already, there were demands being made for a revision of the Constitution. But the PP government remained unwilling to consider any revisions of the constitutional clauses, claiming it would unsettle a fragile national unity. It seems ironic that while debate on the European Constitution was possible and encouraged (albeit with very limited public interest), the PP showed no desire to engage in a debate over the national Constitution.

Another problem concerns the status of the regions themselves within the European Union. Direct representation of the regions at the Brussels level is possible, but it is very much dependent upon the nature of regional/local government in the member-states, and the degree of decentralisation in each case.[21] Representation does not mean the same thing as decision-making, as the regions have discovered from their membership of the European Union's Committee of the Regions (CoR), itself a purely consultative body within the EU institutional framework. For the more independent-minded regional parties, such as the Catalan Convergència i Unió, the CoR has provided no opportunity to develop towards de facto independence.

The EU is still a community of nation-states. It is the latter that exert the power and influence in the European arena. The draft European Constitution does recognise the issue of regional autonomy, and it is still the nation-state that is the real force and voice for all the sub-national regions. Of course, the most effective outcome of national representation is very much dependent upon the central government being able to take all the regional views into account when presenting the national case at the European level – and this unity of voice is in turn dependent upon the autonomous communities being able to form common positions.

Given the privileged status of the state both within the European Union draft constitutional treaty and in the decision-making frameworks of the EU, the status of the regions is ambivalent at best. Consequently, for a country such as Spain with its semi-federal state and strong regional identities, there is a clear imperative for the state to address the challenge posed by the demands for regional autonomy and constitutional change if it is to preserve internal political stability and at the same time to assume the responsibilities of its membership in the future EU-25.

Conclusion – a middle power in the remaking?

The series of bomb attacks in Madrid on 11 March 2004 had a cataclysmic effect on the country in general, and on the political scene in particular. Unexpectedly, the PP lost the election as the electorate slowly came to terms with not only the horror of the carnage in the capital city but also the poorly managed efforts of the Aznar government to capitalise upon the situation in order to gain political advantage. The government was severely criticised for its handling of the events in the wake of the bombings, for attempting to mislead both the national public and the European partners by laying the blame for the attacks on the Basque organisation, ETA, and subsequently attempting to manage the information flow through the media as well as failing to provide full information to the security organisations of its partner states in the European Union. The electorate cast its vote in disapproval of the way that the Aznar administration had responded to the attacks, and returned the Socialist Party to power under the leadership of José Luis Rodríguez Zapatero.

This sudden and unanticipated change in the political landscape had several effects, identifiable at a number of levels. The relationship between Spain and the United States or, more properly, between Aznar and George Bush came apart. The new government withdrew the Spanish troops from Iraq and sought new approaches towards resolving the deteriorating situation within that country. While the new administration declared its commitment towards the war on terrorism, it distanced itself from the Bush administration. The Socialist government was opposed to the doctrine of pre-emptive war and held to the position that terrorism could not be addressed through this doctrine but instead required an understanding of the root causes. Moreover, it supported collective action on international terrorism within the framework of international law.

As a result of the Zapatero decision, the United States could no longer count upon the unconditional support of Spain, which had hitherto been useful in weakening the European Union and preventing the forging of European unity to challenge US dominance. In the months after the war, it had become clear that Aznar's friendship with the leader of the world's only superpower brought him plenty of photo opportunities but little real influence and no power over decision-making. Even the British prime minister showed by his actions that when it came to issues of importance in European affairs, it was Germany and France that he needed to talk to.

The return of the Socialists changed the geo-political balance in Europe, with Spain switching from a pro-US stance to one closer to the core European Union countries. Relations with the European Union also took a dramatic turn, as the Zapatero government announced a change of strategy and declared its support for finding an agreement on the draft EU Constitution. With Spain now willing to negotiate, Poland was left without an ally and its original opposition to the Constitution was replaced by a more conciliatory tone. The new Spanish government wanted to prove it was committed to strengthening the European Union and restoring the confidence of its European partners. Once again, the notion that Europe's interest and the national interest were the same was affirmed publicly by the new prime minister in the course of his first official visit to meet the French and German leaders.

The argument of this chapter has been that, with the changing circumstances in an enlarged European Union, Spain was under pressure to find a new role for itself in the Union, not just because of the external challenges of the new Europe but also because of the internal dynamic of state–region relations.[22] The election result on 14 March 2004 did not remove this challenge, but it did suggest the possibility of alternative courses of action.

What possible actions and strategies are open to the Spanish government? For one thing, it needs to rebuild relations with countries and regions of importance to Spain – in particular, with Latin America and the Mediterranean region.[23] The Euro-Mediterranean Process grew out of the efforts made by Spain when it held the presidency of the European Union in 1995, but was largely sidelined owing to the insecurity in the Middle East and the lack of capacity for action or intervention on the part of the EU, as well as the preoccupation with eastern enlargement.

Given Spain's close geographic proximity to the Mediterranean region in general, with the cultural and economic ties that have built up over time, the country is well placed to take (or perhaps re-take) a leadership role and to reinvigorate the political and economic dimensions of the agreement made in Barcelona in 1995. It would also serve national security interests to have greater influence with the countries of North Africa and along the further reaches of the eastern Mediterranean. In the absence of a European immigration policy, Spain continues to implement its own national policies in the management of the inflows of people from that region, reconciling the competing claims of an economic sector demanding cheap labour with the more political desire to limit the number of immigrants.

The other area where Spain might take an active role in shaping EU policy and also developing new strategies of its own is in Latin America. Aznar's support for the United States in the war with Iraq placed him at odds with many Latin American countries and ultimately damaged the important political and economic ties that had built up between the two. Spain's concern with security especially during the PP's second term of office had meant greater restrictions on the flow of economic immigrants from the traditional sending countries in Latin America, a reversal of earlier policies that allowed immigration from a region with shared historical ties – and to a receiving country with its own history of large-scale emigration.

These are two strategic areas where Spain can define its role within the European Union. Progress on policy towards the Mediterranean, and enhanced cooperation agreements with Latin American countries and Mercosur would create positive spillover for other areas of concern to the European Union as a whole, most notably the area of security (in its broadest sense) and that of trade liberalisation, as well as serve the Spanish national interests.

In this regard, the issue of international presence can be addressed not by separating policy on Europe from policy towards the rest of the world, but by working within the EU framework to enhance Euro-Mediterranean relations and to launch new political initiatives and closer ties with Latin America and the Arab world.[24] In the past decade, Spain has adopted a defensive rather than a constructive position on the European Union, particularly with regard to the current phase of European integration.[25] The stance was based upon an aggressive defence of the national interest, pushing for the retention of existing financial benefits and decision-making rights, while failing to consider substantive policies towards those regions of the world with strategic significance for both the national interest and that of the European Union at large.

Once again there is the opportunity to define the national interests with the European interest. Even as Aznar took his government in a direction contrary to the wishes of the people, popular and elite opinion continued to support the European integration process. A Eurobarometer poll published in February 2004 showed 85 per cent of the Spanish population believed the European Union should adopt the draft Constitution, and 65 per cent thought the Aznar government should make concessions to facilitate its adoption.

However, national support for the European Union is tempered with a more rational calculation of the costs and benefits. Some 61 per cent of Spaniards believed Europe was more important than America in a report published by the Real Instituto Elcano at the end of February 2004, but there was a preference for cooperation rather than rivalry between the European Union and the United States. In the same report, three-quarters of Spaniards thought Spain had benefited from the European Union, though one in two considered the euro had damaged their interests.[26] There is no indication of an emerging European identity.[27] On the contrary, the evidence to date suggests that in Spain the majority of people (including the young) have a stronger regional and local identity (expressed in terms of loyalty and affiliation), with less than 12 per cent claiming European identity. This is broadly in line with the experience in the other European countries.[28]

The search for Spain's role in the new Europe is inextricably linked with the internal search for national unity and stability. For one thing, the flow of financial transfers under the Structural and Cohesion Funds will be reduced in the EU-25 and, as demands for greater regional autonomy continue to escalate, the Spanish state will be under pressure to balance the obligations of EU membership with the demands for financial transfers to its poorer regions. At the same time, it will face new demands for further autonomy, which also have financial implications.

The system of regional autonomous communities constitutes an extra layer of government with an unequal division of autonomy across the regions. Regional identities remain strong, however, and for many of the regions the aspirations for autonomy have yet to be fully realised. Spain is perhaps the one member state in the EU-15 where the political system is still in the process of being defined. In effect, the 1978 Constitution launched a democratic state and a system of regional autonomous communities that continues as work in progress.

Aznar held firm to the principle of national unity and was unsympathetic to any regional aspirations regarding autonomy, other than those that could be fulfilled according to the criteria laid down by the Constitution. The Socialist government led by Zapatero partly reflected a more conciliatory tone on taking office, indicating a new spirit of dialogue and a departure from the previous governmental approach. The commitment of the prime minister to renegotiate the Statutes of Autonomy and amend the Constitution certainly reflects a different line of thinking, and opened the way for the Basque leader, Juan José Ibarretxe, to indicate a willingness to negotiate over the sovereignty proposals set out in the Ibarretxe Plan.

There will be ample opportunity to show how far the rhetoric extends to commitment towards greater decentralisation in the face of escalating demands from the regions. Since the new government does not have an overall majority in parliament, it must remain sensitive to the claims of the small regional parties and restore democratic pluralism in the national parliament. The issue of regional (i.e. sub-national) representation at both the national and supranational level is likely to loom large in the future European Union, with communities and societies seeking to maintain and extend local democratic representation and regional identity in the larger political entity.

What of Aznar's preoccupation with Spain as a 'big country' in the world? The former prime minister had sought new allies and forged new alliances in the search for international presence, and the decision to support George Bush was a key element in the strategy. However, memories of great-power status must suffice in the contemporary world where Spain has neither the resources nor the capacity to exercise this role in the twenty-first century. Lacking both economic and military capacity, national public sector spending remains below that of the other large EU member states, while spending on research and development falls short of the European average.

Limited national capacity and economic strength do not suggest a convincing case for the country to become a member of the G-7, the club of the world's richest (and most influential) countries.[29] In the EU-25, Spain will still be a middle-sized power among the existing large countries (France, Britain, Germany, and Italy) and some nineteen small states, so the issue of strategic alliances will remain paramount in the redefinition of Spain's role and identity in the new Europe.

The one legacy of the Aznar term that is certain to remain under the new government is the choice of economic policy. Under the PP government, economic deregulation, tight monetary policy, and strict fiscal policy were central elements in macro-economic management – in part, a reflection of the government philosophy generally, but also in keeping with its obligations under monetary union. Even the predecessor Socialist government followed a policy of economic liberalisation as a key element of the government programme – privatisation, deregulation and the support of monetary stability, as well as labour market reform – in the anticipation of entry to the European monetary union. The obligations of euro membership mean that with the former European Commissioner for Economic and Monetary Affairs, Pedro Solbes, now holding the national portfolio, the continuity of economic policy is assured. But the government will still have to address the rising economic and social insecurity across the wider society, issues of immigration, poverty and exclusion, and national house price inflation as well as the continued challenge of retaining national competitiveness.

With the new Socialist-led government in office comes a return to the philosophy that shaped the national policy of their predecessors who took the country into the European Community – that it is through constructing and consolidating Europe's role in the world that member states, and Spain in particular, can define the national interest. As *The Economist* magazine remarked during the 2003 IGC negotiations, 'the eagerness of so many countries to join the EU is, in part, a recognition that the period of lone national greatness is now in the past'.[30]

Notes

1 See Carlos Closa, 'The Domestic Basis of Spanish European Policy and the 2002 Presidency', *Notre Europe, European Studies* 16 (2001), hhp://www.notre-europe.asso.fr.

2 J. Tusell, J. Avilés and R. Pardo, *La política exterior de España en el siglo XX* (Madrid: Biblioteca Nueva, UNED, 2000).

3 José Ramón Montero, Richard Gunther and Mariano Torcal, *Democracy in Spain: Legitimacy, Discontent, and Disaffection* (Juan March Institute Working Paper, 1997).

4 Antonio Moreno Juste, 'Del "problema de España" a "la España europeizada": excepcionalidad y normalización en la posición de España en Europa', in Juan Carlos Pereira (ed.), *La política exterior de España 1800–2003* (Barcelona: Ariel, 2003).

5 Tómas Fernández and Juan José Laborda, *España ¿Cabemos Todos?* (Madrid: Alianza, 2002).

6 See M. Farrell, *Spain in the EU. The Road to Economic Convergence* (Basingstoke: Palgrave, 2001). For a more historical perspective, see also Charles Powell, *España en democracia 1975–2000* (Barcelona: Plaza y Janés, 2001).

7 José Torreblanca, 'Ideas, Preferences and Institutions: Explaining the Europeanisation of Spanish Foreign Policy', ARENA Working Paper, WP01/26, 2001; Rafael García Pérez, 'España en un mundo en cambio: a la búsqueda de la influencia internacional 1986–2002', in Juan Carlos Pereira (ed.), *La política exterior de España 1800–2003* (Barcelona: Ariel, 2003).

8 Closa, 'The Domestic Basis of Spanish European Policy'.

9 Ibid., p. 29.

10 Shortly after the September 11 attacks in the United States, the European Union held an extraordinary Council meeting in Brussels and agreed to produce a list of proscribed terrorist organisations. Spain called for the inclusion of ETA and groups with alleged links to ETA on the list, as well as the political organisation Herri Batasuna.

11 See Félix Arteaga, 'The Balance of the Spanish Presidency of 2002 with Regard to Justice and Home Affairs of the European Union'. Paper presented at the Conference on the Spanish presidency of the European Union, Europe in the World Centre, University of Liverpool, 12 October 2002.

12 Carlos Elordi, *El amigo Americano. De Franco a Aznar: una adhesión inquebrantable* (Madrid: Temas de Hoy, 2003).

13 Javier Rubio, '¿Qué ha sido la política exterior para España?', in Juan Carlos Pereira (ed.), *La política exterior de España 1800–2003* (Barcelona: Ariel, 2003).

14 Carmela Martín, José Herce, Simon Sosvilla-Rivero and Francisco Velazquez, *European Union Enlargement. Effects on the Spanish Economy* (Barcelona: La Caixa Economic Studies Series no. 27, 2002).

15 Reported in *El País*, 22 October 2003.

16 Ibid.

17 Elisa Roller, 'Institutional Reform, Quasi-Federalism and Constitutional Ambiguity: Senate Reform in the Spanish State of Autonomies', Manchester Papers in Politics: EPRU Series 6/2002.

18 See Farrell, *Spain in the EU*.

19 The financing arrangement is discussed in M. Farrell, 'Meeting the Conditions of Monetary Union: The Challenge to the Spanish Model of Regionalisation', *Journal of Southern Europe and the Balkans* 4/2 (2002), pp. 171–89.

20 The discussion is well documented in Fernández and Laborda, España.

21 Angela Bourne, 'The Impact of European Integration on Regional Power', *Journal of Common Market Studies* 41/4 (2003), pp. 597–620.

22 See similar and supporting arguments in de José M. Areilza Caruajal, 'La Unión Europea de 2004 y la piedra filosofal', *Política Exterior* 85 (Jan–Feb, 2002); Fernando Delage, 'Una politica exterior para el siglo XXI', in Pereira, *La política exterior de España*.

23 Manuel Montobbio, 'The Spanish Presidency of the Council of the European Union 2002 and the Relaunching of the Barcelona Process'. Paper presented at the Conference on the Spanish presidency of the European Union, Europe in the World Centre, University of Liverpool, 12 October 2002; Carlos Closa, 'The Third Spanish Presidency of the EU in Comparative Perspective'. Paper presented at the same conference.

24 Kalypso Nicolaïdis and Robert Howse, '"This is my Eutopia" . . . Narrative as Power', *Journal of Common Market Studies* 40/4 (2002), pp. 767–92.

25 Esther Barbé, 'La política europea de España 2001–2002', Working Paper 23, Institut Universitari d'Estudis Europeas, Universitat Antonoma de Barcelona, 2002.

26 Reported on the Real Instituto Elcano website, http:www.realinstitutoelcano. org/200403brie.asp.

27 F. Archiles and M. Marti, 'Ethnicity, Region and Nation: Valencian Identity and the Spanish Nation State', *Ethnic and Racial Studies* 24/5 (2001), pp. 779–97; J. D. Medrano and P. Gutierrez, 'Nested Identities: National and European Identity in Spain', *Ethnic and Racial Studies* 24/5 (2001), pp. 753–78.

28 Inger Enkvist, 'Do Northern and Southern Europe Discuss the Same Issues?', Working Paper, Centre for European Studies, Lund University, 2000, http:// www.cfe.lu.se.

29 J. A. Zorilla, 'España y el G-7. Una anómala posición internacional', *Política Exterior* 88 (2002).

30 'The Shadow of Empires', *The Economist*, 18 October 2003.

Index

abortion 10, 148, 155
African National Congress (ANC) 62
Aguirre, Esperanza 156
Ajuria-Enea Pact 88
Alberón, Vicente 43
Alfonso XIII 28–31, 152
Alianza Popular (AP) 10, 147, 183; and
    Constitution 122; UCD 19; see also
    Partido Popular (PP) government
Almunia, Joaquín 186–8
al-Qaeda 191, 203, 209–11
Álvarez, Aida 43
Amedo, José 64, 75–6
Andalusia 17, 20, 43, 52
Arana, Sabino 93
Ardanza, José Antonio 87
Arenas, Javier 152
Arias Navarro, Carlos 36
Armada, Alfonso 37
Armengou, Josep 109
Arriaga spirit 87, 102
Arzalluz, Xabier 103–4 n. 33
Association for the Recuperation of
    Historical Memory 4
Asunción, Antonio 43
Autonomous Communities 53, 81, 122–4,
    126, 129, 131–2, 180, 226, 228, 231
Azaña, Manuel 124, 133, 138, 143,
    151–2
Aznar, José María 151–4, 160, 163–4,
    183, 190, 201, 207–8, 216, 218–19,
    231–2, 234: early career 153; foreign
    policy 161,197, 201–2, 205–8,
    210–11, 215, 224, 230; Iraq War
    160–1, 219–22, 228–30; terrorism
    160, 225, 228; see also Partido
    Popular (PP) government

Banca Catalana 109
Banco Bilbao Vizcaya Argentaria
    (BBVA) 39, 55

Banesto 74
Barrionuevo, José 43, 69
Basque Country 2, 10, 64, 67, 72, 73,
    81–105, 130, 134, 139, 224; and
    Constitution 16; devolution and
    autonomy 81–2, 85–6, 154, 226;
    French Basque Country 63, 69, 72,
    90–1; nationalism 81–104;
    parliament 84–5, 91, 102 n. 12;
    see also Arriaga spirit; Euskadi Ta
    Askatasuna (ETA); Euskera
    (Basque language); Gernika
    Statute, Herri Batasuna (HB;
    Batasuna); Partido Nacionalista
    Vasco (PNV)
Batallón Vasco-Español 67
Batasuna see Herri Batasuna (HB;
    Batasuna)
Behan, Brendan 61
Belloch, Juan Alberto 74, 80
Blair, Tony 114, 152, 154, 161–2, 165,
    206, 218
Blanco, Miguel Ángel 88
Bono, José 115, 189
Borbón, Don Juan de 30–1, 33–4, 38
Borbón Dampierre, Alfonso de 34
Borrell, Josep 187–8
Bouteflika, Abdelaziz 201, 204
Brouard, Santi 71
Bush, George W. 160–1, 228, 232

caciquismo 52
Calvo Sotelo, Leopoldo 37, 177
Cambó, Francesc 115, 129, 151
Campbell, Alistair 154
Cánovas del Castillo, Antonio 137
Carlists 32
Carod Rovira, Josep-Lluís 113
Carrero Blanco, Luis 33–4, 66–7
Carrillo, Santiago 8
cartel parties 51, 55

Cassinello, Andrés 71
Castillo, Pilar del 54, 137, 158
Catalonia 105–18, 130, 131, 138, 139,
   151, 163, 186, 217, 226, 227; Catalan
   language 112–13, 130; devolution
   and autonomy 5, 107, 108, 115;
   economy 109–10, 111, 112; elections
   106–8, 114, 115, 117–18, 163;
   nationalism 2, 3, 107, 109–10, 111,
   113, 115–16, 125–6, 130, 138, 206,
   228; *see also* Convergència i Unió
   (CiU); Convergència Democrática
   de Catalunya (CDC); Esquerra
   Republicana de Catalunya (ERC);
   Generalitat; Iniciativa per
   Catalunya (IC); Partit Socialista de
   Catalunya (PSC); Partit Socialista
   Unificat de Catalunya (PSUC)
Catholic Church and Catholicism 29,
   31–2, 40, 46, 47, 109, 110, 126, 127,
   158, 167, 223
Centro Superior de Información de la
   Defensa (CESID) 75, 79, 153
Christian Democrats 17, 20, 148, 163
Cierva, Ricardo de la 138
Citizens for Change (Ciutadans pel
   Canvi) 114
Civil War 16, 26, 29, 35, 37, 86, 101, 124,
   125, 135–8
clientelism 51–3, 111
Clinton, Bill 152
Comunidad Autónoma Vasca (CAV)
   see Basque Country
Concha, Manuel de la 43
Conde, Mario 74, 80
Confederación Española de Derechas
   Autónomas (CEDA) 152
Confederación Española de
   Organizaciones Empresariales
   (CEOE) 18, 20, 21, 150
Constitution (1876) 137
Constitution (1978) 4–5, 8, 9–10, 15–16,
   23–4, 39, 61, 68, 87, 115, 122–6,
   128–40, 142, 143, 147, 150, 153,
   158–9, 160, 171, 175, 215, 227, 231;
   Autonomous Communities 7, 67, 82,
   83, 84, 90, 91–3, 154, 159, 217, 227;
   monarchy 29–31, 33–4, 36, 37
constitutional patriotism 121, 125–6,
   128–31, 133–4, 138, 158, 159, 164
Convergència Democràtica de
   Catalunya (CDC) 106, 110, 111, 117
Convergència i Unió (CiU) 2, 106–18,
   156, 159, 163, 185, 206

Corcuera, José Luis 43
corruption 2, 39–87, 115, 147, 153, 183,
   185–6, 190, 208
Corruption Perception Index (CPI) 40,
   42, 56
Cortes *see* parliament

Díez, Rosa 189
Domínguez, Michel 64, 74

Eisenhower, Dwight 221
electoral system 8, 13, 14, 22, 23, 188
Elf Acquitaine 53, 54
Elgorriaga, Julen 64–5, 78
Ercros affair 54–5
Ertoil 54
Esquerra Republicana de Catalunya
   (ERC) 111, 119
Etxebarrieta, Txabi 66
European Union/European
   Community (EU/EC) 3, 47, 53, 57,
   82, 90, 97, 107, 125, 127, 131, 156,
   160, 161, 165, 201, 206, 209, 211,
   215–32; Committee of the Regions
   (CoR) 224, 227, 228; Constitution
   116, 161–2, 216, 220, 221, 223–4, 227,
   228–30; enlargement 3, 202, 211,
   212, 216, 218, 220–2, 223, 229;
   Euro-Mediterranean Partnership
   (EMP) 199, 205; *see also* Growth
   and Stability Pact; Maastricht
   Treaty
Euskadi *see* Basque Country
Euskadi Ta Askatasuna (ETA) 2, 37,
   42, 61–78, 81–101, 113, 134, 160–2,
   191, 210, 225, 228; ceasefire 81, 89,
   97, 156; dirty war against 2, 42, 61,
   64–5, 70–3; during Francoism 65–7;
   networks of support 97–8; Spanish
   Army 37, 69; *see also* Euskal Herria;
   Grupos Antiterroristas de
   Liberación (GAL); Herri Batasuna
   (HB; Batasuna); Lizarra Pact
Euskadiko Ezkerra (EE) 68
Euskal Herria 94, 104
Euskera (Basque language) 94, 100
Eusko Alkartasuna 86, 89
Expo 92 43

Falange 150
Fascism 30, 94, 127, 136, 142
Fernández de la Mora, Gonzalo 126
Fernández Díaz, Alberto 154
Fernández, Matilde 189

Fernández Miranda, Torcuato 36
Fomento de Trabajo Nacional 114
Fraga, Manuel 111, 123, 147–50; AP
  President 19, 148–9; President of
  Galicia 129
Franco Dictatorship 4, 7, 47, 50, 52, 65,
  66, 109, 136, 137, 159, 199
Franco, Francisco 27–35, 221
Francoism 122, 124, 127, 136, 138, 151,
  154
Frente Nacional 126
Fuerza Nueva 126
Fundación Francisco Franco 151
Fundación para el Análisis y los
  Estudios Sociales (FAES) 153

Galicia 17, 20, 128, 138, 145 n. 80, 82, 205
García Valverde, Julián 43
Garzón, Baltasar 43–4, 56, 64, 72, 74,
  75, 97
Generalitat 111–12
Gernika Statute 81–2, 85, 92, 147
Gescartera case 39, 55–6
Gesto por la Paz 100
Gibraltar 147, 203, 204
Giménez Reyna, Enrique 56
Giscard d'Estaing, Valéry 36, 216
Gómez de Liaño, Javier 47
González, Felipe 19, 63, 64, 74, 75–6,
  164, 178, 179, 186, 207, 210, 216;
  government 10, 29, 52, 69, 70, 73,
  200, 202, 207; PSOE Secretary
  General 169, 171, 174–5, 184, 185,
  186–7, 192
Growth and Stability Pact 146, 218, 221,
  226
Grupos Antiterroristas de Liberación
  (GAL) 42–3, 45, 55, 63–5, 68–77
Guerra, Alfonso 19, 42, 108, 169, 171,
  179, 183–6
Guerra, Juan 42

Hassan II 203, 207
Hernández Mancha, Antonio 148–9
Herrero de Miñón, Miguel 128
Herri Batasuna (HB; Batasuna) 71, 77,
  89, 92, 97, 98, 99
Hussein, Saddam 160, 161, 168, 215

Ibarretxe, Juan José 103 n. 33, 231;
  Ibarretxe plan 90, 103, 116, 231
Imaz, Josu Jon 92
immigration 3, 112–13, 140, 157, 164,
  206, 208–10, 222, 225, 230, 232

Iniciativa Ciudadana Vasca 86
Iniciativa per Catalunya (IC) 108,
  113,117
IRA (Irish Republican Army) 61, 99
Iraq war 3, 161, 162, 220
Isabel II 31, 136
Isla Perejil *see* Parsley Island

Jiménez Losantos, Federico 132
Juan Carlos de Borbón, King 2, 27–37;
  democratic transition 27, 35–7; and
  Franco 32–5; 1981 coup attempt 37
judiciary 2, 56, 64, 73, 75–7, 100, 190

Kohl, Helmut 53
Kindelán, Alfredo 30, 31

Lasa, Boxean 63–5, 70, 76, 78, 80
Lerrouxism 113, 119 n. 38
Ley de la Jefatura del Estado 29
Ley Orgánica de Armonización del
  Proceso Autonómico (LOAPA) 82,
  108
Ley Orgánica del Estado 34, 35
Libya 198, 200, 205
Lisbon Declaration 218
Lizarra Pact 81, 85, 89–90, 94, 103 n. 28
Lliga Regionalista 109, 111, 113, 115
Lmrabet, Ali 207, 213 n. 21
López Rodó, Laureano 33, 34

Maastricht Treaty 155, 185, 218, 226
Madrid bombings (2004) 1, 3, 162–3, 209
Maghreb 198–200, 202, 204, 205, 211
Mani Pulite 42
Manifesto of Lausanne 30
Maragall, Pasqual 92, 106, 113–17, 227
Martin Artajo, Alberto 31
Martínez Pujalte, Vicente 40
Marxism 17, 65, 136, 175
Mas, Artur 116–17
Matutes, Abel 207
Maura, Antonio 146
media 2, 16, 42, 54, 56–7, 65, 73, 74, 81
  121, 123, 137, 170, 228; Basque
  Country 87, 94, 96–7, 104 n. 38;
  Popular Party 153–5, 163
Mediterranean 3, 134, 198–212, 227,
  229, 320
Menéndez y Pelayo, Marcelino 131
Mercosur 230
Mérida, Declaration of 115
Middle East peace process (MEPP) 3,
  202

Milans del Bosch, Jaime 37
military 17, 19, 22, 28, 37, 69, 70–1, 178
Moa, Pío 137
Mohammed VI 203, 207, 213 n. 21
monarchy 125, 127, 128, 133, 137, 139;
  and Franco 27–31; *see also* Juan
  Carlos de Borbón, King
Moncloa pacts 16
Morocco 200–11; fishing 200, 204–5,
  207; immigration 202, 206, 208;
  Moroccan–Algerian rivalry 200,
  201 204; Parsley Island 161, 201,
  208, 210
Mundo, El 42, 74, 75

Nadal, Miquel 206
National-Catholicism 121–2, 126, 127,
  136
nationalism, Spanish 121–45, 158–9; for
  regional *see* Basque Country;
  Catalonia
Nice Treaty 161, 220, 223
North Africa 200, 204, 205, 225, 230
Northern Ireland 76, 89, 95, 99

ONCE 57
Oniandía, Mario 84, 88
Opus Dei 33, 148, 150
Ortega y Gasset, José 125, 151
Oslo Accords 202
Otero Novás, José Manuel 135

Palacio, Ana 203
parliament, during Aznar government
  10, 162, 164, 206; transition 9–10,
  15; European 223; Iraq War 160,
  162; regional government 190, 197
  n. 64; *see also* Basque Country,
  parliament
Parsley Island (Isla Perejil) 204
Partido Comunista de España (PCE) 8,
  13–16, 22, 36, 107, 108 172, 176
Partido Nacionalista Vasco (PNV) 16,
  65, 68, 81–105, 130, 159; and Euskadi
  Ta Askatasuna (ETA) 89–91, 99;
  Gernika Statute 83–4, 92; *see also*
  Basque Country; Ibarretxe, Juan
  José; Lizarra Pact
Partido Popular (PP) government 3, 5,
  53, 57, 74, 107, 115, 127, 146–65, 216;
  corruption/clientelism 39–40, 53,
  55–6; electoral strategy 146–68;
  foreign policy 160–2, 201–2, 205–8,
  210–11, 215, 218–19, 222–4, 225, 227,

230; Francoism 147, 151, 159; Iraq
  War 160–2, 190; in opposition 77,
  153, 188; origins 147–9; policies:
  (1996–2000) 152, 154–6 (2000–4)
  157–65, 191, 208, 232; *see also*
  Alianza Popular (AP); Aznar, José
  María
Partido Socialista de Euskadi (PSE) 84,
  86
Partido Socialista Obrero Español
  (PSOE) 5, 13, 68, 70, 169–97; and
  Constitution 15–16; corruption/
  clientelism 42–53, 155, 190; electoral
  strategy 15–22, 173, 188–9; factions
  and divisions 183–5, 187; foreign
  policy 69, 200–2, 204, 209, 211,
  229; Marxism 174–5; NATO
  Referendum 177–8; in opposition
  15–16, 17, 19–22, 173, 186–90; party
  organisation 9, 169, 179–83, 192;
  policies 90, 92, 108, 164, 177–85, 190,
  192; terrorism 69–80; *see also*
  Grupos Antiterroristas de
  Liberación (GAL); Guerra,
  Alfonso; González, Felipe;
  Rodríguez Zapatero, José Luis;
  Unión General de Trabajadores
  (UGT)
Partit Socialista de Catalunya (PSC)
  114, 115, 117, 108–9, 111, 113
Partit Socialista Unificat de Catalunya
  (PSUC) 107–9, 114
party system 1, 8, 10–16, 21–2, 84, 146,
  183, 192
Perote, Juan Alberto 74–5
Piñar, Blas 35, 126
Piqué, Josep 133, 166 n. 21, 207
Polisario 207
Pradera, Javier 69–70
Prestige tanker 104, 147
Primo de Rivera, Miguel 28
Príncipe de Asturias 34
Prisa 155
Pujol, Jordi 108–12, 114, 115–7

Rajoy, Mariano 163, 190
Ramírez, Pedro J. 42, 44, 74–5
Repsol 205
Rodríguez Galindo, Enrique 64–5, 76
Rodríguez, Miguel Ángel 154
Rodríguez Zapatero, José Luis 78 n. 2,
  115, 189–90, 228
Roldán, Luis 43
Rubio, Mariano 43

Sahara Western/Spanish 35, 201, 204–5, 207
San Gil, María 133
Santaella, Jesús 95
Sindicato Español Universitario 31
Solana, Javier 213, 225
Solbes, Pedro 222
Solchaga, Carlos 43, 178, 184
Spanish Republic (Second) 28, 137, 152, 176
Spanish Sahara 35, 201, 204, 205, 207, 213 n. 14
Structural and Cohesion Funds 215, 220, 221, 231
Suárez, Adolfo 8–9, 14–15, 17–18, 36–7, 52, 68, 174, 200

Tangentopoli scandals 42
Tejero, Antonio Lt. Col. 37, 67
Telefónica 55, 154
terrorism and counter-terrorism 61–3, 71, 73, 76–8, 81, 84, 88–9, 91–4, 97–100, 130, 160, 161–2, 168, 190, 203, 209, 210, 219–20, 224–5, 228–9; *see also* al-Qaeda; Euskadi Ta Askatasuna (ETA)
trade unions 39, 89, 97; *see also* Unión General de Trabajadores (UGT)

Trillo-Figuero, Federico 162, 225

Unidad Alavesa 86
Unió Democràtic de Catalunya (UDC) 106, 117, 120
Unión de Centro Democrático (UCD) and UCD government 8–23, 150, 174, 176; business elites 20–1; cabinet instability 8; clientelism 52; collapse 12–13, 20–1, 148; and Constitution 15–16; origins 8; policies 9, 17–18, 23; relations with AP 16, 18; with PSOE 15–17, 19, 22; *see also* Suárez, Adolfo
Unión General de Trabajadores (UGT) 172–3, 176, 178, 195 n. 40, 150
United Nations (UN) 160, 168, 207, 215, 219, 220

Valiente, Pilar 56
Vera, Rafael 43, 69, 72, 80
Vidal Quadras, Aleix 131–2, 154
Villalonga, Juan 55

Yesa reservoir 55

Zabala, Joxe 63–5, 70, 76, 78, 80

Routledge/Cañada Blanch Studies on Contemporary Spain

Series editors: Paul Preston and Sebastian Balfour
Cañada Blanch Centre for Contemporary Spanish Studies, London

1. Spain 1914–1918
Between war and revolution
Francisco J. Romero Salvadó

2. Spaniards in the Holocaust
Mauthausen, horror on the Danube
David Wingeate Pike

3. Conspiracy and the Spanish Civil War
The brainwashing of Francisco Franco
Herbert R. Southworth

4. Red Barcelona
Social protest and labour mobilisation in the twentieth century
Edited by Angel Smith

5. British Women and the Spanish Civil War
Angela Jackson

6. Women and Spanish Fascism
The women's section of the Falange 1934–59
Kathleen Richmond

7. Class, Culture and Conflict in Barcelona, 1898–1937
Chris Ealham

8. Anarchism, the Republic and Civil War in Spain: 1931–1939
Julián Casanova

9. Catalan Nationalism
Francoism, transition and democracy
Montserrat Guibernau

10. British Volunteers in the Spanish Civil War
The British Battalion in the International Brigades, 1936–1939
Richard Baxell

11. The Catholic Church and the Spanish Civil War
Hilari Raguer

12. Nazi Germany and Francoist Spain
Christian Leitz

13. Churchill and Spain
The survival of the Franco Regime, 1940–1945
Richard Wigg

Also published in association with the Cañada Blanch Centre

Spain and the Great Powers
Edited by Sebastian Balfour and Paul Preston

The Politics of Contemporary Spain
Edited by Sebastian Balfour

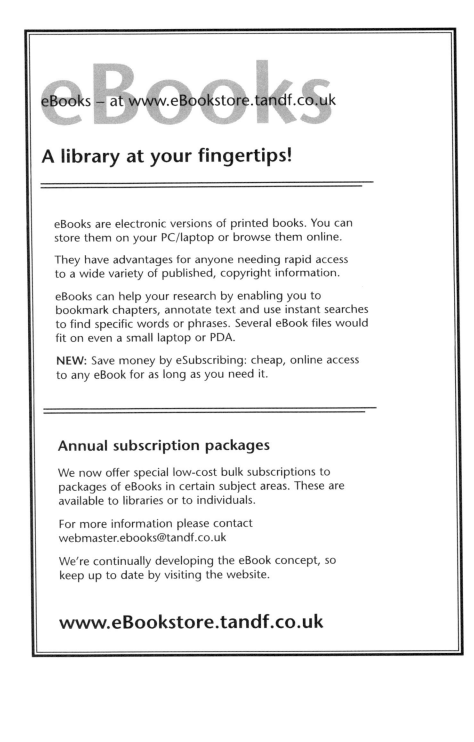